W9-AHM-086

MICROECONOMICS SCOREBOARD

HOW INCOME IS DISTRIBUTED AMONG CANADIANS

Source: Statistics Canada, CANSIM Table 202-0701

	AVERAGE INCOME		
	2006	2011	Increase
Market Income			
Lowest 20% of incomes	11,600	11,500	−1.0%
Second-lowest 20%	40,000	40,500	1.3%
Middle 20% of incomes	66,000	68,500	3.8%
Second-highest 20%	97,800	103,600	5.9%
Highest 20% of incomes	186,200	198,000	6.3%
Income after government transfers and taxes			
Lowest 20% of incomes	27,300	29,200	7.0%
Second-lowest 20%	47,000	49,800	6.0%
Middle 20% of incomes	64,500	68,400	6.0%
Second-highest 20%	86,500	92,900	7.4%
Highest 20% of incomes	146,900	157,900	7.5%

Ecomic family type5= Economic families, two persons or more
Statistic= Average income (Dollars)

MEDIAN AFTER-TAX INCOME, BY ECONOMIC FAMILY TYPE, 2011

Source: Statistic Canada, CANSIM Table 202-0605

Economic families, two people or more	**$68,000**
Elderly families	49,300
Married couples only	48,400
All other elderly families	54,600
Non-elderly families	73,300
Married couples only	66,500
Two-parent families with children	83,600
Married couples with other relatives	103,400
Lone-parent families	41,400
All other non-elderly families	58,600
Unattached individuals	**25,800**
Elderly males	27,800
Elderly females	23,000
Non-elderly males	29,200
Non-elderly females	23,300

MICROECONOMICS SCOREBOARD

AVERAGE HOUSEHOLD EXPENDITURES, 2012

Source: Statistic Canada, CANSIM Table 203-0021

Total expenditures	**75,443**
Total current consumption	**56,279**
Food	7,739
Shelter	15,811
Household operation	4,111
Household furnishings and equipment	2,183
Clothing	3,461
Transportation	11,216
Health care	2,285
Personal care	1,194
Recreation	3,773
Education	1,386
Reading materials and other printed matter	214
Tobacco products and alcoholic beverages	1,274
Games of chance (net amount)	202
Miscellaneous	1,430
Income taxes	**13,060**
Personal insurance payments and pension contributions	**4,272**
Gifts of money and contributions	**1,831**

CANADIAN HOME OWNERSHIP, 2012

Source: Statistics Canada, CANSIM Table 203-0027

	Owned dwelling with mortgage percent	Owned dwelling without mortgage percent	Rented dwelling percent
Canada	**35**	**31**	**35**
Newfoundland and Labrador	31	41	28
Prince Edward Island	36	35	29
Nova Scotia	36	37	28
New Brunswick	34	38	28
Quebec	34	28	38
Ontario	34	30	36
Manitoba	35	32	33
Saskatchewan	32	39	29
Alberta	39	33	28
British Columbia	34	30	36

PEARSON

ALWAYS LEARNING

Brian Lyons

Canadian Microeconomics
Problems & Policies

Eleventh Edition

Pearson Learning Solutions, 330 Hudson Street, New York, New York 10013
A Pearson Education Company
www.pearsoned.com

Printed in Canada

1 2 3 4 5 6 7 8 9 10 V092 18 17 16 15

000200010271960919

SK/SF

ISBN 10: 1-323-09066-5
ISBN 13: 978-1-323-09066-4

For Barb, Marnie, Brent, Dylan, Liam, Ryan, Amber, Colin, Parker and Reid

Brief Table of Contents

Contents

5   The Supply Side of Markets ... 84

6   The Dynamics of Competitive Markets ... 106

7 Market Structures ... 128

8 The Costs and Revenues of the Firm ... 157

12   The Government Sector ... 261

16W The Politics of Economics ... 313

"IN THE NEWS" BOXES

"YOU DECIDE" BOXES

Preface

Introduction

Canadian Microeconomics: Problems and Policies, Eleventh Edition, is an introductory text that addresses itself to economic issues and problems faced by Canada and Canadians today. This text is not oriented toward rigorous, elegant, or abstract theory, or toward a mathematical approach to economics; most students of introductory economics neither want nor need these. Rather, its approach tends to be practical and based in the real world, using economic theory to develop an understanding of the issues and problems being discussed and the policy choices facing governments in dealing with these matters. This text is ideally suited to a student's first course in economics and has been used in this role at the secondary school, community college, and university levels.

New to This Edition

In this eleventh edition, we have tried to *increase the interactivity of the student with the text.* The most visible change is the addition of an **Integrated Study Guide** following the end-of-chapter questions in each chapter. The Integrated Study Guide consists of three types of questions:

(a) **Review Questions** These are based closely on the material in the chapter and are multiple choice or short answer in nature. The answers are provided at the end of the book, making these questions a useful "self-check" for the content of each chapter.

(b) **Critical Thinking Questions** These questions are more complex and lend themselves to discussion and perhaps debate. Some are based on real-world situations; others are based on "what-if" scenarios.

(c) **Use the Web** These investigation/research questions usually require the same thinking skills as the Critical Thinking Questions, but are based on real-world information that can be found on the internet.

Student interactivity is also enhanced by an increase in the number of "In the News" and "You Decide" boxes, many of which are new for the eleventh edition. The questions that accompany these boxes also require critical thinking skills and lend themselves to classroom discussion.

Because what is in the news regarding economics changes so rapidly, new questions based on real-world examples, together with questions that encourage critical thinking, can be accessed in the MyEconLab with eText for Micro-economics, 11/e via www.pearsonmylabs.com with your Pearson created username and password and provided Course ID from your instructor.

In addition to updating the previous edition's material, the revisions for the eleventh edition were undertaken with the following goals in mind:

1. To improve the flow of the material, within chapters and from chapter to chapter.
2. To stress and reinforce certain "themes" across various chapters, such as scarcity, opportunity cost, efficiency and effectiveness, etc.
3. To add current and interesting material, through
   • many new "In the News" and "You Decide" boxes
   • new end-of-chapter questions and Integrated Study Guide questions that add interest and relevance to the material
   • many new "sidebar" items in the margins with examples and colourful facts
   • updated coverage of ebusiness, including Chapter 8's questions on how the costs and revenues of ebusiness firms differ from conventional firms, and the problems and opportunities that this creates

More specifically, Chapter 1 now includes a clarification of the meanings of effec-tiveness and efficiency, and Chapter 2's coverage of the command system has been improved and clarified. Chapter 5 has a new *In the News* box on how the impact of hydraulic fracturing on the supply of crude oil depends upon the price of oil. Chap-ter 6 includes a new *In the News* box on the economic factors underlying the extreme fluctuations in the price of crude oil following late 2014, together with directions to online sources for updating the information. Chapter 6 also includes a new *You Decide* box on why markets for assets such as corporate shares and housing behave differ-ently from markets for goods and services.

In Chapter 8, a new *You Decide* box links the marginal cost and marginal revenue analysis of Chapter 8 to the topic of supply in Chapter 5, by emphasizing how mar-ginal cost and marginal revenue data influence businesses' production and pricing decisions. Chapter 9's coverage of the Competition Act has been clarified and updated, and a new *You Decide* box uses the banking industry to illustrate the real-world complexities of administering competition policy.

Chapter 10's coverage of non-union labour markets has been expanded and strengthened, and a new *You Decide-* box on Canada's shortage of skilled trades work-ers has been added. There is updated and improved coverage of the unionized sector, including unionization rates for various industries and the growing importance of government unions and female membership in the labour movement, and the out-look for Canadian unionism.

In Chapter 11, the coverage of labour force trends has been updated, and a new *In the News* box deals with the changing nature of technological change, the possibility of technology replacing workers in service-industry jobs previously thought to be safe from technology, and the range of possible consequences (from very positive to very negative) of such technological change. There is new coverage of income by family type, and updated coverage of the growing problem of income inequality. Chapter 11 also includes a new section on how the incomes of Canadians and Americans com-pare, with some new information. Another improvement to Chapter 11 is its greatly simplified and clarified coverage of the topic of poverty, with new statistics on pover-ty rates using both the LICOs and Market Basket Measure approaches.

Chapter 12 contains a general updating and clarification of the coverage of the role of government in the economy, particularly the matter of federal budget deficits, and a new *You Decide* box asks students to think through the possible uses of govern-ment budget surpluses. In Chapter 13, there is updated coverage of environmental issues, particularly climate change and Canada's performance regarding environmental protection. The chapter on agricultural economics has been relocated to www.personmylabs.com

The final chapter's look into the future concludes with additional new material on Canada's challenges regarding its aging population and labour force, the retirement the baby boomers, and the development of a labour force with the skills and education needed for the twenty-first century.

Overall, the result of these changes is a text that is more current and that flows more effectively, providing considerably more opportunities for students to interact with the material.

Features

According to both students and teachers, a major feature of this book is its readability, which helps considerably in the learning and teaching of a subject that has an (undeserved) reputation of being rather formidable. Other aspects of the text include

- **Coverage of "The Basics"** Chapters 1, 2, and 4 through 7 provide good coverage of the microeconomics basics of markets and market structure.
- **Flexibility** In addition to these basics, a variety of other topics can be covered, including marginal cost–marginal revenue analysis (Chapter 8), competition policy (Chapter 9), labour markets and unions (Chapter 10), trends concerning jobs and incomes (Chapter 11), the role of government in the economy (Chapter 12), and the economics of the environment (Chapter 13). And additional material on The Politics of Economics or The Agricultural Sector can be accessed on www.pearsonmylabs.com
- **Interactivity** The "You Decide" and "In the News" boxes, together with the end-of-chapter questions and Integrated Study Guide, provide extensive opportunities for students to interact with the material, both on their own and in groups, as well as via the internet.
- **Pedagogical Tools** Learning objectives, "You Decide" boxes, "In the News" boxes, end-of-chapter questions, and current issues on our website all help students to focus on and apply the important points in each chapter.

Organization

To a considerable extent, the text consists of two sections, with the section through Chapter 8 covering mostly the basic elements of microeconomics and the second half of the book presenting specific topics, most of which involve data pertaining to Canada's current economic situation. Following the discussion of the basic problems and questions of economics and an examination of the Canadian economy, the text presents the basic tools of microeconomics—demand and supply—and how these interact to determine output and prices under a variety of conditions, ranging from highly competitive to monopolistic industries. In the second half of the book various topics are covered, including government policy toward business, labour markets and labour unions, trends in employment and incomes, government programs, financial problems and policy choices, and economic issues related to the environment and agricultural sector. The text concludes with a short chapter that ties the text together with a review of Canada's past economic directions and a discussion of future trends.

Supplements

The following supplements have been carefully prepared to aid instructors and students in using this edition:

Resources for Instructors

MyEconlab with eText for Microeconomics, 11/e via www.pearsonmylabs.com

Resources for Students

In addition to the Integrated Study Guide at the end of each chapter in the text, the following online study material is also provided.
* **MyEconlab with eText for Microeconomics, 11/e** via www.pearsonmylabs.com

Acknowledgments

Anyone undertaking a project of this magnitude and duration feels indebtedness to many people. In particular, I would like to express my gratitude to Bill Trimble, who said I should do it, Len Rosen, who refused to let me say I wouldn't, and all those teachers and students who used the first seven editions and offered helpful comments and suggestions. I would also like to thank the people whose reviews of all eight editions of the manuscript were so helpful: for the first edition, Ray Canon, Gord Cleveland, Ward Levine, Jim Thompson, and Ian Wilson; for the second, Alan Idiens and Chuck Casson; for the third, Linda Nitsou, Bo Renneckendorf, Gord Enemark, L.W. Van Niekerk, Stephen Wise, and Ann Dunkley; for the fourth, Carol Ann Waite, Izhar Mirza, John Parry, and Byron Eastman; for the fifth, Valerie Beckingham, Michael Loconte, Pauline A. Lutes, Peter J. MacDonald, Karen Murkar, John Parry, Don Pepper, Judith Skuce, Don Wheeler, and Peter Young; for the sixth edition, Peter Peters, Karen Murkar, Ian Wilson, Don Wheeler, Martin Moy, Bill Gallivan, Terri Anderson, and Jane Taylor; for the seventh edition, Worku Aberra of Dawson College, Frances Ford of New Brunswick Community College (Moncton), Carl Graham of Assiniboine Community College, Donald Howick of St. Clair College, Al Idiens of College of New Caledonia, Peter J. MacDonald of Cambrian College, Raimo Marttala of Malaspina College, Martin Moy of University College of Cape Breton, A. Gyasi Nimarko of Vanier College, John Pirrie of St. Lawrence College, and Charles Walton of Nova Scotia Community College; and for the eighth edition, Aurelia Best of Centennial College, Tatjana Brkic, Allan Green, and Jack Rink of Red River College, Peter J. MacDonald of Cambrian College of Applied Arts and Technology, Martin Moy of Cape Breton University, Ekaterina Gregory, Alan Idiens, and George Kennedy of College of New Caledonia, and Shirley Pasieka of Southern Alberta Institute of Technology.

Finally, I want to express my appreciation to my immediate family—Barb, Marnie, and Amber—who have provided support and understanding over unduly long periods of time.

I have no doubt that there are many improvements that can be made to this book, and welcome suggestions from teachers and students. Please write to me at Sheridan College, 7899 McLaughlin Road, Brampton, Ontario L6Y 5H9, or email me at **brian.lyons@sheridancollege.ca.** or **brianlyons3@gmail.com**.

Brian Lyons
March 2015

MyEconLab provides students with an opportunity to practice solving economics problems in a structured online environment. It also provides instructors with a powerful homework and test manager lets them create and manage online homework assignments, quizzes, and tests that are automatically graded. The 11th edition of this text comes with an associated MyEconLab course. The MyEconLab course includes:

- A robust bank of online questions correlated to the chapters in the textbook.
- Dynamic Study Modules
- Integration with Learning Catalytics
- Please contact your Pearson representative to help gain access to your course.

What Is Economics?

After studying this chapter, you should be able to

1. Explain what is studied in the field of economics.
2. Describe the three basic types of economic resources.
3. Explain the basic *economic problem* of scarcity.
4. Construct a production-possibilities curve from data concerning two products and show on the curve the effect of a change in the efficiency of producing one or both products.
5. Calculate or estimate the opportunity cost of a given economic decision.
6. Define the terms *standard of living, productivity, efficiency,* and *effectiveness.*
7. Calculate worker productivity in a given situation.
8. Explain how a given decision would affect efficiency and/or effectiveness.
9. Identify the three basic questions of economics.

Living in a world of 24-hour news channels and the internet, it is easy to feel overwhelmed by the constant stream of events being reported to us. Many of these events are of an economic nature, and they are often reported only briefly and with minimal explanations of the *reasons why* they have happened. This often leaves people feeling that economic changes just happen to them, and that they are at the mercy of forces beyond their understanding.

This need not be the case. Economic events don't just happen; they happen because something has *caused* them to happen. And a basic understanding of economics will let you perceive not only *what* is happening, but also *why* it's happening. Doing this does not require mastering difficult economic theories. Much of this book involves organizing things that you already know into a "tool kit," or a framework that can help you to understand the cause–effect connections underlying economic events. And this tool kit will help you not only to understand why things have happened, but also (with a little bit of luck) maybe even to foresee what is likely to happen in the future.

Let's start by getting a clear idea of what economics is all about.

What Is Economics?

Economics means different things to different people. To the householder, economics is the difficult task of balancing the family budget so that there is not too much month left over at the end of the money. To the business leader, economics is the problem of producing a product at a sufficiently low cost to be sold profitably in competition with the products of other producers. To a government leader, economics means making difficult policy choices between goals that often conflict with each other; this makes it impossible to please everyone and difficult to ensure re-election. To the general public, economics is usually associated with vague, incomprehensible, and often contradictory pronouncements by people called *economists*, who many people suspect were created in order to make weather forecasters look good.

Each viewpoint, representing a particular group (householders, business leaders, and government leaders), is only one aspect of the real meaning of economics. To the economist, economics deals with the broader question of how well a society's economic system satisfies the economic needs and wants of its people. Since the basic task of an economic system is to produce goods and services and to distribute them among the people of a society, the most common definition of **economics** is "the study of the decisions a society makes concerning the production of goods and services and how the society distributes these goods and services among its members."

This somewhat dry definition will lead us into considering much more interesting questions about Canadian society, employment, incomes, and government policy, such as

- In what occupations will job opportunities be greatest in the future?
- Should the government control the price of gasoline?
- Why are the wages of unskilled workers falling farther and farther behind the wages of skilled workers?
- Why does the price of gasoline fluctuate so much?
- Why do some professional athletes earn $10 000 000 per year, while other people earn only $10 000?
- Would a big increase in the minimum wage rate help to fight poverty?
- Who has the higher standard of living—Americans or Canadians?
- How many Canadians are really living in poverty?

economics

The study of the decisions a society makes concerning the production of goods and services and the division of these among its people.

Some aspects of economic matters, such as those above, raise *philosophical* questions; for instance, is it proper for the government to control apartment rents, or people's wages, or workers' strikes? Other aspects of economics, however, involve more *technical economic analysis.* For example, if the government increased the minimum wage rate by 10 percent, would this cause unemployment to increase by 5 percent? 2 percent? Or 0 percent? Often, economics also becomes involved with *value judgments.* For example, suppose experts agreed that a 10-percent increase in the minimum wage rate would cause youth unemployment to increase by 25 000. *Should* the government increase the minimum wage rate by 10 percent? Some people would favour increasing the minimum wage because of the expected benefits for the *employed.* Others would oppose the wage increase because it would reduce job opportunities for the *unemployed.* There is no "right" answer to this question, because the response to the question depends on the value judgment of the person answering it.

Folklore Versus Economic Analysis

Probably the greatest obstacle to the effective learning (and teaching) of economics is the fact that many people already think that they know a great deal about the subject. In fact, much of this "knowledge" consists of widely believed but not necessarily accurate ideas such as the following:

- Producers' profits add 20 to 40 percent to the prices we pay for products.
- Canadian companies cannot compete with foreign producers.
- Companies locate wherever wages are lowest.
- The key to increasing Canadians' standard of living is for governments to provide more benefits and services to them.
- A major increase in the minimum wage rate would reduce poverty drastically.
- If the rich paid higher taxes, the rest of us could pay much lower taxes and receive many more government services and benefits.
- A government ban on strikes by labour unions would be a simple way to boost Canada's economy.

None of these statements are accurate, but many people *believe* them to be true. One key objective of this book, and its companion text, *Canadian Macroeconomics: Problems and Policies,* is to replace such folklore about economics with the tools for accurate analysis of economic issues of importance to Canadians.

The Limitations of Economic Analysis

Because economics deals with the behaviour of people (consumers, business people, government policy-makers), economics cannot be a precise science such as mathematics. Similarly, economic analysis does not provide clear and simple answers to important questions, such as whether the government should increase the minimum wage rate. However, economic analysis can *clarify the choices* to be made. For example, economic analysis can be used to estimate the benefits and the costs of increasing the minimum wage rate. So, while economic analysis does not provide us with *decisions,* it does provide us with a much better *basis for making decisions.*

Then What Is Economics About?

Economics is about many matters both small and large. On a large scale, *macroeconomics* (after the Greek word *macro,* meaning "big") deals with broad aspects of the performance of the economy as a whole—such as recession, inflation, unemployment, and international trade and finance. These are the subjects of the companion text *Canadian Macroeconomics: Problems and Policies*.

On a small scale, *microeconomics* (after the Greek word *micro,* meaning "small") focuses on particular aspects of the economy such as consumer demand, supply, demand, and prices under various conditions, and the role of big business, labour unions, and government in the economy, as well as the economics of specific industries (such as agriculture) or specific issues (such as the environment). The purpose of this book is to develop an understanding of these microeconomic matters, which are important to all Canadians. Before examining these *specific* issues, however, we will consider the basic problems of economics *in general*. Then, in Chapter 2, we will examine the nature of Canada's economic system.

The Economic Problem: Too Many Wants, Not Enough Resources

The fundamental problem of economics—so basic that it is known as *the economic problem*—is the simple fact that we cannot have everything that we would like. And this reality forces us to make some difficult decisions.

All too often, however, this and other simple but key economic realities become lost in the confusing complexity of our modern economy. And a modern industrial or post-industrial economy can seem very bewildering, because it consists of a myriad of factors such as consumers, small businesses, big businesses, and ebusinesses. In addition, there are labour unions, governments, exports, imports, and the level of output. And to make matters more complicated, there is employment, unemployment, the money supply, interest rates, prices, the international value of the nation's currency, government tax revenues, government spending, consumer spending and saving, banks, profits, stock markets, and many other factors. Furthermore, each of these factors is related to the others in ways that are often subtle and complex. Such complexities often make understanding an issue difficult because they obscure the basic economic principles involved in the issue.

In order to better understand an economic issue, it is helpful to eliminate the many complexities associated with a modern economy, so that we can focus on the basic economic principles involved. To eliminate these complexities and focus on the basics, suppose that a group of people has been stranded on a deserted island. With none of the complexities of a modern economy to distract us, our group must come to grips with the single most basic economic problem: the people in the group have *economic needs and wants*, but there are only certain *economic resources* available to this particular group. The group needs and wants things such as food, shelter, clothing, security, and so on. To produce these things, the group can use the three basic types of economic resources, or **inputs**—the skills of the people in the group, the equipment they have, and the natural resources of the island.

The Skills of People (Labour)

The largest and most important single economic resource of any society is the skills of its people, which economists refer to collectively as **labour**. Labour includes all the skills possessed by a wide range of people, from manual labourers and skilled workers to managers and research scientists. In our island mini-society, people

inputs

Economic resources, such as labour, capital equipment, and natural resources, that are used to produce goods and services.

labour

The largest single productive input available to any economy, labour includes all of the productive talents of the people of a society, mental as well as physical.

would have various useful and necessary skills such as hunting, fishing, farming, building, planning, and managing.

Capital Equipment

Another vitally important economic resource is society's stock of **capital equipment** (also simply called **capital**), by which we mean its factories, equipment, machinery, computers, tools, and so on. Capital equipment is crucially important because it increases *output per worker per hour*, or **productivity**. And when each worker produces more, the society can enjoy more economic prosperity, or a higher **standard of living**—more goods and services per person. Figure 1-1 illustrates the importance of capital equipment.

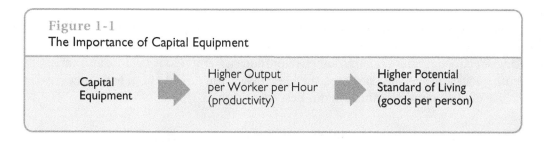

Figure 1-1
The Importance of Capital Equipment

Capital Equipment → Higher Output per Worker per Hour (productivity) → Higher Potential Standard of Living (goods per person)

While a modern industrial economy possesses a vast array of factories, machinery, equipment, and tools, our island mini-society will have only a few basic tools, such as spears, fishnets, and plows. So productivity will be low, and the people of the mini-society will have relatively few goods available to them. This scarcity of goods could make the people want to increase their stock of capital equipment, in order to increase their productivity and their standard of living.

Natural Resources (Land)

The third economic resource available to a society is natural resources, which economists refer to as **land**. In our island mini-society, these natural resources would likely be few and simple—waterways, fish, land, trees, plants, and so on.

People tend to think of natural resources as depletable (and depleting), as is the case with oil. But some natural resources, such as forests and fish, can be renewable if man-aged effectively, and technology is capable of creating entirely new resources, such as nuclear power and wind power. In a similar way, improvements in technology have increased energy supplies by developing new ways of extracting oil from the earth.

The Task of an Economic System

The task of the economic system of any society is to organize and use these economic resources, or productive inputs, to produce goods and services (**output**) of the *types* and *quantities* that will best satisfy the needs and wants of the people of the society. This process is shown in Figure 1-2 on the next page.

In our island mini-society, the process shown in Figure 1-2 would be quite simple: people with different skills would use simple tools, such as spears, nets, and plows, to

capital (equipment)
The tools, equipment, machinery and factories used to increase production per worker.

productivity
Output per worker per hour; a measure of efficiency.

standard of living
A measure of the economic prosperity of the people of a society, usually expressed in terms of the volume of consumer goods and services consumed per household or per person per year.

land
Short form for all the natural resources available to a society's economy as economic inputs.

output
The goods and services produced by a society using its productive inputs.

"If you were asked to choose just one test of an economy's performance, one of the strongest candidates would be growth in productivity. In the long run, increases in productivity—that is, in output per worker—are the only way for a country to raise its living standards."
— THE ECONOMIST

Figure 1-2
The Basic Operation of Any Economic System

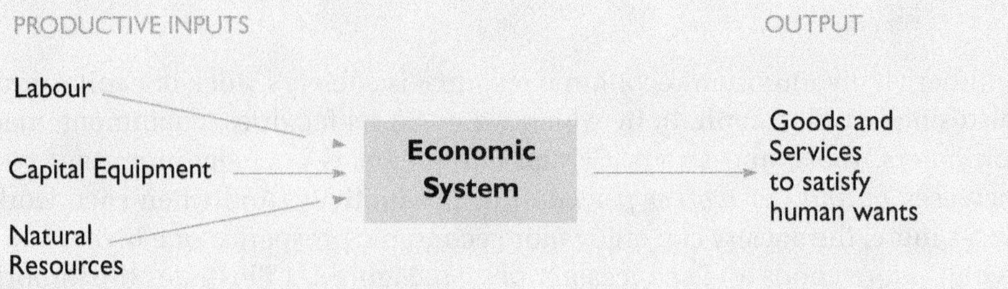

PRODUCTIVE INPUTS   OUTPUT

Labour

Capital Equipment   →   **Economic System**   →   Goods and Services to satisfy human wants

Natural Resources

---

produce products to satisfy basic needs, such as food, shelter, and security. In a modern economy, this process is much more sophisticated, involving a wide range of skills and "high-tech" equipment and resources to produce a tremendous volume and variety of both goods and services. However, the basic task is the same in both economies: to try to use our economic resources to our best advantage.

The Basic Economic Problem of Scarcity

How to use our economic resources to our best advantage is a particularly important question because we do not have enough economic resources to produce everything that we would like to have. This is the basic economic problem of **scarcity**: the economic resources (inputs) on the left side of Figure 1-2 are in *limited* supply, while the amount of goods and services wanted by people on the right side of Figure 1-2 seems to be *unlimited*. Since we cannot have everything that we want, we are forced to *make choices*, some of which might be difficult.

The island mini-economy illustrates this reality particularly clearly, because the choices are so limited. Suppose we have ten people available for work and decide to use five of them for getting food, three for getting fuel, and two for taking care of security by maintaining fences and guarding against certain threatening creatures that roam the island. If we find that we don't have enough food, we can increase food production by 20 percent by *adding* a sixth person to the "food team." However, this addition would require *removing* that person from either the group getting fuel or the group providing security. While we would be better fed, we would have either less comfort or less security. And *more of any one* of these items means *less of another*, forcing us to make difficult choices. This forgoing of one thing in order to enjoy more of another is called **opportunity cost** by economists.

We constantly encounter opportunity costs in our lives. Creating your personal budget is an exercise in managing opportunity costs. Since your income can't buy everything that you would like, you have to *make choices* as to what you will have and what you will forgo. Taking that dream vacation would be wonderful, but it will mean that you cannot buy that car that you also really want.

On a broader level, an entire nation, through its government, must come to grips with the same problems. The public wants the best health care and education systems as well as other government services, but governments lack the tax revenues to provide the ideal levels of all services. Since using more tax resources for one service would leave less for other services, the public must accept that each service will not be provided at an ideal level.

scarcity
The problem that, while economic inputs (and thus potential output) are limited in availability, people's wants and needs are apparently unlimited.

opportunity cost
The concept that the real economic cost of producing something is the forgone opportunity to produce something else that could have been produced with the same inputs.

So the basic economic problem of scarcity is a universal one, affecting all societies. This problem is illustrated in more detail by something called a *production-possibilities* curve, discussed below.

YOU DECIDE

The Scarcity Problem on a Personal Level

On a personal level, the problem of scarcity manifests itself in the form of your income. If your take-home pay is $2000 per month, then you have only $2000 (at most) to spend on consumer goods and services each month. If you spend $200 more this month on new clothes, you will have $200 less to spend on, say, restaurant dinners. Just like on the deserted island, enjoying more of one thing means that you must accept less of something else.

Or must you accept less of something else if you enjoy more of one thing? Unlike the unfortunate people on the deserted island, you have a credit card! You can put the $200 for the new clothes on the credit card, and enjoy $2200 of consumer spending this month. Better yet, put the restaurant dinners on the credit card too, and then you can enjoy $2400 of consumer spending—an increase of 20 percent from your monthly take-home pay of $2000.

QUESTIONS

1. Would you recommend this credit strategy to a good friend? Why?
2. If you would not recommend this credit strategy, how *would* you suggest that credit cards be used?

The Production-Possibilities Curve

One way of illustrating the problem of scarcity is with a **production-possibilities curve**. Suppose our islanders can only produce two items—vegetables and fish. If all their economic inputs were devoted to producing vegetables, they could produce 15 kilograms of vegetables daily, but no fish. This option is shown as combination **A** in Figure 1-3, which indicates vegetable production of 15 kg and fish production of 0 kg. If the islanders went to the opposite extreme and used all their productive inputs to produce fish, the result would be fish production of 5 kg and vegetable production of 0 kg, as shown by combination **F** in Figure 1-3 on page 8.

Of course, it is more likely that the islanders would choose to produce some combination of fish and vegetables, such as combination **B** (14 kg vegetables and 1 kg fish), **C** (12 kg and 2 kg), **D** (9 kg and 3 kg), or **E** (5 kg and 4 kg). In making their choice, however, they will be restricted by the limitations of the production-possibilities curve: since their economic resources are limited, *producing more of one product necessarily means being able to produce less of the other*. The islanders may *want* 4 kg of fish and 12 kg of vegetables (combination **X**), but they will not be able to *have* this combination. Resource scarcity dictates that if they want 4 kg of fish, they can only have 5 kg of vegetables, and if they are to have 12 kg of vegetables, fish production can only be 2 kg. So while it is possible to produce 4 kg of fish or 12 kg of vegetables per day, it is not possible to produce this much of both on the same day. The islanders choose among various combinations of products, and the production-possibilities curve reflects the limitations that resource scarcity imposes upon their choices.

production-possibilities curve
A curve that shows the economy's potential output, assuming that economic inputs are fully employed and efficiently utilized.

Figure 1-3
Production-Possibilities Curve

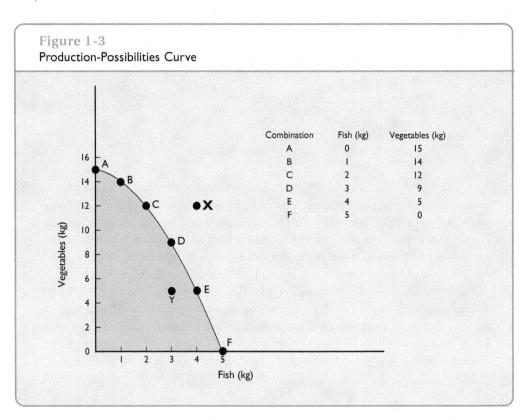

Combination	Fish (kg)	Vegetables (kg)
A	0	15
B	1	14
C	2	12
D	3	9
E	4	5
F	5	0

However, the combinations shown by the production-possibilities curve are based on two important assumptions—that the islanders use all of their available productive inputs, and that they utilize them as efficiently as possible. If some of their productive inputs were not used (if, for instance, some of the workers were sick, or one of their fish spears were broken), output would be below the potential level shown by the production-possibilities curve. Point **Y**, at which fish production is 3 kg and vegetable production is 5 kg, reflects such a situation. With fish production at 3 kg, vegetable production could be as high as 9 kg rather than 5 kg, and with vegetable production at 5 kg, fish production could be as high as 4 kg rather than 3 kg. However, if the islanders do not employ all of their productive inputs, their production will be below its potential. In fact, even if all inputs are employed, production may fall short of its potential. If the islanders' inputs (labour and capital equipment) were not producing fish and vegetables as efficiently as possible, production could be below its potential level and the islanders could still wind up at point **Y**.

It is important to recognize that the production-possibilities curve indicates the economy's *potential* output, assuming that economic inputs are fully employed and efficiently utilized. Production can be at any point *on* the production-possibilities curve (if inputs are fully and efficiently utilized) or *within* the shaded area (if they are not fully and efficiently utilized), but cannot be *outside* the curve.

However, the islanders need not live forever within the limitations imposed by the curve shown in Figure 1-3. This curve represents the situation at a particular point in time, given the economic resources available to the islanders at that time. If, in the future, they were to add to their economic resources, say, by building new capital equipment or developing new technologies, their potential output of *both* fish *and* vegetables could increase. Figure 1-4 shows the new production-possibilities curve that could be created by additions to or improvements in the islanders' economic resources.

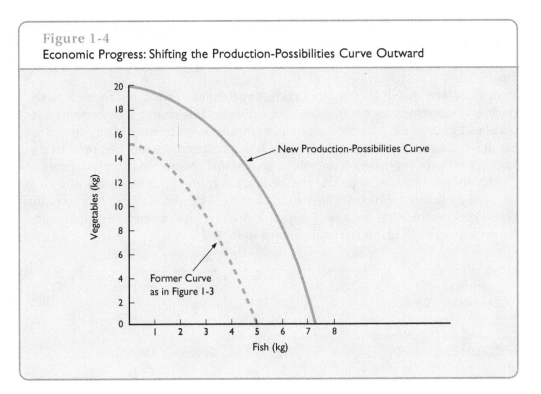

Figure 1-4
Economic Progress: Shifting the Production-Possibilities Curve Outward

The inquisitive reader may wonder why the production-possibilities curve is bowed outward as it is, rather than following a straight line. The shape of the curve reflects the changing efficiency of resources as they are shifted from one use to another. For instance, the table in Figure 1-3 shows that to increase fish production from 0 kg to 1 kg, we must sacrifice only 1 kg of vegetable production, which falls from 15 kg to 14 kg. But as we push fish production higher, we must forgo ever higher amounts of vegetable production to achieve the same increases in fish production. The second kilogram of fish costs 2 kg of vegetables, the third kilogram of fish requires the forgoing of 3 kg of vegetables, and so on.

To produce the first kilogram of fish, we would shift resources (labour and capital) out of their *least efficient use* in vegetable production (say, from the least productive land or using the least efficient capital equipment) into their most efficient use in fishing (say, using the best available equipment to fish the most productive waters). However, as we push fish production higher and higher, the trade-off between fish and vegetable production becomes less attractive. Increasingly, we have to shift labour and capital out of more efficient uses in vegetable production and into less efficient uses in fishing. The fifth kilogram of fish production is particularly costly in terms of vegetable production lost (5 kg of vegetables), as it requires that we shift labour and capital out of our last (and most efficient) use in vegetable production and into our least efficient use in fish production. As a result of these factors, the production-possibilities curve is not a straight line, which would reflect a constant trade-off between fish and vegetable production, but rather a curve which reflects changing efficiencies and trade-offs.

We have used a very simplified situation, involving a production-possibilities curve for only two products, to illustrate the basic nature of the problem of scarcity. While the real world is much more complex, involving many more inputs and outputs, the basic reality shown by our simple production-possibilities curve still exists. Because economic resources are limited, society must somehow make choices between various goods and services. Enjoying more of one thing means having less of something else—we must deal with trade-offs between the things that we want.

Opportunity Cost

These trade-offs shown by the production-possibilities curve bring us back to the concept of opportunity cost that we saw earlier in this chapter. The opportunity cost of using economic resources to produce any item is the amount of any other item that those same economic resources could have produced instead. The production-possibilities curve in Figure 1-3 provides a good visual illustration of this concept.

The opportunity cost of producing the first kilogram of fish is the loss of 1 kg of vegetable production, which declines from 15 kg to 14 kg. The opportunity cost of the second kilogram of fish is the 2 kg of vegetable production lost when their production falls from 14 kg to 12 kg, and so on, as shown in Table 1-1.

Table 1-1
Opportunity Cost

Combination	Fish Production (kg)	Vegetable Production (kg)	Opportunity Cost of
A	0	15	
B	1	14	The 1st kg of fish = 1 kg vegetables
C	2	12	The 2nd kg of fish = 2 kg vegetables
D	3	9	The 3rd kg of fish = 3 kg vegetables
E	4	5	The 4th kg of fish = 4 kg vegetables
F	5	0	The 5th kg of fish = 5 kg vegetables

We can express opportunity cost in terms of vegetable production forgone for *each additional kilogram* of fish, as shown in the table. Alternatively, we can calculate the opportunity cost of *any given amount* of fish production. For instance, the table shows that the opportunity cost of the third kilogram of fish production is 3 kg of vegetables, while the opportunity cost of 3 kg of fish production is 6 kg of vegetables, because if the entire 3 kg of fish had not been produced, vegetable production could have been 15 kg rather than 9 kg.

To calculate the opportunity cost of anything, ask yourself what could have been produced instead of it. For instance, the opportunity cost to society of $3 billion of military equipment is not the $3 billion, but rather the consumer and capital goods that could have been produced by the inputs used to produce the military equipment. And, to a student, the opportunity cost of riotous living on the weekend could be viewed as the 16 extra marks that he or she could have obtained on the economics test if the time had been spent studying.

In summary, scarcity is a basic economic problem that applies to all societies. In the following sections, let's consider some of the implications of the problem of scarcity.

Effectiveness and Efficiency

Because we cannot have everything that we would like, it is very important that we use our scarce economic resources wisely, by producing as much as we can of things that are needed and wanted. These goals are expressed by the terms *effectiveness* and *efficiency*, which are the two most basic measures of the performance of any economic operation, from an individual business to a nation's entire economy.

Effectiveness refers to achieving your goals. For instance, a parcel delivery company might measure its effectiveness by the percent of its deliveries that arrived at their destination on time. **Efficiency** refers to managing your economic resources so as to use the minimum amount of resources in order to achieve your goals—for instance, our parcel delivery company could measure its efficiency by the cost per parcel delivered.

For a nation's entire economic system, the ideas are the same, although on a grander scale: *effectiveness* would refer to the economy achieving the goal of producing goods and services that were wanted and needed, and *efficiency* would mean achieving the goal of producing them at a high volume and low cost per item. One commonly-used measure of efficiency is *productivity*, or output per worker per hour.

To recap, it is important that an economy be *both* effective *and* efficient. The more efficiently and effectively a society uses its economic resources, the more successful it will be in making available to its people larger volumes of goods and services that are needed and wanted and at lower prices. As a result, its people will enjoy a higher standard of living.

effectiveness
A measure of how well an economy performs in terms of producing goods and services that are needed and wanted.

efficiency
A measure of how well an economy performs in terms of producing high volumes of goods and services at a low cost per item.

YOU DECIDE

Measuring Your School's Performance

Our examples of effectiveness and efficiency in this section have dealt with businesses selling goods and services to consumers. However, the tools of effectiveness and efficiency could also be used to assess the performance of your school. ■

QUESTIONS

1. How could you measure the effectiveness of your school?
2. How could you measure the efficiency of your school?
3. Explain three ways to increase the efficiency of your school.
4. How would these ways of increasing efficiency affect your school's effectiveness?

The Three Basic Questions of Economics

As we have seen, the task of any economic system is to use its scarce economic resources efficiently and effectively so as to best satisfy the needs and wants of its people. Since economic resources are scarce and we cannot have everything that we want, we are forced to make certain very basic choices:

- What goods and services should we produce?
- How should we produce these goods and services?
- How should we divide up our output of goods and services among ourselves?

These are the three most basic economic decisions that must be made by every society, regardless of its stage of development or its economic system.

What to Produce?

Because economic resources, or productive inputs, are scarce, no society can have all the goods and services it would like to have. Instead, it must make choices or set priorities. For example, the people in our island mini-society would have to decide whether to produce fish, vegetables, shelter, fuel, or equipment such as spears and plows to help them to be more productive.

What makes such choices difficult is that we have to decide not only what *will* be produced, but also what *will not* be produced. If we decide to use six people to farm vegetables, those six people will not be available to catch fish or build shelter. So a decision to produce *more* of one thing necessarily means accepting *less* of other things. This type of decision forces us to set priorities, or decide what is most important to us. Obviously, making decisions relates to the goal of *effectiveness*, as discussed in the previous section, because the priorities we set will reflect our needs and wants, or how much we value each product.

Consumer Goods or Capital Goods?

One of the most basic "what to produce" decisions that must be made is whether consumer goods or capital goods will be produced. Consumer goods (such as food and fuel) can be enjoyed in *the present*, but are used up quickly and do not contribute to longer-term economic prosperity. Capital goods (such as tools and equipment), on the other hand, cannot be consumed and enjoyed *today*, but they will increase our productive efficiency *in the future*. In this way, capital goods will contribute to our production and prosperity in the longer term, by increasing our productivity for the many years that they will last. Figure 1-5 illustrates this choice.

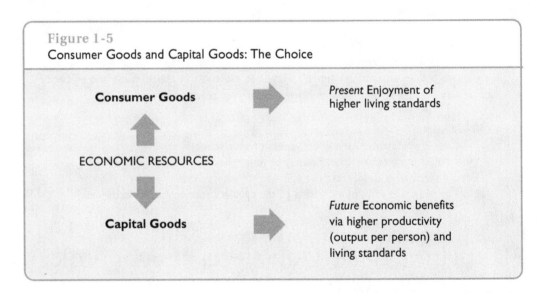

Figure 1-5
Consumer Goods and Capital Goods: The Choice

Consumer Goods → *Present* Enjoyment of higher living standards

ECONOMIC RESOURCES

Capital Goods → *Future* Economic benefits via higher productivity (output per person) and living standards

These decisions will have a crucial influence on the prosperity of a society both in the present and in the future. If our island mini-society emphasizes the production of consumer goods, its people will enjoy a higher standard of living in the present. However, if they emphasize consumer-goods production to the point of neglecting capital-goods production, they will enjoy less prosperity in the future. On the other hand, if its people are willing to do with fewer consumer goods in the present in order to build more capital goods, they can look forward to higher levels of economic prosperity in the future. In recent years, China has achieved rapid economic growth, largely by placing a high priority on the production of capital goods.

How to Produce It?

Once we have decided *what* we want to produce, we must decide *how* each product or service is to be produced. These decisions are a question of production methods:

How should we combine our scarce inputs of labour, capital equipment, and natural resources to produce a product or service?

As a simple example, suppose our island mini-society has decided to produce (cultivate) vegetables. The next question is, How should it do this? Should the vegetables be cultivated by hand? Or should people use simple tools such as hoes? Or more sophisticated equipment such as plows? Before the vegetables that the group wants can be produced, the group will have to decide how to produce them.

Generally speaking, our goal will be to develop production methods that result in *higher efficiency* so as to increase our economic prosperity. However, the decision becomes more complicated if we need to use economic resources to build capital equipment in order to increase output per worker. If the amount of capital equipment we can build is limited, would it be better to build a plow for cultivating vegetables or a net for fishing? This decision would be easier to make if we could find a way to measure the *costs* of building the plow and the net (in terms of the hours needed to build each of them) against the *benefits* of each (in terms of the increased output each would bring).

Obviously, in deciding the answer to this question, we are pursuing the goal of *efficiency* as discussed earlier. By being efficient, we avoid wasting our scarce economic resources, and thus increase our economic prosperity.

Who Gets How Much? (Dividing the Economic Pie)

The last of our three basic questions is this: How will we divide up our output of goods and services among ourselves? Who will receive what share of the output that we have produced?

Should everyone receive an equal share? Or should some people receive more than others? If some are to receive a larger share, why should they get more, and how much more should they get?

We have seen that a society will prosper economically if the work of its people is *effective* and *efficient*. This consideration argues in favour of inequality, with a larger "piece of the pie" providing incentives for people to work more effectively and efficiently. If everyone knew that they were going to receive the same share as everyone else, why should anyone make an extra effort or contribution?

In addition to effectiveness and efficiency, however, there is the goal of *fairness*. How wide a gap between the rich and the poor are we prepared to accept? What if some people cannot produce enough to live decently without help from others? Should the most productive people give up some of what they have produced (earned) in order to help the less productive ones? And if our answer to this question is yes, how much should the better-off people give up in order to help the less fortunate (or less capable)?

This question of how to divide up the economic pie is certainly the most controversial of the three basic economic questions. In a modern economy such as Canada's, a person's share of the "economic pie" depends on his or her *income*. If an accountant's income (*after taxes*, a factor that we will consider in Chapter 12) is twice as large as a labourer's, the accountant's share of the economic pie will be twice that of the labourer.

But by what standards should we *decide* who gets higher incomes and a larger share of the pie? Should NHL hockey players receive a larger share than doctors? Should lawyers have a larger share than social workers? Should firefighters get a larger share than day-care workers? Somehow, every society has to work out the question of how to divide up the economic pie.

Most running shoes are manufactured in Asia with low-wage labour, but New Balance also has plants in the United States that use computerized equipment.

Answering the Three Questions

In this chapter we have considered the three basic questions of economics that every society must answer—what to produce, how to produce it, and how to divide it up. Different societies answer these questions in very different ways. In the next chapter we will begin to examine how Canada's economic system deals with these most basic questions.

Chapter Summary

1. Economics is the study of how societies make decisions concerning the production of goods and services and how these will be distributed among its members. The basic task of an economic system is to use its productive inputs (labour, capital equipment, and land) to produce goods and services so as to satisfy the wants and needs of the people of the society. (L.O. 1, 2)
2. This task encounters the problem of *scarcity*: whereas society's economic resources are limited in quantity, people's wants and needs are apparently unlimited; thus, not all wants and needs can be satisfied. (L.O. 3)
3. The problem of scarcity and the related concept of opportunity cost can be illustrated with a production-possibilities curve. (L.O. 4, 5)
4. The opportunity cost of producing one good is the other goods that could have been produced with the same resources. (L.O. 5)
5. Scarcity makes it important that economic resources be used both effectively (so as to produce goods and services that are needed and wanted) and efficiently (with high productivity, or output per worker), in order to achieve a high standard of living. (L.O. 6)
6. The task of an economic system is to make the best possible use of its scarce economic resources by providing answers to the following three questions:
   (a) what to produce,
   (b) how to produce it, and
   (c) how to divide it among the people in order to best satisfy the needs and wants of the society. (L.O. 9)

Questions

1. "Every society, regardless of the economic system that it has, faces the problem of scarcity." This statement means that
   (a) all economies have depressions during which scarcities exist.
   (b) there are times when some products can be had only by paying high prices.
   (c) there are insufficient productive resources to satisfy all the wants of a society's people.
   (d) in the beginning, every society faces shortages, but a mature and prosperous economy such as Canada's overcomes scarcity over time.
   (e) None of the above.
   Explain your answer.

2. The economic problem facing any society would be less difficult if
   (a) governments provided more benefits for their citizens.
   (b) human wants were limited.
   (c) economic resources were more abundant.
   (d) production technology advanced at a more rapid pace.
   (e) Answers (b), (c), and (d) are all correct.
   Explain your answer.

3. Suppose that in an island mini-economy there were four people working: two people catching a total of six fish per day and two others picking a total of 8 kg of fruit per day. If they decided that they wanted to have three more fish each day, what would be a reasonable estimate of the *opportunity cost* of that decision?

4. John works for 6 hours and picks 12 baskets of berries. Jane works for 4 hours and picks 12 baskets of berries. This means that
   (a) John's productivity and Jane's productivity are equal.
   (b) Jane's productivity is 33 percent higher than John's productivity.
   (c) Jane's productivity is 50 percent higher than John's productivity.
   (d) John takes more rest breaks than Jane.
   (e) None of the above.

5. The following table shows production possibilities for two items—chairs and tables.

Combination	Chairs	Tables
A	0	6
B	8	5
C	15	4
D	21	3
E	26	2
F	30	1
G	33	0

   (a) What is the opportunity cost of producing the first table?
   (b) What is the opportunity cost of producing the third table?
   (c) What is the opportunity cost of producing the sixth table?
   (d) Draw the production-possibilities curve for chairs and tables on a graph, placing tables on the vertical axis and chairs on the horizontal axis.
   (e) If the economy achieved greater efficiency in the production of tables, how would the production-possibilities curve change?
   (f) If a more efficient method of producing chairs were developed, how would the curve change?
   (g) Suppose more economic resources (labour, materials, and capital) became available. How would the curve change?

6. After months of debate over which of its programs should receive more funds, the government decides to spend $2 billion more on health care rather than education, and to allow colleges to increase tuition fees in order to obtain more revenues. Explain the opportunity cost of this decision, from the perspective of:
   (a) college students, and
   (b) society at large.

7. Explain how each of the following management decisions would be intended to affect the *effectiveness* and/or *efficiency* of a firm's operations, and how it would do so.
   (a) A quality control program under which finished products are inspected more thoroughly in order to ensure that they meet quality standards.

(b) A profit sharing plan, under which a portion of the company's profits above a certain level will be shared with the employees.

(c) A restaurant reducing the number of servers it employs, so that each server has to serve 20 percent more tables than before.

8. In some of the situations in the previous question, a conflict could arise between effectiveness and efficiency; that is, a decision that increases efficiency would decrease effectiveness, or vice-versa. Which are these decisions, and why could such a conflict occur?

9. Visit the website of a newspaper or a news agency such as **www.msn.ca**, and look for news items concerning government policy or business decisions that involve the basic economic concept of opportunity cost. Write a brief explanation of the opportunity cost of the decision that you selected.

Study Guide

Review Questions (Answers to these Review Questions appear in Appendix B.)

1. According to the text, economics deals with
   (a) how to spend money more wisely.
   (b) decisions made by society concerning the production of goods and services.
   (c) decisions made by society concerning how goods and services are to be distributed among its people.
   (d) how a society satisfies the material needs and wants of its people.
   (e) Answers (b), (c), and (d) are all correct.

2. Which of the following are the three basic economic resources (inputs) identified in the text?
   (a) labour, entrepreneurship, money, and credit
   (b) labour, capital, and land (natural resources)
   (c) people, equipment, and money
   (d) labour, capital equipment, and money
   (e) None of the above.

3. The basic economic problem is
   (a) to achieve a more equal distribution of income in order to reduce poverty.
   (b) that economic resources are scarce while human wants are unlimited.
   (c) to establish prices that accurately reflect the relative scarcities of goods.
   (d) to establish a fair system of personal and business taxation.
   (e) to increase your exports so that they exceed your imports.

4. In a country such as Canada today,
   (a) *natural resources* are so plentiful that economists would not consider them to be "scarce."
   (b) *labour* is not scarce—there are about 30 million people of working age, and about one-third of them are not working.
   (c) *capital* is the only economic resource that could be considered to be "scarce."
   (d) all three of these economic resources would be described by economists as being "scarce."
   (e) None of the above.

5. Which is the best description of the opportunity cost of a $200 dinner?
   (a) It is not a serious consideration in the decision of whether to enjoy the dinner.
   (b) It is the nice clothes that could have been bought instead of the dinner.
   (c) It is $200.
   (d) It is only a problem if you don't have a credit card with you.
   (e) It is far too large!

6. The term *standard of living* refers to
   (a) the minimum income that a person or family needs in order to not be poor.
   (b) the average family income.
   (c) the economic prosperity of the people of a society.
   (d) the amount of goods and services consumed by an average person or family.
   (e) Both (c) and (d) are correct.

7. The most commonly used definition of *productivity* is
   (a) output per worker per hour.
   (b) the total output (gross domestic product) of a nation.
   (c) profit per unit of output.
   (d) the total number of worker-hours worked per year.
   (e) None of the above.

8. A factory employs 20 workers who work 8 hours per day and produce 800 boxes of candles per day. What is the productivity of workers in that factory?
   (a) 800 boxes of candles per day
   (b) 5 boxes of candles per worker per hour
   (c) 40 boxes of candles per worker per hour
   (d) 100 boxes of candles per hour
   (e) None of the above.

9. The "what" problem in economics means that
   (a) every society must in some way decide what goods it will produce (and not produce).
   (b) economists should tell us what goods should be produced.
   (c) goods and services should be produced as efficiently as possible.
       society should always produce only those goods that it can produce most efficiently with its technology and resources.
   (e) in every society, the government decides what goods will be produced.

10. In economics, the "how to produce" question refers to
    (a) decisions concerning how to go about marketing a product.
    (b) designing products so as to increase their appeal to consumers.
    (c) how much of each product to produce.
    (d) decisions concerning the production methods to be used to produce goods and services.
    (e) None of the above.

11. In economics, the question of "for whom" to produce goods and services means
    (a) how much should be exported and how much should be kept inside the country.
    (b) businesses must research the market for particular products before they produce and market them.
    (c) how should society divide up its total output of goods and services among the population.

(d) poor people buy bicycles; rich people buy big cars.

(e) the more society produces of one product, the less it can produce of other products.

12. A company's decision to introduce a new car that is designed in a manner that will appeal to higher-income women is an example of

(a) a "what to produce" decision.

(b) a "how to produce" decision.

(c) a "for whom" decision.

(d) a "why to produce" decision.

(e) None of the above.

13. The following is a table showing the production possibilities for fish and vegetables.

Combination	kg of Fish	kg of Vegetables
A	0	20
B	1	18
C	2	14
D	3	8
E	4	0

What is the opportunity cost of producing

(a) the first kilogram of fish?

(b) the second kilogram of fish?

(c) 2 kg of fish?

(d) the third kilogram of fish?

(e) 3 kg of fish?

(f) the fourth kilogram of fish?

(g) 4 kg of fish?

14. Imagine a production-possibilities curve for two products. If producers become less efficient at producing both products,

(a) the production-possibilities curve will shift outward (up and to the right).

(b) the slope of the production-possibilities curve will become steeper.

(c) the slope of the production-possibilities curve will become less steep.

(d) the production-possibilities curve will shift inward (down and to the left).

(e) None of the above will happen.

15. Imagine a production-possibilities curve for two products. If producers become more efficient at producing only one of the products,

(a) the production-possibilities curve will not be affected.

(b) the slope of the production-possibilities curve will change, and become either steeper or less steep.

(c) the entire production-possibilities curve will shift outward (up and to the right).

(d) the entire production-possibilities curve will shift inward (down and to the left).

(e) None of the above will happen.

Critical Thinking Questions

(Asterisked questions 1 to 5 are answered in Appendix B; the answers to questions 6 to 10 are in the Instructor's Manual that accompanies this text.)

*1. Suppose that you had only $200 and your mother was expecting a Mother's Day gift (tickets to yet another Rolling Stones concert) that cost $200; however, your car has just broken down and it will cost $200 to repair it.

(a) What would be the opportunity cost of buying your mother the gift?

(b) What would be the opportunity cost of getting your car fixed?

*2. What is the opportunity cost of your attending school this year?

*3. Rajinder wins $1 000 000 in a lottery. Does this mean that Rajinder no longer has to be concerned about the economic problems of scarcity and opportunity cost?

*4. Explain how each of the following management decisions would be intended to affect the *effectiveness* and/or *efficiency* of a company.
   (a) A plan whereby the company's sales representatives provide feedback and suggestions to management based on their experience with customers.
   (b) The introduction of a piece rate incentive plan under which workers are paid $2 for each of the first 50 products they produce, and $3 for each product beyond 50.
   (c) The use of industrial robots that are programmed to perform production tasks repetitively and with great precision.

*5. Explain whether each of the following is mainly intended to improve either the effectiveness or efficiency of a college, and how it is intended to do so.
   (a) a Key Performance Indicator survey of college students asking for their views regarding the quality of the education and services they are receiving.
   (b) an increase in class sizes at a college.

6. How could having an internet website improve the effectiveness and the efficiency of a business firm's operations?

7. The question of how to divide the economic pie can be a difficult one.
   (a) In some societies, old people who are unable to work any longer are given *no* share of the economic pie and are left to die. What economic factors might explain such a custom?
   (b) How does the custom referred to in part (a) compare to Canada's attitudes toward those who are unable to support themselves? What might explain this difference?

8. Regarding the question of how to divide up the economic pie, it has been suggested that the highest paid people in industry and government should receive no more than two-and-a-half times as much take-home pay as the lowest-paid workers. Do you agree with this suggestion? Why? What do you believe would happen if such a policy were implemented?

9. The text notes that although some of the Earth's resources can become depleted, new resources can also be created.
   (a) How can new resources be "created"?
   (b) If you had to pick only *one* new resource that could be created this way, which one would you choose? Why?

10. A common criticism of government departments and agencies is that their operations are *inefficient*.
   (a) What might explain why government operations are often inefficient?
   (b) What is the opportunity cost of any such inefficiency?

Use the Web (Hints for this Use the Web exercise appear in Appendix B.)

1. Visit the website of a newspaper or a news agency such as **www.msn.ca**, and look for news items concerning government policy or business decisions that involve the basic economic concepts of effectiveness and efficiency. Write a brief explanation of how the decision that you selected affects effectiveness and efficiency.

http://ca.msn.com

2

Canada's Economic System

After studying this chapter, you should be able to

1. Explain how a market system economy provides answers to each of the three basic questions of economics.

2. Explain how profits and the profit motive contribute to the effective and efficient use of economic resources.

3. Explain how competition contributes to the effective and efficient use of economic resources.

4. Identify the major strengths of market system economies.

5. Identify three types of problems that tend to occur in market system economies.

6. Describe how a command system operates, and compare its performance regarding effectiveness and efficiency to the performance of a market system.

7. Explain why Canada's economic system is appropriately described as a mixed free-enterprise system.

8. Describe three major types of roles played by government in the Canadian economy.

To overcome the problem of scarcity that we saw in Chapter 1, a society must make the best possible use of its limited economic resources. It must address the three basic questions of what to produce (and not produce), how to produce it, and how to divide it up among the people of the society. To deal with these questions, a society has to use its economic resources (labour, capital equipment, and natural resources) *effectively* (produce things that are needed and wanted) and *efficiently* (produce them in high volume and at low cost and price), thereby generating economic prosperity for its people.

This goal is no small challenge. The Canadian economy—the eleventh largest in the world—comprises over 36 million consumers with their own wants and needs, more than 1 million businesses using a vast array of capital equipment and producing millions of different goods and services, and a labour force of more than 20 million people with a wide variety of skills. How, then, does the Canadian economy organize all these economic resources to produce over $2 trillion ($2 000 000 000 000) of goods and services, and in the process succeed in providing its people with one of the highest standards of living in the world? How does it make the billions of economic decisions required to achieve this success?

The Market System

Most of Canada's economic system is organized according to a market system. In the **market system** (also known as the *free-enterprise system*), privately owned businesses (*free enterprises*) produce goods and services for a profit, in response to the demand of buyers. Nearly 80 percent of the total output of the Canadian economy is produced by such businesses, which are collectively known as the *private sector*. In the private sector, the key economic decisions are made by consumers and businesses.

In addition to its private sector, the Canadian economy has a substantial *government sector*, in which the key decisions are made by governments. The government sector accounts for about 20 percent of the output of the economy, consisting mostly of public services such as health care, education, and public security. In addition, governments play a number of other important roles in the economy, which we will examine later.

First let's examine what a market is and how it operates. Then we can see how a market system functions.

market system
An economic system in which economic decisions are made mainly by consumers and privately owned producers, in a decentralized manner.

What Is a Market?

Simply stated, a *market* is where buyers and sellers come together to exchange goods and services for money, or to buy and sell things. Figure 2-1 on the next page illustrates this concept a little more formally, using the market for pizza as an example.

Figure 2-1 shows that the market for pizza consists of

(a) a number of sellers offering to sell pizzas, in competition with each other (economists call this the *supply side* of the market), and
(b) a number of buyers offering to buy pizzas, in competition with each other (economists call this the *demand side* of the market).

In Figure 2-1, the interaction between buyers and sellers in the marketplace determines that the price of one pizza is $15.00 and 100 000 pizzas are sold each week. But if the willingness of buyers to buy pizzas (demand) or the willingness of sellers to sell them (supply) were to change, the price and sales of pizza would also change.

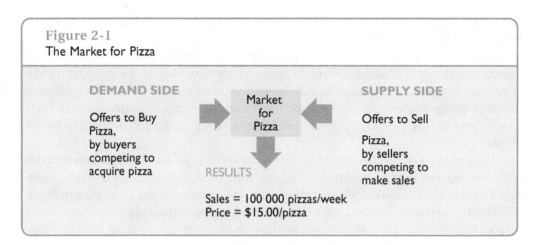

Figure 2-1
The Market for Pizza

DEMAND SIDE

Offers to Buy
Pizza,
by buyers
competing to
acquire pizza

Market
for
Pizza

RESULTS

SUPPLY SIDE

Offers to Sell

Pizza,
by sellers
competing to
make sales

Sales = 100 000 pizzas/week
Price = $15.00/pizza

How Do Markets Work?

Markets respond to changes in buyers' demand. For instance, if the demand for pizza increased (because there were more buyers, or buyers had more money, or they just liked pizza more than before), the increased demand would cause the price of pizza to increase, say, from $15 to $18 per pizza. This higher price, together with higher sales, would make it more profitable to make pizzas. Existing producers would increase their output, and new producers might start up, so that pizza production might increase from 100 000 to 110 000 pizzas per week.

In the same way, if the demand for pizza were to decrease, then the price would fall, making it less profitable to make pizza. With lower prices and lower sales, producers would make fewer pizzas, in response to the lower demand of consumers.

The "classic" form of market is a farmers' market or a flea market, where many producers and consumers come directly together to buy and sell various products. However, markets take many other forms. To most people, the most familiar market is at the retail level, where consumers buy goods and services from retailers. In addition, there are wholesale markets and commodity markets (where the buyers are businesses that bid for the products in an auction environment), labour markets (where people's time and skills are purchased and the price paid is a wage rate or salary), capital markets (or markets for loans, where the use of someone else's money is purchased and the price paid is the interest rate), and stock markets (where the shares of corporations are bought and sold).

Some markets, such as the market for babysitters, are extremely local in nature, while others, such as the market for wheat or oil, are worldwide in scope. In many markets buyers and sellers deal face to face, while in e-markets they deal over the internet without ever seeing each other. Regardless of its particular form, however, each market consists of a supply side and a demand side, as shown in Figure 2-1. In Chapters 4 to 6 we will examine the operation of markets in more detail.

Because demand is such a basic force in markets, the market system is sometimes said to be *demand-driven*. And because of the key role played by prices and price changes in adjusting production to demand, the market system is sometimes referred to as the *price system*.

Some markets are conducted over the internet. For examples, visit www.autotrader.ca and www.expedia.ca.

How a Market System Type of Economy Is Organized

Figure 2-2 illustrates the operation of a market system. The upper flows in Figure 2-2 represent consumers buying goods and services from businesses. These flows

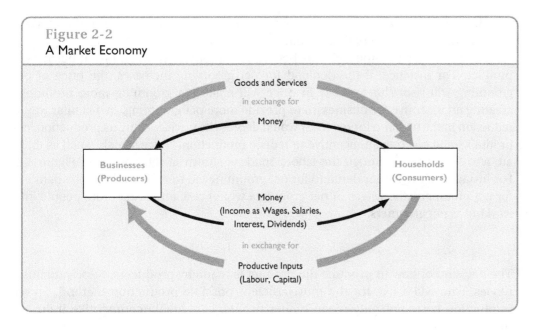

Figure 2-2
A Market Economy

Goods and Services

in exchange for

Money

Businesses
(Producers)

Households
(Consumers)

Money
(Income as Wages, Salaries,
Interest, Dividends)

in exchange for

Productive Inputs
(Labour, Capital)

represent many thousands of markets for specific goods and services, in which millions of consumers buy these items at the prices and in the quantities determined in the marketplace.

In other words, the upper flows would consist of the market for hamburgers, the market for CDs, the market for apartments, the market for baseball tickets, the market for haircuts, and all the other markets for all of the other goods and services that consumers buy. And in each of these markets, a *price* is determined for the good or service involved.

The lower flows in Figure 2-2 represent a different side of the economy, in which businesses buy the inputs for producing the goods and services shown in the top flows.

So the lower flows would include markets for factory workers, for retail clerks, for accountants, for professional athletes, and for all of the other job skills that the economy needs. And in each of these markets, a *price*—in the form of a wage rate or salary level for that type of skill—is established. Also, the lower flows would include markets for the capital needed by businesses; for instance, funds being loaned by people to businesses, for a *price*, or an interest rate.

The operation of a market system such as that shown in Figure 2-2 involves billions of individual decisions by consumers, business firms, and workers about consumer purchases, production levels, prices, the numbers of workers to be employed, wage rates, capital investment, and so on. It is through these innumerable decisions, made in countless markets, that the answers are developed to the three basic questions of what to produce, how to produce it, and how to divide it up.

How the Market System Answers the Three Questions

What to Produce?

Consumers play the largest role in deciding what will be produced. Since the basic goal of business is to earn a profit, businesses will produce those goods and services that are in demand. This process is described by the phrases "consumer sovereignty" (meaning that the consumer is "king of the marketplace") and "dollar votes" (meaning that, by purchasing a product, a consumer is in effect casting a vote in the market-place for the production of that product).

Prices provide an important link between what buyers want and what businesses produce. For instance, if the demand for pet grooming increases, the price of pet grooming will rise. The increase in price will make pet grooming more profitable, creating an incentive for businesses to provide more pet grooming. In a similar way, a reduction in the demand for red meat would depress its price, making its production less profitable and creating an incentive to reduce production. "Price signals" such as these are also transmitted through the labour markets shown at the bottom of Figure 2-2. For instance, if the higher demand for pet grooming led to an increase in the demand for pet groomers, the wages of pet groomers would rise, attracting more people into working as pet groomers.

How to Produce It?

The decision of how to produce the product is made by producers, or private businesses, who will strive for the most efficient possible production method. Lower production costs not only mean higher profits; in a highly competitive industry, they may be the key to survival.

Prices also help to determine the methods for producing goods and services. In determining the most efficient production methods, it makes obvious economic sense to minimize the use of the most scarce inputs. Prices help to minimize using scarce inputs because the *more scarce* an input is, the *more costly* it will be for producers to buy. For instance, if gasoline is scarce, its price will be high. Since it is such a costly input, producers will minimize waste of it, and will use substitutes, if possible. So to maximize their profits, businesses have to manage society's scarce economic resources carefully, economizing the most on the use of the most scarce resources.

How to Divide up the Economic Pie?

As we saw in Chapter 1, a person's share of the economic pie depends on his or her income. For instance, if electricians take home (after taxes) five times as much pay as day-care workers, an electrician's share of the economic pie will be five times as large as that of a day-care worker.

And since your *income* is really the *price* of your productive skills, *prices* play a major role in deciding the question of how to divide up the economic pie. Like other prices, people's incomes (or salaries or wages) are mostly determined by the interplay of supply and demand—in this case, the supply of and the demand for your productive skills. For example, if skilled trades workers are in short supply but in high demand, their incomes (and their share of the economic pie) will be quite high. On the other hand, if there is a large supply of low-skilled workers relative to the demand for them, they will have low incomes and a small share of the economic pie.

How Does the Market System Organize the Use of Economic Resources?

As we have seen, organizing the vast and varied economic resources of an economy such as Canada's to produce millions of goods and services effectively and efficiently is an enormous task. On the face of it, the market system might appear to be ill-suited to such a complex task. The market system has no central plan, and seems to lack any organizing or coordinating forces—rather, it looks more like an economic "free-for-all" in which people buy whatever they want to, produce whatever they want to, and work wherever they want to. Millions of consumers and producers make economic decisions, which are decentralized and apparently uncoordinated, rather than organized according to a centralized plan. Nevertheless, the market system has in practice proven to be the best system for achieving both effectiveness and efficiency in the use of economic resources and in providing a high standard of living for its people.

Then what are the forces within the market system that enable it to organize and mobilize economic resources so effectively and efficiently? The two key features of the market system that promote effectiveness and efficiency are the *profit motive* and *competition*.

The Profit Motive

Profits are those funds from a business's sales revenues that are left after all expenses and taxes have been paid. Profits are therefore available for reinvestment in the business or to be paid out as dividends to the shareholders who own the business.

The *profit motive* plays two vital roles in the operation of a market system. First, profits provide incentives for businesses to use economic resources both effectively and efficiently. By producing goods and services that consumers will buy—that is, by using economic resources *effectively*—a business will increase its sales and profits. And by producing those goods and services at the lowest possible production cost—that is, by using economic resources *efficiently*—a business will also increase its profits.

The second important role of profits is that they provide funds for the *purchase of capital equipment*. Each business purchases capital equipment to improve its own efficiency and profitability. But when many businesses do this, the result is improved productivity across the economy, which is the basic source of higher living standards for society generally. So the reinvestment of profits by businesses makes an important contribution to a society's economic prosperity.

In addition, many Canadians have a large stake in the profitability of corporations. Nearly half of adult Canadians own shares of corporations, many in registered retirement savings plans. In addition, about three dollars of every eight in *pension funds* in Canada are invested in corporate shares, so many people who do not think of themselves as shareholders have a stake in the success of Canadian corporations. In fact, millions of Canadians have billions of dollars invested in shares. These people not only receive part of corporate profits as dividends but also depend on the prosperity of those corporations for financial security in their retirement.

Despite the financial importance of profits, there is a great deal of misunderstanding and even hostility among the public concerning profits. The very word *profit* evokes for many people images of exploitation of workers and consumers, or *profiteering*. One misconception concerns the *level* of profits. Many people believe that manufacturers' profits amount to 30 cents or 40 cents per dollar of sales, whereas before-tax profits are actually about 7 cents to 10 cents per dollar of sales, and after taxes, most manufacturers' profits amount to only 4 cents or 5 cents per dollar of sales. Ironically, the public believes 20 cents per dollar of sales to be a "fair" profit, indicating that there is a great deal of confusion regarding this matter.

The public also has misconceptions concerning the *uses* of profits, which are widely regarded as being hoarded away in corporate coffers or being paid out in lavish dividends to vulgarly wealthy shareholders. In fact, about 30 percent of corporation profits goes to taxes, and most of the remainder is reinvested by businesses in capital equipment. Dividends to shareholders generally amount to a modest return on their

profits
Those funds left from a business's sales revenues after all expenses have been paid; such funds are therefore available (after taxes have been paid) for dividends to shareholders and reinvestment in the business.

Different Views of Profits
Suppose a corporation has annual sales of $600 million, profits after taxes of $24 million, 4000 employees, and $600 million of shareholders' capital invested in the company.

The *employees* might feel that they are underpaid. If the $24 million of profits were divided among them, each would receive $6000 more ($24 million ÷ 4000).

Consumers might feel that $24 million in profits shows that they are being overcharged by this company. Realistically though, the total elimination of the manufacturer's profits would only reduce prices by 4 percent ($24 million ÷ $600 million).

From the viewpoint of the *shareholders* of the company, their capital is earning a rate of return (after tax) of only 4 percent ($24 million ÷ $600 million). Compared to other investments, this is not a very attractive rate of return.

So while employees and consumers complain about its high profits, investors might be thinking of selling their shares in the company.

investment, and these "capitalist" shareholders include not only the wealthy but also ordinary Canadians. Because of the public's misconceptions about profits and the negative emotional overtones attached to the word, many companies prefer to call their profits *earnings*.

Competition

Competition, which is the other key element in a market system, plays three vitally important roles in a market economy. First, competition forces businesses to provide consumers with what they want in order to increase their sales and profits. In this sense, competition *promotes effectiveness* in the use of economic resources. Second, competition *promotes efficiency* in the use of economic resources. To prosper in a competitive marketplace, a producer must keep its operating costs low, by being as efficient as possible. And third, competition forces producers to *keep prices as low as possible*, in order to compete successfully for business. So, competition ensures that the advantages of higher efficiency/lower production costs are passed along to the consumer, allowing the maximum possible number of people to enjoy them.

Competition is closely linked with *information* in the effective functioning of markets. A free marketplace provides a wide variety of goods and services, of various qualities and at different prices. If consumers are well-informed about what items are available and at what prices, they will be better able to take advantage of the opportunities offered by a free and competitive marketplace. By contrast, poorly informed consumers will be more likely to get poor value for their money.

In summary, a highly competitive marketplace pushes private profit-making producers to serve the interests of consumers by being effective and efficient and by keeping prices down. By contrast, in situations in which there is little or no competition, producers tend to be less responsive to consumers' preferences (less effective), to be less efficient than they could be, and to charge consumers excessive prices.

Together, the two incentives of profits and competition tend to push producers to use economic resources both effectively and efficiently. The ability of the market system to coordinate the decisions of millions of businesses and individuals automatically in response to changes in consumer demand has been referred to as "the miracle of the market." As long ago as 1776, in *The Wealth of Nations*, Adam Smith, the earliest advocate of this economic system, described business people as being led by an "invisible hand" (the profit motive) "to promote (the interest of) the society more effectually than when they really intend to promote it."

Figure 2-3 summarizes the market system's powerful incentives for efficiency and effectiveness, which contribute greatly to productivity and prosperity.

For an indication of the role of information in markets, visit www. autotrader.ca and "shop" for a used car.

Figure 2-3
Incentives in a Market System

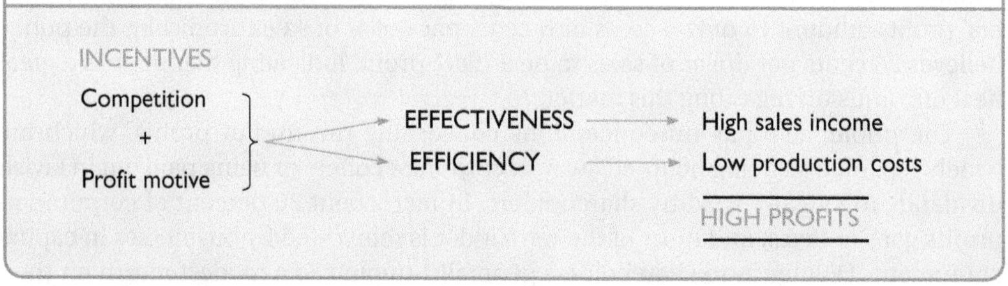

INCENTIVES

Competition
+
Profit motive } → EFFECTIVENESS ────→ High sales income
              → EFFICIENCY ────→ Low production costs

HIGH PROFITS

Figure 2-3 also shows how the basic concepts of effectiveness and efficiency relate to the income statement and the profits of a business. A business that is *effective* in the sense of producing what buyers want will enjoy a *high sales income*. If that business is also *efficient*, it will have *low production costs* and other expenses. The more effective and efficient a business is, the higher its profits will be.

Strengths and Weaknesses of the Market System

We have seen that about four-fifths of the Canadian economy—the private sector—is organized as a market system. How well does this sector of the economy perform?

According to the criteria of *effectiveness* and *efficiency*, the market system performs very well. With respect to effectiveness, there is no economic system that is more responsive to consumer demand than the market system, which is marvellously flexible in adjusting its production automatically in response to changes in consumer preferences. And with respect to efficiency, no system provides greater incentives for efficient use of economic resources than the combination of the profit motive and competition.

However, the market system also has certain weaknesses. A basic problem is that a free market will tend to produce too little of key *public services* such as health care and education. For instance, if college costs $10,000 per year, only 100 000 people will attend college, because they consider the high cost of attending college to be justified by the *benefits to them*. However, having more college graduates is of significant *benefit to society*, in the form of more productive and educated citizens. So society would benefit if *more* people attended college, making it logical for the government to *intervene in the market* and reduce the cost of college education, which would encourage more people to attend college. The most common way for government to do this is to operate colleges itself, and finance them partly with grants. Reducing the cost of public services also increases the access of citizens to higher education and health care, which many view as an important social policy.

Another problem that can develop in a market system is **market power**, or monopoly-like power in some markets. Sometimes, producers may be able to band together and agree to limit competition among themselves, resulting in higher prices and profits. In the same way, some workers may be able to band together into labour unions that achieve essentially the same result—less competition and higher prices (wages) for their members. In both cases, an organized group (of businesses or workers) reduces competition in the marketplace for its own benefit, at the expense of others.

And while free markets for labour provide strong incentives for people to acquire skills that are in demand and to work efficiently, it is also true that in a market system there is a tendency for great *inequality in incomes*, as some people enjoy very high incomes, while others live in poverty.

While the profit motive provides strong incentives to be effective and efficient, it also provides incentives to do some things that are less beneficial to society. These things include unfair competitive practices, misleading of consumers, unfair treatment of vulnerable employees, and pollution of the environment.

On a larger macroeconomic scale, another fundamental problem with the market system is *economic insecurity*. Market economies sometimes slump into a **recession**, during which the economy's output falls and unemployment rises. During a typical recession in Canada, the number of unemployed people rises by more than half a million.

market power
The ability to raise one's prices; usually associated with a dominant or monopolistic position in the market.

In 2011, the top 20 percent of Canadian families earned an average income of $198 000 in the marketplace, while the bottom 20 percent of families earned only $11 500 on average.

recession
A period during which the economy's output is falling and unemployment is high.

The Command System

command system

An economic system in which economic decisions are made mainly by the government, in a centralized manner.

The major alternative to the market system is known as the **command system**. In a market system, we have seen that the key economic decisions are made by millions of consumers and businesses in a very *decentralized* manner. However, in a command system, all major economic decisions are made in a *centralized* manner, by the government.

All of the major production facilities such as factories and farms are owned and operated by the government. Government economic planners draw up a central economic plan that sets out the government's priorities and maps out all major economic activities for the nation. The economic planners decide *what to produce* through detailed instructions to plant managers that tell them what products to produce. Since the government owns all major production facilities, the planners also decide *how to produce* those products, because the planners determine the production technology and methods. And since the government is the only employer, the planners also can decide the incomes of various groups, and so decide *how the economic pie is divided.* The most famous example of a command system was, of course, the economy of the former Soviet Union.

The command system appears simple in principle, and organizing all of society's economic resources according to a central economic plan sounds attractive. However, the command system was not the success that its advocates expected. The system enjoyed some early successes in the production of capital goods and military goods, largely because the government gave these areas generous resources since they contributed to the government's priorities of economic development and national security.

But with respect to the production of consumer goods, the command system ultimately proved to be a failure. A major problem was that a system in which all decisions are made in a centralized manner was simply unable to cope with the countless millions of decisions required to organize effectively and efficiently all of the resources needed to produce a wide array of consumer goods. The result was numerous errors in planning, which would cascade through the production system. For instance, an error in the planning of the production of a particular metal would make it impossible for another factory to produce its quota of a particular part for television sets, which would make it impossible for the television factory to produce workable television sets.

Another basic weakness of the command system was its *lack of incentives.* Most producers were monopolies, so they had no competition to push them to be effective and efficient, and no feedback regarding how satisfied their customers were. The profit motive was also lacking—if a plant manager did an excellent job of being efficient and so had money left in the plant's account at the end of the planning year (in other words, "profit"), the government would take those funds, and probably give the plant *less* money for next year's operations, because it had revealed that it didn't need all the funds than it had been given.

Russians joked that in their planned economy, "We pretend to work and they pretend to pay us."

As a result, producers tended to be neither effective nor efficient in their use of economic resources. Most of the consumer goods that were available were of low quality and limited usefulness, and shortages of many goods and waiting lists for goods were common.[1]

---

[1] Another reason for shortages of consumer goods was that the government placed higher priority on capital goods and military goods.

By the time of the collapse of the Soviet Union in the late 1980s, its command system was failing miserably to produce goods and services efficiently and effectively, and the standard of living of the people had been falling for some time.

Ultimately, the command system proved incapable of organizing and coordinating through a central planning process the countless millions of decisions needed to run a complex modern economy. The central planning process was simply unable to deal with the gigantic task of organizing the resources of such a vast economy. As the Soviet command system was collapsing, one of its economic planners said, "The latest index of products has 20 million articles. The plan can't detail that amount." And to make matters worse, it failed to motivate its people to work effectively and efficiently.

Following the failure of the Soviet economy around 1990, many countries that had been using the command system (including China) shifted significantly in the direction of the market system approach.

Russians joked that "Our economy is perfectly planned—you can be sure that when there are no eggs, there will also be no bacon."

The Ubiquitous Nature of the Market System

A strong argument can be made that markets are a natural aspect of human behaviour. People have different abilities, needs, and wants, so it is only natural for them to exchange (buy and sell) what they produce. For instance, when the former Soviet Union's command system failed to produce the goods wanted by consumers, an illegal but very active black market for many such goods developed. Some of these were smuggled from Western nations into the Soviet Union, where they sold on the street for very high prices. Other goods were produced illegally by Russians themselves in secret plants and sold to consumers through the underground economy. In both cases, the unfulfilled demand of Soviet consumers created a market opportunity for enterprising (and risk-taking!) Soviet "entrepreneurs."

"Unofficial" markets also developed in the industrial sector of the Soviet economy. Often, the central planning system would fail to deliver the materials needed by plant managers for their operations—sometimes managers would get too little or none at all, while at other times they would receive more materials than they needed. In order to meet their production quotas, plant managers set up a "parallel market," through which managers would trade surplus materials with each other, receiving in return materials that were needed or credits for future materials when these became available.

The Market System in Perspective

Perhaps the most outstanding feature of the market system is the high degree of *economic freedom* for both consumers and businesses. This freedom underlies the key strengths of the market system, such as the ways in which its incentives of the profit motive and competition drive producers to be both efficient and effective managers of economic resources. The result is that market economies tend to be the best at generating high levels of productivity and a high standard of living.

Ironically, this freedom also underlies the most serious weaknesses of the market system. If producers are free to dominate industries and markets, the problem of market power (or monopoly power) will tend to arise in some situations. Because individuals and groups are free to earn (take?) as big a share of the pie as they can get, some can wind up with a very large share of the pie, while others get only crumbs. And because consumers and businesses are free to spend—and not spend—as they see fit, there are times when spending is inadequate and the economy slides into recessions and high unemployment. These weaknesses of the market system have led governments to take corrective action in various ways that introduce into the market system some elements of governemt decision-making.

The Mixed Economic System of Canada

Canada's economic system can best be described as a *mixed free-enterprise system* because, while this type of system is basically a market system, it also includes a large government sector and a great deal of government involvement in its private sector.

The Private Sector

As we have seen, nearly 80 percent of the total annual output of the Canadian economy is produced by the private sector. In this sector, in which the vast majority of Canadians are employed, businesses produce goods and services in response to market demand and for a profit. In the private sector of the economy, households (or consumers) and businesses make the key economic decisions.

The Government Sector

In the government sector, the key economic decisions are made by governments. The government sector accounts for more than 20 percent of the annual output of the economy, most of which consists of public services such as health care and education. In broad terms, governments play three major roles in the economy.

First, governments are involved heavily in the provision of *public services*. From health care, education, and law enforcement, to traffic control, public transit, and postal service, Canadian governments provide the public with a wide range of services in various ways. In most cases, such as health care, police protection, and elementary and secondary education, the public pays for these services with its tax revenues. In effect, then, the government is buying these services collectively on the public's behalf from the government's own employees (such as teachers) and from others (such as doctors) who provide the services. In some cases, governments *operate enterprises* that provide services, including Crown corporations (such as Canada Post and the Canadian Broadcasting Corporation) and public commissions that provide services (such as public transit and electricity). In many cases, such as public transit and post-secondary education, governments *subsidize public services*. **Subsidies** use tax revenues to pay part of the cost of the service, making the cost to the user lower. The grand total of these government-provided services is impressive—when the services of all government employees are counted as government purchases, Canadian governments account for nearly 25 percent of all the goods and services produced by the economy.

Second, governments *regulate* in many ways the economic behaviour of the various "players" in the economy. Because a free marketplace can be a rough game in

subsidies

Payments by the government of part of the cost of a service in order to reduce the cost to the user of the service.

YOU DECIDE

To Subsidize or Not to Subsidize?

As noted in this chapter, a market system will tend to produce less than the ideal amount of public services such as education and health care. To correct for this shortcoming, the government can *subsidize* such services, by giving taxpayers' funds to providers of the services. This government assistance permits these organizations to provide more of these services and to reduce their prices, which encourages citizens to make greater use of these services. ▪

QUESTIONS

1. What is the opportunity cost of subsidizing public services?
2. If the government had only enough funds to subsidize two of the following services, which ones would you choose to subsidize? Explain the reasons for your answers.
   (a) public transit in a major city
   (b) a city's symphony orchestra
   (c) government campsites at provincial parks
   (d) college programs in business and technology

which some players can be hurt by the unfair tactics of others, governments establish—and enforce—rules, in the form of laws and regulations. There are so many of these regulations that only a few will be mentioned here, as examples.

The purpose of many laws is to **protect consumers**. Examples of such regulations are laws prohibiting monopolistic pricing by sellers, outlawing misleading advertising, protecting borrowers, and setting safety standards for products.

Other laws **protect workers**, by establishing standards for employers to follow, such as minimum wage rates and safety standards, and guaranteeing their right to join labour unions. There are also laws to **protect investors**, such as laws requiring financial disclosure by businesses, laws governing banking, and laws against fraud. Some laws **protect the environment**, by regulating how producers deal with the toxic by-products of their operations.

While many government regulations limit the actions of businesses, some regulations **protect producers**, particularly farmers, many of whom suffer from low and unstable prices. Also, governments protect some producers from foreign competition.

In addition, some prices are regulated by government, including electricity rates, tobacco and alcohol prices, some transportation rates, and apartment rents in some areas.

In summary, governments at all levels—federal, provincial, and local—play an active role as "referees" in the marketplace.

The third major area of government involvement in the economy is the *redistribution of income* through programs that transfer income from people with higher incomes to those with lower incomes. These programs include transfer payments such as employment insurance, welfare, old age security allowances, and assistance to farmers and other groups. In addition, various features of the income-tax system (tax credits) reduce the taxes payable by those with lower incomes, or entitle them to tax refunds, such as the sales tax credits received by many students.

In 2011, government programs increased the average income of the poorest 20 percent of Canadian families from $11 500 to $29 200.

gross domestic product (GDP)
A measure of the total value of goods and services produced and incomes earned in a country in one year.

Taken together, these government programs amount to a great deal of government involvement in the Canadian economy. The grand total of spending by Canadian governments (on goods and services, transfer payments to persons, and interest on government debt) usually amounts to nearly 40 percent of Canada's **gross domestic product** (GDP), which measures the total of goods and services produced and incomes earned in Canada in any one year. When the many government regulations of economic activity as described earlier are added, the Canadian economy is accurately called a "mixed" system—still mostly "market" in nature, but with a large amount of government involvement.

A Preview of Microeconomics

In Chapter 3, we will take a closer look at parts of the Canadian economy, particularly the various forms of business organization, as well as the "small business" and "big business" sectors of the economy. In Chapters 4 through 6, we will cover the basics of demand and supply, and examine how prices are determined in markets. In the ensuing chapters, we will see how demand and supply interact to determine prices and incomes in a wide variety of markets under a wide range of conditions. In Chapters 7 and 8, we will examine how the prices of goods and services are determined in various types of industries, ranging from highly competitive industries that have a large number of small firms to industries with only a few firms, to monopolies. In Chapter 9, we will consider government policy regarding these various types of industries. In Chapters 10 and 11, we will consider markets for labour and trends in the distribution of income and employment, and in Chapter 12 we will examine the role of government in the economy in more detail. This will complete our microeconomic study of the four major sectors of the economy—consumers, business, labour, and government.

Chapter Summary

1. A market system type of economy (also called the price system and the free enterprise system) operates through markets. In these markets, what to produce is decided by consumer demand, how to produce it is decided by producers, and the division of the economic pie is decided by people's incomes. (L.O. 1)
2. Profits play a vital role in the operation of a market system. Profits provide incentives for the efficient and effective use of economic resources and are a major source of funds for capital investment, which contributes to economic prosperity by increasing output per worker. (L.O. 2)
3. Competition is essential to the effective operation of a market economy. Competition keeps prices and profits down and forces producers to be both efficient and responsive to consumers. (L.O. 3)
4. The main strength of the market system is its high living standards, which are the result of the strong incentives this system provides for efficient and effective use of resources. (L.O. 2, 3, 4)
5. The main weaknesses of the market system are its tendency toward periodic recessions, a lack of competition in some markets, and a tendency for incomes to be distributed very unevenly. (L.O. 5)

6. In a command system, the government decides the answers to the three basic questions of economics. Command systems tend to be less effective and efficient than market systems, due to their lack of incentives. (L.O. 6)

7. Canada's economic system is called a *mixed* or *mixed free enterprise* system: while it is basically a market or free-enterprise system, it includes significant elements of government involvement in the economy. (L.O. 7)

8. Major aspects of government involvement in the Canadian economy are the provision of various public services, the regulation of economic activity, and the redistribution of income from those with higher incomes to those with lower incomes. (L.O. 8)

Questions

1. In a *market* type of economic system, the questions of *what to produce, how to produce it*, and *how to divide up the economic pie* are basically decided by
   (a) the people, working consciously for the social good rather than for their own self-interest.
   (b) social custom and tradition.
   (c) the free decisions of households and businesses, made out of self-interest.
   (d) the government.
   (e) economists.

   Explain the reason for your answer.

2. The market type of economic system would correct a shortage of lumber by
   (a) lowering the price of lumber and the profits of the lumber producers who are causing the shortage.
   (b) the government paying a subsidy to lumber producers to encourage them to increase their production of lumber.
   (c) the government instructing producers to increase their production of lumber.
   (d) increasing the price of lumber and the profits of producers of lumber.
   (e) the government establishing a government-owned lumber company.

   Explain your answer.

3. Everyone knows that child care is far more important than hockey, yet hockey players are paid far more than daycare workers. Why is this so?
   (a) Hockey players are really entertainers rather than producers of a service.
   (b) There are fewer professional hockey players than daycare workers.
   (c) Hockey players are more skilled than persons who get less pay.
   (d) The demand for hockey players is greater than for daycare workers.
   (e) Compared to the demand for them, good hockey players are more scarce than daycare workers.

   Explain your answer.

4. Write a paragraph that evaluates the accuracy of the following statement.
   "Profits serve no useful purpose and contribute nothing to society economically. All that profits do is make prices much higher and take vast amounts of money from consumers and give it to businesses and their wealthy shareholders."

5. The sixteenth-century philosopher Michel de Montaigne asserted that, "No man can profit except by the loss of others, and by this reasoning all manner of profit must be condemned." Do you agree with his position? Does every economic transaction necessarily involve a winner and a loser?

6. Explain how a development in communications technology such as the internet could improve the way in which some markets function.

7. Canada has a mixed economic system, in which both the marketplace and government play a role. For each of the following situations, explain why you think that it would be best dealt with by the market, or by government action.
   (a) There are too many restaurants in a town, and several are losing money.
   (b) The gap between the rich and the poor is very wide, and the poorest citizens are unable to afford even the bare necessities of life.
   (c) The largest supermarket chain in the country is planning to buy the second-largest chain, which would give it a near-monopoly in many communities.
   (d) A trend toward healthier eating has driven the price of chicken up so sharply that many consumers are complaining to the government about the increased prices.
   (e) Several manufacturers are cutting costs by dumping waste into a local river.

8. The internet has brought markets into your home as never before. Visit **www.autotrader.ca** and look for the best price that you can find on a used 2013 Honda Accord. Before the internet, how did people shop for a used car? How has the internet changed the effectiveness and the efficiency of the market for used cars?

Study Guide

Review Questions (Answers to these Review Questions appear in Appendix B.)

1. A *market system* type of economy is one in which
   (a) most economic decisions are made by consumers and privately owned businesses.
   (b) most economic decisions are made in a decentralized manner.
   (c) the dominant influence on economic decisions is the government.
   (d) private and government decision-makers have an equal influence on economic decisions.
   (e) Both (a) and (b) are correct.

2. The "what to produce" problem in economics means that
   (a) the government decides what goods will be produced.
   (b) if we produce more of one good, we must accept less of something else.
   (c) goods and services should be produced as efficiently as possible.
   (d) we should produce only those goods that we can produce most efficiently with our technology and resources.
   (e) every society must somehow decide what goods it will (and will not) produce.

3. In a market system type of economy, which of the following best describes how the question of *what to produce* is decided?
   (a) The most important factor is the government, which through its own purchases and the regulations it places on businesses, is the dominant influence concerning what is produced.
   (b) Privately owned businesses (producers) make the decisions as to what to produce, in the final analysis.

    (c) The most important factor is consumer demand, which influences prices and profits, and thus incentives for businesses to increase or reduce production.

    (d) This decision is made by the people, because everybody works consciously for the social good rather than for his or her own self-interest.

    (e) None of the above.

4. *Consumer sovereignty* means that

    (a) consumers do not have legal liability for their misuse of products.

    (b) the question of how products are produced is decided mainly by consumers.

    (c) the question of "what to produce" is decided mainly by consumers.

    (d) the customer is always right.

    (e) None of the above.

5. A market system type of economy would correct a surplus (oversupply) of running shoes by

    (a) raising the price of running shoes and the profits of manufacturers of running shoes.

    (b) government instructing running shoe manufacturers to reduce their production of running shoes.

    (c) reducing taxes on running shoes, to encourage people to purchase them.

    (d) lowering the price of running shoes and the profits of their manufacturers.

    (e) None of the above.

6. In economics, the "how to produce" question refers to

    (a) how to design products so as to increase their appeal to consumers.

    (b) decisions concerning how to go about marketing a product.

    (c) decisions concerning the production methods to be used to produce goods and services.

    (d) how much of each product to produce.

    (e) None of the above.

7. In a market system type of economy, which of the following best describes how the question of *how to produce* goods and services is decided?

    (a) Those productive inputs that are particularly scarce will be used more efficiently, because they will cost producers more.

    (b) The actual decisions regarding the production methods to be used are made by producers (businesses).

    (c) The consumer decides this question, through the demand for goods and services.

    (d) The major factor influencing this decision is the government.

    (e) Both (a) and (b) are correct.

8. In economics, the question of "for whom" to produce goods and services means

    (a) businesses must research the market for particular products before they produce and market them.

    (b) how much should be exported and how much should be kept inside Canada.

    (c) how society should divide up its total output of goods and services among the population.

    (d) poor people buy bicycles; rich people buy big cars.

    (e) the more society produces of one product, the less it can produce of other products.

9. In a market system type of economy, the question of *how to divide up the economic pie* is basically decided by
   (a) the social status of individuals and groups.
   (b) the marketing departments of businesses.
   (c) how much income is received by individuals and groups.
   (d) the government.
   (e) economists.

10. In a market system type of economy, *prices* play an important role in determining
    (a) what will be produced.
    (b) the production methods to be used.
    (c) how the "economic pie" will be divided.
    (d) Both (a) and (b).
    (e) (a) and (b) and (c).

11. State whether each of the following assertions regarding business profits is *true* or *false*.
    (a) T or F
       They provide strong incentives for businesses to produce what consumers want.
    (b) T or F
       They provide strong incentives for businesses to produce goods and services as efficiently as possible.
    (c) T or F
       Most profits are paid out as dividends to shareholders.
    (d) T or F
       They are an important source of funds for capital investment, which increases productivity and our standard of living.
    (e) T or F
       They are considerably larger than many people believe them to be.

12. State whether each of the following assertions regarding competition in a market economy is *true* or *false*.
    (a) T or F
       It results in higher profits for businesses.
    (b) T or F
       It promotes the efficient use of economic resources.
    (c) T or F
       It promotes the effective use of economic resources.
    (d) T or F
       It is not considered to be an important element in the operation of a market economy.
    (e) T or F
       It keeps down the prices paid by consumers.

13. State whether each of the following assertions regarding the market system type of economy is *true* or *false*.
    (a) T or F
       It makes effective use of economic resources for meeting the wants of consumers.
    (b) T or F
       It provides strong work incentives for businesses and for people.
    (c) T or F
       It makes efficient use of economic resources (or productive inputs).
    (d) T or F

It grows steadily, and is not prone to economic fluctuations and crises, such as recessions or depressions.

(e) T or F

It tends to generate a high material standard of living.

14. Which *one* of the following criticisms of the market type of economic system is *inaccurate*?
   (a) It tends to result in a very unequal distribution of income, with a few very rich people and many living in poverty.
   (b) It suffers from economic instability—periods of recession and inflation.
   (c) It fails to produce goods and services efficiently.
   (d) Private economic power groups can become established, and enrich themselves at the expense of less powerful groups.
   (e) It tends to create economic insecurity, particularly due to periodic increases in unemployment.

15. In a *command economy*, the questions regarding *what to produce, how to produce it*, and *how to divide it up* are basically decided by
   (a) the people, working consciously for the social good rather than for their own self-interest.
   (b) tradition.
   (c) the free decisions of households and businesses.
   (d) the government.
   (e) None of the above.

16. Command systems generally use economic resources
   (a) less effectively but more efficiently than market economies.
   (b) more effectively and more efficiently than market economies
   (c) as effectively and as efficiently as market economies.
   (d) more effectively but less efficiently than market economies.
   (e) less effectively and less efficiently than market economies.

17. A key reason for the situation in the previous question is that
   (a) command economies carefully plan the use of economic resources.
   (b) command economies lack the incentive of profit.
   (c) command economies lack the incentive of competition.
   (d) in market economies, producers have the advantage over consumers.
   (e) Both (b) and (c) are correct.

18. Canada's economic system is best described as
   (a) a command system for capital goods decisions and a market system for consumer goods decisions.
   (b) a market system with extensive elements of government involvement.
   (c) a market system for capital goods decisions and a command system for consumer goods decisions.
   (d) a command system with elements of market involvement.
   (e) None of the above.

19. The three major roles played by governments in Canada's mixed economic system are
   (a) national defence, health care, and education.
   (b) environmental protection, income security, and health care.
   (c) income security, health care, and education.
   (d) income security, health care, and national defence.
   (e) environmental protection, public safety, and gun control.

Critical Thinking Questions

(Asterisked questions 1 to 4 are answered in Appendix B; the answers to questions 5 to 8 are in the Instructor's Manual that accompanies this text.)

*1. Explain why you think that each of the following represents a market or command element of Canada's mixed economic system.
   (a) Growing demand for goat meat causes its price to increase sharply.
   (b) Primary and secondary education is provided at no cost to students and their families.
   (c) An oversupply of computers causes their price to decrease considerably.
   (d) The government stops the largest corporation in an industry from buying its largest competitor.
   (e) The poorest Canadians are able to receive welfare benefits.
   (f) Following a year-long work stoppage, hockey players accept pay reductions.
   (g) The 10 percent of Canadians with the highest incomes pay 53 percent of all personal income taxes paid.

*2. Suppose that a manufacturer is selling two products (product A and product B) for $100 each, and is making a profit (before taxes) of $7 on each product.
   (a) If strong demand increases the price of product A by 2 percent, by what percentage will the profits from product A rise?
   (b) If weak demand for product B causes its price to fall by 1 percent, by what percentage will the profits from product B decrease?
   (c) Given these facts, what would be the logical decision for the management of the company to make?

*3. Three of the following are essential to the operation of a free-enterprise market economy; one is not essential. Which one might a market economy operate *without*?
   (a) the profit motive
   (b) markets
   (c) corporations
   (d) prices

*4. In Chapter 9, we will see that Canada's federal government enforces legislation that is intended to promote competition in Canadian markets.
   (a) Why is competition among producers necessary for a market system economy to operate effectively and efficiently?
   (b) What dangers arise if there is a lack of competition in markets?

5. Suppose there were a shortage of apartments.
   (a) How would a market system correct this situation?
   (b) If the government passed a law that made it illegal to increase rents, how would this law affect how the market for apartments worked?

6. Suppose that, due to an interruption of international crude oil supplies, gasoline became so scarce that its price became too high for many people to afford. Suppose that the government decided that instead of letting the marketplace decide through very high prices who would—and would not—get gasoline, it would be fairer to low-income households to use a command approach, by *rationing* gasoline. For a low price, the government would sell each household a limited number of coupons that could only be redeemed for gasoline.
   (a) If you were administering such a rationing system, how would you decide

who gets how many gas coupons, and at what price?

(b) Suppose that some people received more gas coupons than they really needed, while others received fewer than they needed. What would probably happen in these circumstances?

7. What do you like the least about how Canada's economic system answers the three questions of what to produce, how to produce it, and how to divide it up? Why do you think this problem exists? What would you do to correct this problem?

8. Explain to someone who lives in a country with a command system why your standard of living is higher because you live in a country with basically a "market system" type of economy.

Use the Web (Hints for this Use the Web exercise appear in Appendix B.)

1. Gather some classmates and have a contest. Visit **www.expedia.ca** and see which of you can find the lowest-cost flight from Halifax to Vancouver that flies during the next four weeks. How has the internet changed the market for travel?

http://ca.msn.com

2. Think of something that you would really like to have. Now visit **www.ebay.ca** and see if you can find it. Can you find this textbook on eBay? What was the price? How did people shop for used items *before* the internet? (It's okay to ask your parents; this will be regarded as research rather than cheating.)

3

Business Organization in Canada

After studying this chapter, you should be able to

1. Summarize the advantages and disadvantages of the sole proprietorship, the partnership, and the corporation.

2. Describe the importance of small business in the Canadian economy, particularly in terms of producing services and providing employment.

3. Identify three of the most serious problems facing small businesses in Canada.

4. Explain how the Canadian Federation of Independent Business (CFIB) assists Canada's small business community.

5. Describe the importance of the *big business* sector of the Canadian economy, in terms of output, employment, and exports.

6. Define the terms *multinational enterprise* and *corporate concentration*, and describe the significance of each for the Canadian economy.

7. Explain why control of the modern large corporation usually does not lie in the hands of its shareholders.

8. Describe the role of government enterprises in the Canadian economy and assert the arguments in favour of the government retaining them and the arguments in favour of privatizing them.

We have seen that prices are determined by supply and demand, a process that we will examine in detail in Chapters 4, 5, and 6. In this chapter, we will examine some of the structural aspects of the supply side of the economy—the various forms of business enterprise in Canada—to gain more insight into the business sector that supplies most goods and services.

The most common forms of business enterprise are the sole proprietorship, the partnership, and the corporation, each of which has certain characteristics, advantages, and disadvantages. Listing and describing the pros and cons of the different forms of business organization can be pretty dull, so we will try to enliven the discussion with the story of Dan's Doughnut Den instead.

Dan's Doughnut Dens

Dan, an enterprising young man employed by a large multinational corporation, decided that he was tired of working for someone else and would go into business for himself. He found it quite simple to start up his own business—after obtaining a licence from the municipal government, he rented an appropriate building and purchased equipment and supplies with $25 000 of capital obtained from his own savings, a small inheritance, and some loans from his relatives. Before long, "Dan's Doughnut Den" opened. The business was a **sole proprietorship**; that is, it was totally owned by Dan.

At first, things went exceptionally well: enjoying his newfound freedom and independence, Dan worked harder than he ever had, and sales were good and the business seemed headed for success. As the business grew more complex, Dan was working very long hours, many of which were spent recruiting, training, and supervising staff, and dealing with his bank manager. Dan found financial matters a continual hassle— his bank manager was reluctant to provide as much credit as Dan felt he needed, and was always pestering Dan for financial information, which Dan was too busy to prepare carefully. Actually, keeping financial records for the business was a constant and time-consuming chore, and one at which Dan was not too skilled. Partly as a result of this problem, preparing his income tax return was a nightmare that tied up much of his time for about a month each year. Finally, he hired an accountant to sort it out, and was horrified to learn that he owed nearly $4000 in taxes, most of which he didn't have—he had invested practically all of the earnings back into the business, including the opening of another Doughnut Den across town. The sales at the new location were good, too, but having two outlets put an even greater strain on Dan's limited time and talents. For Dan, the crunch came when some of his suppliers and the Canada Revenue Agency (CRA) threatened to sue him for unpaid debts and taxes. Upon consulting his lawyer, Dan learned, to his dismay, that as the sole proprietor of a business he was subject to *unlimited liability*. That is, if the business went bankrupt, he could lose not only the assets of the business but also his personal assets, such as his house.

Still, Dan thought, the business had a lot of promise, with strong sales at both locations. What was required, he concluded, was more than just hard work; he needed more management experience and more capital. So Dan decided to change the business from a sole proprietorship to a **partnership**. One of his new partners was Sally, an old high-school friend of Dan's who had a diploma in Business Administration from Sheridan College. Sally was able to contribute $40 000 to the capital of the business. Perhaps more importantly, Sally brought a more systematic approach to the management of the business, which soon began to show up in the profit figures. These figures were calculated (much more proficiently) by the other new partner, Ed, who also con-

sole proprietorship
A business firm owned (and usually managed) by a single person who bears full legal liability for the firm's debts.

partnership
A business firm owned by two or more persons, with each person bearing full legal liability for the firm's debts.

limited partner
A partner who invests in a business but takes no active part in the management of it, and whose liability is limited to the amount invested.

general partners
Partners who take an active part in the management of the business and who have unlimited personal liability for its debts.

tributed $50 000 to the capital of the business. Ed kept the books, working on weekends and in the evening after working at his regular job in an accountant's office. Unlike Dan and Sally, Ed took no active part in the management of the business and was therefore a **limited partner**: if the business went bankrupt, his liability was limited—all he could lose was the $50 000 he had invested. Dan and Sally, on the other hand, were **general partners** who had unlimited liability and could therefore lose their personal assets if the business went bankrupt. As is customary in partnerships, all of the partners took out life insurance policies on each other's lives, so that if one died, the others would have sufficient cash from the insurance to buy the deceased partner's share from his or her heirs. This practice ensured that the death of a partner would not force the business to dissolve. The three partners signed an agreement outlining their respective rights and responsibilities, and the proportions of the profits that each would receive.

The infusion of new capital and managerial expertise improved the operation of the business considerably, and things went quite well for a while. However, after a period of time, disagreements began to develop among the partners. Dan continued to work almost as hard as before, and began to resent the share of the profits taken by the others who, he felt, weren't working as hard as he was. He found this particularly hard to accept because he was the one who had undertaken the effort and risk necessary to start the business originally. Sally felt that, if anything, she was contributing more to the business than Dan, due to her superior business knowledge. Sally's increasingly frequent reminders to Dan that her capital and know-how had saved the business only aggravated the situation (Sally's grade in Human Relations at Sheridan College had been a well-deserved low D, and she had fought with the teacher over it). Ed was annoyed by these attitudes on the part of his partners: while he didn't work full-time at the business, his after-hours accounting tasks on their behalf made for many a long day for him. Furthermore, he knew that without the accounting data and analysis that he prepared, Sally couldn't manage the business nearly as effectively as she did. Also, he had contributed more money to the business than either of the other two (the $50 000). The disagreements came to a head when, after a heated exchange with Ed, Dan learned that Sally had signed certain long-term contracts on behalf of the business, which Dan believed to be unwise. Since Sally was a partner, there was no way Dan could cancel these contracts—he was bound by Sally's decisions. Worse yet, as a partner, he was personally liable for the debts of the business. Dan was furious that unilateral decisions by someone else could possibly cause the bankruptcy of *his* business and the loss of *his* personal assets. The other two partners threatened to pull out of the partnership, which would almost certainly mean the end of the business. Dan went home that night wishing that there were some way that he could collect on the insurance on the lives of his partners.

corporation
A business firm that is a separate legal entity from its owners, or shareholders, each of whose liability is limited to the amount of his or her investment in the firm.

Finally, Dan decided that too much was enough; the partnership just couldn't work over the long term. On the advice of his lawyer, Dan decided to change the form of the business into a **corporation**. As his lawyer explained to him, the corporation would be owned and controlled by **shareholders**, and would be a separate legal entity from the shareholders. This meant that if the corporation went bankrupt, the shareholders' liability would be limited to their investment in the corporation's stock. Control of the corporation would lie with its **board of directors**, which would be selected by the shareholders, who would have one vote per share held. As the lawyer pointed out, Dan could control the board of directors, and thus the corporation, by owning (or controlling the votes of) 51 percent of the shares of the company.

shareholders
The owners of shares (stocks) in a corporation; shareholders may or may not have voting rights and their liability is limited to the amount invested.

The corporation was set up so that Dan and his wife held 85 percent of the shares, with Dan owning 45 percent and the other 40 percent being registered in his wife's name, in order to split their dividend income and reduce their total personal income

board of directors
A group of people elected by the shareholders of a corporation to provide direction to the management of the corporation.

taxes. A few family friends bought the other 15 percent of the shares. The friends were attracted not only by the prospects for the success of the business but also by the limited liability of shareholders and the tax treatment of the gains from their investments, since both dividend income from their shares and any capital gains realized from sale of their shares for a profit would be subject to favourable tax rates. In addition, as the lawyer pointed out, if the business were ever to expand, the corporate form of organization could prove advantageous for raising the necessary capital, because the corporation could sell shares to the public.

The incorporation process was complex and quite costly, but it seemed like an excellent idea. The two partners were bought out, improved equipment was purchased, and the facilities were renovated. A qualified manager was hired, a website and online purchasing system was implemented, and a sophisticated sales promotion campaign was undertaken. Sales and profits rose, and there were bonuses for the managers and substantial dividends for the shareholders. Dan found that incorporation brought tax advantages to the business, too. When the business was first a sole proprietorship and then a partnership, its income (profit) was taxed as personal income, at personal income tax rates, which became quite high as the income of the owners rose. However, the profits of the corporation were taxed at *corporate income tax rates*, which were lower unless profits were quite low. (On the other hand, the shareholders were somewhat disappointed to find that they were subject to "double taxation"—not only were the profits of the corporation taxed, but the dividends they received out of after-tax profits were also taxed, although at reduced rates, as their personal income.) Bank credit became more available as the business prospered, with the opening of three more outlets. After talking to his investment advisor, Dan also considered selling an issue of shares to the public to raise capital to finance expansion into other provinces.

While Dan found being president of a successful and rapidly growing corporation exciting (not to mention financially rewarding), he also found that, as president, he seemed to spend all of his time in his office, doing paperwork and meeting with managers, committees, and lawyers to talk about financing arrangements, short-, medium-, and long-range plans, reorganization plans, controls systems, and seemingly endless government regulations that had to be followed. At times, Dan longed for the days when he worked in the shop, where he had spent time talking with his customers, and when life was simple.

Dan's wishes were soon to be answered. Fed up with Dan's heavy responsibilities and long working hours (as well as impressed by the assets he had accumulated), his wife established a relationship with the manager of Dan's largest outlet (an ambitious young man anxious to get ahead in the organization) and divorced Dan. She then teamed up with the other shareholders (her friends) against Dan at a shareholders' meeting. While Dan's 45 percent of the shares made him the largest single shareholder, the other shareholders (including his ex-wife) were able to outvote him and remove him from the presidency. The new board of directors was kind enough to offer Dan a job as manager of the company's largest outlet (an opening created by the very recent promotion of its former manager to the presidency of the company), but Dan had lost interest in the business. He declined the offer and went to work as a letter carrier for Canada Post, where, he had been told, he wouldn't ever have to worry about anything. As a shareholder in Dan's Doughnut Dens, Ltd., Dan is entitled to any dividends per share that are paid to the other shareholders, and he lives quite comfortably on this income, plus his Canada Post salary. While he still owns 45 percent of the company's shares, he does not attend shareholders' meetings of the company. Now see the accompanying "You Decide" box for an update to Dan's story.

Small Business in Canada

www.industrycanada.ca

55 percent of small businesses have only 1–4 employees.

Because small business includes a wide range of enterprises, various definitions are used to describe it. According to a definition used by Industry Canada, a small business is any goods-producing firm employing fewer than 100 workers and any service-producing firm with fewer than 50 workers. Firms between these sizes and 500 employees are considered medium-sized, and firms with 500 or more employees are classed as large.

There are between 1.1 and 1.2 million employer businesses (businesses that have employees) in Canada. Over 98 percent of these, or about 1.1 million, are classed as small businesses, because they have 1–99 employees. Small business includes a tremendous variety of individuals, firms, and economic activities: professionals such as doctors and lawyers; farmers; small-scale manufacturers producing toys, boats, clothing, furniture, and a host of other products; retailers such as drug stores, gift shops, grocery stores, clothing stores, bookstores, music stores, and variety stores; service industry operations such as dry cleaning, hairdressing, restaurants, motels, real estate, insurance, services to business, employment agencies, repairs, and landscaping; and construction, which is characterized by large numbers of small contractors and sub-contractors. To gain a quick impression of the small business sector in your community, just visit www.yellowpages.ca.

Small businesses may be small, but collectively they make a big contribution to Canada's economy. Small businesses employ nearly 8 million people, or about 70% of Canada's private-sector labour force, and it is estimated that in recent years they have accounted for about 80 percent of job creation in the private sector of the economy. The output of small businesses amounts to over 40 percent of the output of all private businesses, and the Business Development Bank of Canada has estimated that they account for as much as 20–25 percent of the exports that are so important to Canada's economy.

private corporation

A private corporation has fewer than 50 shareholders.

Small businesses use all the forms of business organization: while over half are sole proprietorships or partnerships, many are corporations. Many of these corporations are **private corporations**, meaning that they have fewer than 50 shareholders.

Private corporations are not required by law to publish considerable financial information in the same way as **public corporations** must, because private corporations do not sell shares and bonds to the general public to raise capital.

public corporation

A public corporation has 50 or more shareholders.

Canadian Federation of Independent Business

Until the early 1970s, small business owners in Canada felt that they lacked a voice in the federal and provincial governments. As a result, they believed, government policies were often formulated without consideration of their effects on small business, which was being threatened by the expansion of taxation and regulations, and the proliferation of bureaucratic "red tape" associated with these. In response to these problems, several organizations of small businesses developed, the most important of which is the Canadian Federation of Independent Business (CFIB).

www.cfib.ca

The CFIB was formed in 1971, and by 2014 it included 109 000 small and medium-sized Canadian-owned businesses in its membership. With offices located across the country, the federation employed a staff of about 300, including legislative specialists, economists, and a field staff engaged in selling memberships nationwide. A major function of the CFIB's staff is conducting surveys and other research with the small business membership. The analysis of this information on the views of the small business community provides the basis for the CFIB's presentations to governments.

The CFIB acts as the small business lobby with government, raising issues such as taxation, financing, government regulations, and red tape. It claims to have saved small business several billions of dollars through its influence on government decisions. The CFIB's stated objective is to promote and protect a system of free competitive enterprise in Canada and to give the independent business owner a greater voice in the laws governing business and the nation. With its sizable cross-country membership base and its lines of communication with each provincial government as well as the federal government, the CFIB is by far the most important and influential of the groups representing small business in Canada.

Problems of Small Business

While over 100 000 new businesses start each year, the failure rate is high, especially in the first year of operations. About 15 percent of new firms do not make it through their first year, and about half of them survive past five years.

One of the main reasons for failures of small businesses is that management is often stretched too thinly. In many small businesses, a single owner-manager is required to perform more functions than time or expertise permit; as a result, the business often suffers from inadequate management.

According to surveys by the Canadian Federation of Independent Business (see Figure 3-1), taxation and government regulation are the major impediments to the operations and growth of small and medium-sized businesses in Canada.

Nearly 80 percent of CFIB members report that the *total tax burden* is the most important issue facing small businesses. While smaller businesses pay a *lower income tax rate* on profits below a certain level, the *total taxes* that they pay often amount to a *higher* percentage of their profits than larger firms pay.

This is largely due to **payroll taxes**, such as premiums for Canada Pension Plan, Employment Insurance, and Workers' Compensation, which are calculated *as a per-*

payroll taxes

Taxes paid by employers based on the number of their employees or the amount of their payroll.

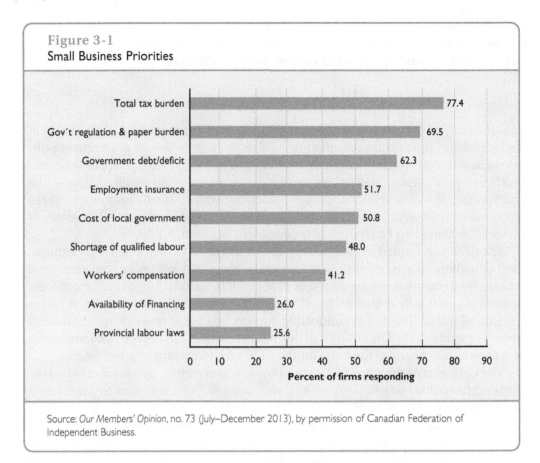

Figure 3-1
Small Business Priorities

Priority	Percent
Total tax burden	77.4
Gov't regulation & paper burden	69.5
Government debt/deficit	62.3
Employment insurance	51.7
Cost of local government	50.8
Shortage of qualified labour	48.0
Workers' compensation	41.2
Availability of Financing	26.0
Provincial labour laws	25.6

Percent of firms responding

Source: *Our Members' Opinion*, no. 73 (July–December 2013), by permission of Canadian Federation of Independent Business.

centage of a firm's total payroll. The effect of payroll taxes is therefore to increase the labour costs of a firm by a certain percent. For a large high-technology manufacturing corporation whose labour costs are a quite small percentage of its sales income, such an increase in its labour costs is not burdensome. But for small businesses in labour-intensive service industries whose labour costs are a big proportion of their sales income, payroll taxes can cut significantly into profits, the moreso because they must be paid whether the firm is earning profits or not.

Another major concern of small business is *government regulation and paper burden,* as cited by 70 percent of the respondents. For small business owners who spend a great deal of time managing their enterprise, the time required to fill out government forms relating to statistical information and tax collection (which in many cases consumes 5 to 10 hours per week) can be a real burden.

Shortages of qualified labour are another problem for many small businesses. Small firms have traditionally given young entrants into the workforce their first job. However, for a number of years, small business owners have reported problems with attracting and retaining qualified workers.

Financing problems often create serious handicaps. Small firms face considerable problems in attempting to raise sufficient equity and risk capital, and also tend to lack the access that larger businesses have to banks and other credit sources. Not only are small businesses considered by lenders to be a greater risk than larger firms, but also owner-managers of small firms often have difficulty identifying sources of funds.

IN THE NEWS

Self-Employment in Canada

According to Statistics Canada (CANSIM Table 282-0012),

- In 2014, 2 710 000 Canadians were self-employed, representing more than 15 percent of the total number of employed people in Canada.
- Self-employment has grown in importance. From 1976 to 2014, the number of self-employed Canadians more than doubled. Over the same period, the number of paid workers not working for themselves grew by a little more than one-half.
- Self-employment is more common among men than women; however, self-employment is growing more rapidly among women. In 1976, 26 percent of the self-employed were women; by 2014 this number had increased to over 36 percent.

QUESTIONS

1. Why has self-employment been growing so rapidly in recent years?
2. What could explain the increasing participation of women in this trend?
3. Would you expect these trends to continue?

Big Business in Canada

As Table 3-1 shows, big business in Canada is a very different world from the small business sector, a world dominated by corporate giants that are household names. All such large businesses are incorporated, mostly in the form of *public corporations* that have the ability to raise capital through the sale of stocks and bonds to the public. Public corporations' shares are traded on stock exchanges such as the Toronto Stock Exchange and the TSX Venture Exchange. Through these stock exchanges, corporations can issue new shares to raise capital, and the investing public can buy and sell shares. The ability to buy and sell corporate shares freely, together with the limited liability of shareholders, makes it possible for public corporations to raise the vast amounts of capital they need, not only from the general public but also from large institutional investors such as pension funds and mutual funds.

http://www.tsx.ca

Large corporations such as those listed in Table 3–1 play a major role in the Canadian economy—usually, the sales of the largest 50 corporations (Including foreign sales) amount to about half of all the goods and services produced in Canada. Over 20 percent of Canada's largest 50 companies are in the energy sector, and a similar number are financial institutions such as banks and insurance companies.

Many of Canada's large companies, including financial institutions, are major exporters; in fact, it is often by exporting to larger foreign markets that these corporations attain their large size.

The ownership of these large enterprises is quite diverse. About half are widely held, meaning that ownership is spread among a large number of relatively small shareholders. In many control is very concentrated, in the hands of another corporation or family. Over one-quarter of Canada's largest nonfinancial corporations are foreign-owned, mostly by U.S.-based parent companies.

Table 3-1
Canada's 50 Largest Corporations by Sales Revenue, 2013

Rank	Company	Revenues $000	Profits $000
1	Suncor Energy Inc., Calgary	$39,784,000	$3,911,000
2	Royal Bank of Canada, Toronto (Oc13)	$38,766,000	$8,331,000
3	Magna International Inc., Aurora, Ont.	$35,880,048	$1,607,830
4	Alimentation Couche-Tard Inc., Laval, Que. (Ap13)	$35,650,032	$574,518
5	The Toronto-Dominion Bank, Toronto (Oc13)	$33,800,000	$6,557,000
6	George Weston Ltd., Toronto	$33,582,000	$674,000
7	Enbridge Inc., Calgary	$32,918,000	$629,000
8	Imperial Oil Ltd., Calgary	$32,722,000	$2,828,000
9	Power Corp. of Canada, Montreal	$29,642,000	$1,029,000
10	The Bank of Nova Scotia, Halifax (Oc13)	$28,799,000	$6,422,000
11	Onex Corp., Toronto	$28,643,270	-$364,620
12	Caisse de dépôt et placement du Québec, Quebec City	$23,323,000	$23,036,000
13	Husky Energy Inc., Calgary	$23,317,000	$1,829,000
14	Walmart Canada Corp., Mississauga, Ont. (Ja14)	$23,200,000	n.a.
15	Brookfield Asset Management Inc., Toronto	$22,919,560	$2,183,600
16	Bank of Montreal, Montreal (Oc13)	$20,851,000	$4,183,000
17	BCE Inc., Verdun, Que.	$20,400,000	$2,106,000
18	Bombardier Inc., Montreal	$18,695,530	$580,920
19	Manulife Financial Corp., Toronto	$18,672,000	$3,130,000
20	Cenovus Energy Inc., Calgary	$18,657,000	$662,000
21	Empire Co. Ltd., Stellarton, N.S. (My13)	$17,612,700	$384,800
22	Canadian Imperial Bank of Commerce, Toronto (Oc13)	$17,139,000	$3,403,000
23	Costco Wholesale Canada Ltd., Nepean, Ont. (Au13)	$16,492,709	n.a.
24	Agrium Inc., Calgary	$16,198,810	$1,093,860
25	Canadian Natural Resources Ltd., Calgary	$16,145,000	$2,270,000
26	Catamaran Corp., Schaumburg, Ill.	$15,223,497	$270,035
27	Sun Life Financial Inc., Toronto	$13,874,000	$1,060,000
28	Thomson Reuters Corp., New York	$13,083,060	$141,110
29	Rio Tinto Alcan Inc., Montreal	$12,836,890	$573,710
30	Rogers Communications Inc., Toronto	$12,706,000	$1,669,000
31	Barrick Gold Corp., Toronto	$12,555,700	-$10,676,980
32	Air Canada, St-Laurent, Que.	$12,382,000	$6,000
33	Valero Energy Inc., Montreal	$12,242,973	n.a.
34	Hydro-Québec, Montreal (De12)	$12,228,000	$860,000
35	Canadian Tire Corp., Ltd., Toronto	$11,785,600	$561,200
36	Honda Canada Inc., Markham, Ont. (Mr13)	$11,600,000	n.a.
37	TELUS Corp., Vancouver	$11,404,000	$1,294,000
38	METRO INC., Montreal (Se13)	$11,402,800	$712,900
39	Canada Mortgage and Housing Corp., Ottawa (De12)	$11,258,000	$1,716,000
40	Canadian National Railway Co., Montreal	$10,575,000	$2,612,000
41	McKesson Canada Corp., St-Laurent, Que.	$10,280,430	n.a.
42	CGI Group Inc., Montreal (Se13)	$10,084,624	$455,820
43	Direct Energy Marketing Ltd., Toronto	$10,020,600	n.a.
44	Novelis Inc., Atlanta, Ga. (Mr13)	$9,821,812	$202,202
45	Federated Co-operatives Ltd., Saskatoon (Oc13)	$9,423,000	$879,000
46	Teck Resources Ltd., Vancouver	$9,382,000	$961,000
47	Ford Motor Co. of Canada, Ltd., Oakville, Ont.	$9,084,600	n.a.
48	Cargill Ltd., Winnipeg (My13)	$9,063,000	n.a.
49	TransCanada Corp., Calgary	$8,797,000	$1,786,000
50	The Jim Pattison Group, Vancouver	$8,100,000	n.a.

Source: Reprinted from the *Financial Post 500*, June 2014, by permission of National Post/Postmedia Network Inc.

YOU DECIDE

Sales and Jobs

In 2013, Canadian Tire had sales of $11.8 billion and approximately 58 000 employees. Honda Canada's sales were almost the same ($11.6 billion), but Honda had only about 4 600 employees.

QUESTION

1. What might explain why Honda and Canadian Tire have similar *sales*, but Canadian Tire has more than 12 times as many *employees* as Honda?

Multinational Enterprises

Many of Canada's large corporations are what are known as *multinational enterprises*, or corporations that conduct business internationally. Multi-national corporations first attracted attention in the 1960s and 1970s; however, following the shift in the 1980s toward freer international trade, their growth became spectacular. Worldwide, there are estimated to be more than 37 000 multinationals with more than 170 000 affiliates, and more than one-third of world trade is conducted between related companies. Over half of all Canada–U.S. trade takes place between multinational affiliates.

The strategic significance of these firms is great—it is estimated that North America's 1000 largest multinationals employ 30 million people and account for about 25 percent of all the goods and services produced in Canada and the United States. Most of the largest multinationals are U.S.-owned; however, approximately 12 percent of the top North American firms are Canadian-controlled, providing Canada with a good presence in this large and growing aspect of business enterprise.

Corporate Concentration

In Canada, much business activity is concentrated in the hands of relatively few very large corporations. In broad terms, the largest 25 enterprises (ranked by sales) have tended to control about one-third of all corporate non-financial assets in Canada. In particular industries, such as automobile manufacturing, steel, and breweries, concentration is especially high. This corporate concentration is the result of various factors, including the growth of the sales and assets of the most successful corporations and the tendency of corporations to purchase control of, or merge with, other corporations. As a result, as we will see in Chapter 7, some industries and markets in Canada have come to be dominated by a few large corporations, and to a greater degree than in the United States. When a few firms dominate an industry, concerns are raised about whether there is sufficiently strong competition in the industry. The handful of "competitors" may tend to agree among themselves not to compete too strongly, especially with respect to prices, so that all of them can live together more comfortably and profitably. In these cases, it is viewed as necessary for the government to set down rules for corporate behaviour that, in effect, prohibit anticompetitive practices, as we will see in Chapter 9.

Who Controls the Modern Large Corporation?

In theory, this is a simple question, since the shareholders of a corporation vote to elect the board of directors, which in turn selects top management and directs them as to the corporation's objectives and the policies to be followed. In reality, however, the matter is often not so simple. In many large corporations, the shares are so widely held that the shareholders are too numerous and too dispersed to exercise any effective control. A typical shareholders' meeting of a large corporation attracts only a handful of shareholders, few of whom ever seriously question or challenge the executive officers of the corporation.

If the small shareholders are often not in a position to exercise control over the large corporation collectively, then who does control it? Given the importance of large corporations in the economy, this is an important question. Unfortunately, the answer is not always clear, since it depends on the circumstances.

If the corporation's stock is so widely held that there is no major shareholder or organized group of shareholders, it will be impossible for the shareholders to exercise control through their meetings. Rather, control will often fall to the *top management* of the corporation, which can control the shareholders' meetings through **proxies**. (A proxy is a legal instrument whereby a shareholder, in effect, delegates to another person authority to vote on his or her behalf.) Under these circumstances, the top management of a corporation can control the firm, even to the point of nominating and selecting the members of the board of directors to which top management reports. In such cases, the management of the corporation can usually retain control as long as the corporation performs well enough to keep the shareholders content. Those shareholders who disagree strongly with management's decisions will generally sell their shares rather than engage in a struggle for control that will probably prove futile.

In Canada, it is often the case that, in many large corporations, the *board of directors* takes a more active part in company policies and decisions than is suggested in the preceding paragraphs. Sometimes such control is exercised through boards of directors by majority shareholders, such as family interests or other corporations that own a majority of the shares. However, the situation is not always so clear-cut—under certain conditions, a group of shareholders (individuals or other corporations or investment funds) can exercise strong influence on a corporation's board of directors even though it does not hold a majority of the total shares outstanding. Such control can be achieved through proxy votes or simply through personal relationships between the people involved.

While corporate directorships have in the past been thought of as sinecure positions involving status and perks but relatively little responsibility, the situation has changed. Directors now face significantly increased responsibilities due to changes in the law that place much more liability upon them for their companies' actions. Under a variety of laws (by one count, more than 100 in Ontario alone), directors of companies are now exposed to a wide range of both civil and criminal penalties including claims for employees' wages and infractions of environmental laws. In fact, in recent years there was growing concern that governments had taken the concept of directors' liability too far. In several cases, directors of companies that were in difficulty resigned when the possibility arose that they could be held personally liable for millions of dollars of claims. This event raised the concern that the laws relating to directors' liability could discourage capable people from serving on the boards of corporations.

Partly as a result of this concern, and partly in response to increasing concerns that board members be impartial and independent in providing shareholders with information about their companies, corporations are seeking directors with more expertise and dedication than ever before, and are increasingly going outside their own companies for them. So the question of who controls the large corporation is not a simple one. What can be said is that large corporations play a very important role in the Canadian economy, even greater relative to the size of the economy than in the United States, and that in these large corporations, *control is often separated from*

proxies

Legal instruments that allow a shareholder's right to vote at shareholders' meetings to be delegated to another person, either with or without specific instructions as to how that vote will be exercised.

ownership. Widespread small shareholders are not in a position to exercise active control. As a result, control tends to shift, depending on the circumstances, to the top management of the corporation or to groups of influential members of the board of directors. Generally, neither top managers nor directors are major shareholders in their corporation; their claim to control over the corporation is based on their expertise rather than on ownership.

Government Enterprises

No discussion of big business in Canada would be complete without reference to government-owned enterprises. Comprising about 10 percent of Canada's very large corporations, government enterprises often take the form of **Crown corporations**. Crown corporations, like other corporations (federal or provincial), are legally independent, separate entities. However, their shares are owned by a government, and they are ultimately responsible to the government through a cabinet minister. In addition to Crown corporations, government enterprises often take the form of *boards* or *commissions*, such as hydroelectric commissions.

Crown corporations
Corporations owned by a government and that are ultimately responsible, through a cabinet minister, to that government.

Whatever legal forms they take, government enterprises constitute an important part of big business in Canada. Their largest single activity is the *provision of electricity:* the combined sales of the 10 provinces' electricity utilities would place them among Canada's largest enterprises. Traditionally, government enterprises have also been important in the fields of *transportation and communications* in Canada, including, at various times. Canada Post, provincial and national railways, airlines, and communications networks. Government enterprises play a key role in the generation and distribution of electricity and public water supply, and have at times been involved in the *energy and resources* sector, such as, nuclear energy, petroleum, and other resources.

Attitudes toward government enterprises in Canada have changed over the years. For many years, government enterprises such as the Canadian Broadcasting Corporation, the Canadian National Railway, and Air Canada (originally Trans-Canada Airlines) were warmly regarded as the providers of vital transportation and communications links that for many decades knitted together Canada's diverse and far-flung people and regions, and provided services to more remote areas even when this was not profitable. Because of the nation's small population and the vast distances between population centres, it was not economical for private profit-making businesses to provide these services, so by providing them, government enterprises contributed considerably to the economic development and unity of the nation. And because these government enterprises were subsidized by government they could provide more of their services to Canadians at a lower cost to the users of those services.

However, as time passed, some of these government enterprises came to be seen as less essential to the nation. The development of alternatives such as other airlines, railways, highways, and communications networks raised the question of whether the government should continue to subsidize money-losing enterprises such as railways, airlines, and communications networks. Critics of government enterprises stressed that many government enterprises paid above-market wages to their employees and/or operated inefficiently, losing money regularly and falling back on taxpayers for subsidies. As the federal government's budget deficits mounted in the 1980s and 1990s, pressures to reassess the government's commitment to many of its money-losing enterprises grew.

In the 1980s the federal government undertook a critical review of the performance of its Crown corporations. It decided to sell some of them to private interests, or **privatize** them. The privatization program started with the high-profile sale of De Havilland

Privatization
The process of selling government enterprises (usually Crown corporations) to private interests.

Aircraft of Canada Ltd. to Boeing Corp. of the United States. In 1989, the sale of Air Canada to private interests was completed, and in the 1990s Petro-Canada and the Canadian National Railway were privatized.

Governments have also generally owned and operated most educational institutions at all levels. Some people have suggested, however, that this government "monopoly" should be changed to a situation in which schools have to compete for customers in the same ways as other businesses do (see the accompanying "You Decide" box).

YOU DECIDE

A Competitive Market for Education?

In most elementary and secondary school systems, students have no choice as to which school they will attend—they are assigned to the school in the area in which they live. Some critics would like to see competition introduced into the education "industry." They want the government to give students (or their parents) vouchers for each year's education and allow them to "spend" these vouchers at any school they wish. In such a system, schools would function partly like businesses—the more students (and vouchers) a school attracted, the more revenue it would have. The theory is that this competition would put pressure on schools to improve the quality of their education. ◼

QUESTIONS
1. What advantages do you see in such a system?
2. What disadvantages or potential dangers do you see in it?
3. What would be required for such a system to operate effectively and improve the quality of education?

To summarize, government enterprises are big business in Canada, many of them being household names and major forces in the economy. The objectives of these enterprises are not only profits—some of them, such as the Canadian Broadcasting Corporation, are intended to provide particular services throughout the country whether doing so is profitable or not, or to aid in the development of particular industries, products, or regions. The matter of government enterprises has always been a controversial one; critics argue that such operations tend to be inefficient and costly because of political interference and the absence of the profit motive, and supporters argue that they are an essential component of the Canadian economy, performing functions that private enterprise would not or could not.

Big Business, Small Business, Government Enterprises and Prosperity

Together, the three major types of enterprises discussed in this chapter contribute strongly to the economic prosperity of Canadians, with each making its own special contribution.

Big business is a particularly efficient *producer of goods* (manufactured goods, food products, energy and resource products, etc.). Such efficient production of goods means that relatively few workers are needed in goods industries, making a high proportion of Canada's labour force available for work in service industries. Meanwhile, efficient production of goods makes their prices low, leaving consumers with ample funds for buying a wide range of services.

The small business sector is a major producer of these services (restaurants, entertainment, travel, etc.) that enrich the lives of Canadians, and provides *employment for many Canadians* in the process.

Finally, government enterprises support Canadian producers by providing both the required *infrastructure* and *an educated and trained labour force*; these enterprises also provide key *public services* such as health care to Canadians.

Market Structure

In this chapter we have considered the nature of the business sector of the economy, which produces most of the supply of goods and services. In Chapters 4 through 7, we will see how supply and demand interact to determine prices. This task is complicated somewhat by the fact that supply—the production of goods and services by business—occurs under various conditions ranging from industries comprising large numbers of small firms to industries dominated by a few large firms to industries in which there is only one producer (a monopoly). These different conditions—referred to as *market structures* by economists—have a significant impact on the supply of goods and services. If there is only one firm in an industry (a monopoly), it is in a position to control the supply of the product, thereby raising the price of the product and increasing its profits. In industries dominated by a few large firms, it is sometimes possible for these firms to get together to avoid competing on prices and thus increase their profits. On the other hand, in industries in which there are many small firms, such collective action is very difficult or impossible to achieve. As a result, competition in such industries tends to be more intense, and prices and profits are lower than in either of the first two cases. In Chapter 4, we will examine the concept of demand, and then in Chapter 5 we will begin our examination of supply (and its interactions with demand) in those industries that have a large number of small firms—industries that economists call *competitive*.

Chapter Summary

1. The advantages of the sole proprietorship and the partnership are that they are easily formed and provide strong motivation and a high degree of independence. Disadvantages include lack of access to financing, lack of managerial expertise, the unlimited personal liability of the owner(s), and higher tax rates once the income of the business exceeds a certain amount. An added disadvantage of the partnership is the possibility of disagreements among the partners. (L.O. 1)

2. One advantage of the corporation, the typical form taken by larger businesses, is that it can raise larger amounts of capital due to the limited liability of its share-

holders. Another advantage is the lower tax rates on income above a certain level. Disadvantages include the initial costs of incorporation and a greater degree of government regulation, especially with respect to public corporations. (L.O. 1)

3. Small business is an important and dynamic sector of the Canadian economy, consisting of many hundreds of thousands of firms and providing over one-third of all private sector employment and a high proportion of new private sector job creation in recent years. (L.O. 2)

4. Major problems faced by small business include high tax rates, lack of management expertise, financing problems, government regulations and paperwork, and difficulties attracting and retaining skilled employees. (L.O. 3)

5. The Canadian Federation of Independent Business (CFIB) assists the small business community by lobbying with governments and providing research. (L.O. 4)

6. Big business is another major component of the Canadian economy, accounting for particularly high proportions of the country's output and exports. Multinational enterprises are an important aspect of Canada's big business sector. (L.O. 5, 6)

7. While these large corporations are important to the Canadian economy, the domination of some industries by a few large corporations raises questions as to whether such corporate concentration is in the public interest. (L.O. 6)

8. Control of the modern large corporation is not usually in the hands of the shareholders as a group; rather, it tends to rest with top management and/or the board of directors, neither of which are usually major shareholders. (L.O. 7)

9. A significant number of Canada's large corporations are government-owned, particularly in the areas of electrical utilities, transportation and communications, and energy and resources. Advocates of these enterprises argue that they provide important services to the public, while others argue that they are inefficient and ineffective and therefore should be privatized. (L.O. 8)

Questions

1. Which of the following best describes the contribution of small business to the economic prosperity of Canadians?
   (a) They are major producers of goods.
   (b) They are major exporters.
   (c) They have provided most of the employment growth of recent years.
   (d) They provide a wide range of services to consumers.
   (e) Both (c) and (d) are correct.

2. Which of the following best describes the contribution of big business to the economic prosperity of Canadians?
   (a) They are major producers of goods.
   (b) They have provided most of the employment growth of recent years.
   (c) They are major exporters.
   (d) Both (a) and (c) are correct.
   (e) Answers (a), (b), and (c) are correct.

3. Which of the following best describes the contribution of Crown corporations to the economic prosperity of Canadians?
   (a) They are major producers of goods.
   (b) They are major exporters.
   (c) They provide Canadians with various important public services.
   (d) They have provided most of the employment growth of recent years.
   (e) They make no significant contribution to Canadians' prosperity.

4. Large corporations are owned by their shareholders. In most cases, effective control of such corporations tends to be in the hands of
   (a) the president.
   (b) the shareholders.
   (c) the individual owning the greatest number of shares.
   (d) the top management and/or board of directors.
   (e) None of the above.

   Explain your answer.

5. The text notes that many service industries consist of large numbers of small business firms.
   (a) Why do you think that this is so often the case?
   (b) Name some exceptions to this generality; that is, service industries that are dominated by a few large corporations. What explains why *these* service industries consist of a few large firms?

6. In your opinion, what is the future for small business in Canada? Do you think its importance will grow or decline? Why?

7. What is *industrial concentration*, and why do both consumer groups and economists consider it to be concern? Include in your answer references to the terms *effectiveness* and *efficiency*, and provide at least one example of such concerns.

8. What is meant by *privatization*, and why do critics of government enterprises believe that privatization would improve their performance in terms of both efficiency and effectiveness?

9. Visit the website for the Canadian Federation of Independent Business at **www.cfib.ca**. What issues are currently of concern to CFIB and the small business community? Why are CFIB and its members concerned about these matters?

Study Guide

Review Questions (Answers to these Review Questions appear in Appendix B.)

State whether or not the story of *Dan's Doughnut Dens* illustrates that each of the following statements is *true* or *false*.

1. T or F
   The sole proprietorship often involves a great deal of strain on the owner-manager.

2. T or F
   Sole proprietorships are usually very well-managed, because the owner-manager knows the business so well.

3. T or F
   It is possible to be a partner in a business and *not* have unlimited liability for the debts of the business.

4. T or F
   Partnerships are often subject to severe strains due to differences among the partners.

5. T or F
   The corporate form of business enterprise can involve the risk of the original founder/owner losing control of the business.

6. T or F

   A risk of the partnership form of organization is that if one of the partners dies, the business has to be sold so that the deceased partner's heirs can receive their share of the firm.

7. T or F

   To preserve the continuity of the firm after the death of a partner, partners often take out life insurance policies on each others' lives.

State whether each of the following statements concerning the sole proprietorship as a form of business organization is *true* or *false*.

8. T or F

   The owner of the business is protected from liability for the debts of the business.

9. T or F

   It provides strong incentives to be effective and efficient.

10. T or F

    It is inexpensive and easy to form and get started.

11. T or F

    It can readily raise capital in order to buy assets and grow.

12. T or F

    It typically has strong management expertise.

State whether each of the following statements concerning the corporation as a form of business organization is *true* or *false*.

13. T or F

    It is inexpensive and easy to form and get started.

14. T or F

    Its owners (shareholders) have limited liability for the debts of the corporation.

15. T or F

    It is able to raise large amounts of capital.

State whether each of the following four statements concerning Crown corporations in Canada is *true* or *false*.

16. T or F

    They are very few in number and therefore not a major part of the Canadian economy.

17. T or F

    Only the federal government has the power to create Crown corporations.

18. T or F

    They are an important part of the Canadian economy, comprising about 10 percent of Canada's very large corporations.

19. T or F

    Their objective is not only to make a profit, but also in some cases to provide certain services for the public.

20. Which of the following problems is/are commonly faced by small businesses?
    (a) financing problems
    (b) lack of managerial expertise
    (c) government regulations and the extensive paperwork associated with them
    (d) difficulties attracting and retaining capable employees
    (e) All of the above.

21. A *multinational* enterprise is one in which
   (a) shareholders are spread throughout many different countries.
   (b) resources are imported from one country to be processed in another.
   (c) business is conducted internationally, in different countries.
   (d) shareholders are Americans and workers are Canadians.

Critical Thinking Questions

(Asterisked questions 1 to 5 are answered in Appendix B; the answers to questions 6 to 10 are in the Instructor's Manual that accompanies this text.)

*1. Small business operators are known for their independent nature. So why does the small business community believe that it needs the Canadian Federation of Independent Business? To illustrate your answer, explain two key functions that the CFIB carries out for its members.

*2. Many small business owners earn less than they could by working for a large corporation. Why, then, do you think that they have chosen to be small business owners?

*3. What are payroll taxes? Why are small businesses particularly concerned about payroll taxes?

*4. What are the key arguments *in support of* government ownership and operation of enterprises such as Canada Post and the Canadian Broadcasting Corporation?

*5. Explain the arguments *against* government ownership and operation of such enterprises, referring in your explanation to *efficiency, effectiveness,* and *opportunity cost.*

6. Each year in Canada, many small businesses fail, for one reason or another.
   (a) Provide at least one example of an industry that consists largely of small businesses and has a high failure rate.
   (b) What would explain the high failure rate for smaller businesses in Canada?
   (c) Does the lack of success of so many small businesses represent a failure of our economic system?

7. Explain how your own personal economic prosperity is enhanced by
   (a) big businesses.
   (b) small businesses.
   (c) Crown corporations.

8. Some people propose that community colleges should be operated as private profit-making businesses rather than as government enterprises. State arguments both *for* and *against* privately-run community colleges, and decide whether you think college education should be provided by private firms or by governments.

9. Check the most recent Financial Post 500 listing of the largest Canadian corporations, ranked by sales revenue. What changes in the rankings have occurred since 2013, and what might explain these changes?

Use the Web   (Hints for these Use the Web exercises appear in Appendix B.)

www.tsx.com

1. Divide your class into teams of three or four students. Each team has $10 000 to invest in shares listed on the Toronto Stock Exchange. Buy $10 000 worth of shares now, and over the remainder of your course, keep track of the changing value of the stocks purchased by each team on the Toronto Stock Exchange website.

2. In 1980, there were only 12 business "incubators" in North America; currently there are more than 900. What are incubators, and what sorts of assistance do they provide to small business? For information on incubators, visit the Toronto Business Development Centre at **www.tbdc.com**.

The Demand Side
of Markets

After studying this chapter, you should be able to

1. Draw a demand curve for a product, given a demand schedule showing the quantity demanded at various prices, and explain the buyer behaviour underlying the demand curve.

2. Explain the meaning of the term *complementary good*.

3. Explain whether a given event would increase or decrease the demand for a particular product, and show how the event would affect the demand curve.

4. Explain the difference between *elastic* and *inelastic* demand.

5. Calculate whether the demand for a product is elastic or inelastic over a specific price range, given the demand schedule for that product.

6. Use the concepts and tools in this chapter to analyze given situations relating to demand and to elasticity of demand.

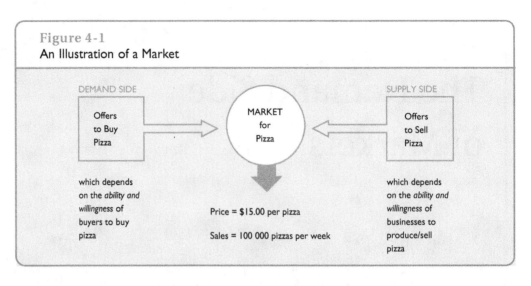

Figure 4-1
An Illustration of a Market

In Chapter 2, we saw how markets consist of
- a demand side, or offers by buyers to purchase products, and
- a supply side, or offers by sellers to sell products.

Figure 4-1 illustrates in a general way how, in a market, the supply side and demand side interact to determine the price and sales of a particular item.

In this chapter, we will consider in more detail the *demand side* of markets, or factors that affect the ability and willingness of buyers to *purchase* particular goods or services. In the next chapter, we will cover the *supply side* of markets, or factors that affect the ability and willingness of businesses to *produce and sell* particular goods or services.

Part A: What Is Demand?

Generally, people will buy more of a product if its price is lower, all other things being equal. Suppose we took a survey of all the households in Cantown to determine how many pizzas people would buy each week in March 2015 if the price were $20 per pizza, $16 per pizza, $12 per pizza, $8 per pizza, and $4 per pizza, respectively. While surveys such as this one are an imprecise way of gathering information, especially when they ask people to estimate what they *might* do under different circumstances, we would expect that the results of the survey would show that people would buy more pizza at lower prices than at higher prices, as shown in Table 4-1.

Table 4-1
Demand Schedule for Pizza in Cantown, March 2015

If the price per pizza were	The quantity sold (bought) per week would be
$20	20 000
16	30 000
12	50 000
8	80 000
4	120 000

Table 4-1 shows the relationship between the price of a pizza and the quantity of pizzas sold (bought): as the price *increases*, the quantity demanded *falls*. This drop occurs for two reasons: higher prices cause some people to become *unwilling* to buy pizza, and others to become *unable* to buy pizza. Those who do not buy pizza at the higher prices can either substitute another product (such as submarine sandwiches) for pizza, or they can do without some pizza (that is, buy pizzas less often, or not at all).

This relationship between price and quantity demanded, known as **demand**, can be shown in a table, or *demand schedule* as in Table 4-1, or a *demand curve* as in Figure 4-2. The demand curve is simply another way of showing the same information in the demand schedule. The demand curve also shows that if the price increases, the quantity demanded will fall (assuming that no other factor affecting demand changes).

It is important to recognize that Table 4-1 and Figure 4-2 are different from most tables and graphs. They do not represent *facts*, but rather a series of *"what if"* scenarios: *if* the price were $20, 20 000 pizzas would be bought, *if* the price were $16, 30 000 pizzas would be bought, and so on.

demand

The entire relationship between the various possible prices of a product or service and the quantity demanded at each price, expressed through either a schedule or a graph.

If Dell changes prices on its website, changes in its customers' buying patterns can be seen within a minute.

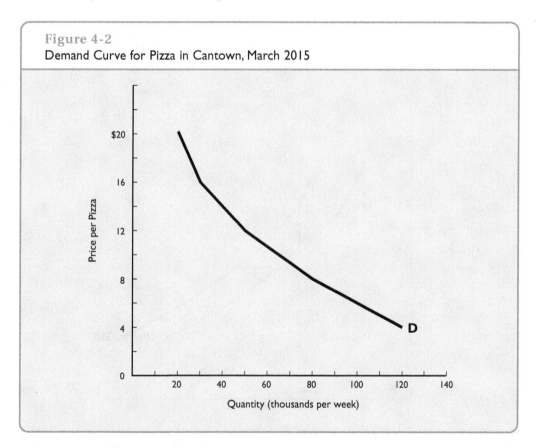

Figure 4-2
Demand Curve for Pizza in Cantown, March 2015

What Demand Is Not

Suppose that, in the example discussed above, the *actual* price of a pizza was $12, and that the *actual* quantity sold was 50 000 pizzas per week. Under these circumstances, it is tempting to conclude that the demand for pizza is 50 000 pizzas, but this conclusion would be incorrect. Demand refers to much more than the *actual* price and quantity bought; it also includes the idea that *if* the price of pizza *had been* higher, less *would have been* sold, and that lower prices would have generated higher sales. When we say "demand," we mean the entire relationship between the *various possible prices* and the quantity demanded at each price. Think of *demand* as the entire results of our hypothetical survey, or as the entire demand schedule or curve, as shown in Table 4-1 and Figure 4-2, respectively.

Shifts in the Demand Curve

In Figure 4-3 the information in the second column of the demand schedule and the demand curve labelled D is the same as that in our previous example. But suppose that some time after we did the original survey, we did another similar survey.

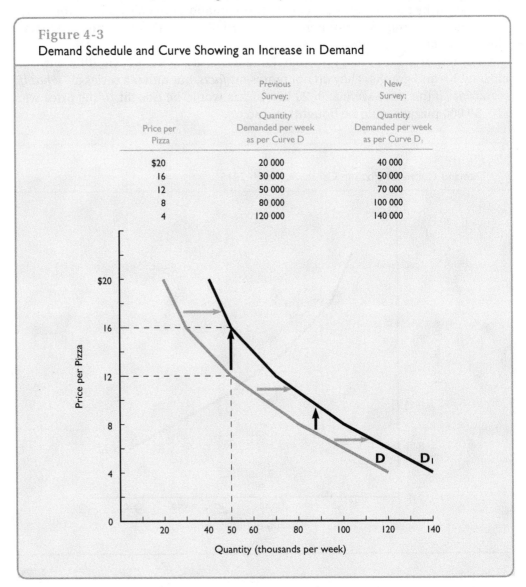

Figure 4-3
Demand Schedule and Curve Showing an Increase in Demand

Price per Pizza	Previous Survey: Quantity Demanded per week as per Curve D	New Survey: Quantity Demanded per week as per Curve D₁
$20	20 000	40 000
16	30 000	50 000
12	50 000	70 000
8	80 000	100 000
4	120 000	140 000

Quantity (thousands per week)

This new survey shows a change in the demand for pizza, which is shown in the third column of the demand schedule. At every possible price, consumers *will buy more* pizza than before. At a price of $20 per pizza, people used to buy 20 000 pizzas per week but will now buy 40 000; at a price of $16, people will increase their purchases from 30 000 to 50 000 pizzas per week; at a price of $12, weekly sales used to be 50 000 pizzas but will now be 70 000, and so on. The demand for pizza has *increased.*

On the graph, this increase in demand causes the demand curve to move to the position shown by the new demand curve D_1. This shift in the demand curve can be seen in two ways. First, as the horizontal arrows show, the demand curve has shifted *to the right*. This shift reflects the fact discussed in the previous paragraph: at every possible price, consumers are prepared to *buy more* pizza per week than before. Second, as the vertical arrows show, the demand curve has shifted *upward*. This reflects the fact that consumers are prepared to *pay higher prices* for pizza. For instance, to get 50 000 pizzas, they will now pay $16 per pizza, whereas before they would only pay $12.

So demand curve D_1 shows that consumers are prepared both to buy more pizza and to pay higher prices for it. Clearly, there has been an *increase in demand*.

Causes of an Increase in Demand

For buyers' behaviour to change in these ways, there has to have been an increase in their *ability* and/or their *willingness* to buy pizza. What could cause such changes?

One possible explanation could be an *increase in consumer income*. Total incomes in the marketplace could increase either because the average incomes of consumers had increased, or because there were more buyers in the market. Such an increase in income would increase the demand for pizza.

Another possible explanation is a *change in people's tastes*. If people's preferences changed so that they prefer pizza to other foods more strongly now than in the past, their willingness to buy pizza would increase and the demand for it would increase, shifting the demand curve to the right.

Another explanation for such an increase in demand could be an *increase in the price of substitutes* for pizza. For example, an increase in the price of submarine sandwiches, hamburgers, or tortillas would make pizza a better buy by comparison, causing an increase in the demand for pizza that would shift the demand curve for pizza to the right. The demand for pizza could also be increased by a *decrease in the price of a* **complementary good** that is bought along with pizza, such as garlic bread.

Another explanation for an increase in the demand for a product is a *change in consumer expectations* concerning its price or availability. If consumers expect that a product will be in shorter supply and/or become more expensive, some of them will buy it *now*, before its price increases. In the case of pizza, this is pretty unlikely; however, in some markets such as housing, the prospect of rising prices can—and does—cause an increase in demand, as some buyers try to beat the price increases by buying now.

complementary good
A good that is bought in combination with another good.

In summary, the causes of an *increase* in demand include changes in
- buyers' incomes,
- buyers' tastes,
- the prices of substitutes,
- the prices of complementary goods, and
- buyers' expectations.

Causes of a Decrease in Demand

Everything discussed in the preceding sections about increases in demand can be reversed for the purpose of discussing decreases in demand. As Figure 4-4 shows, when the demand for pizza decreases, less pizza is bought at every possible price (as shown by the demand schedule), and the demand curve shifts to the left (as shown by the horizontal arrows) to the new location D_2. The change can also be interpreted as a downward shift of the demand curve, as shown by the vertical arrows. This downward shift means that consumers are not prepared to pay as high a price for pizza as they were before.

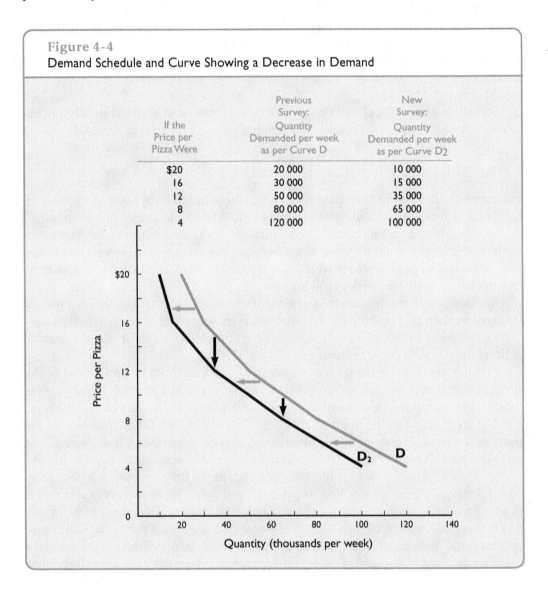

Figure 4-4
Demand Schedule and Curve Showing a Decrease in Demand

If the Price per Pizza Were	Previous Survey: Quantity Demanded per week as per Curve D	New Survey: Quantity Demanded per week as per Curve D2
$20	20 000	10 000
16	30 000	15 000
12	50 000	35 000
8	80 000	65 000
4	120 000	100 000

A shift of the demand curve to the left and down indicates that the factors underlying the demand for pizza have changed in such a way that the demand for pizza has decreased. Such a change can be explained by reference to the same factors discussed earlier. Perhaps people's *incomes have fallen*, leaving them less able to buy as much pizza as before, or perhaps their *tastes have changed*, and they find pizza less attractive than before. Or, perhaps the *prices of substitute products* have fallen—if other foods became less costly, consumers would buy more of them, causing a decrease in the demand for pizza. An increase in the *price of complementary* goods could also cause a decrease in the demand for pizza. Finally, a *change in people's expectations* could cause a decrease in the demand for a product. If people expect lower prices in the future, they may reduce their purchases now, and wait for the lower prices that are anticipated. The housing market provides a better example than the pizza market of the role of expectations. In the housing market, both house prices and mortgage interest rates (the prices of the loans used to buy houses) periodically increase to very high levels, then fall again. When house prices and mortgage rates are believed to be near one of their periodic peaks, many house buyers postpone purchases, expecting that the future will bring lower prices and interest rates.

Whatever the cause, the decrease in demand shown by the shift in the demand curve from D_1 to D_2 reflects the fact that buyers are not as *able* and/or *willing* to buy as much pizza and pay as much for it as before.

In summary, the causes of a *decrease* in demand include changes in
- buyers' incomes,
- buyers' tastes,
- the prices of substitutes,
- the prices of complementary goods, and
- buyers' expectations.

Changes in Demand Versus Changes in Quantity Demanded

We have seen that, if the tastes, incomes, or expectations of consumers change, or the prices of other products change, the demand for a product will change—the demand curve will *shift*, either to the left or to the right.

But what if the *price* of that product changes—will the *demand* for the product also change? Certainly, the *quantity demanded* (or purchases) will change, as Figure 4-5 shows: an increase in the price from $1 to $3 causes a reduction in quantity demanded (purchases) from 400 to 200.

But "demand," as we have explained it in this chapter, has *not* changed. The price/quantity preferences of consumers that are shown by the "what if" scenarios in the demand curve remain the same. So there will be no *shift* of the demand curve as occurs when demand changes, only a *movement along* the demand curve, from point A to point B. So while a change in price does cause a change in *quantity demanded* (sales), it does not alter *demand,* by shifting the demand curve to the right or to the left. Instead, there is merely a movement to a different point on the same demand curve.

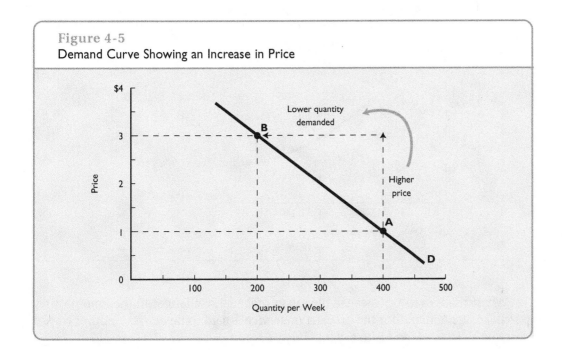

Figure 4-5
Demand Curve Showing an Increase in Price

Factors Underlying Demand

In summary, demand is the relationship between the *price* of a product and the *quantity demanded* by buyers. This relationship can be expressed numerically, in a demand schedule, or graphically, in a demand curve. The location of the demand curve for a product depends on such factors as buyers' tastes and incomes, the prices of other products, and buyers' expectations of future price changes. Should these factors change so as to increase the demand for the product, the demand curve will shift to the right and up, whereas changes that reduce the demand for the product will cause the demand curve to shift to the left and down.

Part B: Elasticity of Demand

In Part A of this chapter, we saw that at higher prices buyers will purchase less of a product than at lower prices. A very important question, which we will now consider, is *how much will purchases fall* when the price increases? Since the answer to this question will depend on the nature of a specific product or service, we will examine two different cases.

Elastic Demand

Figure 4-6 shows a hypothetical demand schedule and demand curve for chicken. As the price increases, consumers reduce their purchases of chicken considerably—for instance, an increase in price from $1.20 to $1.50 per 100 g will reduce purchases from 500 kg per week to only 100 kg. We could also say that if the price of chicken were to decrease, consumers would increase their purchases of it a great deal.

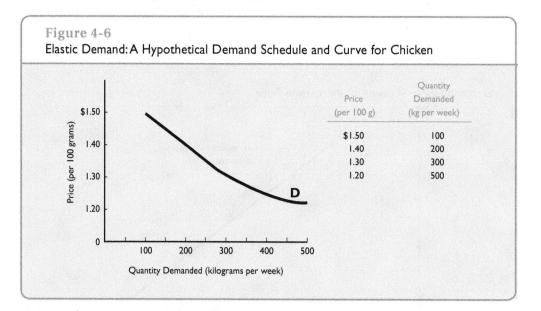

Figure 4-6

Elastic Demand: A Hypothetical Demand Schedule and Curve for Chicken

Price (per 100 g)	Quantity Demanded (kg per week)
$1.50	100
1.40	200
1.30	300
1.20	500

elastic demand

The term used to describe demand if a price increase causes a reduction in total sales revenue.

When changes in price cause buyers to make large changes in the amount they purchase, the demand for the product or service is said to be *elastic.* Another way to describe **elastic demand** is to say that buyers are *price-sensitive.*

Inelastic Demand

Figure 4-7 shows a hypothetical demand schedule and demand curve for gasoline. The demand for gasoline is different: as the price increases, buyers do not reduce their purchases of gasoline by that much. For instance, an increase in price from $1.20 to $1.50 per litre would reduce sales from 220 000 L to 190 000 L per week—a much smaller decrease than in the case of chicken. And if the price of gasoline were to fall, consumers would not increase their purchases of it by very much.

The inelastic demand curve in Figure 4-7 is much steeper than the elastic demand curve in Figure 4-6—this reflects the fact that if the price moves upwards or downwards, buyers do not change their purchases by much.

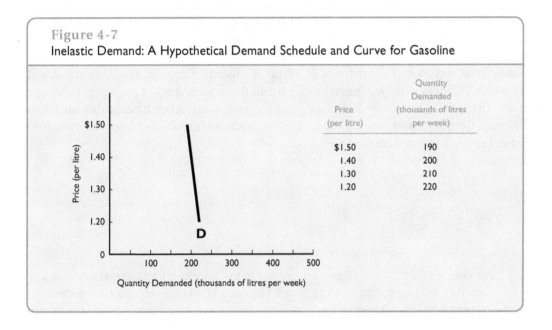

Figure 4-7

Inelastic Demand: A Hypothetical Demand Schedule and Curve for Gasoline

Price (per litre)	Quantity Demanded (thousands of litres per week)
$1.50	190
1.40	200
1.30	210
1.20	220

When changes in price do not cause buyers to change the amount that they purchase by much, the demand for the product or service is said to be *inelastic*. An **inelastic demand** means that buyers are not price-sensitive.

inelastic demand
The term used to describe demand if a price increase causes an increase in total sales revenue.

What Makes Demand Elastic?

For demand to be elastic, buyers have to be able and willing to reduce their purchases substantially if the price increases by a small percentage. Two things could make this situation possible:
(a) a reasonably close substitute could be available, making it easy for buyers to switch to the substitute,
(b) buyers could readily do without the product because it is not a necessity or treated as such.

For the demand for chicken to be elastic, buyers do not need to *completely* do without chicken or *completely* switch to a substitute. Instead, they could buy smaller cuts of chicken, and buy it less frequently. By combining these two responses, they could reduce their purchases of chicken considerably if its price increases by a small percentage, making the demand elastic. But buyers do not necessarily need to make *both* of these adjustments—by *either* substituting *or* cutting back (partially doing without), they can reduce their purchases considerably.

What Makes Demand Inelastic?

If demand is inelastic, buyers will not reduce their purchases by much even if the price increases considerably. They would behave this way because:

(a) there are no close substitutes available, and

(b) they are unable or unwilling to do without the product because it is a necessity or is treated as such.

Both of these conditions need to exist in order for demand to be inelastic. For instance, there may be no substitutes for a product, but if buyers can and will do without it, the demand for it would be elastic rather than inelastic.

Also, a product need not *be* a *physical* necessity for its demand to be inelastic; it need only be *treated* as a necessity. For instance, consumers may be able to survive without cell phones, but if they *want* them strongly enough, the effect will be the same as if they were a necessity—if the price goes up, people will still buy them.

It is important to be very specific about the product in question when analyzing elasticity of demand. If the price of gasoline *in general* increased, the demand would be inelastic, because buyers need gasoline and there is no ready substitute. However, if the price of a *particular brand* of gasoline rose (and other brands did not), the demand for that brand would be very elastic, because buyers could readily switch to other brands as substitutes.

YOU DECIDE

The Economics of Smoking

It has been estimated that a 10 percent increase in the price of tobacco causes adults to reduce their tobacco consumption by 3 to 4 percent, and causes youths to reduce their consumption by about 8 percent. ■

QUESTIONS

1. For which age group is the demand for tobacco more inelastic?
2. What explains the difference in elasticity of demand for the two age groups?
3. To reduce youth smoking by about half, what sort of price increase would be required?

Defining *Elastic* and *Inelastic*

The preceding examples provide an *illustration* of the concepts of elastic and inelastic demand, but they do not give precise *definitions* of these terms. To define *elastic* and *inelastic* more precisely, we will use as an example the demand for Supersmooth Shaving Cream, as illustrated in Table 4-2 on the next page.

In Table 4-2, we have added a third column—*total revenue per week*, which is the total sales revenue, or price times quantity demanded per week. If we assume that the Supersmooth Shaving Cream Company is currently selling 90 000 cans per week at a price of $1.20 per can, Table 4-2 provides some interesting information.

First, while a price cut from $1.20 to $1.00 would increase sales from 90 000 cans to 100 000 cans per week, it would actually reduce the company's total revenue from $108 000 to $100 000 per week, making such a price reduction an unattractive

> ### Table 4-2
> #### Demand Schedule and Total Revenue for Supersmooth Shaving Cream
>
> | Price per Can | Quantity Demanded (thousands of cans per week) | Total Revenue ($ thousands per week) (price × quantity demanded) |
> |---|---|---|
> | $1.80 | 60 | $108 |
> | 1.60 | 70 | 112 |
> | 1.40 | 80 | 112 |
> | 1.20 | 90 | 108 |
> | 1.00 | 100 | 100 |

decision.[1] On the other hand, a price increase from $1.20 to $1.40 would have the opposite effect: while it would *reduce weekly sales* from 90 000 to 80 000 cans, it would *increase the total revenue* of the company from $108 000 to $112 000 per week.

So, increases in price within the $1.00 to $1.40 price range cause total revenue to increase. Within this price range buyers are not particularly sensitive to price changes—when the price increases, purchases are not reduced by so much that total revenue falls. We have said that when buyers are relatively unresponsive to price changes, demand is said to be *inelastic*. Our formal definition, then, is that

> ### *if a price increase causes total revenue to increase, demand is inelastic.*

However, increases in the price of Supersmooth Shaving Cream beyond a certain point cause total revenue to *fall*. An increase in price from $1.60 to $1.80 causes total revenue to decrease from $112 000 to $108 000, as this higher price cuts more deeply into sales. In this price range, where buyers are quite sensitive to changes in price, demand is *elastic*. Our definition then is that

> ### *if a price increase causes total revenue to fall, demand is elastic.*

In summary, elasticity of demand refers to the responsiveness of buyers to changes in price. Demand is said to be elastic if a price increase causes total revenue to fall, and inelastic if a price increase causes total revenue to increase.[2] Similar rules can be worked out for the effects of price reductions, but these tend to be confusing. A simple rule of thumb is that if the *price* and the *total revenue* move in the same direction (up or down), demand is inelastic. These definitions are illustrated in the Supersmooth Shaving Cream demand schedule in Table 4-3.

In the Supersmooth Shaving Cream example, demand is inelastic over the lower price ranges, presumably because at low prices buyers are not very sensitive to price increases. Beyond a certain price, however, the demand becomes elastic, as such high prices drive away more and more buyers. So the elasticity depends on the price range we are discussing. In the real world, when we say that the demand for a product is elastic or inelastic, we are implicitly referring to the price range around its *present actual price*.

---

[1] Note that we say *total revenue*, not *profits*. The effect on profits is more complex—it depends on the combined effect of the increased sales and output on total sales revenue *and* total production costs, respectively. This concept is covered in Chapter 8; however, at this point we can simply assume that higher total revenue means higher profits, and vice versa.

[2] When the price increases from $1.40 to $1.60, total revenue remains unchanged at $112 000. In this borderline case, when the effects of the higher price per unit sold are exactly offset by effects of the reduced number of units sold so that total revenue remains unchanged, we say that the demand has "unitary elasticity."

Table 4-3
Elasticity of Demand for Supersmooth Shaving Cream over Various Price Ranges

Price per Can	Quantity Demanded (thousands of cans per week)	Total Revenue ($ thousands per week) (price × quantity demanded)	Elasticity of Demand (over price range shown)
$1.80	60	$108	elastic from $1.60 to $1.80
1.60	70	112	unitary[a] elasticity from $1.40 to $1.60
1.40	80	112	inelastic from $1.20 to $1.40
1.20	90	108	inelastic from $1.00 to $1.20
1.00	100	100	

[a] Unitary elasticity means there is no change in total revenue as a result of a price increase.

Real-World Elasticity

Elasticity of demand is a very important factor in many business and economic decisions. One obvious area is that of *business pricing policies,* since the elasticity of demand will determine whether a price change will increase or reduce the firm's total revenue. Suppose, for instance, that the Cantown Ice Turkeys hockey team is currently pricing tickets to its games at an average price of $4 each, and that average ticket sales per game are 2400, which is well below the arena's capacity of 3000. Should the Ice Turkeys' management seek to increase ticket sales to 3000 and fill the arena for their games? The answer is not as simple as it seems if increasing attendance requires the kind of price reductions shown in the demand schedule in Table 4-4. If the demand for tickets is as shown, ticket prices will have to be cut to $3 to lure 3000 people to support the Ice Turkeys—a price that would *reduce* the club's total revenue by $600 per game, or more than 6 percent.

Table 4-4
Hypothetical Demand Schedule for Tickets to Cantown Ice Turkeys' Home Games

Average Price per Ticket	Quantity of Tickets Demanded per Game	Total Revenue per Game
$6.00	1650	$9900
5.00	2000	10 000
4 00	2400	9600
3.00	3000	9000

Table 4-5
Another Hypothetical Demand Schedule for Tickets to
Cantown Ice Turkeys' Home Games

Average price per Ticket	Quantity of Tickets demanded per game	Total Revenue per game
$6.00	1500	$9000
5.00	1900	9500
4.00	2400	9600
3.25	3000	9750

In fact, the demand schedule indicates that, financially, the Ice Turkeys would be better off if they *raised* the ticket price to $5, as the loss of sales would be more than offset by the higher price per ticket. Even at a price of $6 per ticket, there are still enough die-hard Ice Turkeys fans to make a nearly half-empty arena more profitable for the club than one with 2400 fans paying $4 each.

On the other hand, suppose the demand schedule is as shown in Table 4-5. In this case, it would pay the club to *reduce* the ticket price. A price reduction would increase total revenue as well as attendance, whereas price increases would have the opposite effect.

Obviously, the Ice Turkeys' management would like to know the elasticity of the demand for their tickets. However, in the real world, sellers do not have neat and precise demand schedules to guide them in their pricing decisions. While the market research departments of larger corporations may expend considerable effort in attempts to estimate the elasticity of demand for their products,[3] many smaller businesses operate on a trial-and-error basis, gaining a rough idea of the elasticity of demand by testing the market with small price increases or reductions. But this lack of a reliable method for determining elasticity of demand does not mean that sellers operate in the dark in their pricing decisions. Large corporations might sense that their position in the market is so dominant that the demand for their product is quite inelastic. And small retailers sense that if their prices increase above those of their competitors, the demand for their products will prove to be quite elastic. For similar reasons, discount retailers operate on the basis that at least a certain segment of consumers is quite sensitive to prices.

In a similar way, elasticity of demand influences the *ability of workers to increase their wages.* For instance, the demand for certain highly skilled workers, such as professional athletes, is inelastic. Such work is in demand, and there is no alternative way of doing it. Consequently, such people are in an excellent position to bargain for higher wages— which they do. By contrast, people in the lawn-mowing industry probably face a more elastic demand since their service is not essential and buyers have the alternative of mowing their own lawns. As a result, the demand for lawn mowing would be more elastic, making it more difficult for people who mow lawns to raise their prices and incomes.

---

[3] Usually, the elasticity is expressed numerically as a **coefficient of elasticity**. For instance, a coefficient of 1.2 means that a 1-percent increase in price causes a 1.2-percent reduction in quantity demanded, while a coefficient of 0.4 means that if the price increases by 1 percent, quantity demanded declines only 0.4 percent. Demand is *elastic* if the coefficient is greater than 1.0 and *inelastic* if the coefficient is less than 1.0. For example, the coefficient of elasticity for food has been estimated at 0.4, while for durable goods the coefficient has been estimated at 1.1.

coefficient of elasticity
The percentage change in quantity demanded that results from a 1-percent change in price.

Elasticity of demand is also an important consideration underlying the *taxation policies* of governments. Three of the most heavily taxed products are alcohol, tobacco, and gasoline. Moral, health, and ecological considerations aside, a major reason for these products being singled out for exceptionally high taxes is that the demand for all three is inelastic, so sales (and tax revenues) hold up quite well even after tax increases have raised these products' prices considerably. There is little point in imposing heavy taxes on products whose demand is elastic, because sales would fall drastically, devastating those industries, as well as the government's own tax revenues from their products.

Elasticity of demand is also a factor underlying certain social problems, a good example of which is the low incomes of many farmers over the years. Farmers have advanced technologically, raising productivity and the total output of farm products, but most still find themselves in a difficult position economically. While the increased output has depressed farm prices, the lower prices have not led to increased sales of farm products, because the demand for food is inelastic—people do not buy much more food just because it is a bargain. Farmers receive lower prices for their crops, but are unable to sell more crops to offset the lower prices, leaving them with lower total revenue, which means lower incomes for the farmers. Largely as a result of these problems, many groups of farmers have had to rely upon various types of government programs to support their prices and/or incomes, as we will see later.

Conclusion

This chapter has considered demand—the first part of the demand-and-supply process that determines prices in markets. In Chapter 5, we will consider supply, and then how supply and demand interact to determine prices.

Chapter Summary

1. A demand schedule or curve reflects the fact that, as the price of a good or service increases, the quantity demanded generally decreases, other things being equal. (L.O. 1)
2. A complementary good is a good that is bought in combination with another good. (L.O. 2)
3. If consumer tastes, incomes, or expectations change, or the prices of other products change, the demand for a product will increase (in which case the curve shifts to the right) or decrease (in which case the demand curve shifts to the left). (L.O. 3)
4. If buyers can do without a product or find a close substitute, a price increase will cause the seller's total sales revenue to fall, and demand will be elastic. (L.O. 4, 5, 6)
5. If buyers cannot or will not do without a product and cannot find a close substitute, a price increase will cause the seller's total sales revenue to increase, and demand will be inelastic. (L.O. 4, 5, 6)

Questions

1. If the incomes of Canadian families increased significantly, how would the demand curve for vacation packages be affected? Explain the reason for your answer.
2. If the price of electricity increased sharply, how would the demand curve for electric heaters be affected? Explain the reason for your answer.

3. How would a significant increase in the price of chicken affect the demand curve for fish? Explain the reason for your answer.

4. Following is the demand schedule for tickets to a show:

If the price were	The quantity demanded would be
$10	700 tickets
9	800
8	900
7	1000

   (a) For a price increase from $7 to $8, is demand elastic, inelastic, or unitary elastic?
   (b) For a price increase from $8 to $9, is demand elastic, inelastic, or unitary elastic?
   (c) For a price increase from $9 to $10, is demand elastic, inelastic, or unitary elastic?

5. State whether each of the following will make the demand for the product or service involved *more elastic* or *more inelastic*, and explain *why* it would do so.
   (a) The development of a new good-quality Canadian-produced white wine would tend to make the demand for imported white wine more _____, because _____.
   (b) Rising consumer incomes should make the demand for restaurant dinners more _____, because
   _____.
   (c) The use of freezers in more homes should make the demand for foods that can be frozen more _____, because
   _____.
   (d) In the summer, the demand for steak would become more _____, because _____.

6. Which product has the more inelastic demand—barbecues or propane gas for barbecues? Explain the reason for your answer.

7. Ticket prices to Toronto Maple Leafs hockey games are not only the highest in the National Hockey League, but also have increased faster than other teams' prices in recent years.
   (a) What makes it possible for the Maple Leafs to charge such high prices, and then increase them even further?
   (b) Could a team such as the Edmonton Oilers or Columbus Blue Jackets imitate the Maple Leafs' pricing policies? Why or why not?

8. A customer is about to buy 4 shirts at $20 each. When she finds that they have just gone on sale for $15, she buys 5 shirts instead. Is her demand for these shirts elastic or inelastic? Explain the reason for your answer.

9. Visit the Statistics Canada website at www.statcan.ca and search the site for "new motor vehicle sales."
   What has been the trend in the demand for new motor vehicles in Canada over the past five years, and what might explain this trend?

10. Visit the Statistics Canada website at www.statcan.ca and search *The Daily* for "new motor vehicle sales." What have been the most recent developments in the demand for new motor vehicles, and what are the reasons for these?

Study Guide

Review Questions   (Answers to these Review Questions appear in Appendix B.)

1. Which of the following portrays a typical demand curve?

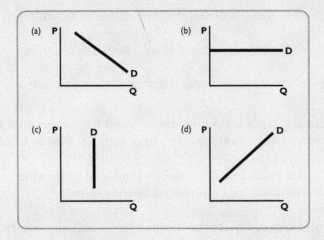

2. The demand curve shows that (for most products), an increase in price causes the quantity demanded to _____.

3. The effect in question 2 happens for two reasons:
   (a) some buyers become _____ to buy as much as before, and
   (b) some become _____ to buy as much as before.

4. Buyers who reduce their purchases have two basic alternatives: they can _____, or they can _____.

5. Following is the demand schedule for rowboat rentals on Lake Canmore.

Price per Day	Quantity Demanded per Week
$30	10
25	20
20	30
15	50
10	70

   On graph paper, draw the demand curve for rowboat rentals on Lake Canmore.

6. If family incomes increased, the demand curve for restaurant dinners would
   (a) shift to the left.
   (b) shift to the right.
   (c) not be affected.

7. If the price of imported wine decreased, the demand curve for Canadian-produced wine would
   (a) shift to the left.
   (b) shift to the right.
   (c) not be affected.

8. As a result of a successful advertising campaign for butter, the demand curve for margarine would
   (a) shift to the left.
   (b) shift to the right.
   (c) not be affected.

9. As a result of an increase in the price of margarine, the demand curve for margarine would
   (a) shift to the left.
   (b) shift to the right.
   (c) not be affected.

10. If sales of sport utility vehicles (SUVs) were to decrease, the demand curve for gasoline would
    (a) shift to the left.
    (b) shift to the right.
    (c) not be affected.

11. If many people expected the price of houses to increase over the next year or two, the demand curve for houses would probably
    (a) shift to the left.
    (b) shift to the right.
    (c) not be affected.

12. If a serious recession caused family incomes to fall, the demand curve for travel to Caribbean resorts would
    (a) shift to the left.
    (b) shift to the right.
    (c) not be affected.

13. As a result of the development of DVDs, the demand curve for tickets to movie theatres
    (a) shifted to the left.
    (b) shifted to the right.
    (c) was not affected.

14. For which one of the following would the demand be *most inelastic*?
    (a) electric heaters
    (b) electricity
    (c) stoves
    (d) lamps
    (e) TV sets

15. In the winter, Canadians' demand for vacations in the south
    (a) becomes more elastic.
    (b) becomes more inelastic.
    (c) Neither (a) nor (b)—elasticity of demand is not affected by the season.

16. Place the following in order of elasticity of demand, the *most elastic* coming first.
    • chocolate ice cream
    • dairy products
    • Neilson's chocolate ice cream
    • ice cream

Critical Thinking Questions

(Asterisked questions 1 to 6 are answered in Appendix B; the answers to questions 7 to 14 are in the Instructor's Manual that accompanies this text.)

*1. Which of these demand curves (**A** or **B**) shows an *elastic* demand? Explain fully the reasons for your answer, and show any calculations that you used.

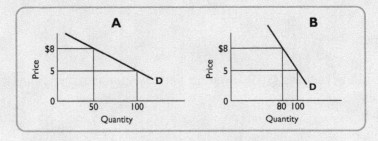

*2. Following is the demand schedule for a dozen cobs of corn:

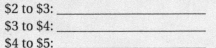

If the price were	The quantity demanded would be
$5	20 thousand per week
4	30 thousand per week
3	40 thousand per week
2	50 thousand per week

(a) Over the price ranges shown below, is the demand for cobs of corn *elastic* or *inelastic*?
$2 to $3: _____
$3 to $4: _____
$4 to $5: _____

(b) What could explain the *change* in the elasticity of demand as the price increases?

*3. Explain whether each of the following will make the demand for the product or service involved *more elastic* or *more inelastic*, and *why* it would do so.

(a) At Christmas, the demand for turkey should become more _____, because _____.

(b) The development of DVDs would make the demand for movie tickets more _____, because _____.

(c) The opening of a new pizzeria in town would make the demand for the existing pizzerias' products more _____, because _____.

*4. For each of the following pairs of goods, state which one of the pair has the more *elastic* demand, and explain the reason for your choice.

(a) air conditioners/furnaces
(b) automobiles/licences for automobiles
(c) telephone service/electricity
(d) new automobiles/replacement parts for automobiles

*5. Suppose the price of gasoline were to rise to record levels in the future.

(a) How would this affect the demand curve for SUVs?
(b) What is the economic term for the relationship between gasoline and SUVs?

*6. When the price of gasoline soared after 2004, economists pointed out that a major reason why the price went as high as it did was that the demand for gasoline was inelastic.

(a) Explain the reasoning behind this argument, in terms of the behaviour of buyers.
(b) If the price of gasoline remained high, might the elasticity of demand for gasoline change?

7. By 2004–05, the prospect of higher gasoline prices was generating interest in alternatives such as hybrid engines and alternative fuels. Describe *two* ways in which the development of such alternatives would affect the demand curve for gasoline, and show both of these changes on a graph.

8. If you were selling a product with an *inelastic* demand, what would you emphasize and not emphasize in your advertising?

9. If you were selling a product with an *elastic* demand, what would you emphasize in your advertising?

10. Would you expect the demand for dinner reservations at the most exclusive restaurant in the city to be elastic or inelastic?

11. "The dilemma posed by the demand curve is that, to increase *sales*, you must lower your *price*. This means that you will have to charge *less* to some buyers than they would have been prepared to pay, thus forgoing some sales revenue." Is there any way for a seller to get around this dilemma? (*Hint: Think Canadian Tire.*)

12. Many economists (and merchandisers) believe that the demand curve for some products is the type of curve shown in the following graph rather than the simple downward-sloping demand curve discussed in this chapter.

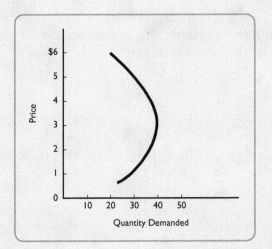

    (a) What is the relationship between price and quantity demanded, as shown by this curve?

    (b) What could explain this peculiar type of consumer behaviour?

    (c) How could merchandisers use this type of consumer behaviour to their advantage?

13. The following graph portrays some very unusual buyer behaviour.

(a) What is the buyer behaviour shown by this graph?

(b) What could explain such unusual buyer behaviour?

(c) Can you think of a product that might have a demand curve like this one?

14. What is the product with the *most elastic* demand that you can think of? Compare your choice with the choices of other students, and debate which choice is the best.

15. What is the product with the *most inelastic* demand that you can think of? Compare your choice with the choices of other students, and debate which choice is the best.

Use the Web   (Hints for these Use the Web exercises appear in Appendix B.)

1. Housing building contractors start building new houses in response to trends in buyers' demand. Visit the Statistics Canada website at **www.statcan.gc.ca** and click on Summary Tables, then search for housing starts by province.

   (a) What has been the trend in the demand for new housing in Canada over the past five years, and what might explain this trend?

   (b) Has the trend in your province differed significantly from the Canadian trend? If so, what might explain any differences?

2. Visit www.statcan.ca and search *The Daily* for "residential construction investment." What have been the most recent developments in the demand for new housing, and what are the reasons for these developments?

Appendix 4A
Graphs as Tools

In economics, graphs are frequently used, not only to illustrate statistical data but also as tools of analysis. This appendix is intended to introduce students who are not familiar with graphs to the types of graphs we will use in the remainder of this text.

The simplest and most common graph, and the one with which most people are quite familiar, is the *historical series graph*, which shows the behaviour of a statistic over a period of time. Figure 4A-1 is an example of such a graph. It

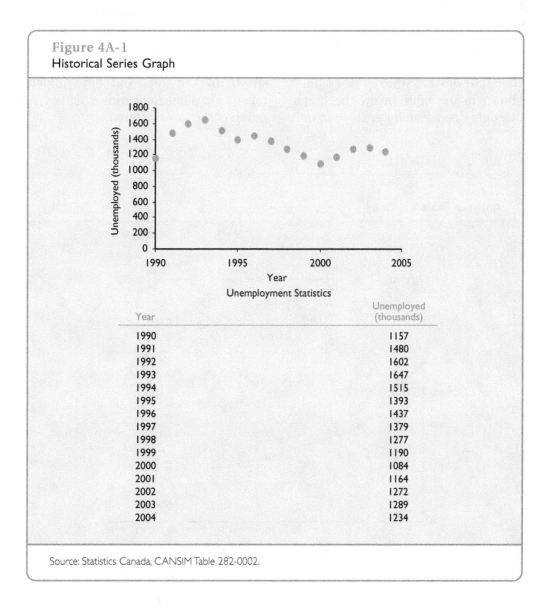

Figure 4A-1
Historical Series Graph

Unemployment Statistics

Year	Unemployed (thousands)
1990	1157
1991	1480
1992	1602
1993	1647
1994	1515
1995	1393
1996	1437
1997	1379
1998	1277
1999	1190
2000	1084
2001	1164
2002	1272
2003	1289
2004	1234

Source: Statistics Canada, CANSIM Table 282-0002.

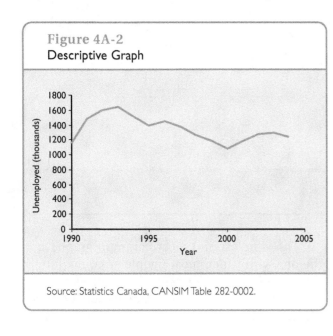

Figure 4A-2
Descriptive Graph

Source: Statistics Canada, CANSIM Table 282-0002.

the dots can be drawn on the graph with certainty. However, to allow the graph to give us a better visual presentation of the trends it shows, we usually join the dots together as a line, as shown in Figure 4A-2. Because such a time series graph simply describes a trend in a visual manner, it can be called a *descriptive graph*.

There is, however, another type of graph that we use in economics, particularly in microeconomics. Such a graph partly *describes* a situation, but can also be used to help to *analyze* the situation. Suppose that we wish to show how many coats Kathy's Coat Shop could sell at various prices. This information could be shown in a *table*, as in the first part of Figure 4A-3. This table tells us that at low prices, Kathy can sell more coats per week than she can sell at higher prices. The same information can also be shown on a graph, as in the second part of Figure 4A-3. This graph shows the same information as the table does, but this graph shows the information visually. (Again, we have only the five specific pieces of information as shown by the dots, but have joined the dots together as a line to provide a better visual presentation of the information.)

shows the fluctuations in the number of Canadians unemployed in each year from 1990 to 2004.

The actual statistics on which the graph is based are shown in the table below the graph. Since we have only one figure for each year, only

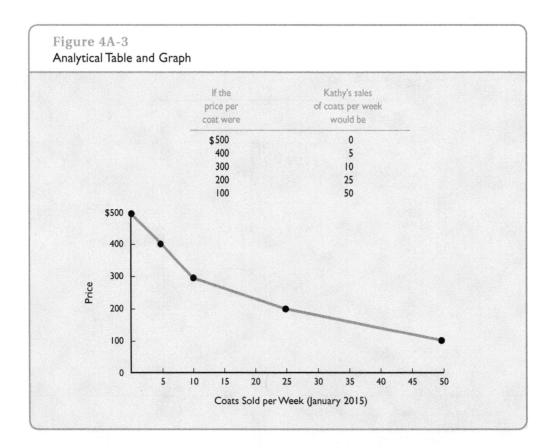

Figure 4A-3
Analytical Table and Graph

If the price per coat were	Kathy's sales of coats per week would be
$500	0
400	5
300	10
200	25
100	50

Coats Sold per Week (January 2015)

It is important to understand the nature of graphs such as the one in Figure 4A-3, because it is quite different from graphs such as the one in Figure 4A-2. Figure 4A-2 shows the behaviour of unemployment *over a period of time*—the 1990–2004 period, as shown on the horizontal axis. Figure 4A-3, by contrast, shows the relationship between the price of coats and coat sales *at a particular point in time* (January 2006 in our example). As time changes and the behaviour of buyers changes, so will this relationship change—for instance, in July we would expect coat sales to be much lower at each price shown on the graph.

Figure 4A-3 shows the sort of "what if" relationship explained earlier in Chapter 4—it shows that *if* the price were $300, the quantity demanded would be 10 coats, and *if* the price were $400, the quantity demanded would be 5 coats. But the information in Figure 4A-3 also implies a *dynamic cause-effect relationship* between the two variables; that is, if the price increased from $300 to $400, this would *cause* a decrease in the quantity demanded from 10 coats to 5 (assuming that no other variables affecting buyer behaviour change).

The most important function of graphs such as the one in Figure 4A-3 is to show the relationship between two variables—the price of coats (on the vertical axis) and sales of coats (on the horizontal axis). The two basic types of relationships that can be shown on such a graph are *inverse* and *direct*. Figure 4A-4 shows an inverse relationship—the higher the price goes, the lower the sales go and vice versa. When higher amounts of one variable are associated with lower amounts of the other variable in this way, the line on the graph slopes down to the right, and we say that the two variables are *inversely related*.

Conversely, if higher quantities of one variable are associated with higher quantities of the other, the two variables are said to be *directly related*. An example of a direct relationship in economics would be the relationship between the wage rate offered for part-time student help by a college's athletic department and the number of hours of work offered by students—the higher the wage rate, the greater the number of hours the students will be prepared to work. Such a relationship is shown in Figure 4A-5.

Finally, while graphs such as Figure 4A-4 and 4A-5 can describe a relationship between two variables, they can also help to analyze, or explain, that relationship. That is, the graph can portray a *cause-and-effect relationship* between two variables such as the price of coats and sales of coats. If Kathy raises her price from $200 to $300, the increase will *cause* sales to decline from 25 coats to 10 coats per week. Because they can be used to analyze relationships in this way, graphs such as Figure 4A-4 and Figure 4A-5 are sometimes referred to as *analytical graphs*, as distinct from the simpler descriptive graphs, such as Figure 4A-3.

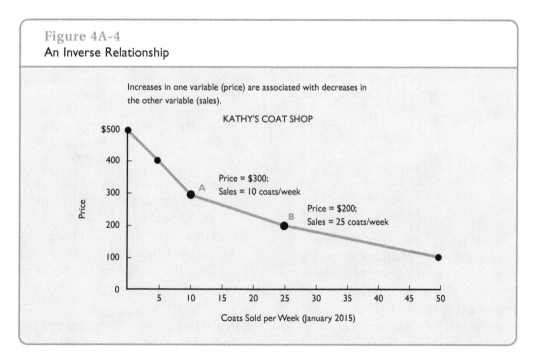

Figure 4A-4
An Inverse Relationship

Increases in one variable (price) are associated with decreases in the other variable (sales).

KATHY'S COAT SHOP

Price = $300; Sales = 10 coats/week

Price = $200; Sales = 25 coats/week

Coats Sold per Week (January 2015)

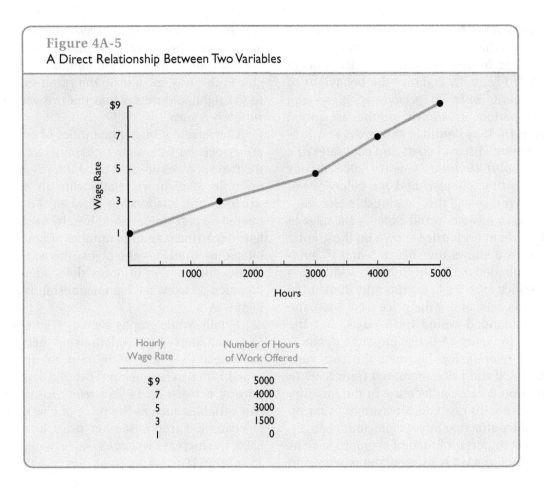

Figure 4A-5
A Direct Relationship Between Two Variables

Hourly Wage Rate	Number of Hours of Work Offered
$9	5000
7	4000
5	3000
3	1500
1	0

Study Guide

Review Questions

(Answers to these Review Questions appear in Appendix B.)

1. The following table shows the number of American travellers entering Canada over a 5-year period.

Year	Number of Travellers
2000	44 million
2001	43 million
2002	41 million
2003	36 million
2004	35 million

 (a) Use the statistics in the table to draw a graph of the number of American travellers entering Canada from 2000 to 2004.

 (b) What information does the graph convey to someone who reads it?

 (c) Does the graph help the reader to understand *why* the number of American travellers entering Canada changed?

2. The following table shows how many tickets people would buy to a concert at various prices.

If the price were	People would buy
$50 per ticket	4000 tickets
40 per ticket	5000 tickets
30 per ticket	6000 tickets
20 per ticket	7000 tickets
10 per ticket	8000 tickets

 (a) Use the statistics in the table to draw a graph showing these data, with the price on the vertical axis.

 (b) What information does the graph convey to someone who reads it?

 (c) Does the graph help the reader to understand *why* the number of tickets sold changes?

3. In a resort area with recreational fishing, children pick worms and sell them at a roadside

stand. The following table shows how many dozens of worms will be offered for sale by the children at various prices.

If the price were	The children would supply
$5 per dozen	100 dozen per week
4 per dozen	80 dozen per week
3 per dozen	60 dozen per week
2 per dozen	40 dozen per week
1 per dozen	20 dozen per week

(a) Use the statistics in the table to draw a graph showing these data, with the price on the vertical axis.

(b) What information does the graph convey to someone who reads it?

(c) Does the graph help the reader to understand *why* the number of worms offered for sale changes?

5

The Supply Side of Markets

LEARNING OBJECTIVES

After studying this chapter, you should be able to

1. Identify industries as either *competitive* or *concentrated* according to the criteria in the text.

2. Differentiate between the nature of supply in competitive and concentrated industries, using the terms *price-taker*, *price-maker*, and *market power* in your explanation.

3. Draw a supply curve for a product from a supply schedule showing the quantity supplied at various prices.

4. Explain whether a given event would increase or decrease the supply of a particular product, and show how this would affect the supply curve.

5. Explain the difference between *elastic*, *inelastic*, and *perfectly inelastic* supply.

6. Explain why a given event or situation or makes the supply of an item more elastic or more inelastic.

7. Draw the demand and supply curves for an item and show the equilibrium price and quantity, given the demand schedule and the supply schedule for that item.

8. Use the concepts and tools in this chapter to analyze given situations relating to supply and to elasticity of supply.

As we have seen, markets consist of
- a demand side, or offers by buyers to purchase products, and
- a supply side, or offers by sellers to sell products, as shown in Figure 5-1.

In Chapter 4, we saw how, on the demand side of markets, the demand for particular products is determined by the ability and willingness of buyers to *purchase* those products. In this chapter, we will consider the supply side of markets and factors that affect the ability and willingness of businesses to *produce and sell* particular goods and services.

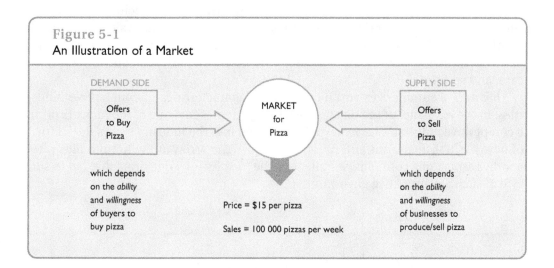

Figure 5-1
An Illustration of a Market

DEMAND SIDE

Offers to Buy Pizza

which depends on the *ability* and *willingness* of buyers to buy pizza

MARKET for Pizza

Price = $15 per pizza

Sales = 100 000 pizzas per week

SUPPLY SIDE

Offers to Sell Pizza

which depends on the *ability* and *willingness* of businesses to produce/sell pizza

Competitive Conditions

Before we examine how demand and supply interact to determine prices, we have to take a closer look at the supply side of the market—the right panel of Figure 5-1. In particular, we need to examine how different types of industries and firms[1] are organized and operate.

As we saw in Chapter 3, the process that we call *supply* takes place under different conditions. Some industries have many small firms, while other industries are dominated by a few large firms, and in a few markets there is only one producer (a monopoly). These different conditions—which economists refer to as **market structures**—have a significant effect on the supply of various products. There is a great deal of difference between the ways in which a small vegetable farmer and a huge automobile manufacturer make their decisions as to how much output to produce and what price to charge for it.

market structure
Term used to describe the organization and nature of a market or an industry, particularly whether it is competitive or concentrated in nature.

Competitive Industries

One basic market structure consists of what economists call **competitive industries**. Competitive industries have the following two basic characteristics:
- they consist of a large number of small firms, and
- it is easy for new firms to enter (and exit) the industry.

competitive industry
An industry that consists of many small firms and is easily entered by new competitors.

---

[1] The term *firm* refers to a business; the term *industry* refers to the group of business firms producing a particular product or service. For example, Ford is one *firm* in the North American automobile *industry*.

As a result, competition among producers is strong, and the strong competition holds prices and profits down to relatively low levels. If prices and profits *were* to increase to higher levels, new producers would be attracted into the industry, which would increase supply and push prices and profits back downward. While this situation is not to the advantage of the producers in the industry, they are unable to do anything about it; because they are so numerous, it is impossible for them to get together and agree to restrict competition among themselves. And even if they did manage to agree to increase their prices, new competitors would enter their market anyway. Examples of competitive industries include much of the small business sector described in Chapter 3, such as small-scale retail stores, many small agricultural producers, small-scale manufacturing, and many service industries, such as restaurants, barbershops, repair shops, home renovations, lawn care, and so on.

Figure 5-2 summarizes and illustrates the characteristics of competitive industries. In the left panel of the diagram, each circle represents one of the many firms in a competitive industry. The arrow pointing down into the industry shows the "births" of newly established firms entering the industry. The arrow at the bottom illustrates another aspect of a competitive industry—the "deaths" of some firms that fail to survive in such a competitive environment.

Figure 5-2
Characteristics of Competitive and Concentrated Industries

Competitive Industries	*Concentrated Industries*
Producers have very little control over prices and profits	Producers are sometimes in a better position to influence prices and profits
because	*because*
1. there are many small firms in the industry; and 2. it is easy for new firms to enter (and exit) the industry;	1. there are only a few firms in the industry; and 2. It is difficult for new firms to enter;

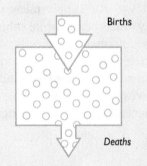

Births

Deaths

so that	*so that*
the producers are unable to control the supply—if profits become high, new firms start up, causing supply to rise and prices and profits to fall;	existing producers may be able to reach agreements to limit supply and increase prices;
with the result that	*with the result that*
prices and profits tend to be held down to low levels.	prices and profits tend to be maintained at above-competitive levels.

Concentrated Industries

Not all industries are competitive in this sense; in some industries, a few large firms dominate the market. In these industries, it is much more difficult for newcomers to enter the market, due to obstacles such as the amount of capital required and the established position of the existing firms in the market. Such obstacles put these established firms at a greater advantage than firms in competitive industries. First, because they are few in number, the dominant firms will be in a better position to agree among themselves not to compete vigorously on prices. As a result, profits in such **concentrated industries** are often higher than those in competitive industries. Second, because it is so difficult for new firms to enter the industry, there is much less risk that the industry's high profits will attract newcomers who would increase competition and erode their high profits. Examples of concentrated industries include banking, steel, breweries, and petroleum refining, as well as government monopolies such as Canada Post.

The panel on the right side of Figure 5-2 on page 86 shows the characteristics of concentrated industries. The industry is dominated by a few large firms, and there are few if any "births" of new entrants or "deaths" of firms.

concentrated industry
An industry that is dominated by a few large firms and is not easily entered by new competitors.

Price-Makers, Market Power, and Price-Takers

Prices are determined by demand and supply. If a group of producers/sellers in a concentrated industry can restrict the supply of their product by agreeing to restrict their production of it, they can increase its price. Sellers who possess the ability to influence the supply of their products are called **price-makers** because they have the ability to determine (or at least influence) the price of the product. Another way of describing this situation is to say that such producers have **market power**. In this way, organized groups have been able to maintain high price levels, at various times, for a wide variety of products, including diamonds, oil, coffee, and cell phone service.

By contrast, in an industry that is competitive, there are many sellers, who are too numerous to organize and reach agreements among themselves in the way that a few large producers can, and new producers can enter the industry easily, which makes it impossible for producers to control the supply or the price. Such producers are described as **price-takers**, because the market, not the producers, determines the price, and each producer must accept that price. Since each individual producer cannot control the price, the economic incentive is for each producer to produce as much as possible, as efficiently as possible, and sell it for the going price.

Because the production and pricing decisions associated with supply in concentrated industries are different from those in competitive industries, we will consider the two separately. In this chapter, our first look at supply will be limited to the case of competitive industries, which includes a wide range of industries, from farming to small-scale manufacturers to a vast array of services such as restaurants, home repair contractors, barbershops, and so on. Later, in Chapter 7, we will consider the case of concentrated industries.

price-maker
Term used to describe the position of the dominant firm(s) in a concentrated industry, which can influence the price of the product.

market power
The ability to raise one's prices; usually associated with a dominant or monopolistic position in the market.

price-taker
Term used to describe the position of the individual small firm in a competitive industry, which is unable to influence the price of its product and is forced to accept (take) whatever price is determined in the market.

Supply Under Competitive Conditions

As a general rule, in a competitive industry, an increase in the *price* of the product will lead to an increase in the *quantity supplied*. By making it more profitable to produce the product, higher prices will generate higher output by

- leading existing firms to increase their output, and also
- attracting new firms into the industry, which will also increase output.

This important characteristic of competitive industries is illustrated in Figure 5-3, in which a price increase from $6 to $8 causes the quantity supplied (offered for sale) to increase from 50 000 units per week to 80 000 units per week.

Finally, it should be clarified that the concept of *supply* does not refer to the physical *quantity* of a product in existence but rather to the quantity of it that is *offered for sale*. For instance, the supply of used mountain bicycles in a city is not the 300 000 such bicycles that *exist* there, but rather the number that would be *offered for sale* at various possible prices. And the 300 used mountain bicycles that are presently on the market (offered for sale) is the *quantity supplied* at the current market price of, say, $120.

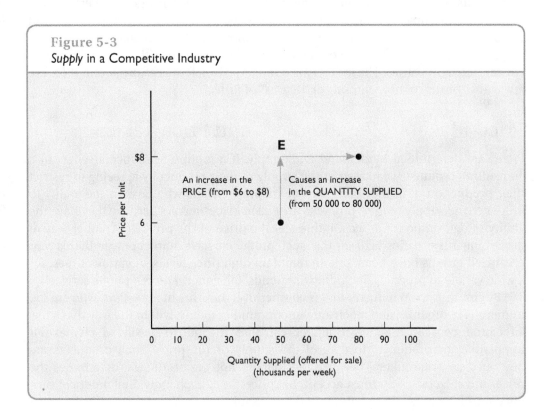

Figure 5-3
Supply in a Competitive Industry

An increase in the PRICE (from $6 to $8)

Causes an increase in the QUANTITY SUPPLIED (from 50 000 to 80 000)

Price per Unit

Quantity Supplied (offered for sale)
(thousands per week)

Back to the Pizza Example

Now let's revisit the market for pizza that we used in Chapter 4 to illustrate the demand side of markets. Suppose that the supply side of the pizza market is a "competitive" industry consisting of a large number of pizzerias in competition with each other, and that it is easy to enter the industry. Now suppose that pizza prices *increase*. What effect will this increase have on the amount of pizza offered for sale?

We should expect the higher prices to induce producers to offer *more* pizzas for sale, by making it more profitable to sell pizzas. Existing pizzerias will increase their output, and new pizzerias might start up, attracted by the industry's higher profits.

The supply of pizzas is illustrated in the **supply schedule** in Table 5-1 on the next page, and graphically in a **supply curve** in Figure 5-4 on the next page. Both the supply schedule and the supply curve reflect the fundamental fact that we have stressed: in a competitive market, increases in price will tend to cause increases in the quantity that producers will supply.

supply schedule
A table depicting the relationship between the price of a product and the quantity supplied (offered for sale).

supply curve
A graphical representation of a supply schedule.

Table 5-1
Supply Schedule for Pizza in Cantown, March 2015

If the price per pizza were	The quantity supplied (offered for sale per week) would be
$20	100 000
16	80 000
12	50 000
8	20 000
6	0

As we saw with demand in Chapter 4, the table and the figure show a series of "what-if" scenarios. *If* the price were $6 per pizza, no one could make a profit selling pizza, so the quantity supplied would be zero. But *If* the price were $8, 20 000 could be supplied profitably, *If* the price were $12, the quantity supplied would be 50 000, and so on.

As with demand, the concept of supply includes the entire supply schedule or curve—that is, *supply* refers to the amounts that would be offered for sale at every possible price. If the actual price were $12 per pizza and the actual quantity supplied were 50 000 pizzas, the supply would not just be 50 000 pizzas—supply also includes the amounts that *would have been offered* for sale if the price had been higher or lower. See the accompanying "In the News" box for a look at the relationship between price and supply.

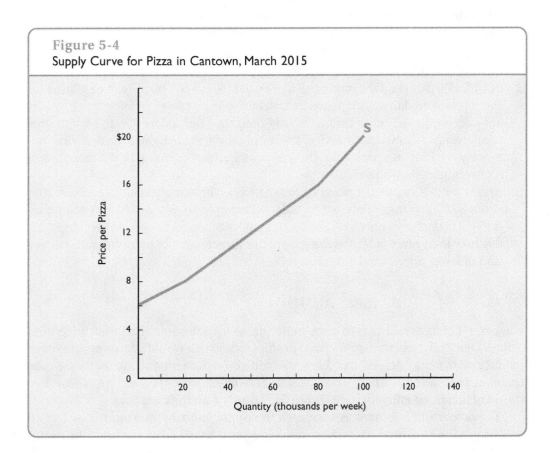

Figure 5-4
Supply Curve for Pizza in Cantown, March 2015

Changes in Supply

An Increase in Supply

In Chapter 4, we saw that, if demand increased, the demand curve shifted to the right. In a similar way, increases in supply cause the supply curve to shift to the right, as shown by the new supply curve S_1 in Figure 5-5 on the next page.

There are two ways of looking at the changes shown in Figure 5-5:

(a) *Sellers are offering more pizza for sale.* The supply schedule at the top of Figure 5-5 shows that at a price of $20, sellers used to offer 100 000 pizzas for sale, but will now put 130 000 pizzas on the market; at a price of $16, 110 000 pizzas will be offered for sale as compared to 80 000 pizzas before, and so on. At every possible price, sellers are offering 30 000 more pizzas for sale than they did before. On the graph, this relationship is shown by the shift of the supply curve to the right, to its new location, as shown by the new curve S_1. The horizontal arrows pointing in the direction of higher output show this change.

(b) *Sellers are willing to sell pizza at lower prices.* The supply schedule shows that when 80 000 pizzas are offered for sale, sellers used to charge $16 for each pizza, but will now charge only $12. Similarly, for 50 000 pizzas, they used to charge $12, but now their price is $8. On the graph, the vertical arrows pointing in the direction of lower prices show this change.

Causes of Increased Supply

What could *cause* producers to offer more pizzas for sale, and at a lower price than before? One likely reason is *an increase in efficiency,* which would enable producers to *produce more pizza.* Increased efficiency would also *reduce production costs per pizza,* enabling producers to offer pizza for sale at a *lower price* than before. These two effects of increased efficiency are shown in Figure 5-6 on the next page.

Technology often generates increases in supply, both by making it possible to produce more of a product and by reducing production costs per unit. In recent

Figure 5-5
An Increase in Supply

Price per Pizza	Previous Quantity Supplied (S)	New Quantity Supplied (S₁)
$ 20	100 000	130 000
16	80 000	110 000
12	50 000	80 000
8	20 000	50 000
6	0	30 000

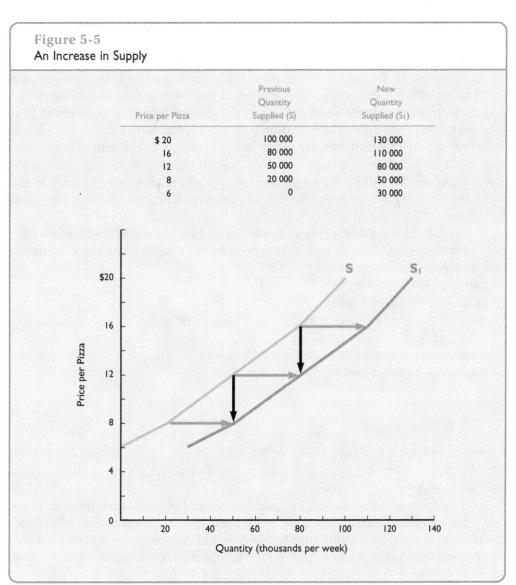

Figure 5-6
Higher Efficiency as a Cause of Increased Supply

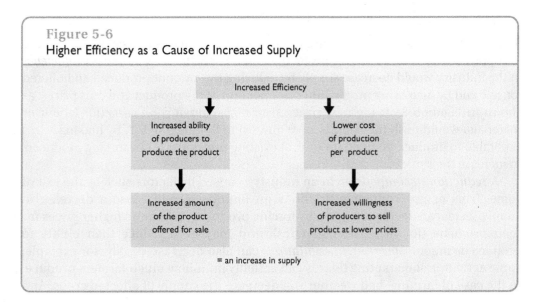

years, computer technology has been a strong force in increasing productivity in may industries.

There are various other possible causes of an increase in supply. If *new producers* (either domestic or foreign) were to enter the market, the increased *competition* would bring both a higher supply of the product and lower prices, as has happened recently with freer trade between nations. If the government paid *subsidies* to producers such as public transit commissions, they could afford to expand and charge lower prices, both of which represent an increase in supply. In the case of farm products, weather is a factor, as when a *good harvest* causes an increase in supply. *Expectations* can also affect supply—if higher sales and profits were expected in the near future, existing producers might produce more, and new producers might enter the industry.

In general, anything that increases the ability and willingness of producers to offer more of their product for sale and/or reduce prices will cause an increase in supply. Such factors include the following:
- increases in efficiency,
- improvements in technology,
- increased competition, such as from new firms or imports,
- subsidies from governments,
- weather, in the case of agricultural products, and
- producers' expectations.

A Decrease in Supply

A decrease in supply is shown in Figure 5-7 on the next page. This figure shows the opposite of everything that is covered in the previous section, in terms of what happens and the causes of these changes.

As the supply schedule shows, less pizza is offered for sale at each possible price. This relationship is shown on the graph by the horizontal arrows pointing in the direction of lower output. Also, as the supply schedule and the vertical arrows show, sellers will only sell their pizza at higher prices than before. As a reflection of these changes, the supply curve shifts to the left, to its new location S_2.

Causes of Decreased Supply

Such a decrease in supply would be caused by the same factors that cause an increase in supply, but operating in the opposite direction. For instance, a *decrease in efficiency* in the industry would decrease supply by reducing the amount produced and offered for sale and by increasing production costs per unit of the product and thus prices, as shown in Figure 5-8 on the next page. Also, *higher production costs* (for labour or materials) would push the supply curve upward to S_2 in Figure 5-7, by making it less profitable to produce as much product at existing prices and/or by forcing producers to increase their prices.

A *reduction in competition* in an industry, caused by factors such as the exit of some firms or government restrictions on imports, would cause a decrease in supply. *Taxes* can decrease supply, by forcing producers to require higher prices for their products (for instance, cigarettes), and may even reduce their ability to produce as much. *Government regulations* can also decrease supply; for example, some agricultural marketing boards can actually limit how much farmers produce. In the case of farming, bad weather will decrease the supply of affected crops. And

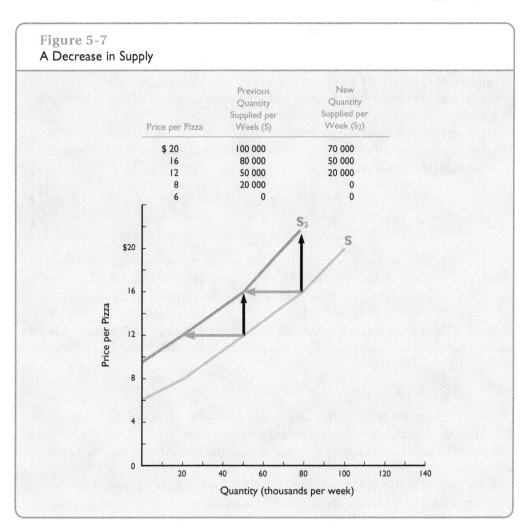

Figure 5-7
A Decrease in Supply

Price per Pizza	Previous Quantity Supplied per Week (S)	New Quantity Supplied per Week (S₂)
$ 20	100 000	70 000
16	80 000	50 000
12	50 000	20 000
8	20 000	0
6	0	0

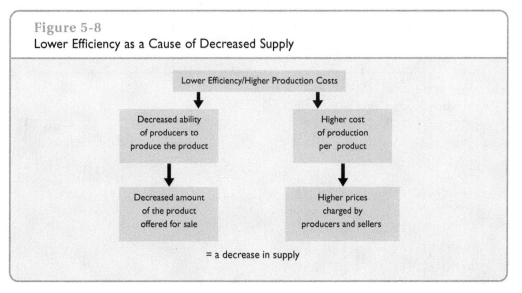

Figure 5-8
Lower Efficiency as a Cause of Decreased Supply

Lower Efficiency/Higher Production Costs

Decreased ability of producers to produce the product

Higher cost of production per product

Decreased amount of the product offered for sale

Higher prices charged by producers and sellers

= a decrease in supply

expectations can generate a decrease in supply. If lower sales and profits were expected, supply might be reduced as firms cut back on output or as some of them even leave the industry.

In general, anything that reduces the ability and/or willingness of producers to produce the product and/or increases their production costs will reduce the supply of the product, and shift the supply curve to the left or upward. These factors include the following:

- reductions in efficiency and increases in production costs per unit;
- reductions in competition, such as restrictions on imports or firms leaving the industry;
- taxes on the product or the producers;
- government regulations that limit output and/or increase costs per unit; and
- producers' expectations.

Elasticity of Supply

We have seen that, as the price of a product produced in a competitive industry increases, the quantity supplied will increase. We must now consider the question of *how much* the quantity supplied will increase in response to a higher price. In some cases, the higher price will cause prompt and large increases in the quantity supplied, while in other cases, even very large increases in price will not cause the quantity supplied to change significantly, at least in the short run.

Inelastic Supply

inelastic supply
A situation in which quantity supplied does not increase readily when the price increases.

If rising prices do not cause significant increases in quantity supplied, supply is said to be inelastic. Figure 5-9 shows an **inelastic supply**: here, even a fivefold increase in price (from $2 to $10) only causes the quantity supplied to increase by one-half (from 40 to 60 units).

Such an inelastic supply is usually caused by obstacles to increasing production of the product, at least in the short run. These obstacles could include shortages of labour or materials, limited plant capacity, or rising costs such as overtime wage rates. For instance, the supply of strawberries in January would be inelastic: no locally grown strawberries would be available at any price, so any additional strawberries would have to be imported, at high costs and in limited quantities.

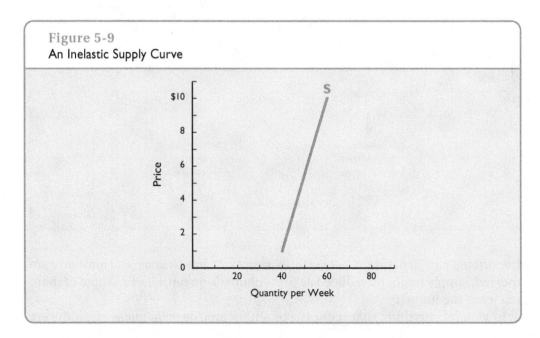

Figure 5-9
An Inelastic Supply Curve

The most extreme case of inelasticity of supply—*perfectly inelastic supply*—is illustrated in Figure 5-10: here, despite very large price increases, *no* increase in the amount offered for sale takes place. The best example of such a situation would be a unique item such as an original work of art—no matter how high the price goes, there can be only one of it.

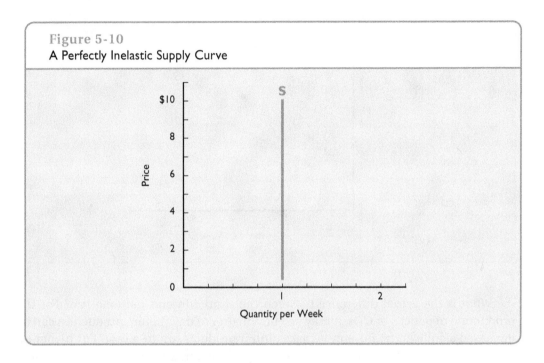

Figure 5-10
A Perfectly Inelastic Supply Curve

Elastic Supply

If an increase in price brings forth onto the market a large increase in the quantity supplied, supply is referred to as **elastic supply**.

Figure 5-11 shows an elastic supply curve. Here, tripling of the price (from $2 to $6) causes a fivefold increase in the quantity supplied (from 20 to 100). An example of such a situation could be the production of pencils or compact discs—with the machinery already in existence and the labour and materials readily available, it is a simple and low-cost matter to increase production of pencils or CDs if price increases made it profitable to do so.

elastic supply
A situation in which the quantity supplied increases readily when the price increases.

Elasticity of Supply Over Time

Finally, as with elasticity of demand, elasticity of supply tends to increase with the passage of time. When the price of the product first increases, limited amounts of equipment or trained labour may make it impossible (or quite costly) to increase the quantity supplied by much for a while. However, given more time, producers can often overcome these obstacles by obtaining equipment and training workers to increase the quantity supplied in response to price increases. How elasticity of supply can change from the short run to the long run is illustrated in Figure 5-12, which shows the supply becoming much more elastic as time passes.

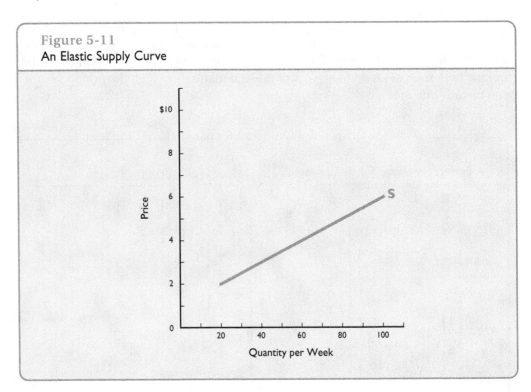

Figure 5-11
An Elastic Supply Curve

What is the actual difference between the short run and the long run? For the production of pencils or CDs, it may just be a matter of days before production can be increased significantly; for annual agricultural products, up to a year. For higher oil prices to stimulate increased exploration, development, and production of oil on a large scale, 10 to 15 years may be required.

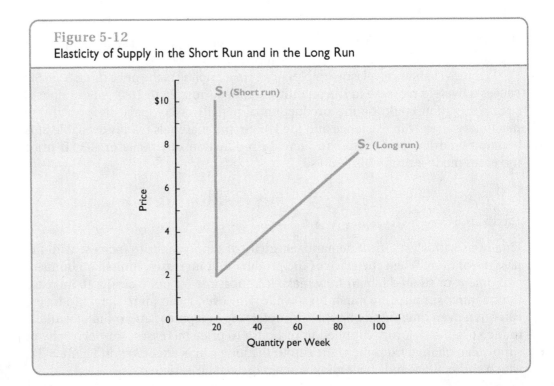

Figure 5-12
Elasticity of Supply in the Short Run and in the Long Run

The Market: Supply, Demand, and Prices

We have now examined both demand (in Chapter 4) and supply under competitive conditions (in this chapter); these two concepts are summarized in Table 5-2. We are now ready to consider how demand and supply interact, by combining them, as in Table 5-3.

Table 5-2

Supply and Demand Schedules for Pizza in Cantown, March 2015

DEMAND		SUPPLY	
The relationship between the price of the product and the number of units buyers will offer to buy.		The relationship between the price of the product and the number of units producers will offer to sell.	
Price per Pizza	Quantity Demanded per Week	Price per Pizza	Quantity Supplied per Week
$20	20 000	$20	100 000
16	30 000	16	80 000
12	50 000	12	50 000
8	80 000	8	20 000
4	120 000	4	0

As the supply and demand schedules in Table 5-3 show, the price of pizza will tend to stabilize at $12 each. This price is called the **equilibrium price**. It is not possible for the market to clear at any other level because all other prices lead to either a shortage or a surplus, which would cause the price to change. For instance, at a price of $20, the quantity supplied exceeds the quantity demanded, generating a surplus of 80 000 pizzas on the market. Under these circumstances, competition among sellers will drive the

equilibrium price

A price determined in the marketplace by the interaction of supply and demand.

Table 5-3

Supply and Demand Interacting to Determine the Price of Pizza in Cantown, March 2015

Price per Pizza	Quantity Demanded per Week	Quantity Supplied per Week	Balance	Price Will Tend to
$20	20 000	100 000	Surplus of 80 000	Fall
16	30 000	80 000	Surplus of 50 000	Fall
12	50 000	50 000	No surplus/no shortage	Remain stable
8	80 000	20 000	Shortage of 60 000	Rise
4	120 000	0	Shortage of 120 000	Rise

price down toward the equilibrium level of $12. Similarly, prices below $12 discourage production but encourage demand, causing shortages on the market. As buyers compete for the limited supply, the price will be bid up toward the equilibrium level of $12. Only at a price of $12 are the actions of both buyers and sellers in harmony so that there is neither a surplus nor a shortage. As a result, the price will tend to settle at the equilibrium level of $12.

The interaction of supply and demand can also be shown on a graph, as in Figure 5-13. On the graph the equilibrium price of $12 is determined by the intersection of the supply curve and the demand curve at the *equilibrium point* (E). The intersection of the curves also determines the quantity that will be bought (and sold), that is, the **equilibrium quantity** of 50 000 pizzas per week.

equilibrium quantity

The quantity sold (bought) at the equilibrium price.

To summarize, the way in which supply and demand interact to determine the price of a product or service can be represented on a schedule such as Table 5-3, or on a graph such as Figure 5-13. Both the schedule and the graph depict the behaviour of buyers (demand) and sellers (supply) in the market for a particular good or service, and the equilibrium price and quantity that will emerge in that market.

Figure 5-13 is a very *static* representation of a market, showing the demand for and supply of pizza *at a particular point in time* (March 2015). In reality, however, markets are very *dynamic,* with constant changes in supply and demand occurring, causing continual changes in equilibrium prices and quantities. In effect, then, Figure 5-13 is a *snapshot* of a dynamic, changing situation at a particular point in time. In the next chapter, we will consider the more realistic situation of how markets change and adjust in response to changes in both supply and demand.

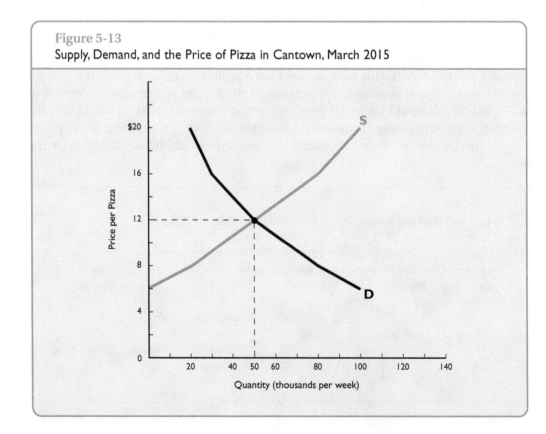

Figure 5-13

Supply, Demand, and the Price of Pizza in Cantown, March 2015

Chapter Summary

1. Competitive industries consist of many small firms and are easy to enter; in concentrated industries, a few large firms are dominant and it is difficult for new firms to start. (L.O. 1)
2. In competitive industries, producers are unable to restrict the supply of the product, so increases in the price of a product will cause increases in the quantity supplied. In concentrated industries, producers may be in a position to agree to restrict output and increase prices. (L.O. 2)
3. Increases in supply will shift the supply curve to the right, while decreases in supply will shift the curve to the left. (L.O. 4)
4. If the quantity supplied does not increase significantly in response to a small increase in price, supply is *inelastic*, while supply is *elastic* if small price increases cause large increases in the quantity supplied. (L.O. 5, 6)
5. In competitive markets, supply and demand interact freely to determine the equilibrium price and quantity, which will change as supply or demand changes. (L.O. 7)

Questions

1. Would economists consider Canada's banking industry to be *competitive* or *concentrated*? Explain the reasons for your choice.

2. Would economists consider the restaurant industry to be competitive or concentrated? Explain the reasons for your choice.

3. Explain why economists consider the distinction between competitive and concentrated industries to be an important matter, using the terms *price-taker*, *market power*, and *price-maker* in your answer.

4. Suppose that the prospect of low mortgage interest rates led builders to expect that the demand for new houses would increase considerably next year. Explain how this would affect the supply curve for new houses.

5. Suppose the government imposed heavy new taxes on cigarettes. Explain how this would affect the supply curve for cigarettes.

6. One hour before closing for the evening, your local supermarket cuts the price of its fresh barbecued chickens by half. How would you show this change on a supply curve for barbecued chicken?

7. Which would be more inelastic—the supply of crude oil or the supply of paper clips? Explain the reason for your answer.

8. Explain the logic behind the following statement: "The more inelastic the supply of a product is, the more likely it is that its price will increase."

9. The table below shows the demand and supply schedules for cashew nuts.

Price per Can	Quantity Demanded ('000s cans per week)	Quantity Supplied ('000s cans per week)
$8	10	55
7	20	50
6	30	45
5	40	40
4	50	30
3	70	10

(a) On graph paper, draw the demand and supply curves for cashews.

(b) What will the equilibrium price of cashews be? Explain why it will be this price, and not any of the other possible prices.

(c) Suppose that, due to increased imports of cashews, the quantity supplied at each possible price increases by 20 000 cans per week. How would the price be affected? Show these changes on your graph.

10. The internet can provide an indication of the number of sellers competing in a market. Visit **www.bizrate.com** and "shop" for a product that is of interest to you. Does this seem to be a "competitive" industry, as described in chapter 5? How many sellers did you find? What was the range of prices?

Study Guide

Review Questions   (Answers to these Review Questions appear in Appendix B.)

1. What are the two basic characteristics that cause an industry to be classified as competitive? (Select *two* answers.)
   (a) There is competition from foreign imports.
   (b) There are many small firms.
   (c) Competing firms do a lot of advertising.
   (d) Most firms in the industry have been in business for a long time.
   (e) It is easy to start up a new firm in the industry.

2. Because of the characteristics described in question 1, in competitive industries
   (a) producers can control the price of their products, but not the supply of them.
   (b) producers can control the supply of their product so as to increase its price and their profits.
   (c) producers are unable to control either the supply of their product or its price, and profits tend to be low.
   (d) product prices tend to be high because there are too many producers in the industry.
   (e) None of the above.

3. Which of the following best describes the characteristics and behaviour of concentrated industries?
   (a) With only one producer in the industry, prices and profits tend to be unusually high.
   (b) With only a few large producers in the industry, prices tend to be lower than in competitive industries, because firms spend less money on competition.
   (c) The few firms in the industry are able to make price agreements among themselves and thus earn high profits, but they are unable to keep out new firms attracted by the industry's high profits.
   (d) Because there are only a few firms in the industry and it is difficult for new firms to enter the industry, producers may be able to agree to avoid price competition and restrict supply, thus forcing prices and profits to high levels.
   (e) None of the above is a reasonable description of concentrated industries.

4. Indicate whether an economist would classify each of the following industries as competitive or concentrated.
   (a) steel manufacturing _____
   (b) window washing _____
   (c) airlines _____
   (d) travel agencies _____

5. Which of the following is the supply curve for a competitive industry?

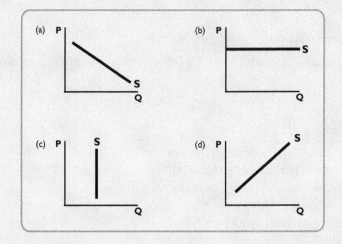

6. The supply curve described in question 5 reflects the fact that in competitive industries, as the price increases, the quantity supplied will
   (a) increase.
   (b) not be affected.
   (c) decrease.

7. The effect described in question 6 takes place because
   (a) when prices increase, producers hold down their production in order to keep prices and profits high.
   (b) when prices increase, the increased profitability of the product gives existing producers an incentive to increase the amount of it that they produce/supply.
   (c) when prices increase, the increased profitability of the product attracts new producers into the industry, which increases the amount produced/supplied.
   (d) an industry can only produce/supply a certain amount of output, regardless of the price of the product.
   (e) Both (b) and (c) are correct.

8. If there were an increase in the cost of the leather from which shoes are made, the supply curve for shoes would
   (a) shift to the right.
   (b) shift to the left.
   (c) not shift in either direction.

9. If there were an influx of low-price imported shoes from Asia, the supply curve for shoes would
   (a) shift to the right.
   (b) shift to the left.
   (c) not shift in either direction.

10. If new technology improved the efficiency of shoe manufacturers, the supply curve for shoes would
    (a) shift to the right.
    (b) shift to the left.
    (c) not shift in either direction.

11. If several shoe manufacturers were to go out of business, the supply curve for shoes would
    (a) shift to the right.
    (b) shift to the left.
    (c) not shift in either direction.

12. If the government restricted imports of clothing from Asia, the supply curve for clothing would
    (a) shift to the right.
    (b) shift to the left.
    (c) not shift in either direction.

13. Supply is said to be *inelastic* if an increase in the price of the product
    (a) causes a large increase in the quantity supplied.
    (b) causes a small decrease in the quantity demanded.
    (c) causes no increase in the quantity supplied.
    (d) causes a small increase in the quantity supplied.
    (e) None of the above.

14. Supply is said to be *elastic* if an increase in the price of the product
    (a) causes no increase in the quantity supplied.
    (b) causes a small increase in the quantity supplied.
    (c) causes a large increase in the quantity supplied.
    (d) causes a small decrease in the quantity demanded.
    (e) None of the above.

15. Supply is said to be *perfectly inelastic* if an increase in the price of the product
    (a) causes a large increase in the quantity supplied.
    (b) causes a small increase in the quantity supplied.
    (c) causes no increase in the quantity supplied.
    (d) causes a small decrease in the quantity demanded.
    (e) None of the above.

16. Which of the following is the best example of a product with a perfectly inelastic supply?
    (a) pencils
    (b) crude oil
    (c) lumber
    (d) an original oil painting
    (e) corn on the cob in January

Answer questions 17–20 on the basis of the following demand and supply schedules for carrots:

Price	Quantity Demanded ('000s kg per week)	Quantity Supplied (per kg) ('000s kg per week)
$5	10	50
4	20	40
3	30	30
2	40	20
1	50	10

17. On graph paper, draw the demand and supply curves for carrots.

18. In the market represented by the above diagram,
    (a) the equilibrium price will be $ ___ per kilogram and
    (b) the equilibrium quantity will be _____ kilograms.

19. If the price were $4, the result would be
    (a) a shortage of 20 000 kilograms, causing the price to increase.
    (b) a surplus of 10 000 kilograms, causing the price to increase.
    (c) a surplus of 20 000 kilograms, causing the price to fall.
    (d) a balance between supply and demand, making the price stable.
    (e) None of the above.

20. If the price were $2, the result would be
    (a) a surplus of 20 000 kilograms, causing the price to increase.
    (b) a shortage of 20 000 kilograms, causing the price to increase.
    (c) a shortage of 10 000 kilograms, causing the price to increase.
    (d) a balance between supply and demand.
    (e) None of the above.

Critical Thinking Questions

(Asterisked questions 1 to 5 are answered in Appendix B; the answers to questions 6 to 10 are in the Instructor's Manual that accompanies this text.)

*1. Suppose that there were large inventories of unsold summer shoes in the hands of retailers in August. How would such a situation probably affect the supply curve for summer shoes?
Explain your answer, and illustrate it with a graph.

*2. Which would be more elastic—the supply of medical doctors or the supply of retail clerks?
Explain your answer fully.

*3. Following are the supply and demand schedules for candles.

Price	Quantity Demanded	Price	Quantity Supplied
$6	20	$6	50
5	40	5	40
4	60	4	30
3	80	3	20
2	100	2	10

    (a) On graph paper, draw the supply and demand curves for candles, and indicate the equilibrium price.
    (b) Suppose that improvements in efficiency cause the supply of candles to increase by 30 at each price shown. Draw the new supply curve and indicate the new equilibrium price.

*4. The graph below represents the world supply curve for crude oil, in which the current price is $50 per barrel and production is 85 million barrels per day.
Suppose that the current production level of 85 million barrels per day represents the maximum daily production rate from existing oil fields. Additional output could be obtained from more remote and difficult sources; however, the production cost per barrel of such oil would be higher, and it would take time to increase production of it.
    (a) On graph paper, draw the supply curve for oil for quantities beyond 85 million barrels per day.

(b) What are the implications of this supply curve for the price of oil if demand increases?

(c) What could prevent the developments in part (b) from occurring?

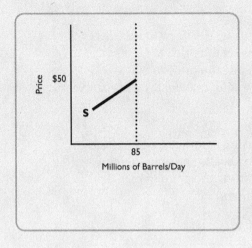

*5. In 2004–05, the price of gasoline increased faster than the price of crude oil from which gasoline is made. It was then reported that no new oil refineries (which process crude oil into gasoline) had been built in North America for many years. Using the concept of elasticity of supply, explain how this situation could contribute to rapidly rising gasoline prices.

6. A good example of government subsidizing a service is *public transit.* In this case, subsidies keep public transit fares low, with the objective of encouraging the public to use public transit in order to reduce automobile traffic congestion and pollution. These social benefits are the justification for using taxpayers' money to subsidize transit riders.

(a) How would government subsidies affect the supply curve for public transit? Another example of a subsidized public service is *college and university education.*

(b) How does the government subsidize post-secondary education?

(c) What are the social benefits that the public is intended to derive from these subsidies?

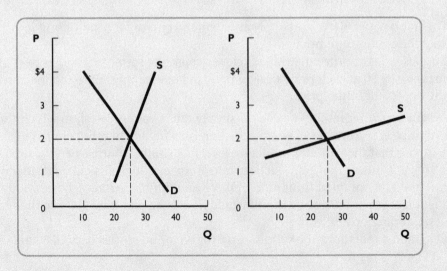

7. In the graphs at the bottom of page 104, the demand curves are identical and the equilibrium price is $2 in each case. However, the supply curves are of different shapes.
   (a) What might explain the different shapes of the two supply curves?
   (b) How would this affect the price of the products if the demand for each were to increase?
   (*Hint: Draw a new demand curve on each graph showing an identical increase in demand.*)

8. The text says that, generally, the supply of a product becomes more elastic as time passes.
   (a) Why would supply become more elastic as time passes?
   (b) Can you think of any exceptions to this generality?
   (c) What would be the implications for the prices of such products?

9. You are managing a factory that is capable of producing a maximum of 100 products per day. If you use overtime labour, you can produce up to 150 products per day. Due to equipment maintenance requirements, 150 products per day is the absolute maximum that you can produce. At present, there is a recession—business is slow, and you are producing only 80 products per day.
   (a) Suppose that sales of your product increase, and so does its price. Your employer asks you to increase production from 80 to 100 products per day. Would the term *elastic* or *inelastic* best describe your ability to supply more of the product? Why?
   (b) Suppose that the economy is booming, unemployment is low, and the sales and price of your product continue to increase. Your employer asks you to increase production from 100 to 150 products per day. How will the elasticity of your supply change, and why? What are the implications of this change for the price of the product?
   (c) Suppose that the sales and price of your product increase even further, and your employer requests production of 180 products per day. What has happened to the elasticity of your supply, and why? What are the implications of this change for the price of the product?
   (d) What can be done to overcome the problems in part (c)?

10. Some ebusinesses produce and sell electronic products, such as software and games. Once the "original" product has been produced, buyers can simply download additional copies of it from the firm's website, without any of the costs associated with physical products, which must be produced and delivered. Describe the supply potential of such ebusinesses in terms of *elasticity of supply*, and compare and contrast it to the situation of the factory in the previous question.

Use the Web (Hints for this Use the Web exercise appear in Appendix B.)

1. Supply consists of sellers offering products for sale. Visit **www.amazon.ca** and find a book that is of interest to you. Then click on "New and used" beside the picture of the book's cover and see the various offerings of copies of that book in the marketplace. Does this market appear to be very competitive?

2. Suppose you are thinking of buying a used car of particular year, make, and model, but are uncertain of what is available on the market and at what prices. Visit **www.autotrader.ca** and see how many of that car are presently being offered for sale, and at what prices. Does this market appear to be very competitive?

6

The Dynamics of
Competitive Markets

After studying this chapter, you should be able to

1. Explain with the aid of a graph how a market will adjust to factors that cause an increase in demand, a decrease in demand, an increase in supply, and a decrease in supply.

2. Explain why a change in supply will have a larger effect on price if demand is inelastic rather than elastic, using a graph to illustrate your explanation.

3. Explain why a change in demand will have a larger effect on price if supply is inelastic rather than elastic, using a graph to illustrate your explanation.

4. Logically determine the changes in demand and/or supply that are occurring in a market, given information on changes in price and sales, plus other market information.

5. Explain with the aid of a graph the effects on a market of a government price support that holds the price above its equilibrium level.

6. Explain with the aid of a graph the effects on a market of a government-imposed price control that holds the price below its equilibrium level.

In Chapter 5, we considered how supply and demand interact in competitive markets to determine equilibrium prices and quantities, using as our example the market for pizza, reproduced in Figure 6-1.

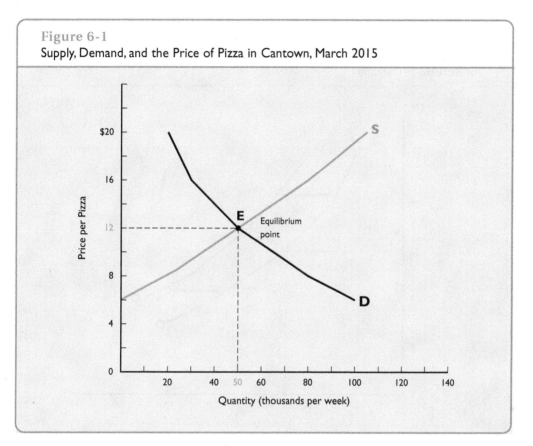

Figure 6-1
Supply, Demand, and the Price of Pizza in Cantown, March 2015

To see a market "live and in action," visit www.tmxmoney.com, where you can see changes in stock prices updated every minute.

www.tmxmoney.com

The equilibrium price ($12) and equilibrium quantity (50 000 pizzas) in Figure 6-1 must be interpreted carefully. They do not mean that the "proper" price is $12, or that the price will necessarily *stay* at $12. All they mean is that, given the behaviour of sellers (supply) and buyers (demand) *at that time* (March 2015), the equilibrium price will be $12. However, the behaviour of buyers and sellers does not remain static; rather, it continually changes. As a result, the supply and demand curves in Figure 6-1 are best viewed as a "snapshot" of a dynamic, changing situation. As supply and/or demand change, the supply and demand curves will shift, causing changes in the equilibrium price and quantity. In the following sections, we will consider a few such changes, and in doing so, we will see how competitive markets actually operate.

Changes in Supply and Demand

An Increase in Demand

The demand curve in Figure 6-1 depicts buyer behaviour in March 2015. Suppose that a change in consumers' tastes leads to an increase in demand so that the demand curve shifts to the right, as shown in Figure 6-2. Assuming no change in supply, the new demand curve, labelled D_1, intersects the supply curve at a higher point, resulting in a higher equilibrium price of $14 per pizza. This higher price creates an incentive for pizza-makers to offer more pizzas for sale. As a result, there is an increase in quantity supplied, to 65 000 pizzas. So an increase in demand (without a change in supply) will cause increases in *both* the *equilibrium price* and *quantity* as the market responds to the higher demand.

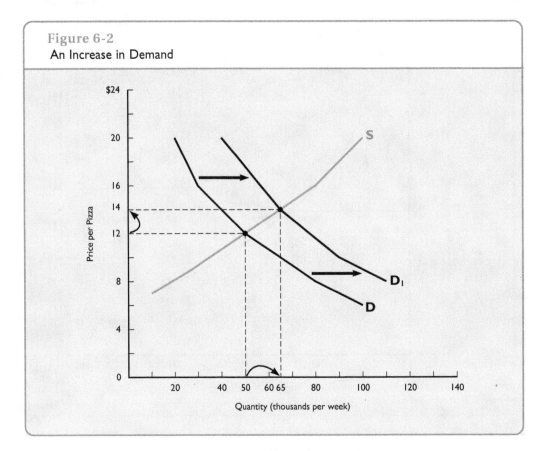

Figure 6-2
An Increase in Demand

In the Greater Toronto Area housing market in 2014–15, rising demand generated strong increases in both prices and quantity.

A Decrease in Demand

Figure 6-3 on the next page shows the results of a decrease in demand for pizza, such as might occur if consumers switched to buying other types of food that had become more popular. As the graph shows, such a decrease in demand will shift the demand curve to the left (to D_2), causing the equilibrium price to decline (from $14 to $12), and leading pizza-makers to reduce the quantity supplied (from 65 000 pizzas to 50 000 pizzas). So the market responds to a decrease in demand by reducing *both* the *equilibrium price* and *quantity.*

An Increase in Supply

Suppose that, for some reason such as the establishment of new pizzerias, the supply of pizzas increased. Such an increase in supply would cause the supply curve to shift to the right, as shown by curve S_1 in Figure 6-4 on the next page. This increase in supply would decrease the equilibrium price from $12 to $9, and this price reduction would induce an increase in the quantity demanded, from 50 000 pizzas to 70 000 pizzas. So the market's response to an increase in supply is to *reduce the equilibrium price* and *increase the equilibrium quantity.*

Figure 6-3
A Decrease in Demand

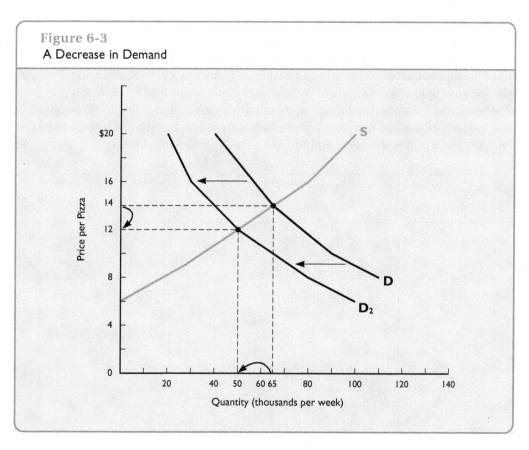

Falling demand for golf and golf equipment has in recent years led to a similar situation to that shown in Figure 6-3

Figure 6-4
An Increase in Supply

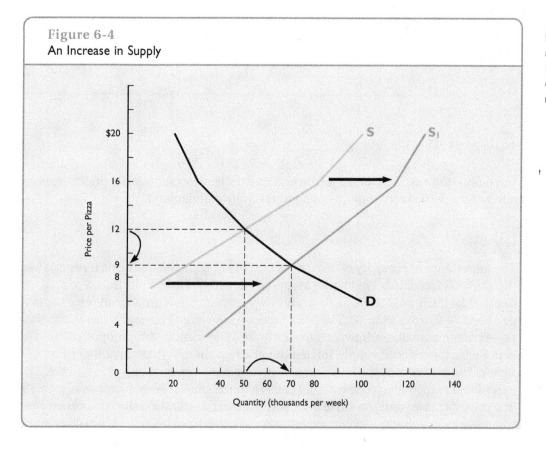

In the early 2000s, the market for computers provided a dramatic illustration of Figure 6-4, due to falling production costs and a growing number of producers.

A Decrease in Supply

If factors such as increases in production costs led to a decrease in the supply of pizzas, the supply curve would shift to the left, as shown by curve S_2 in Figure 6-5. With the lower supply, the equilibrium price would increase from $12 to $14 and this price increase would induce a reduction in the quantity demanded from 50 000 pizzas to 40 000 pizzas. When the supply of a product decreases, the market's response is to *increase* the *equilibrium price* and to *reduce* the *equilibrium quantity*.

Bad weather that reduced harvests has in some years caused the wholesale price of coffee on world markets to *double*.

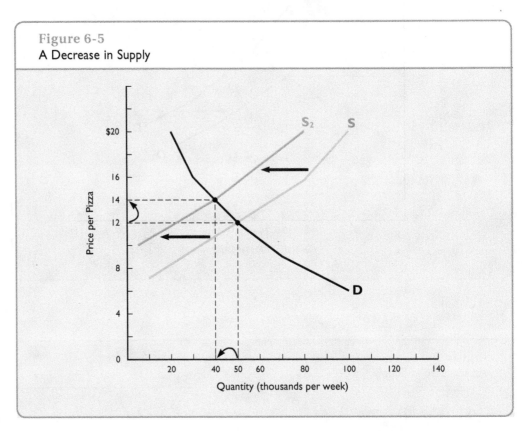

Figure 6-5
A Decrease in Supply

Elasticity

Elasticity—the responsiveness of buyers and sellers to changes in prices—greatly affects how markets respond to changes in supply and demand.

Elasticity of Demand

The importance of elasticity of demand is shown in Figure 6-6 on the next page. When the market is faced with a reduction in supply, the supply curve shifts from S to S_1. If the demand for the product is *inelastic*, as shown in graph (a), the equilibrium price increases a great deal, from $5 to $8. The price increase is so large because demand is inelastic—buyers are unable or unwilling to substitute or do without this product, so they bid actively for the reduced supply, forcing the price up sharply. If, on the other hand, the demand were *elastic*, as shown by graph (b), the situation would be quite different. The exact same reduction in supply would cause a much smaller price increase, to only $6. The price increase would be small because the demand is elastic—since buyers are able to substitute for this product or do without it, they do not bid up its price nearly as much

In the market for crude oil, the inelastic demand for gasoline is a major contributor to the sharp fluctuations in prices that often occur.

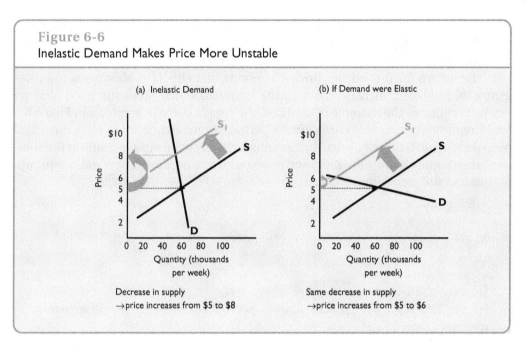

Figure 6-6
Inelastic Demand Makes Price More Unstable

(a) Inelastic Demand

(b) If Demand were Elastic

Decrease in supply
→price increases from $5 to $8

Same decrease in supply
→price increases from $5 to $6

when it is in short supply. So how a change in supply will affect price depends to a great extent on the elasticity of demand—the more inelastic demand is, the larger the price changes will be.

Elasticity of Supply

Elasticity of supply also has a large effect on how changes in demand affect prices. Figure 6-7 shows the effect of an increase in demand (from curve D to D₁) on the price of the product when supply is inelastic and when supply is elastic. If supply is inelastic, as shown by graph (a), the increase in demand causes the price to increase greatly, from $50 to $80. An example of such an inelastic supply would be crude oil, when pro-

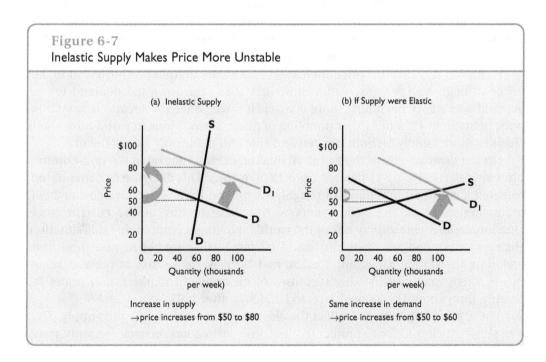

Figure 6-7
Inelastic Supply Makes Price More Unstable

(a) Inelastic Supply

(b) If Supply were Elastic

Increase in supply
→price increases from $50 to $80

Same increase in demand
→price increases from $50 to $60

The inelastic supply of commodities such as copper causes their price to rise considerably during economic booms.

The first two "space tourists" each paid US$20 million for a week in space.

In May 2004, Picasso's painting "Boy with a Pipe (The Young Apprentice)" sold at auction for US$104.1 million.

ducers are pumping as much oil as possible and it is difficult to produce more oil, regardless of how high demand and prices go. However, if the supply had been elastic, as shown by graph (b), the price increase would have been much smaller, rising to only $60. The reason for the smaller price increase is that supply is elastic—as the price increases, producers increase the quantity supplied, which holds the price increase down. To continue the example of crude oil, the supply curve in graph (b) in Figure 6-7 could represent the supply curve after a period of time, when more oil sources had been developed. Generally, price fluctuations are likely to be most extreme in the short run, when supply is most inelastic, and more moderate over the longer run, when supply has had sufficient time to adjust.

IN THE NEWS

Commercials During the Super Bowl

For the 2015 Super Bowl game, advertisers paid *US $4.5 million* for just *30 seconds* of commercial time. ■

QUESTIONS
1. What factors on the demand side of this market would help to explain such a high price?
2. What factors on the supply side of this market would help to explain such a high price?
   (*Hint: Define exactly what it is that advertisers buy from television networks.*)

How Markets Adjust: An Example

World oil markets provide a good example of how markets adjust over time to changed circumstances.

The first major increase in oil prices by the Organization of Petroleum Exporting Countries (OPEC) in 1973–74 caught consumers unaware. Because many were unprepared to cut back on their consumption of gasoline, demand was quite inelastic. This inelastic demand made it possible for OPEC to impose a major price increase that generated the greatest international transfer of wealth in the history of the world.

Following the 1973–74 price increases, consumers gradually adjusted to higher prices through energy conservation measures that held down the demand for oil; demand was slowly becoming more elastic. However, after the second major OPEC price increase in 1979 (a further doubling of prices), conditions in world oil markets changed more rapidly on both the demand side and the supply side of the market.

On the *demand side* of the world oil market, demand for oil in the non-communist world decreased by 11 percent from 1979 to 1985. This decrease in demand represented a cut in oil purchases of roughly six million barrels per day, leaving OPEC producing more oil than consumers were willing to buy at the current price. Developments on the *supply side* of the world oil market compounded this situation. High oil prices had attracted into world oil markets a number of new producers, including the United Kingdom, Mexico, and Norway. As a result of these developments, there were considerable surpluses of oil on world markets, and prices fell sharply, from about US$34 per barrel to US$12–20 after 1985.

These price adjustments reflect the elasticity of both demand and supply. They also show why it is naive to project that because a price *has increased* sharply, it will

www.opec.org

continue to increase rapidly. If anything, it is more likely that it will *not* continue to increase rapidly (and may actually fall) as the higher prices cause more of the product to be supplied and less to be demanded.

IN THE NEWS

The World Market for Oil

We have seen that *inelastic demand* will cause prices to be more unstable. And we have seen that *inelastic supply* will make prices more unstable. So how would a market behave if *both* demand *and* supply were inelastic?

The answer would be that prices could be *very* unstable, and world market for crude oil has for many years provided an example of just such a market, as shown by the graph.

To appreciate why prices in this market can be so unstable, visualize on the graph how the price of $90 per barrel would be affected by a relatively small shift to the right or the

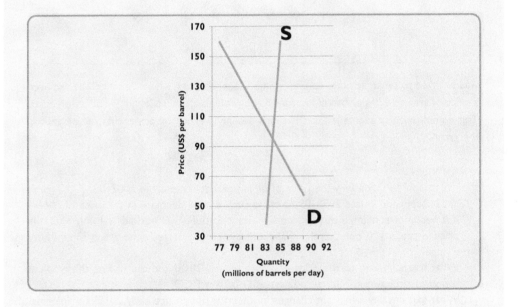

left of *either* the demand curve *or* the supply curve—combination of these would cause a significant increase or decrease in the price.

This instability can be seen in the graph of the actual price of oil, which has fluctuated from as low as $19 per barrel to as high as nearly $140 over a period of less than seven years, then plunged sharply in 2008–09, and again in 2014–15.

Following mid-2014, the crude oil market was hit by a "perfect storm" consisting of a combination of a major increase in the supply of oil <u>and</u> falling demand for it.

The increase in supply came mostly from the United States, due to increased use of hydraulic fracturing ("fracking") as a method of recovering oil. The falling demand was mainly the result of slower economic growth in China and Europe.

As one of the world's largest oil producers, Saudi Arabia might have tried to stabilize the price, by reducing its own output. However, Saudi Arabia maintained its output, in what

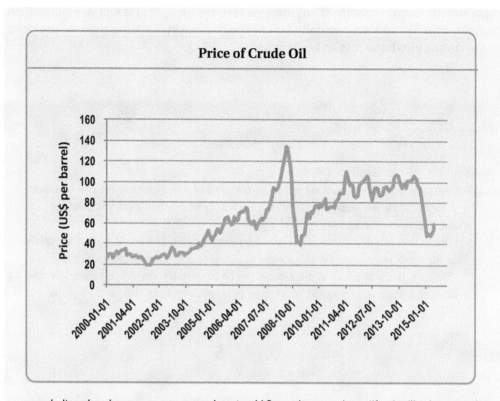

Price of Crude Oil

was believed to be an attempt to undermine U.S. producers, whose "fracked" oil required a price of around $70 per barrel in order to be profitable, due to its high production costs. This combination of events led to the sharp decline in crude oil prices that can be seen in the graph. ▪

QUESTIONS

1. What would explain why the price of oil increased so rapidly in 2007–08?
2. What happened in late 2008–09 to cause such a rapid decrease in the price of oil?
3. If it becomes profitable to produce significant amounts of "fracked" oil only after the price exceeds $70 per barrel, how would the supply curve in the graph shown here change?
4. What has happened to the price of oil since early 2015? You can update the graph at http://research.stlouisfed.org/fred2/series/DCOILWTICO.
5. What explains any significant changes in the price of oil since early 2015? For information, Google "oil price".

Summary

It can be said that, in many markets, equilibrium prices and quantities are constantly changing in response to changes in supply and demand. In those cases where supply and demand are elastic, the market's adjustment to changing conditions occurs quite completely and quickly, while in cases where supply or demand is inelastic, the adjustments will be less complete and/or will take longer. In any case, it is through these markets, and through price adjustments in these markets, that the economy adjusts to fluctuations in consumer demand, the cost and availability of products, and other changes.

YOU DECIDE

Markets for Assets

In markets for goods and services, increases in the price of an item tend to discourage buying of it, and encourage more production and selling of it. These adjustments tend to stabilize the market and the price of the item.

The situation is often quite different in *markets for assets* such as corporate shares, because people often buy such assets with the intention (or hope) that they will be able to *resell* them at a higher price.

As a result, *expectations* concerning *future price movements* often play an important role in markets for assets. For instance, if the price of a corporation's shares were expected to rise, this could lead to *increased demand* for its shares, which would drive the price of those shares even higher.

But how would the *supply side* of such a market react? If people who already own that asset also expect its price to increase, they will be less likely to offer it for sale—that is, the *supply would decrease*.

So the same event (here, the expectation of a higher price) could cause an *increase in demand* <u>and</u> a *decrease in supply* in the market for an asset. The result could be a sharp increase in the price of the asset, generated in large part by people's expectations concerning that price—a sort of self-fulfilling expectation. And as long as people expected the price to rise, this dynamic would continue.

Similar effects sometimes occur in the markets for other assets, such as gold, silver, art, and real estate.

QUESTIONS

1. Suppose that the price of an asset were expected to *fall*—how would this expectation affect the demand, the supply, and the price of that asset?
2. How would the role of expectations in these markets for assets affect the behaviour over time of the prices of those assets, compared to the prices of ordinary goods and services?
3. If the price of an asset were rising because people expected it to rise, it could rise to very high levels. What would eventually *stop* it from rising, and what might happen then?

Real-World Supply and Demand: Interpreting Signs from Markets

In the real world (as distinct from textbooks), we do not have neat supply and demand curves that show us the *causes* of changes in the prices of products and the quantities of them bought and sold in markets. Instead, what we have are certain facts concerning changes in prices and quantities bought and sold, together with other information relevant to demand and supply in those markets. From such information, it is usually possible to interpret what *has happened* concerning demand and supply in those markets. More interestingly, it is sometimes possible to use such information to predict *what will happen* concerning demand, supply, prices, and sales volumes. In the following sections, we will consider a few examples of how this can be done.

Rising Sales and Prices

In the late 1980s, both *sales* of houses (the quantity demanded) and the *prices* of houses increased very sharply. What would likely have caused these two trends? It is logical to conclude that *rising demand* was driving both sales and prices up. And, indeed, that is what happened—in the late 1980s, many of the "baby boomers" (the very large group of Canadians born between 1946 and 1966) reached the age at which people tend to buy homes, driving the demand for houses to unprecedented levels.

But what happened next to house prices? Many people assumed that prices would continue to rise, but the information in the previous paragraph could be used to predict that the opposite would happen. Once the baby boomers had bought their homes, the demand for housing would fall considerably. When this happened, housing prices would also fall—as they in fact did. People who understood these market dynamics were able to take advantage of them by selling or buying at the right time. Those who did not understand the market might buy or sell a home at the wrong time—an error which in that market could have cost them a great deal of money.

Rising Sales and Falling Prices

If the *sales* of an item were higher than usual but its *price* were falling, the logical conclusion would be that the *supply of that product had increased*. For example, large harvests sometimes lead to high inventories of unsold wheat that depress prices.

Does this mean that prices will continue to fall even lower? Not likely—the lower prices will lead farmers to plant less wheat, and they will help to increase sales and reduce inventories. Eventually, it can be expected that this combination of forces will cause prices to recover.

Falling Sales and Prices

If *both* the *sales* of an item and its *price* fall, the logical conclusion is that *falling demand* is pulling both down. This situation happened in the early 1990s in the housing market, when demand fell not only because the baby boomers had purchased their homes but also because of very high interest rates on mortgage loans. In some markets, the prices of homes fell by as much as 40 percent.

Does this mean that housing prices would continue to fall? Again, not likely—such low prices would discourage not only new home construction but also resales of homes, as homeowners would wait for the market to improve before selling. And, as buyers returned to the market (encouraged, in part, by low prices), sales and prices would begin to recover.

Falling Sales and Rising Prices

A combination of *falling sales* and *rising prices* would indicate that the *supply of the item had decreased*. For instance, if weather conditions or crop disease caused a low supply of strawberries, the volume sold would fall and the price would increase. Again, however, it is not likely that the price would continue to increase. The higher price would not only curb demand but also would create an incentive for farmers to increase their production of strawberries.

In summary, from the information available concerning the sales and the price of an item, together with other information concerning the demand for and/or supply of that item, it is possible to determine what has caused the changes in the sales volume and price. More importantly, it is often possible to forecast future trends in the market for that item. And finally, it is often the case that due to changes in demand and/or supply, the probable future trend is the opposite of the past one.

YOU DECIDE

The Internet and Markets

With more and more businesses using the internet, consumers are able to research purchases by visiting the websites of a large number of sellers from the convenience of their home.

A related development is that some people in large urban areas use the internet to post notices that they will be holding garage sales.

QUESTIONS

1. What effect would you expect the internet to have on the average prices paid by buyers who shop online, and why?
2. What effect would you expect their internet postings to have on the prices received by the people holding garage sales, and why?
3. Why is the effect of the internet on prices different in the situations presented in questions 1 and 2?

Government Intervention: Price Supports and Price Ceilings

We have been describing markets in which prices are free to increase or decrease to their equilibrium level in response to changes in demand and supply. However, sometimes markets are not allowed to operate freely in this way; sometimes, governments will intervene in markets in order to keep prices either above or below their equilibrium levels.

For instance, if apartment rents (which are the price of using an apartment) are rising rapidly, tenants may put political pressure on the government to pass laws that hold rents below their market rate. In the case of some farm products, the opposite has happened—prices have been so low that the government has tried to keep them above their equilibrium level, so as to help the farmers. On the surface, this seems like a fairly simple solution to problems of prices that are seen as "too high" or "too low," but as we consider each of these policies in turn, we will see that they are not as simple as they appear.

Price Supports (Price Floors)

A good example of a government **price support** program designed to hold prices above their equilibrium level is one of the methods used to subsidize farmers. For many years, North American farmers have suffered from a tendency to oversupply the market. Improved technology and farming methods greatly increased the productivity

price support (floor)
An artificially high price, held above the equilibrium level by the government.

of farmers, oversupplying the market and driving prices down. The problem was aggravated by the inelastic demand for food generally; as prices fell, people would not buy significantly more food, so the increased supply of food drove prices down more. In some cases farm prices and incomes were depressed to the point that they threatened the long-term survival of parts of Canada's agricultural sector.

Unable to solve the problem on their own, some groups of farmers turned to the government, which provided assistance in a number of ways. One such program is *farm price supports*, under which the government would prevent the price of a farm product from falling below a certain level. The government could achieve this by *offering to buy the product* from the farmers at a certain price. Then no farmer would have to sell for a lower price, so all farmers would be guaranteed at least that price for their entire crop.

While such a program would support farm prices and incomes, it would have complicating side effects, which are illustrated in Figure 6-8. As the graph shows, the equilibrium point would have been E, making the equilibrium price of wheat $1.25 per bushel and the equilibrium quantity 50 million bushels. However, if the government supported the price at $2, two adjustments would take place. First, at the higher price, somewhat less wheat would be demanded: on the graph, point A shows that at a price of $2, 45 million bushels would be bought, which represents a decline in sales of 5 million bushels.

This decrease is a fairly small change because the demand for wheat is quite inelastic. The second change, however, could be considerably greater: assured of a price of $2, farmers would *increase their production*. On the graph, point B shows that the quantity supplied would increase from 50 million to 65 million bushels as farmers responded to the incentive of a guaranteed higher price. The combined effect of these

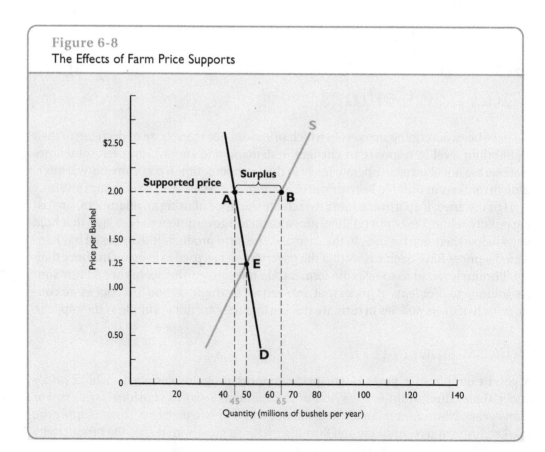

Figure 6-8
The Effects of Farm Price Supports

two adjustments to the new, higher price (a 15-million-bushel increase in quantity supplied and a reduction of 5 million in the quantity demanded) would be a *surplus* of 20 million bushels—20 million more bushels of wheat will be produced than people would be willing to buy at the $2 price.

Where would this surplus go? It would wind up in the possession of the government, which would act as a *reserve buyer* in the wheat market, supporting the price by buying whatever the farmers produced at a price of $2 per bushel. In some cases, such surpluses grew to sizes that they became costly and caused political embarrassment. This situation led governments to try other ways of supporting farm prices and incomes, such as paying farmers *not* to grow certain crops and setting up marketing boards empowered to set maximum production limits for farmers so as to reduce the supply of products.

Price Controls (Price Ceilings)

Sometimes, governments want to hold a price *below* its equilibrium level. Controls of this sort are known as **price controls** (or **price ceilings**). *Rent controls* (legal limits on the level of rents and/or on the rent increases charged by landlords) are probably the best illustration of such policies. In response to the complaints of tenants (who constitute a significant political pressure group in some areas), governments have imposed various sorts of rent controls to limit the rents charged by landlords to lower levels than could have been charged under prevailing market conditions. While rent controls benefit tenants who are already in apartments, they can have the unfortunate side effect of creating shortages of rental accommodation, as illustrated in Figure 6-9 on the next page.

> **price control (ceiling)**
> A legal limit on a price or on increases in a price, which holds the price below its equilibrium level.

While the graph shows an equilibrium rent of $900 per month and a government-controlled rent of $700 per month, this information should not be interpreted as meaning that the government arbitrarily *reduced* rents by $200 per month. Rather, it should be interpreted as meaning that rent controls were imposed some time ago and have held rents to $700 per month, but since then demand has increased to the point where, without the controls, rents *would now be* $900 per month in a free market. Point E represents *what would have happened* if rents were not controlled—the equilibrium price (rent) would have been $900 and the equilibrium quantity would have been 55 000 rental units on the market.

At the controlled rent of $700 per month, the situation is quite different. As point B shows, the lower rent has caused a small (5000-unit) increase in the quantity demanded, from 55 000 units to 60 000 units. There is a much more important adjustment on the supply side. Here, as point A shows, the quantity supplied at the controlled rent of $700 is only 30 000 units, whereas at the uncontrolled rent of $900 the quantity supplied would have been 55 000 units. In other words, there are 25 000 fewer rental units on the market at the $700 controlled rent than there would have been without the rent controls. When this 25 000-unit reduction in quantity supplied is added to the 5000-unit increase in quantity demanded due to the lower rents, the effect of the rent controls is to create a shortage of apartments to the extent of 30 000 units. The reason for the shortage is not that the landlords of existing buildings refuse to rent their apartments at the controlled rents—they have little choice but to accept the situation (although some landlords may convert their apartments to condominiums, which they can sell as private residences at prices not subject to government controls).

Rather, the shortage will occur mainly because the construction of new apartments will be depressed by the rent controls, which make apartments a less attractive

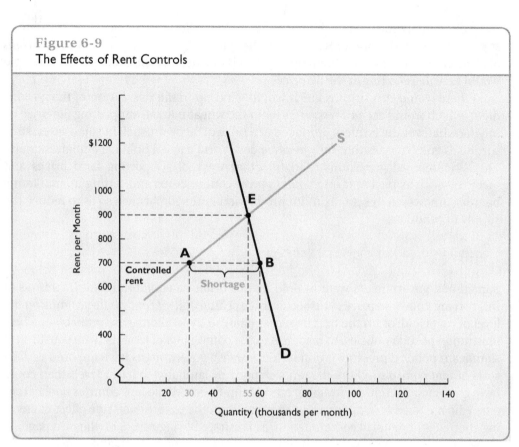

Figure 6-9
The Effects of Rent Controls

investment. Developers will invest less capital into apartments and more into projects on which their returns are not controlled, such as single-family dwellings, townhouses, condominiums, shopping malls, and offices. Because of this problem, governments often use what are called "soft controls," which exempt new buildings from controls for several years and/or allow rents to rise when landlords' costs increase.

Prices: A Final Perspective

Prices are much more than tags on items telling buyers how much they must pay to get those items. Rather, prices play the role of *a key link in a market system* between the demand side and the supply side of markets. If the demand for an item increases, higher prices will create incentives to produce more of it. Conversely, falling demand will depress prices and discourage production of an item. Another perspective on this process is that, as demand and supply constantly change, changes in prices send *signals to buyers and sellers* that indicate how much of an item they should buy or produce and sell. And if government policies increase the price of an item or decrease it, those policies will interfere with these signals. Once a competitive market has established an equilibrium price, governments cannot change that price without affecting the amounts that buyers are willing to buy and sellers are willing to offer for sale. Programs to support prices above the equilibrium level will have the side effects of generating surpluses of that product, while controls that hold prices below their equilibrium level will create shortages of those products.

Chapter Summary

1. In competitive markets, supply and demand interact freely to determine the equilibrium price and quantity, which will change as supply or demand changes. (L.O. 1)
2. Markets adjust more rapidly to changes in supply when demand is more elastic. (L.O.2)
3. Markets adjust more rapidly to changes in demand when supply is more elastic. (L.O.3)
4. By using information concerning the sales volume and price of an item, together with other information on market developments, you can determine what has caused those changes in price and sales volume and often forecast future changes. (L.O. 4)
5. If the government intervenes in a market to hold the price of a product above its equilibrium level, the result will be a surplus of that product. (L.O. 5)
6. If the government intervenes in a market to hold the price of a product below its equilibrium level, the result will be a shortage of that product. (L.O. 6)

Questions

1. Suppose you hear that the price of new housing has increased by 10 percent over the past year and that sales of new houses have been growing rapidly.
   (a) What is the most logical explanation for these changes?
   (b) Draw a graph that shows these changes in the market for new housing.
   (c) How will elasticity of supply affect how much new housing prices rise?

2. Suppose you hear that the price of tomatoes has increased by 10 percent over the past year and that sales of tomatoes have decreased.
   (a) What is the most logical explanation for these changes?
   (b) Draw a graph that shows these changes in the market for tomatoes.
   (c) How will elasticity of demand affect how much the price of tomatoes rises?

3. The present price of crabapples is $2 per kilogram, and crabapple farmers are insisting that the government set a legal minimum price of $4 in order to cover their costs and let them earn a modest profit.
   (a) With the aid of a graph of the market for crabapples, explain to the government why setting a minimum legal price for crabapples will not be a simple solution to this situation.
   (b) If the government does not assist the farmers in any way, what will be the market's solution to this situation?

4. From 1997 to 2001, the price of coffee on world markets fell from $1.60 U.S. per pound to $0.56 U.S. per pound—a decrease of *65 percent*.
   (a) What is the most logical explanation for such a decrease in price?
   (b) What explains the large size of the price decrease?
   (c) Draw a graph representing the factors in (a) and (b).

5. The graph below shows that, in August, Canadians can buy corn on the cob for about $3.50 per dozen.
      In the winter, packages of five cobs sell for prices that work out to about $11 per dozen.
   (a) Draw a graph that explains this seasonal increase in corn prices.
   (b) Why does the government not attempt to protect consumers against such price increases by placing legal limits on corn prices? On the graph, show the effect that a legal limit on prices in the winter would have on this market.

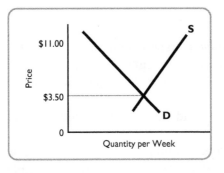

6. For World Series baseball games, ticket prices are approximately triple the prices for the same seats during the regular season. These price increases are decided by Major League Baseball (the Commissioner's Office), in consultation with the players' association (MLBPA).

   (a) Why do ticket prices increase so much for World Series games? Consider not only changes on the demand side of this market but also the nature of the supply side. On graph paper, draw a graph of the market, showing the demand and the supply for regular-season games, and how the market changes during the World Series.

   (b) Do you agree with those who say that it is "highway robbery" to increase prices for these games? If prices were *not* increased by the clubs, what would happen?

   (c) What could prevent prices from increasing so much?

7. One of the key prices Statistics Canada monitors is the price of new housing. The statistics do not show the actual price of housing in dollars, but rather an "index" of prices that is set at 100.0 in 2007, with the index in each year after 2007 showing how much prices have increased since 2007. To see how the price of new housing has changed over the past 5 years, visit the Statistics Canada website at **www.statcan.gc.ca**, and search for New housing price index. Calculate the percentage increase in new housing prices each year over the past five years. What trends do you see in new housing prices, and what demand side or supply side factors might explain these?

8. To see the most recent developments in new housing prices, visit Statistics Canada's website and search *The Daily* for "new housing prices." What has been the most recent trend in new housing prices? Does *The Daily* indicate whether the main reason for the recent trend lies on the demand side of the housing market or on the demand side?

Study Guide

Review Questions   (Answers to these Review Questions appear in Appendix B.)

In answering questions 1–4, you may find it helpful to refer to the diagram on the next page.

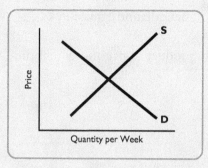

1. If the demand for the product increased (and the supply remained unchanged), the equilibrium price would _____ and the equilibrium quantity would _____.

2. If the demand for the product decreased (and the supply remained unchanged), the equilibrium price would _____ and the equilibrium quantity would _____.

3. If the supply of the product increased (and the demand remained unchanged), the equilibrium price would _____ and the equilibrium quantity would _____.

4. If the supply of the product decreased (and the demand remained unchanged), the equilibrium price would _____ and the equilibrium quantity would _____.

5. When the supply of a product changes, the resultant change in its price will be greater,
   (a) the more elastic the demand for the product is.
   (b) the more inelastic the demand for the product is.
   (c) the larger the demand for the product is.
   (d) the smaller the demand for the product is.
   (e) None of the above.

6. When the demand for a product changes, the resultant change in its price will be greater,
   (a) the more inelastic the supply of the product is.
   (b) the more elastic the supply of the product is.
   (c) the larger the supply of the product is.
   (d) the smaller the supply of the product is.
   (e) None of the above.

   Answer questions 7–11 on the basis of the following graph.

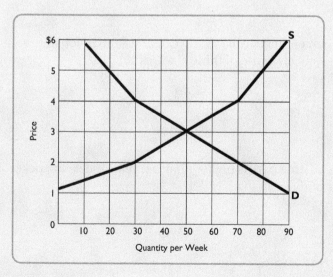

7. The equilibrium for this market is a price of $ ____ per unit and a quantity of ____ units per week.

8. If the government supported the price of this product above the equilibrium price, at a price of $5, the result would be
    (a) a surplus of 20 units.
    (b) a surplus of 30 units.
    (c) a surplus of 60 units.
    (d) a shortage of 60 units.
    (e) reduced profits for producers of this product.

9. The two reasons for the situation described in question 8 are
    (a) _____ and
    (b) _____.

10. If the government placed controls on the price of this product to hold it below the equilibrium price, at a price of $2, the result would be
    (a) a shortage of 20 units.
    (b) a shortage of 40 units.
    (c) a surplus of 40 units.
    (d) a surplus of 20 units.
    (e) increased production of the product.

11. The two reasons for the situation described in question 10 are
    (a) _____ and
    (b) _____.

12. The price of movie tickets is 5 percent lower than last year, and sales of movie tickets are also lower than last year. The most likely cause of these changes is
    (a) an increase in demand.
    (b) a decrease in demand.
    (c) an increase in supply.
    (d) a decrease in supply.
    (e) None of the above.

13. The price of strawberries is 5 percent lower than last year, and sales of strawberries are higher than last year. The most likely cause of these changes is
    (a) an increase in demand.
    (b) a decrease in demand.
    (c) an increase in supply.
    (d) a decrease in supply.
    (e) None of the above.

14. The price of lobsters is 20 percent higher than last year, and sales of lobsters are lower than last year. The most likely cause of these changes is
    (a) an increase in demand.
    (b) a decrease in demand.
    (c) an increase in supply.
    (d) a decrease in supply.
    (e) None of the above.

15. The price of tickets to a new theme park is higher than last year, and so are ticket sales. The most likely cause of these changes is
    (a) an increase in demand.
    (b) a decrease in demand.
    (c) an increase in supply.
    (d) a decrease in supply.
    (e) None of the above.

Critical Thinking Questions

(Asterisked questions 1 to 5 are answered in Appendix B; the answers to questions 6 to 9 are in the Instructor's Manual that accompanies this text.)

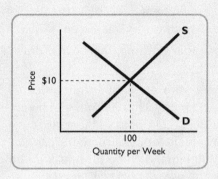

*1. Using the above graph as a starting point,
    (a) draw a graph showing the new demand and/or supply curve(s) associated with each of the following events, and
    (b) explain the changes that occur in the market as a result of that event.

    Events:
    (i)   The prices of substitutes for the product increase.
    (ii)   A technological advance enables producers to make the product more efficiently, at a significantly lower production cost per unit.
    (iii)   New substitutes for this product come onto the market.
    (iv)   The cost of producing this product increases considerably.
    (v)   The government puts price controls on this product, making it illegal to charge more than $5 per unit for it.
    (vi)   A severe recession occurs, reducing the consumer income available for purchasing this product.
    (vii)   The government imposes a $2 per item tax on this product.
    (viii) A strike at several producers limits the production of this product (temporarily). No more than 70 units per week can be produced.
    (ix)   The government supports the price of this product at $15 per unit by standing ready to purchase it at that price.
    (x)   This item becomes much more popular with consumers *and* many new producers enter the industry.

*2. Following are four descriptions of changes occurring in markets. For each of these, explain what would be the most likely cause the changes, and draw a graph showing the changes in that market.
    (a) Compared to a year ago, sales of corn are up 8 percent and corn prices are 6 percent lower.
    (b) Over the past three months, sales of natural gas (used for heating homes) have risen by 12 percent and the price of natural gas has increased by 6 percent.
    (c) Compared to the same period last year, the number of boats being rented has decreased by 15 percent and boat rental rates have fallen by 10 percent.
    (d) Compared to last year, strawberry sales are down 20 percent and prices are 25 percent higher.

*3. Suppose that after a large employer locates near a town, an influx of people causes apartment rents to increase sharply. In turn, residents of the town press the town council to pass a law limiting how high rents can be.
   (a) Draw a graph that shows the market for apartments and the reason for the increase in rents.
   (b) Explain to the town council why limiting apartment rents will not be the simple matter that it may seem to be. Use your graph to show why this is true.

*4. Gasoline prices are sometimes highest early in the morning, then come down later in the day. What could explain this pattern?

*5. Draw a graph showing the market for houses with an equilibrium price of $300 000. Now suppose that housing prices are currently $300 000 and that media reports of soaring house prices make people expect that prices will increase considerably next year because no more land is available for construction. Show on the graph how this expectation would affect the demand curve for housing, the supply curve for housing, and the price of housing *over the next few months*.

6. For several years, the prices of personal computers decreased sharply, and sales of computers grew rapidly.
   (a) What is the most logical reason for these changes in the market for personal computers?
   (b) Draw a graph of the market for personal computers that shows these changes.
   (c) Why was the increase in sales so large? Does your graph make this clear?

7. Ticket "scalping" is buying tickets to an event with the intention of reselling them at higher prices, usually at the scene of the event. At the Super Bowl, some scalpers sell tickets for more than $5000.
   (a) Explain, with the aid of a graph, why scalpers could charge such high prices.
   (b) The popular view of scalpers is that they are getting away with "highway robbery," by selling tickets for far more than they are worth. Is this necessarily correct?
   (c) Can you make an argument that scalpers actually *increase* the total benefits enjoyed by fans at the game?
   (d) What could the government do to prevent ticket scalping?

8. One example of unusual market behaviour is the so-called "Monday effect" that occurs in the stock market. Typically, share prices fall somewhat on Mondays, whereas they rise during the rest of the week. Also, over a 25-year period, seven of the fifteen worst one-day declines in stock prices occurred on Mondays. Two additional facts are that four of every five share-price declines on Mondays happened after a fall on the previous Friday, and the "Monday effect" is really a Monday-*morning* effect: after 1:00 p.m., share prices tended to edge up. Finally, most of the selling on Mondays that caused stock prices to decline was by small shareholders.
   (a) Why would stock prices have a greater tendency to fall on Mondays?
   (b) Why would a decline in stock prices on Monday apparently often be related to a decrease on the previous Friday?
   (c) After falling on Monday morning, why would stock prices tend to recover after 1:00 p.m.?

9. China is suffering from severe water shortages, with over 100 big cities short of water and half of these "seriously threatened." Prices in China are set by the government, and until 1985, most users paid nothing for water. Today, water is still heavily subsidized by the government, and most users pay only about 60 percent of the cost of the water that they use.

(a) Explain to the Chinese government the connection between its water shortages and the government's own pricing policies.

(b) Why do you think the Chinese government continues to subsidize water prices under these circumstances?

(c) How could the market help to avoid a future water crisis in China?

Use the Web (Hints for this Use the Web exercise appear in Appendix B.)

1. Statistics Canada keeps track of the average prices of various *categories* of goods and services (e.g., food, transportation, etc.) in its *Consumer Price Index*. To see how the average prices of items in various categories have changed over the past five years, visit the Statistics Canada website at **www.statcan.gc.ca**, and search for *Consumer Price Index, by province*, then select *Consumer Price Index, by province* (not the page with monthly statistics).

(a) Calculate the percentage price increase in each category over the past five years.

(b) Which category has increased in price the most rapidly? What do you think might explain why the prices of items in this category increased so rapidly?

(c) Which category has increased in price the least rapidly? What do you think might explain why the prices of items in this category increased so slowly?

7

Market Structures

After studying this chapter, you should be able to

1. State the three characteristics of a perfectly competitive industry, sketch the demand curve for an individual firm in that industry, and explain the strategies that such firms will tend to pursue.

2. State the three characteristics of a monopolistically competitive industry, sketch the demand curve for an individual firm, and explain the strategies that such firms will tend to pursue.

3. Define *market power*, and identify the three things that a group of firms must achieve in order to exercise market power.

4. Define *oligopoly*, sketch the demand curve for an oligopolist, and explain the types of competitive strategies that oligopolists tend to favour and those that they tend to avoid.

5. Identify five barriers to entry into industries, and explain the relationship of such barriers to oligopolistic market power.

6. List four factors that could prevent oligopolists from raising prices as much as they might like.

7. Define *monopoly*, and explain how a monopolist maximizes profits.

8. Explain why some industries are considered to be natural monopolies.

9. Identify industries as examples of perfect competition, monopolistic competition, oligopoly, or monopoly.

10. Apply the concepts of market structure to various real-world situations.

We have seen how prices are determined through the interaction between the demand side (buyers) and the supply side (sellers) of markets. In this chapter, we will examine in more detail the supply side of markets—that is, the industries that produce goods and services. The supply side of markets varies widely: in some industries such as restaurants and farming, the supply side consists of large numbers of small producers, while in other industries such as electricity, there is only one seller (in any given market). Also in this chapter, we will organize industries according to how much competition there is between producers/sellers, as shown in Figure 7-1. The most competitive industries are at the left end of the spectrum in Figure 7-1, while the least competitive are at the right end.

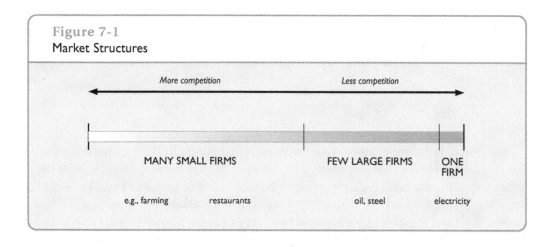

Figure 7-1
Market Structures

The left side of Figure 7-1 represents industries in which there is strong competition among large numbers of producers/sellers. Such competitive industries comprise a large and important part of the Canadian economy—the small business sector as described in Chapter 3. To the right are industries that are dominated by a few large firms, and at the far right are monopolies, in which there is only one seller. Together, these last two types of industries comprise the big business sector of the economy, as was also discussed in Chapter 3.

In this chapter, we will see how these different supply-side conditions (market structures) can affect the decision making of producers/sellers about pricing, output levels, marketing, and product design. In addition, we will see how different market structures can result in quite different results for consumers. We will start by considering the "competitive" industries on the left side of Figure 7-1.

Part A: Competitive Industries

In Chapters 5 and 6, we saw how, in competitive markets, supply and demand interact to determine the prices of goods, services, and labour. In such markets, there are large numbers of both buyers and sellers, and neither buyers nor sellers are organized so as to be able to influence the price. As a result, the price will be determined impersonally and automatically by the *total supply* of all sellers and the *total demand* of all buyers in the marketplace, as illustrated in Figure 7-2. Once the market price for the product has been determined in the marketplace, all producers and sellers must keep their prices at or very near the market price. If a firm's price is too high, there are many competitors to whom the firm's customers can readily switch.

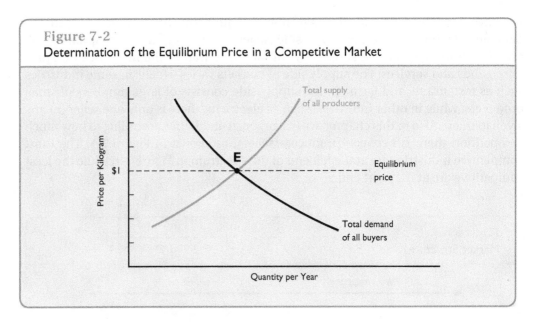

Figure 7-2
Determination of the Equilibrium Price in a Competitive Market

This, then, is the essence of what we have called *competitive* industries—industries in which there are so many small firms and it is so easy for new firms to enter the industry that producers have little or no influence over the price. The market determines the price, and each individual producer is a *price-taker*, that is, each producer has no choice but to charge a price equal to or very near the market price. Economists divide competitive industries into two types: *perfect competition* and *monopolistic competition*.

Perfect Competition

perfect competition
A term describing industries that consist of a large number of small firms, where entry to the industry by new firms is easy, and where all firms in the industry sell identical products.

Perfect competition is the most competitive situation imaginable. It is considered to exist only if the following three conditions are met:
(a) there are *many small firms* in the industry,
(b) it is *easy for new firms to enter* (and exit) the industry, and
(c) all firms in the industry sell *identical products.*

It is the last condition that makes perfect competition so extremely competitive and quite rare. If each producer's product is *identical* to those sold by the other producers, each producer will be forced to charge *exactly the same price* as the others; in Figure 7-2, all producers will have to charge the market price of $1 per kilogram. If any producer charges more than $1, that producer's sales will *fall to zero*, as buyers will buy instead from the numerous competitors who would be charging less for an identical product.

For example, suppose the product is carrots, the buyers are wholesalers, canners, and processors, and the sellers consist of a large number of very small farmers, each selling identical products—carrots. If the market price for carrots is $1 per kilogram, each farmer will be able to sell his or her entire output of carrots at $1 per kilogram, *but only* if his/her price is $1. If any one farmer were to try to charge more than $1 per kilogram, that farmer's sales would be zero. The buyers will be able to get all the carrots they need from the other farmers, and will simply not find it necessary to buy that farmer's output.

A Canadian farm that produces 35 000 bushels of wheat might seem large. Total world wheat production would be about *600 000 times* that farm's output.

Figure 7-3 illustrates the position of one single producer in this market—Vera's Vegetable Farm. Vera operates one of many small farms in the industry, with a maximum

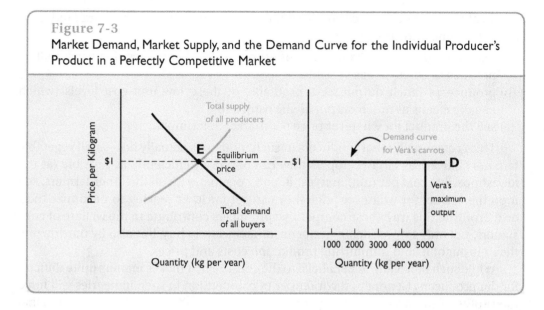

Figure 7-3

Market Demand, Market Supply, and the Demand Curve for the Individual Producer's Product in a Perfectly Competitive Market

("capacity") production of 5000 kg of carrots per year. If Vera produces 1000 kg, she will get a price of $1 for each kilogram; if she produces 2000 kg, the price would be the same; and if she produces all she can (5000 kg), the price she receives will still be the same. The price remains the same because Vera is such a small part of the overall supply that variations in her output will have no effect on the total market supply and therefore on the price. By contrast, if a mojor oil producer such as Saudi Arabia boosted its production to its maximum possible level, there would be so much oil on the market that prices would have to fall in order to sell it all.

As a result, the demand curve for Vera's carrots will consist of a *perfectly horizontal line* at a price of $1, as in Figure 7-3. This unusual demand curve illustrates an unusual situation. At the market price of $1, Vera can sell all the carrots that she can produce. However, if Vera tries to charge more than $1, her sales will fall to zero. This demand curve illustrates **perfectly elastic demand**, reflecting the fact that *any* increase in price will cause *all* sales to be lost. Obviously, the case of perfect competition is the most competitive situation imaginable, where the seller has no *control over the price* of the product, because there are so many sellers competing to sell identical products.

Because perfect competition is restricted to situations involving industries with many small firms, easy entry into the industry, and identical products, this type of extreme competition is rare. It is, for the most part, restricted to markets for certain agricultural products and natural resource products, and to markets in which the buyers are mostly processors or wholesalers buying food items, or manufacturers buying parts for their products.

perfectly elastic demand
A situation in which any price increase above the market price will cause a firm's sales to fall to zero; represented by a horizontal demand curve.

Incentives and Strategies for Producers

What types of business strategies can Vera utilize so as to make as much profit as possible? As we have seen, she cannot *increase her price* because her sales would collapse. And a *price reduction* would serve no purpose—she can already sell all that she can produce, so why reduce her price? A strategy of *product differentiation* (making her product different from those of her competitors) is out of the question—a carrot is, after all, a carrot. For the same reason, *advertising* would be futile—Vera's carrots are identical to everyone else's carrots, and the buyers know this. All that Vera (and all of her many competitors) can do is

(a) reduce production costs per unit of output to the lowest possible level; that is, produce as efficiently as possible;

(b) produce as much output as is profitable at these low unit-cost levels (which usually means as much output as she can); and

(c) sell the product for whatever price the market determines.

This is essentially what producers in such industries actually do—small vegetable farmers cultivate as large a crop as they can afford, as efficiently as possible (at the lowest possible cost per unit), harvest it, and, together with all the other farmers, sell it on the market for whatever price they can get for it. In seeking to maximize their own profits in this way, these competitive producers contribute to the welfare of consumers, not only by producing what consumers want to buy, but also by maximizing their output of it, and minimizing production costs and prices.

While such behaviour is beneficial to the consumer, it makes matters quite difficult for the producers. Generally, the intensity of competition in such industries will force the profits of the average firm to very low levels, and there will be many marginal producers who are barely able to stay in business. Unable to develop a product that is different from its competitors' and unable to charge a higher price, the only way a producer in such industries can earn an above-average profit is to increase productive efficiency so as to reduce production costs per unit and thereby increase profits per unit of output. Those producers who are able to achieve these goals will be able to earn profits above the average for the industry, representing a reasonable rate of return on their capital. However, if the rest of the producers in the industry also increase their efficiency, the supply of the product will increase, which will drive prices lower, and profits back down to minimal levels.

As noted above, perfect competition is a rare situation. Much more common (but still very competitive) is the case of monopolistic competition, which is discussed in the next section.

Monopolistic Competition

Typically, even in competitive industries, each producer is not selling an identical product or service. While there may be large numbers of sellers selling products that are very similar, each seller's product is usually at least a little different from the rest, particularly in industries that cater to the consumer. We will use the term **monopolistic competition**[1] to describe such industries. Monopolistic competition has three characteristics:

(a) there are many small firms in the industry,

(b) it is easy for new firms to enter the industry, and

(c) all firms' products are not identical—each firm's product or service is in some way different from those of its competitors.

The facts that there are many small firms and that it is easy to enter the industry ensure that there will be strong competition and that prices and profits will be held down to low levels. However, the fact that each firm sells a product that is in some way

---

Many small farmers earn most of their income from sources off the farm, mostly from off-farm employment.

monopolistic competition

A term describing industries that consist of many small firms, where entry to the industry by new firms is easy, and where the products or services of individual firms, while basically similar, are differentiated from each other to a degree.

---

[1] This is a very confusing name for describing this type of industry. The term *monopolistic competition* is meant to convey the impression that, while the industry is highly *competitive* (due to the large number of firms), each producer's position can be regarded (to a *slight* degree only) as similar in a small way to that of a monopoly, because it is the only firm whose product or service has its particular characteristics. However, the basic nature of the industry is very competitive. It is essential to avoid confusing this with the position of a real monopoly, such as Canada Post, which is the *only* firm in the market for first-class mail.

different from the other firms' products adds a new dimension to the situation: because the *products* of different firms are not identical, their *prices* do not need to be identical. So a firm in a monopolistically competitive industry has some (small) opportunity to increase the price of its product—although not by much, because with so many competitors selling similar products, a firm would lose too many sales if it increased its price by much.

Product Differentiation

To the extent that a firm can make its product or service *more different* from those of its competitors—that is, practise **product differentiation**—it can increase its ability to raise prices (within limits) without losing too many sales.

product differentiation
Attempts by individual firms to distinguish their products or services from those of their competitors.

For instance, Harry's Hamburg Haven is a firm in a monopolistically competitive industry (fast foods) comprised of a large number of small outlets, each with its own characteristics such as product, service, and location. Harry's Hamburg Haven is differentiated by its location (between the beer store and the drive-in theatre), its product (Harry's hamburgers are not prepackaged, but charbroiled and dressed to the customer's taste), its service (Harry's employees are carefully selected), and its ambience (Harry's is somewhat of a sports bar/hamburger place, and Harry has a personal following in town because he was the highly popular penalty minutes leader for the local minor-pro hockey team for several years). At a price of $5 per meal (the average price in the area), Harry sells 2000 meals per week, as indicated by the dot on the diagram in Figure 7-4.

The demand curve in Figure 7-4 is generally quite elastic, due to the competitiveness of the industry. However, around the market price of $5, it is *less elastic*, due to the fact that Harry's product is differentiated from his competitors' products. This differentiation would allow Harry to raise his price *a little* (say, to $5.50) without losing so many sales that his total revenue will fall. While some of his customers would abandon him, the vast majority would stay with him. Although perhaps not delighted about paying the premium price, they would feel that the combination of location, product, service, and atmosphere made eating at Harry's worth a little more. So for a small price increase, the demand for Harry's meals could be *inelastic*, making it profitable for Harry to raise his price a little. However, if Harry were to raise his price *a lot* (say, to $6.50), he would likely find that the demand for his burgers becomes *elastic*, as numer-

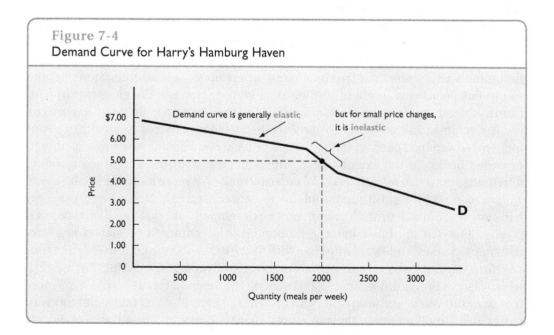

Figure 7-4
Demand Curve for Harry's Hamburg Haven

Demand curve is generally elastic

but for small price changes, it is inelastic

Quantity (meals per week)

ous customers decide that Harry's burgers are not worth the extra $1.50 each to them, and switch to other eating places, causing Harry's sales (and probably his profits) to fall. At prices above $7.00, not even his mother will eat at Harry's. So, in monopolistic competition, the fact that each firm's product is somewhat different from its competitors' can give it an opportunity to raise its price, but only by a quite limited amount.

A similar effect occurs with price reductions—a *small* price cut by Harry will not likely attract many more customers from his competitors. These people are patronizing Harry's competitors because they prefer their product, location, or other features, and will not likely be lured away by the prospect of saving a few cents per burger at Harry's. A *large* price cut is out of the question in an industry as competitive as this— while it would increase Harry's sales greatly, he would lose money on every burger sold, and go bankrupt, at a record level of sales.

In summary, then, the demand curve for the differentiated product of a firm in monopolistic competition is basically very elastic, but for small changes around the market price, it will probably be inelastic. As a result, the firm might have the opportunity to increase its price by a small amount. Whether or not it actually decides to *do* so is a matter of business strategy.

Incentives and Strategies for Producers

What business strategies are available to Harry for increasing his profits? Like Vera's situation of perfect competition, the highly competitive nature of Harry's industry limits his ability to raise prices. This restriction creates a strong incentive for producers in monopolistic competition to *increase productive efficiency*, so as to produce at the lowest possible cost per unit.

However, Harry can adopt some strategies that Vera could not. A firm in monopolistic competition can practise *product differentiation* in order to widen the difference between its product and its competitors', and so gain an advantage in the marketplace. Also, it can use *advertising*, to stress to consumers the advantages of its products or services.

If Harry's customers prefer his place, he may have an opportunity to *raise his prices*, at least a little. So Harry can choose between making a smaller profit per unit on a larger volume of units sold, or making a higher profit per unit with a lower volume of sales. Vera did not have this choice.

Not surprisingly, many sellers in monopolistically competitive industries will try hard to differentiate themselves from their competitors. A key differentiating factor for many small businesses, especially in service industries, is their *location*. Restaurants also stress their special menus, atmosphere, type of entertainment, and so on. Retailers strive to establish their own identity through the character of their shops, special product lines, and special services (parking, delivery, exchanges, returns, refunds, and so on). Some businesses providing services (such as dry cleaning) emphasize the speed of service, while other service businesses stress quality or extended hours. To the extent that a firm is successful in these efforts at product differentiation, it can alter its demand curve by making it more inelastic. For instance, Harry's competitive position would be enhanced strongly if his were the only hamburger stand in a prime location, or if he developed a unique and highly popular product line. On the other hand, a monopolistically competitive market is a very dynamic situation, and Harry must live with the risk that his competitors—or a brand-new firm starting up—may successfully imitate his advantages, reducing the degree to which Harry's firm is differentiated and making the demand for his hamburgers more elastic again. Worse yet (from Harry's viewpoint), some of them may come up with better ideas to differentiate their products, placing Harry at a disadvantage. People

The Big "IF": Suppose that Harry earns $10 of profit on $100 of sales. If he increased his prices by 1 percent, his profits would grow by $1 (10 percent), *but only if* the price increase did not reduce the number of meals people would buy.

who have operated small businesses successfully for years tend to downplay flashy promotional stunts as short-term tactics, and stress instead the importance of establishing a reputation as an honest, reliable firm, if long-term success is to be achieved. They believe that providing "value" in this way is the best type of product differentiation that a firm can establish.

In conclusion, product differentiation, however achieved, can benefit the firm in two ways. First, it can build *consumer loyalty* to the firm and its products, and thus protect the firm against competition; and second, it can provide an opportunity for the firm to *charge higher prices* for its products, to the extent that consumers believe the product differentiation to be worth a higher price. All firms welcome the advantages of consumer loyalty; some will also charge a higher price.

Product differentiation can introduce a slight degree of monopoly power into a very competitive situation, in the sense that each firm's product or service is, in a small way, unique. Obviously, the degree to which this occurs will vary from situation to situation: it is one thing to be the only one of eight hamburger stands in town with a particular location, and quite another to be the only Chinese restaurant or the only restaurant in the town's indoor mall that has a liquor licence and entertainment. Nonetheless, new restaurants can easily open, emphasizing the fact that, while monopolistic competition is less competitive than perfect competition, it still represents a highly competitive situation. As a result, profits in monopolistically competitive industries generally tend to be relatively low, with many firms earning only marginal profits. However, firms that enjoy cost advantages, or that have succeeded in practising product differentiation to their advantage, will earn above-average profits, and some can be very profitable indeed.

Competitive Industries in Review

Let's review and compare the two types of competitive industries that we have discussed. While the large number of firms and ease of entry into the industry make both perfect competition and monopolistic competition highly competitive, product differentiation gives firms in monopolistic competition somewhat more room to manoeuvre. Harry can at least try to make his Hamburg Haven more different from his competitors and possibly charge a slightly higher price, whereas Vera has no such opportunity—the only strategy open to her is to produce as much as she can and sell it on the market for whatever she can get for it.

Economists' descriptions of competitive industries sometimes place such emphasis on *prices* that students get the impression that an industry cannot be classified as competitive unless producers practise aggressive price-cutting tactics against each other on a day-to-day basis, to the point of nearly driving each other out of business. Since few industries fit this description, the concept of competitive industries can seem more theoretical than realistic.

However, the economics of competitive industries are more subtle. Because it is so easy for new producers to enter competitive industries, such industries tend to become crowded with large numbers of producers. And because producers as a group are unable to control supply (partly because there are so many of them and partly because it is easy to enter the industry), the incentive for each is to produce as much as possible. When all producers do so, the result is a *high supply*, which generates downward pressure on prices and profits.

The result—low prices and profits—is the same. However, the origin of this situation lies in the *inability of producers to control supply* rather than in any extraordinary tendency on their part to wake up in the morning with an uncontrollable urge to slash prices.

The Extent of Competitive Industries

Determining the actual number and extent of competitive industries is not a simple matter, because of the difficulties in defining *small business* and deciding whether a particular firm is in a competitive industry or not. As we have said, perfect competition is a rare situation because of the requirement that products be identical; however, monopolistic competition is a very common form of market structure that includes most of the small business sector of the economy discussed in Chapter 3. Taken together, competitive industries probably account for more than half of the economy's output, concentrated for the most part in some sectors of agriculture and fishing, retail trade, small-scale manufacturing, and especially the large number of service industries (restaurants, fast-food outlets, retail shops, travel agencies, and so on) that have expanded rapidly in recent years.

Part B: Concentrated Industries

In Part A of this chapter, we examined competitive industries in which strong competition constantly pushes downward on prices and profits. In this section, we will examine industries of a different nature—industries where there is often less competition and where producers can influence the supply and the price of their product. These industries are described as *concentrated industries* because the supply side of such industries is concentrated in a small number of firms.

The Concept of Market Power

In Chapter 2, we introduced the concept of market power, which was described as the ability of producers or sellers to increase prices. In this chapter, we will examine more closely the concept of market power and how producers obtain it and exercise it. In order for the firms in an industry to exercise market power, the following conditions are necessary:
  (a) the producers make an agreement concerning price and output;
  (b) the producers maintain that agreement;
  (c) newcomers and foreign competition are kept out of the industry; and
  (d) the demand for the product is inelastic.

An Agreement Concerning Price and Output

The producers need to agree on the price to be charged, and not to undercut each other on price. Because less output can be sold at this higher price, the agreement must apply to *output* as well as to *price*. That is, each producer must agree to limit its production so as to avoid over-supplying the market. If output were not restricted, inventories of unsold product would accumulate, which could lead to an outbreak of price-cutting and the collapse of their agreement. (It should be noted that such agreements to restrict competition are illegal; however, at this point the focus is on the economics of this matter. The legalities will be considered in Chapter 9.)

Maintaining the Agreement

The producers must stick to their agreement. While this condition may sound obvious, there is considerable temptation for producers to enter into such an agreement and then break it, especially if it would be difficult for the other producers to know that this has been done. For instance, in the case of products sold by private contract to industrial buyers, one of the firms selling the product might be able to cut its price without its competitors knowing that it was breaking their price agreement.

Keeping Out Newcomers and Foreign Competition

An agreement among oligopolists could collapse if new competitors entered the market, either from new firms starting up or from foreign producers who were not party to the agreement. As we will see shortly, there are various obstacles that can prevent new domestic firms from starting up in many industries. Fending off foreign competition is more difficult and usually requires government assistance in the form of tariffs and other barriers to imports.

Because concentrated industries often have high prices and profits, they do tend to attract new competition from outside. For instance, many major North American industries that in the past had experienced relatively little competition have been more recently subject to considerable foreign competition, especially in the manufacturing sector.

Inelastic Demand

A final key to market power—and one over which the producers do not have much influence—is that the demand for the industry's product must be *inelastic*. With an inelastic demand, price increases will not reduce sales by too much, so that the industry's income will be increased if prices are raised. Generally, if demand is to be inelastic, there must be no close substitutes available.

As the conditions outlined above indicate, it is not an easy task for a group of firms to develop—and maintain—market power. What can be said, however, is that the fewer firms there are in an industry (or the more concentrated the industry is), the more likely they will be able to exercise market power. In this part of Chapter 7, we will consider two types of concentrated industries—**oligopoly**, in which an industry is dominated by a few large firms, and **monopoly**, in which there is only one firm. We will begin by examining the larger and more important of these—oligopoly.

Oligopoly

Oligopoly refers to a situation in which a few sellers (or producers) dominate a market (or industry). More specifically, an industry is called oligopolistic if four (or fewer) producers account for 50 percent or more of the industry's sales.

Behind this dry and quantitative definition lie certain economic realities that are important to understand. When only a few firms dominate an industry, it's possible that they will band together to increase their prices and profits. For such oligopolistic power to exist, it is not necessary that the industry consist of *only* four or fewer firms. As long as the dominant four firms account for half the industry's sales, the rest of the sales could be split up among a considerable number of small firms. In these circumstances, the dominant firms would probably decide the price and the smaller firms would very likely follow along, making the industry oligopolistic, despite the presence of considerably more than four firms. Similarly, there could be dozens of firms in an industry *across Canada*, but if they are fragmented into relatively small local markets with *only a few firms selling in each local market*, each of these markets will be oligopolistic. There are probably dozens of road-paving firms in Canada, but all do not serve a national market: if a municipality offers a contract for road paving, bids may be received from only four or five local firms, a situation that certainly looks oligopolistic. In deciding whether an industry is oligopolistic, then, the total number of producers is less important than the number that buyers actually have to choose from.

oligopoly
A situation in which four or fewer firms account for at least half of the sales of an industry.

monopoly
A situation in which there is only one seller of a particular good or service.

This is the key aspect of oligopoly: unlike the competitive situations we looked at earlier, in an oligopoly the market is dominated by a few firms that together have a strong grip on a large share of the market. This limitation on buyers' choices increases the potential market power of the producers.

The Extent of Oligopoly

Oligopolistic industries have historically comprised an important part of the Canadian economy. We can get an indication of their importance by listing some of them: steel, automobile manufacturing, banking, airlines, heavy machinery, farm implements, pulp and paper, tobacco, beer, liquor, soft drinks, electrical apparatus, aircraft, transportation equipment, explosives and ammunition, sugar, petroleum refining, cement, meat packing, and soap. As these examples show, a substantial proportion of the goods and services produced and consumed in the Canadian economy comes from industries that are quite different from the small businesses discussed in the first part of this chapter.

Barriers to Entry

Because they have more market power, oligopolistic industries will generally enjoy higher rates of profit than competitive industries. In competitive industries, such above-average rates of profit would attract new producers into the industry, causing output (supply) to rise and putting downward pressure on prices and profits. This does not happen so readily in oligopolistic industries because of the *barriers to entry* into these industries—factors that make it difficult for new competitors to start up.

A major barrier to entry into many oligopolistic industries, such as steel mills and automobile manufacturing, is the vast amount of *capital* required to start business on a large enough scale to be efficient and competitive. A related problem for newcomers is in winning a sufficient *volume of sales* to support an efficient level of production. A very high sales/production volume and *extensive advertising* are often required to compete with industry leaders in many manufacturing industries. Another problem facing a newcomer is *consumer acceptance*. Consumers have become familiar with the products of the established firms over the years, and this familiarity is strongly reinforced by the heavy advertising that oligopolists usually do. It can be quite difficult for a newcomer to break down these attitudes.

When the patent on a widely-used drug expired in 2010, its price fell by about 80 percent.

Another problem that prevents newcomers from imitating an established producer's product can be *patents*, through which a firm gains a legal monopoly over a product or process for a period of time. While patents are intended to provide incentives for the development of new products and processes, another effect is to give monopolies to those firms that hold patents. The drug industry is probably the most notable for using patents to protect firms against imitators.

In Toronto in recent years, people who owned a government-issued taxi licence could sell it for over $100 000.

Another obstacle facing new entrants to some industries is *government licensing*, for example, the need to obtain a taxi licence, a commercial airline licence, or a farm product quota poses major barriers to entry into these fields. While government licensing is intended to protect the consumer against unqualified businesses, it can also have the effect of reducing competition and supporting higher prices.

Small regional airlines attempting to start up in competition with Air Canada have frequently complained that Air Canada cuts its fares in a deliberate attempt to drive them out of business.

In the past, it was quite common for the established firms to engage in *predatory pricing*, or price wars, to drive newcomers out of business. Today, such tactics are illegal, and it is much more common for the established firms to buy out new competitors, through *mergers*. Some mergers are "friendly," in that the owners/managers of the firm are offered generous terms for surrendering control of their firm. Alternatively, there may be a *hostile takeover*, in which one firm buys enough of another's shares to give it a controlling interest, after which it elects its own board of directors and replaces the management of the firm.

The problem of foreign competition is more difficult, because foreign competition is beyond the direct control of oligopolists. Traditionally, industries hold off foreign competition by enlisting the assistance of their government in the form of *tariffs or other barriers to imports.* However, in recent years this tariff protection has been decreasing, exposing Canadian producers to considerably stronger foreign competition. This trend has been the result of a worldwide trend toward freer trade and increased international competition, and, of course, the North American Free Trade Agreement between Canada, the United States, and Mexico. This trend is extremely important, as it means that some industries that formerly enjoyed powerful tariff-protected oligopolistic positions within the Canadian market are now being faced with strong import competition that can reduce or even eliminate their market power.

The barriers to entry described above provide formidable obstacles to the entry of new firms into some industries, and are less formidable in other cases. Generally, their effect is to limit competition and increase profits. Studies have shown that, as a general rule, the higher the barriers to entry into an industry are, the higher the profits (expressed in terms of rate of return on investment) of the firms in that industry tend to be.

Price-Fixing

When an industry is dominated by a few producers and is not subject to foreign competition, these producers will have an opportunity to reach an agreement among themselves for avoiding price competition, so that all of them can earn higher profits than otherwise would have been possible. As a result, the pricing policies of oligopolists sometimes reflect a "live-and-let-live" approach to competitors, rather than the strong competition that often characterizes competitive industries.

The control of prices by producers is sometimes referred to as **price-fixing**, or administered prices. In order to control prices successfully, oligopolists must *control the supply* of their product. Therefore, price-fixing agreements must include an agreement concerning how much of the product should be produced by the oligopolists.

> **price-fixing**
> Agreements among oligopolists to raise their prices above levels that would prevail in a competitive situation.

Typically, then, once the oligopolists have set the price of the product for a given period (say, one year, as with steel), they make every effort to maintain that price for the entire period. Such **administered prices** tend to be particularly resistant to downward movements. Should the demand for their product prove weaker than expected, the oligopolists will usually cut back their production rather than reduce their prices and risk an outbreak of price-cutting.

> **administered prices**
> A term used to describe prices that have been fixed by sellers. See *price-fixing.*

Price Stickiness

The reason why oligopolistic prices, once set by the industry, tend to remain unchanged for considerable periods is shown in Figure 7-5. The demand curve in Figure 7-5 represents the demand for the product of one firm in an oligopolistic industry in which it and three other companies are all pricing their product at $100.

The unusual "kink" in the oligopolist's demand curve is the result of the following two situations.

First, if this one oligopolist *increases* its price, and the others do not, the oligopolist that raised its price will lose a considerable volume of sales. That is, for each firm, demand will be *elastic* for price increases, making a unilateral price increase an unattractive strategy.

Then what about a unilateral *price reduction* by one of the oligopolists? We must assume that any price cut by one oligopolist (in violation of their agreement, of course) would be matched by the other oligopolists, so that our oligopolist's strategy would not gain many sales. That is, for price reductions, demand will be *inelastic.* With the demand for a product elastic for price increases and inelastic for price

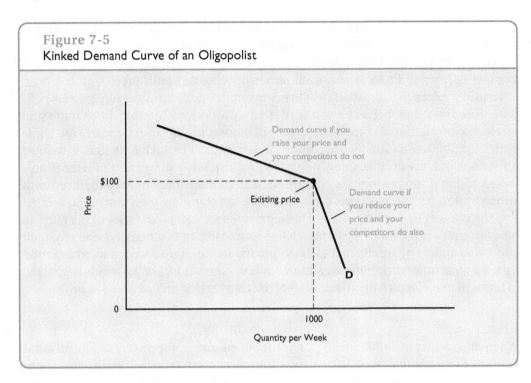

Figure 7-5
Kinked Demand Curve of an Oligopolist

reductions, the oligopolist finds that *neither* price increases *nor* price reductions are profitable.

Rather, the most profitable—and safest—strategy is to let the price remain at the present level of $100, until the producers *as a group* decide to change it. So, once they are set by the producers, oligopolistic prices tend to be quite *sticky,* or resistant to change. This price behaviour is quite different from the behaviour of prices in competitive markets, which fluctuate frequently as supply and demand change.

Oligopolistic Versus Competitive Price Behaviour

Generally, the prices of the products in highly competitive industries tend to fluctuate considerably more than oligopolistic prices. In competitive markets prices vary as supply and demand fluctuate; a good example is seasonal vegetable prices. By contrast, the administered prices of oligopolists tend to remain at the level set by the producers until the oligopolists decide to change them, which generally happens only periodically.

Also, competitive and oligopolistic industries respond quite differently to recessions during which demand decreases. In competitive industries, producers cannot control supply, so *prices* tend to decrease during a recession. In oligopolistic industries, on the other hand, producers often cut back on *output* (and lay off workers) in order to maintain prices during periods of weak demand.

Price-Fixing Techniques

price leadership

A technique of price-fixing in which one firm (the price leader) sets its price and the rest of the firms in the industry follow suit.

There are various ways in which oligopolists can actually go about fixing prices, including the following:

(a) **Price leadership** is probably the most common technique for fixing prices. Under price leadership, the price leader in the industry (usually the largest firm) announces an increase in prices, and all the other firms follow suit in short order.

The technique is especially well-suited to situations in which all firms are selling undifferentiated products, such as gasoline or steel, whose prices need to be identical because the products are identical.

(b) *Formal agreements* are sometimes worked out by oligopolists to avoid competition. Such agreements generally cover matters such as prices, product quality, the division of the market into territories to be reserved for each firm, and techniques for fixing bids on government contracts. These agreements are sometimes quite complex, requiring meetings between executives of the firms and/or written communications and agreements. Because price-fixing is illegal, and such agreements increase the risk of detection, they tend to be used less frequently than price leadership. A group of oligopolists bound by a formal agreement is also known as a **cartel**.

(c) *Informal understandings* about prices are sometimes reached between oligopolists. In these situations, there is no apparent communication among the oligopolists and no clear indication of price leadership, yet the firms' prices come out remarkably close to each other. The automobile industry is believed to be an example of such a situation: knowing each other's costs reasonably well, knowing the general economic situation, knowing how each other calculates prices and each other's plans for model changes, each firm could work out its own prices in reasonable confidence that they would be quite close to the prices of the other firms. This process will not yield identical prices in the way that price leadership does, but automobiles themselves are a quite differentiated product, so identical prices are not necessary.

cartel
A formal agreement among producers to coordinate their price and output decisions for the purpose of earning monopoly profits.

Non-Price Competition Among Oligopolists

As a means of competing, price-cutting has major disadvantages for the firms involved. First, price cuts are easily imitated; if one firm cuts its price, its competitors can quickly match its price cut, removing any competitive advantage that the firm might have gained. Second, price-cutting can escalate into costly price wars, in which all the companies lose. And third, the costs of price-cutting fall on the producers through lower profit margins. With other forms of competition, known as **non-price competition**, these disadvantages are less of a problem.

While oligopolists may tend to avoid price competition, they certainly do not refrain from other types of competition. In fact, the marketing rivalry between firms in oligopolistic industries such as soft drinks, automobiles, soaps, detergents, beer, and so on is a well-known and highly visible feature of our economy. This rivalry, which uses a variety of methods other than price competition, is directed toward *increasing sales and market share.* One measure of the success of an oligopoly is its market share, which means its percentage of the total sales of the industry. Oligopolistic firms tend to be quite concerned with the size of their market share and whether it is growing or falling.

To increase their sales and market share, oligopolists extensively use non-price competition, such as *product differentiation, advertising,* and *sales promotion.* Product differentiation makes a product distinctive from the products of competitors, while advertising is used to persuade consumers that these differences are important. Sales promotion is a short-term tactic for boosting sales and market share.

Some efforts at product differentiation, such as more fuel-efficient cars, will serve real consumer needs; others, such as minor styling changes, will be trivial; and others, such as the "feeling" one supposedly gets from using a product, will be contrivances of advertising imagery. Many of them will be costly, as will the advertising and promotion campaigns associated with them. Generally, oligopolists are heavy spenders in the areas of market research, product design/differentiation, and advertising. Non-

non-price competition
Competition between sellers based not on price but rather on factors such as product differentiation and advertising.

price competition is not cheap competition, but for oligopolists it is preferable to price competition for a few reasons.

First, an advantage gained through effective non-price competition, such as a new product or a unique advertising appeal, cannot be quickly offset by your competitors' simply imitating it, as they can with price reductions. Second, there is much less of a risk of non-price competition escalating in a costly manner, as can happen with price wars. The costs of non-price competition are more readily kept within limits; for instance, many oligopolists set their advertising budgets as a certain percentage of their sales. And third, assuming that the industry has a price-fixing arrangement, at least part of the cost of advertising and product differentiation can be passed on to the consumer through higher prices. As a result, oligopolists prefer, when possible, to practise non-price competition rather than price competition.

Predicting Behaviour

Earlier, we noted that once oligopolists have set the price of their product, the price tends to be "sticky," or resistant to change. However, we have not yet considered how oligopolists *actually decide* what price to charge and what output to produce in the first place. Considering the importance of oligopolistic industries in the economy, this is an important question.

Research has shown that the widely held belief that oil companies regularly raise gasoline prices as long weekends commence is untrue.

Unfortunately, it is quite difficult to generalize about, or predict, the pricing behaviour of most oligopolistic industries. In competitive industries, we can predict that prices will be driven downward toward a minimum level. But oligopolists often have considerably more discretion over the prices of their products, which makes it much more difficult to analyze and predict their pricing decisions.

While the domination of an industry by a few firms creates the *potential* for price-fixing, several factors will influence the *actual* pricing decisions of these firms and industries. The possible range of oligopolists' power over prices is quite wide. At one extreme, a tightly organized group of oligopolists without any foreign competition and facing an inelastic demand for its product is in an excellent position to raise prices to very high levels. At the other extreme, oligopolists facing strong foreign competition may find themselves without any real power over prices at all. In the following section, we will consider some of the factors that limit the power of oligopolists to raise prices.

YOU DECIDE

Coffee Crop Control

At times in the past, the world's major coffee producers have agreed to burn a considerable portion (as much as 20 percent) of their harvests. ▪

QUESTIONS

1. What would be the purpose of destroying so much coffee?
2. What would be required in order for such a plan to achieve its objective?
3. What could prevent the plan from being successful?

Limits on Prices

Foreign competition has in recent years become the most important factor limiting the market power of many oligopolists, especially in the manufacturing sector of the economy. As international trade agreements have reduced tariffs both in North America and globally, many Canadian manufacturers have found themselves facing increasingly strong competition from imports. In many major industries, such as automobiles, steel, electronic equipment, and textiles, the market power of Canadian (and American) industries has been sharply reduced or even eliminated by competition from imports.

Lack of cooperation among oligopolists can also limit their control over prices. If any of the firms in the industry has a tendency to use price competition, either openly or by cheating on the agreement, the other firms will have to respond in kind, or face a decrease in their market share. Price-cutting is more likely during recessions, when sales are slow.

Elasticity of demand for the product is another factor that can limit the ability of oligopolists to raise prices. If substitutes for the product make the demand for it elastic, sales will fall by so much that it will be futile for the oligopolists to raise prices. Usually there are few if any substitutes, since the oligopolists control the entire market for a given product; however, this is not always the case. For instance, in some uses, steel has to contend with competition from aluminum, plastics, and even glass, and the airline industry is to some extent in competition with other vacation packages. And, as technology generates new materials, processes, and products, this kind of inter-product and inter-industry competition has been presenting some previously secure industries with competition from new and unexpected quarters. This trend has been particularly evident in the communications field recently.

Fear of prosecution for price-fixing may also act as a deterrent to oligopolists. As we will see in Chapter 9, price-fixing is illegal under Canadian law, so companies that fix prices face a risk of being prosecuted and fined. While the law has not stopped price-fixing, it seems likely that it has acted as a deterrent.

IN THE NEWS

OPEC

The Organization of Petroleum Exporting Countries (OPEC) is an organization of 12 countries that produce and export oil. OPEC countries produce roughly 40 percent of the world's oil. Periodically, the media report that OPEC is considering reducing production by its member countries in order to increase world oil prices. These media reports often include two other interesting comments. The first is that a seemingly small reduction in OPEC's production is expected to lead to a surprisingly large price increase. The second is that in the opinion of oil industry experts, OPEC will have great difficulty in achieving its objectives.

www.opec.org

"All players are competitors on the market, but before that they are partners within OPEC."
— HOSSEIN KAZEMPOUR ARDEBILI, IRANIAN OPEC REPRESENTATIVE

QUESTIONS

1. What does this information tell us about the elasticity of the demand for oil?
2. Why do you think that OPEC has often failed to achieve the increases in the price of oil that oil-consuming nations had feared?

How Much Market Power?

There is no simple answer, to the question of how much market power oligopolists possess—it varies widely from industry to industry and from time to time, so it is impossible to generalize. In some situations, in which the oligopolists are well-organized and face no foreign competition, they can have considerable market power. In other cases, one or more of the factors outlined in the previous section can take away most or even all of their ability to charge high prices.

Furthermore, the effectiveness of these limits on prices can vary from time to time, as conditions change. For instance, the automobile industry was for many years considered a classic example of a powerful oligopoly as a few dominant firms kept competition within bounds and both workers' wages and companies' profits were well above average levels. However, over the past 40 years, import competition has limited the market power of both the companies and their unions.

Regardless of the factors that may—or may not—restrain the market power of oligopolists, the fact remains that some large corporations do possess considerable power over prices, particularly when economic conditions are favourable. These large corporations, and the market power that some of them possess, are a long way from the competitive industries described in the first part of this chapter. This difference is reflected in the fact that, on average, the profits of larger corporations represent a significantly higher rate of return on the owners' investment than do the profits of smaller businesses.

Monopoly

Suppose that as the result of a patent,[2] Global Gadgets, Inc., is the only producer of a particular component used in snowmobiles. Since Global Gadgets is the only producer of this product, the total market demand for the product and the demand for Global Gadgets' product are the same thing. This demand is illustrated in Figure 7-6, in both schedule and graph form.

What price will the monopoly charge for its product? While our initial response may be that the monopoly will select the highest price, Figure 7-6 shows that the *highest* price may not be the *most profitable.* By charging a price of $5 and producing 700 units per week, the monopoly can make a higher total revenue than if, for instance, the price were raised to $6, and sales dropped to 500 units per week. (Note that we are looking at only the *revenue* side of the picture, and are ignoring the *costs.* In effect, we are assuming that if the monopoly maximizes total revenue, it is also maximizing profits. In Chapter 8, we will consider costs.)

Under these assumptions, the monopoly will raise its price as long as the demand is inelastic. At prices above $5, the demand becomes elastic as buyer resistance to such high prices cuts sales and revenues.

At a price of $5, only 700 products can be sold per week. If more were produced, they could not be sold without lowering the price. So the key to the monopolist's ability to raise the price to $5 lies in the fact that the monopolist *controls the supply* of the product, and can restrict the supply to 700 per week.

Monopoly Compared to Competition

By making *prices higher* and *output lower* than they would otherwise be, monopoly imposes a twofold burden on society economically. In Figure 7-6, suppose that the

---

[2] A patent gives the inventor of a product a legal monopoly over the production of it for a certain period.

Figure 7-6
Demand for Global Gadgets' Product

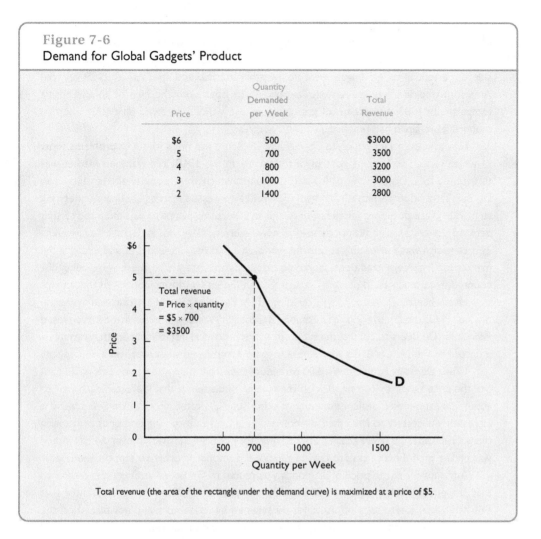

Price	Quantity Demanded per Week	Total Revenue
$6	500	$3000
5	700	3500
4	800	3200
3	1000	3000
2	1400	2800

Total revenue
= Price × quantity
= $5 × 700
= $3500

Total revenue (the area of the rectangle under the demand curve) is maximized at a price of $5.

minimum price for which the product could be sold profitably were $3. If there were strong competition in the industry, the price would fall to $3 (instead of $5) and production would be 1000 units (instead of 700). But with a monopoly in the industry, the public is burdened with *both* higher prices *and* lower output than would exist under competition (see the "You Decide" box below).

YOU DECIDE

The International Diamond Monopoly

One of the most famous monopolies of all time is the international diamond monopoly organized by De Beers, a South African corporation. For most of the twentieth century, De Beers owned or controlled all the diamond mines in South Africa and owned diamond-trading companies in various countries.

De Beers' success stemmed not only from its control of the *supply* of diamonds, but also from its ability to influence the *demand* for them. Starting in 1938 (at which time diamond prices had declined badly due to the Depression), the demand for diamonds in the United States was promoted by a sophisticated advertising campaign that virtually *created* a "tradition": the diamond engagement ring, and the association of diamonds with romance and permanence—"A Diamond Is Forever." By the late 1950s a diamond was generally considered essential to an engagement in North America, and in 1967 this 29-year-old American tradition was successfully "exported" to Japan with the help of an advertising campaign. By 1980, 60 percent of engaged Japanese women received diamonds, and diamond sales in Japan had reached $1 billion per year.

However, even a monopoly as powerful as De Beers was not without its problems, most of which related to keeping control of the supply. In the 1960s the diamond market was threatened by a large inflow of Russian diamonds, which were considerably smaller than De Beers' traditional South African gems. To avoid a depressed market, De Beers undertook to market these diamonds for the Soviets, and an advertising campaign was mounted to shift demand toward smaller diamonds sold in new "eternity rings" for older married women. This campaign was remarkably successful; however, it had the side-effect of undercutting the market for De Beers' traditional larger diamonds. By the late 1970s, these were being discounted by as much as 20 percent—a sign that De Beers was losing control of the supply.

www.debeers.com

Meanwhile, other developments threatened De Beers' control of the diamond market. In the late 1970s the discovery of vast diamond deposits in Western Australia made it even more difficult for De Beers to control the supply. In addition, political instability in South Africa made it uncertain whether De Beers would be able to hold together the key suppliers in that region.

When De Beers had controlled 80 percent of the world supply of diamonds, it could control the price simply by cutting back on the volume of diamonds that it allotted each year to about 300 hand-picked dealers. However, as other suppliers came into play, De Beers found it increasingly necessary to keep their diamonds off the market, by buying diamonds and storing them. Over time, De Beers accumulated an inventory of diamonds worth over $4 billion, and was finding itself short of cash to buy up additional diamonds in order to support the price.

And support of the price of diamonds was crucial to De Beers' strategy. It is estimated that the public holds more than 500 million carats of gem diamonds. It is essential that this half-billion carat stock of diamonds be retained by its owners, and not placed on the market. If only a small proportion of this stock were sold in any one year, the price could collapse. While it is unlikely that people would sell their engagement rings (a diamond is, after all, forever), there was an increasingly large stock of "investment diamonds" in the hands of both wealthy individuals and financial institutions. In the event of price decreases, these investment diamonds might be dumped onto the market, depressing prices further.

Ironically, only by maintaining the price of diamonds (described by some observers as the "diamond illusion") could De Beers prevent such a sell-off of diamonds, and the risk of a price collapse that this could bring. Yet, as additional suppliers came onto the diamond market, it became more difficult to preserve that price by controlling the supply.

Finally, with its market share down to 63 percent, De Beers decided that it could no longer control the supply of diamonds. Instead, De Beers repositioned itself in 2000 as a seller of high-quality diamonds *and* luxury products, using advertising to influence consumer demand for its own products. ■

QUESTIONS

1. Why might diamonds be considered a risky long-term investment?
2. According to some economists, monopoly can never be more than a temporary market condition. Explain the reasoning behind this theory, and why you agree or disagree with it.

The Extent of Monopoly

Monopoly is a relatively rare form of market structure. Most monopolies in the Canadian economy are in public utilities or public services such as electricity, water, postal service, natural gas, and cable television. Such industries are called **natural monopolies** because by having only one producer, the high costs of the capital equipment that is required can be spread over the maximum number of users, reducing the cost of these services to each user. In order to protect the public against the market power of such monopolies, the government has usually either regulated the rates that they charge or taken over ownership and operation of them. In Chapter 9, we will examine in more detail the issues and the arguments concerning the question of government policy regarding these natural monopolies.

natural monopoly
An industry, such as public utilities, that by its nature lends itself to a monopolistic form of organization.

In Conclusion

Figure 7-7 summarizes and compares the four basic types of market structures, ranging from perfect competition to monopoly.

It should be noted that these four market structures represent only *types* of market structures, and that any particular real-life industry may consist of some combination of these types. For instance, an industry with three major Canadian firms that have 50 percent of the market, several smaller Canadian firms, and imports from several large foreign firms would look something like Figure 7-8 on page 149.

The industry in Figure 7-8 would fall very near the middle of the spectrum of industries shown in Figure 7-1 at the start of this chapter. While it might fall under the strict definition of *oligopoly* (four firms or less having 50 percent of the market), there would be considerably more competition and less opportunity for price-fixing in it than in a classic oligopoly. Indeed, it might well be sufficiently competitive that firms in it would have to behave more like firms in a competitive industry than like oligopolists.

In addition, it should be noted that the market structure of an industry can *change* over time, especially when larger size (economies of scale) allow larger firms to enjoy lower production costs. In the 1920s, there were 241 automobile manufacturing firms in North America. Over the years, competition reduced this to three giant companies that enjoyed economies of scale that smaller firms could not achieve.

Competition in the Canadian Economy

Historically, there has been less competition in Canada's economy than in many other countries. In part, this has been the natural result of Canada's small market, since in some industries there was only room in the market for a few firms. However, government policies have also played a role in limiting competition. Many manufacturing industries were protected from foreign competition by tariffs, and government regulation of some sectors of the economy, such as communications and transportation, prevented competition.

More recently, however, the situation has been changing as the intensity of competition in the Canadian economy has increased since the 1980s. In part, this change has been due to changing government policies. As tariffs on imports have come down under *trade agreements* such as the North American Free Trade Agreement and the WTO (World Trade Organization) agreements, some industries that were dominated by a few Canadian oligopolists have become much more like competitive industries. In addition, the *deregulation by governments* of some industries such as communications and transportation has allowed more competition in sectors previously dominated by

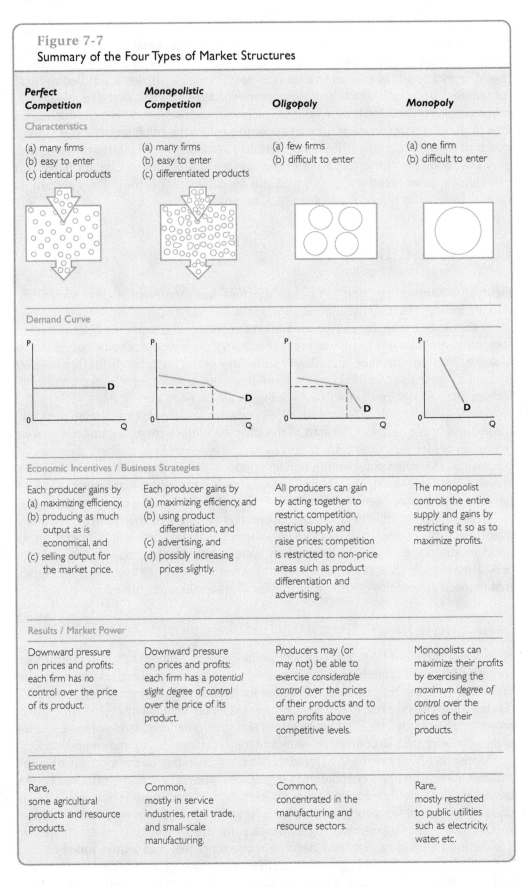

Figure 7-7
Summary of the Four Types of Market Structures

Perfect Competition	Monopolistic Competition	Oligopoly	Monopoly
Characteristics			
(a) many firms (b) easy to enter (c) identical products	(a) many firms (b) easy to enter (c) differentiated products	(a) few firms (b) difficult to enter	(a) one firm (b) difficult to enter
Demand Curve			
Economic Incentives / Business Strategies			
Each producer gains by (a) maximizing efficiency, (b) producing as much output as is economical, and (c) selling output for the market price.	Each producer gains by (a) maximizing efficiency, and (b) using product differentiation, and (c) advertising, and (d) possibly increasing prices slightly.	All producers can gain by acting together to restrict competition, restrict supply, and raise prices; competition is restricted to non-price areas such as product differentiation and advertising.	The monopolist controls the entire supply and gains by restricting it so as to maximize profits.
Results / Market Power			
Downward pressure on prices and profits: each firm has *no* control over the price of its product.	Downward pressure on prices and profits: each firm has a *potential slight degree of control* over the price of its product.	Producers may (or may not) be able to exercise *considerable control* over the prices of their products and to earn profits above competitive levels.	Monopolists can maximize their profits by exercising the *maximum degree of control* over the prices of their products.
Extent			
Rare, some agricultural products and resource products.	Common, mostly in service industries, retail trade, and small-scale manufacturing.	Common, concentrated in the manufacturing and resource sectors.	Rare, mostly restricted to public utilities such as electricity, water, etc.

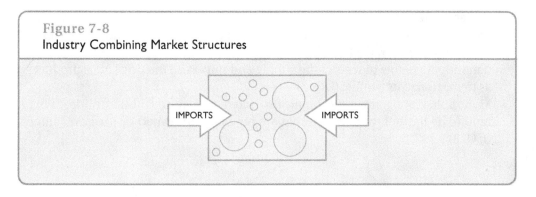

Figure 7-8
Industry Combining Market Structures

monopolies. In part, the trend toward increasing competition has been the result of changes in the economy itself. Another important trend has been the *growth of the service sector* of the economy. Service industries tend to consist of large numbers of smaller businesses, creating a highly competitive environment. As a result of these factors, there is more competition in the Canadian economy today than in the past.

By introducing new products and services, *technological change* has increased competition in some markets, particularly in the communications and entertainment fields, And, of course, *the internet* has increased competition, by allowing buyers to very conveniently compare products and various sellers' prices for those products. For an illustration of how the internet boosts competition, see question 9 in the "Questions" section following this chapter.

PayPal has more than 160 million account-holders worldwide.

Chapter Summary

1. In perfect competition, the most competitive situation possible, many small firms sell identical products, and no individual firm has any influence over the price of its product since it faces a perfectly elastic demand curve. Prices and profits tend to be low. (L.O. 1)

2. The incentives for a firm in perfect competition are to minimize production costs per unit (maximize efficiency), produce as much output as it can afford to, and sell its output for whatever price the market determines. (L.O. 1)

3. Monopolistically competitive industries are also very competitive but differ from perfect competition in that these firms have an opportunity to practise product differentiation, thereby making demand somewhat less elastic and (possibly) enabling the firms to increase prices a little. (L.O. 2)

4. To exercise market power, firms have to make and keep an agreement concerning both price and supply and have to keep out new competitors and foreign competition. Also, demand for their product must be inelastic. (L.O. 3)

5. Oligopolies consist of sufficiently few firms that they are often able to act together so as to fix prices, using various techniques. However, they often do compete strongly in non-price areas. (L.O. 4)

6. The high profits of some oligopolistic industries are protected by various barriers to entry that keep new entrants out of these industries. (L.O. 5)

7. Under some circumstances, oligopolists can possess considerable power over their prices. However, various factors, especially foreign competition, can restrict their market power. (L.O. 6)

8. A monopoly is able to restrict the supply and thus raise the price of its product so as to maximize its profits. (L.O. 7)

9. Monopolies are quite rare, being restricted mainly to public utilities, which tend to be natural monopolies that are regulated or owned by the government. (L.O. 8)

Questions

1. Pat is one of many small farmers in the potato farming industry, which is perfectly competitive.
   (a) Why is this industry described as perfectly competitive?
   (b) If Pat increases his price by a small amount, what will happen to Pat's sales, and why?
   (c) Draw a graph showing the demand curve for Pat's potatoes.

2. Pierre is one small operator in the barbershop industry.
   (a) How is Pierre's industry different from Pat's in question 1, and what name would economists use to describe the barbershop industry?
   (b) If Pierre increases the price of his haircuts by a small amount, what will happen to Pierre's sales, and why?
   (c) Draw a graph showing the demand curve for Pierre's haircuts.

3. (a) What does the term *market power* mean?
   (b) What are the conditions required in order for a group of producers to be able to exercise market power?
   (c) Is it necessary for *all* of the conditions in part (b) to exist in order for the producers to possess market power? Why or why not?
   (d) How much market power does Pat (in question 1) possess? Why?
   (e) How does the market power of Pierre (in question 2) compare to Pat's? Why?

4. Suppose that three companies control 80 percent of the sales in the Canadian fertilizer industry.
   (a) What concerns would this situation raise?
   (b) Explain four factors that could prevent the concerns in part (a) from becoming a reality.

5. Classify each of the following as an example of *perfect competition, monopolistic competition, oligopoly,* or *monopoly.*
   (a) water supply to homes _____
   (b) home repair contractors _____
   (c) steel mills _____
   (d) small farmers selling turnips _____
   (e) pizzerias _____

6. Generally speaking, convenience stores carry the same merchandise as each other. Would you therefore consider the convenience stores in your community to be in "perfect competition" with each other? Why or why not?

7. (a) How do the prices charged by a gas station in a large urban area compare to prices at a gas station located on a limited-access superhighway?
   (b) What explains the difference in their prices?

8. The text notes that over about 50 years, the automobile manufacturing industry evolved from 241 firms to 3 vast companies.
   (a) How did the evolution of the barbershop industry over the same period differ from that of the auto industry?
   (b) What explains the difference between the histories of these two industries?

9. For an indication of how the internet increases competition, visit **www.bizrate.com** and "shop" for a digital camera (or any other product of your choice). First, compare the various *products* available, and make your choice of product. Then, check out all the *sellers of that product*, and compare not only their prices, but also their ratings. If *you* were one of those sellers, how could you use Bizrate, and how would this affect the competitiveness of the marketplace?

Study Guide

Review Questions (Answers to these Review Questions appear in Appendix B.)

1. Name the three characteristics of *perfect competition*.
   (a) _____
   (b) _____
   (c) _____

2. As a result of the situation described in question 1, if an individual seller in a perfectly competitive industry increases the price of its product,
   (a) its sales will fall to zero.
   (b) other sellers will increase their prices, too.
   (c) its profits will increase.
   (d) some buyers will switch to other sellers.
   (e) None of the above.

3. Which of the following industries most closely approximates perfect competition?
   (a) railroads
   (b) steel manufacturing
   (c) vegetable farming
   (d) clothing
   (e) automobile manufacturing

4. *Monopolistic competition* and perfect competition are similar in that
   (a) profits are higher than in other types of industries.
   (b) if producers raise their prices, their sales will fall to zero.
   (c) producers restrict the supply of their product in order to raise prices.
   (d) there are many sellers and it is easy for new firms to enter the industry.
   (e) None of the above.

5. In what way is monopolistic competition different from perfect competition? In monopolistic competition,
   (a) profits are lower than in perfect competition.
   (b) there are fewer sellers than in perfect competition.
   (c) it is more difficult for new firms to enter the industry.
   (d) there is only one seller.
   (e) the product of each producer is not identical to the products of its competitors.

6. Which of the following industries would be classed as monopolistic competition?
   (a) railroads
   (b) aircraft manufacturing
   (c) wheat farming
   (d) restaurants
   (e) cable television

7. In monopolistic competition,
   (a) each seller has a great deal of control over the price of its product.
   (b) while profits are still quite low on average, individual sellers may be able to raise their price by a small amount without losing many sales.
   (c) the demand for each seller's product is more elastic than in perfect competition.
   (d) producers usually make agreements not to compete on prices.
   (e) the one seller has total control of the market.

8. If a producer in a monopolistically competitive industry succeeds in differentiating its product from those of its competitors, the demand for its product will tend to
   (a) become more inelastic.
   (b) become more elastic.
   (c) become neither more nor less elastic.
   (d) None of the above.

9. *Market power* refers to the ability of producers/sellers to _____.

10. The conditions necessary for a group of producers to exercise market power are
   (a) _____
   (b) _____
   (c) _____
   (d) _____

11. *Oligopoly* refers to a situation in which
   (a) an industry is dominated by a few large firms.
   (b) prices and profits are above competitive levels.
   (c) two or three firms do all of the business in a particular market.
   (d) one very large corporation is the largest (but not the only) firm in a particular market.
   (e) None of the above.

12. According to the text, the demand curve faced by oligopolists often creates an incentive for each individual oligopolist to
   (a) increase its price.
   (b) leave its price at the present level.
   (c) change its price only if the other firms in the industry do so.
   (d) reduce its price.
   (e) (b) and (c) are both correct.

13. Which statement best describes the competitive behaviour of most oligopolists?
   (a) They engage in vigorous competition of all sorts: advertising, price cutting, etc.
   (b) They focus mostly on price competition, using relatively little advertising and other non-price methods.
   (c) They use extensive advertising, in order to save money and increase profits.
   (d) They generally avoid all forms of competition of any sort: advertising, price cutting, etc.
   (e) They often seek to avoid price competition so as to protect prices and profits, and instead use other forms of competition, such as advertising and product differentiation, to compete for sales and market share.

14. *Monopoly* is a situation in which _____.

15. Generally, a monopolistic producer will
   (a) charge a lower price and produce a higher output than a competitive industry.
   (b) charge a lower price and produce a lower output than a competitive industry.
   (c) charge a higher price and produce a lower output than a competitive industry.
   (d) charge a higher price and produce a higher output than a competitive industry.
   (e) charge a higher price and produce the same output as a competitive industry.

16. The most basic reason why a monopoly has the greatest amount of market power is that it is able to _____.

Critical Thinking Questions

(Asterisked questions 1 to 5 are answered in Appendix B; the answers to questions 6 to 10 are in the Instructor's Manual that accompanies this text.)

*1. Ed Harasymchuk is one of thousands of grain farmers who produces only #1 grade Northern wheat. His farm can grow up to 40 000 bushels of wheat per year. Last year he harvested and sold 40 000 bushels for a price of $4 per bushel. Total world production of wheat last year was 21 000 000 000 bushels.
   (a) Would you describe this industry as an example of
      (i)   monopoly?
      (ii)   monopolistic competition?
      (iii) perfect competition?
      (iv)   oligopoly?
   (b) Why did you make the choice that you made in part (a)?

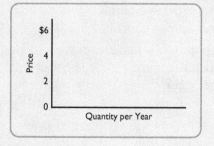

(c) Draw the demand curve facing Mr. Harasymchuk.

(d) How much wheat should Mr. Harasymchuk produce?

(e) What would happen if he were to increase his price slightly above the market price of $4 per bushel?

(f) Should he lower his price below $4 in order to capture more of the wheat market? Why or why not?

(g) Should he spend money on advertising in order to boost his sales?

(h) If you could make *only one* suggestion to Mr. Harasymchuk that would increase his profits, what would that suggestion be?

*2. Pietro's Pizzeria operates in a city in which there are dozens of pizzerias. In this market, Pietro's combination of good pizzas, special toppings, and entertainment have given him a base of loyal customers. In an average week, Pietro sells 2000 pizzas for an average price of $15.

(a) Would you describe this industry as an example of

    (i)   monopoly?

    (ii) monopolistic competition?

    (iii) perfect competition?

    (iv) oligopoly?

(b) Why did you make the choice that you made in part (a)?

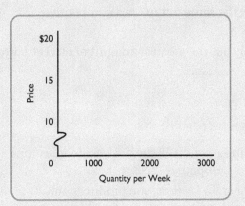

(c) On the above graph, draw the demand curve faced by Pietro's Pizzeria.

(d) To increase his profits, what should Pietro do regarding

    (i)   his product design?

    (ii) his production methods?

    (iii) his advertising?

    (iv) his pricing?

*3. What is the *most basic reason* why competitive industries (both perfect competition and monopolistic competition) generally have low prices and low profits?

*4. (a) What are barriers to entry to an industry? Provide examples.

   (b) Why are barriers to entry a key to the market power of oligopolists?

*5. (a) On the graph below, draw the general shape of the demand curve for a single firm in an oligopolistic industry in which the market price is currently $50. The firm is currently selling 100 units per week.

(b) If the firm increases its price, what will happen to its sales and sales revenue?

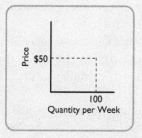

(c) If the firm decreases its price, what will happen to its sales and sales revenue?

(d) What incentives do the situations in parts (a) and (b) create for firms in this industry regarding their pricing strategies?

6. The text notes that service industries are generally very competitive.
   (a) Why is this generally the case?
   (b) Can you think of some exceptions to this generality?
   (c) What explains why some service industries are concentrated?

7. In Toronto in recent years, a taxi licence (by which the government gives its owner the legal right to operate a cab) has sold for about $90 000. What would explain such a high price?

8. Over a period of several weeks, monitor the prices in your local supermarket of a popular breakfast cereal and fresh lettuce. What differences do you observe in the behaviour of the price of these products? How do you explain these differences?

9. Two of the most fundamental forces driving change in recent years have been free trade agreements (such as the North American Free Trade Agreement and the World Trade Organization) and communications technology (such as telecommunications and the internet). What are the implications of these changes for market structure and the degree of competitiveness in the Canadian economy?

10. At the end of Chapter 7, we saw that the number of firms in the North American automobile manufacturing industry decreased from over 240 in the 1920s to only three giant companies less than 40 years later.
    (a) What might explain *why* this dramatic change in the market structure of this industry occurred?
    (b) What would be the implications of this change for North American consumers?
    (c) Did this mean that consumers would have to live indefinitely with such a limited degree of competition in such an important industry?

11. In 1973, the Organization of Petroleum Exporting Countries (OPEC) *quadrupled* the price of crude oil, in arguably the most impressive display of market power in history. At that time, OPEC's share of world oil production was over 50 percent.
    (a) By the mid-1980s, OPEC's share of world oil production had fallen to around 30 percent. What would explain this sharp reduction in OPEC's market share?
    (b) What were the implications for OPEC's market power of this decrease in its market share?

Use the Web   (Hints for this Use the Web exercise appear in Appendix B.)

1. Let's look into how much competition there is in various markets for used cars. Visit AutoTrader at **www.autotrader.ca** and go shopping for cars.

    (a) First, select a very common make of used car (Honda Civic is an excellent example; leave the model and price range unspecified). For the age of the car, specify a year four or five years ago, then click on "Update search." How many of this car were offered for sale?

    (b) Now click on "Browse all makes" and click on the name of a very unusual make of used car (Bentley, Ferrari, and Lamborghini are good examples, but Alfa Romeo and Aston Martin are good, too; after all, this is a matter of taste!). How many of this car were offered for sale?

    (c) What would you probably conclude about the degree of competition in these different markets for used cars?

8

The Costs and Revenues of the Firm

LEARNING OBJECTIVES

After studying this chapter, you should be able to

1. Identify a firm's costs as either fixed costs or variable costs, and describe how fixed cost per unit and variable cost per unit change as output is increased.

2. Explain the *Law of Diminishing Returns*.

3. Using sales revenue data for a firm, calculate and graph the average revenue per unit and marginal revenue per unit over a range of output and sales.

4. Using cost data for a firm, calculate and graph the average fixed, variable, and total cost per unit and the marginal cost per unit over a range of output and sales.

5. Using revenue and cost data for a firm, identify the level of output at which profits will be maximized, and calculate this maximum level of profits.

6. Using revenue and cost data, calculate the output/sales level above which a firm will make profits (its break-even point).

7. Using revenue and cost data, calculate the output/sales level below which a firm should shut down.

8. Apply the cost and revenue concepts used in this chapter to a variety of situations.

In Chapter 7, we examined the behaviour of the individual business firm under the four basic types of market structures: perfect competition, monopolistic competition, oligopoly, and monopoly. While we discussed various strategies whereby firms could increase their profits under various conditions, we focused our attention on the total (sales) *revenue* of the firm more than its *profits*; indeed, we treated total revenue as if it were the same as profits, speaking in terms of the firm maximizing its total revenue rather than its profits. While this approach allowed us to discuss the limitations facing the business firm and its behaviour under various conditions, it is not really accurate to consider total revenue to be the same as profits. Total revenue is the result of the firm's sales, while profits are the net result of the firm's sales revenues *and* its production costs. In this chapter, we will examine the nature and behaviour of production costs and how they interact with sales revenues to determine not only the business firm's profits but also its decisions regarding prices and output.

As we saw in Chapter 1, the more effectively and efficiently a society's economic resources are used, the more economically prosperous its people will be. In a market economy, business firms make many of the key decisions about the use of economic resources. In seeking to increase their sales and sales income, business firms are trying to use economic resources *effectively*, by producing what buyers want. And in seeking to minimize their costs, business firms are trying to use economic resources *efficiently*, by getting the maximum output from the resources employed. So the more effectively and efficiently business firms use their resources, the higher their profits will be.

Suppose you were managing a business and were considering whether or not to increase your output. Before making that decision, it would be good to know *how much revenue* the additional output would bring you, and *how much it would cost* to produce the additional output. In the following, we will first consider the costs associated with such a decision, then the revenues that would result from it.

Production Costs

To illustrate the nature and behaviour of the production costs of the firm, we will use the example of Barry's Bolts Ltd., one of many small manufacturing firms selling an undifferentiated product (bolts) to industrial buyers in a highly competitive market. Since competition limits Barry's price to $3 per 100 bolts, his success is mainly dependent upon his ability to keep his production cost per 100 bolts as low as possible, by producing bolts as efficiently as possible. From Barry's business, we can learn some of the basic facts related to the production costs of a firm.

Fixed Costs

fixed costs
Production costs that remain constant, regardless of the level of output (for example, rent).

We will suppose that Barry has leased a building and equipment for his business, and that the cost of these, plus other overhead items such as light and heat, amounts to $120 per day. These are called Barry's **fixed costs**, meaning that they will remain at $120 per day regardless of how much he produces. Whether he produces only a few bolts per day or a large number of bolts per day, his fixed costs will be $120. This fact makes it essential that Barry produce and sell a certain number of bolts per day because if his production is too low, the fixed costs *per unit* (a unit is a box of 100 bolts) produced will be so high that he will be unable to make a profit. Barry's research into this matter is shown in Figure 8-1, which shows that fixed costs per 100 bolts are extremely high at low volumes of output. Considering that the market price of 100 bolts is $3, it is apparent that Barry can succeed only if he attains a sufficiently high volume of sales and production to spread his fixed costs over a large number of units. And by doing so, he will keep the fixed costs per 100 bolts low. Generally, then, fixed costs per unit of output are very high at low volumes of output, and decrease as output is increased.

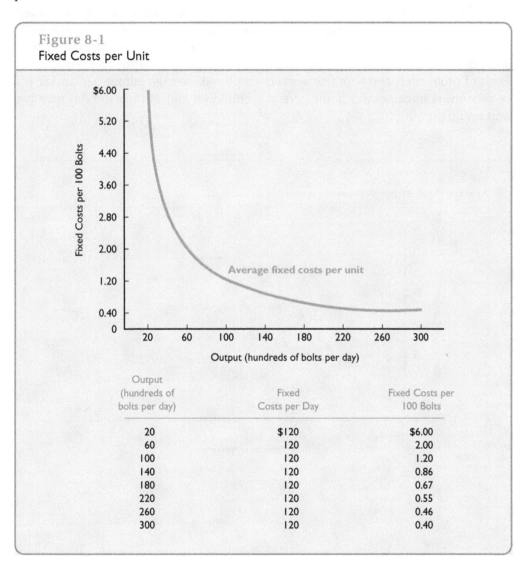

Figure 8-1
Fixed Costs per Unit

Output (hundreds of bolts per day)	Fixed Costs per Day	Fixed Costs per 100 Bolts
20	$120	$6.00
60	120	2.00
100	120	1.20
140	120	0.86
180	120	0.67
220	120	0.55
260	120	0.46
300	120	0.40

Variable Costs

In addition to his fixed costs, Barry will have **variable costs**. These are costs, such as direct labour and materials, that will increase as Barry's output of bolts increases.[1] To simplify our illustration, we will assume that there are no material costs, so that the only variable cost with which we will be concerned is direct labour.

The labour cost per unit (100 bolts) will depend on two factors: how much the average worker is *paid* per day, and how many bolts he or she *produces* per day. At first glance, we might expect both of these factors to be constant regardless of how many bolts the plant produces. That is, hiring additional workers should not affect either the daily wages

variable costs
Production costs that vary with the level of output (for example, direct labour and materials).

---

[1] *Direct* merely specifies that such labour is directly used for producing the product, as distinct from office labour, which is more like fixed or overhead costs.

or the average daily output of the workers. However, the average daily output of each worker will, in fact, change as additional workers are added to Barry's plant.

The reason for this change is that the plant is of a certain size and is best suited to a certain level of production. If production is too far below or too far above this level, efficiency will suffer, and the average daily product of each worker will be below its peak. This relationship between average output per worker and the number of workers is illustrated in Figure 8-2. If only one or two people are working in the plant, the workers will not be able to specialize at particular tasks. Each worker will have to perform so many different tasks as to be unable to do any of them very efficiently. As a result, at low levels of production and with few workers employed, average output per worker will be very low (4 units per day if one person is employed and 14 units per day with two workers on the job).

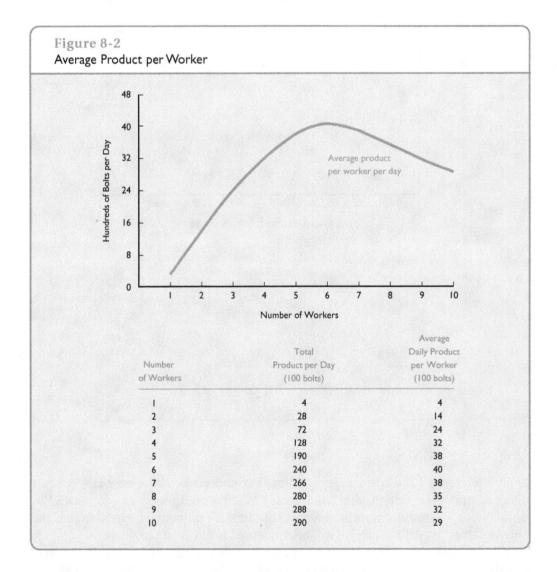

Figure 8-2
Average Product per Worker

Number of Workers	Total Product per Day (100 bolts)	Average Daily Product per Worker (100 bolts)
1	4	4
2	28	14
3	72	24
4	128	32
5	190	38
6	240	40
7	266	38
8	280	35
9	288	32
10	290	29

Barry will find, however, that as he increases production and hires additional workers, average output per worker improves significantly. With more workers in the plant, each can become more specialized. Some can prepare materials for production, some can operate the bolt-making machinery, some can finish and paint the bolts, while others can package them for shipping. As each worker becomes more specialized, efficiency increases and average output per worker rises considerably, reaching 40 units per day when six workers are employed.

However, Barry will find that hiring additional workers improves output per worker only up to a certain point. As Figure 8-2 shows, once Barry hires additional workers beyond the sixth, average output per worker *decreases*, because Barry's plant is only so large, and we have moved beyond the point at which it operates at *peak efficiency*. The addition of more workers does not increase the opportunities for specialization as it did earlier; in effect, the additional workers are crowding the fixed amount of equipment in the plant, and therefore are actually reducing the efficiency of the workforce, or average output per worker. As Figure 8-2 shows, the addition of the seventh through tenth workers causes the plant's *total* output to rise, but *average output per worker* decreases once production is past the level of peak efficiency for that plant.

This phenomenon is known as the **Law of Diminishing Returns**, which can be stated in general terms as follows: "If additional units of one productive input (here, labour) are combined with a fixed quantity of another productive input (here, capital equipment), the average output per unit of the variable input (labour) will increase at first, and then decrease."

The Law of Diminishing Returns places an important limitation on Barry's production decisions. While Barry *physically can* increase output to certain levels, doing so may reduce efficiency to such an extent that it becomes *unprofitable* to increase output, because the cost of producing each additional unit would be too high.

Marginal Productivity

We can analyze the data in Figure 8-2 in another useful way: rather than looking at total output, or average output per worker, we can examine the *increase* in production resulting from the hiring of *one additional worker*, or the **marginal productivity** (marginal output) per worker. This information is presented on the next page in Figure 8-3, which shows that the hiring of the fifth worker increases production by 62 units, and the sixth worker adds 50 units to total output. After that, additional workers add much less. The seventh worker only increases production by 26 units, the eighth and ninth only add 14 units and 8 units, respectively, while the tenth worker barely adds to total output at all—his/her marginal output is only 2 units. It is important to remember that this does not mean that the quality of the workers is declining. The reason for the decrease in marginal output per worker is the Law of Diminishing Returns: once production in Barry's plant moves past the point of peak efficiency, average output per worker will decrease because each additional worker will not add as much to output as previous workers did. This diminishing return will have an important impact on production costs because the cost of the extra units (marginal output) produced by additional workers will rise very rapidly beyond a certain point, making it uneconomical to hire workers and increase output beyond that point. For instance, it is very doubtful that the small marginal output of the ninth and tenth workers (8 units and 2 units, respectively) would make it profitable to hire them. Or, viewed differently, the cost per unit of increasing output from 280 units to 290 units would be so high as to be uneconomical.

The cost and productivity factors that we have been discussing restrict Barry's production decisions. Because fixed costs per unit are very high at low levels of output, he must achieve a certain level of production (and sales) in order to operate economically. However, due to the Law of Diminishing Returns, it will not prove economical to increase his output beyond a certain point, since the variable costs per unit (labour costs) will rise to higher levels, as Figure 8-4 shows.

Law of Diminishing Returns
A physical law stating that, if additional units of one productive input (such as labour) are combined with a fixed quantity of another productive input (such as capital), the average product per unit of the variable input (labour) will increase at first and then decrease.

marginal productivity (per worker)
The increase in production resulting from the hiring of one additional worker.

Figure 8-3
Average and Marginal Productivity per Worker

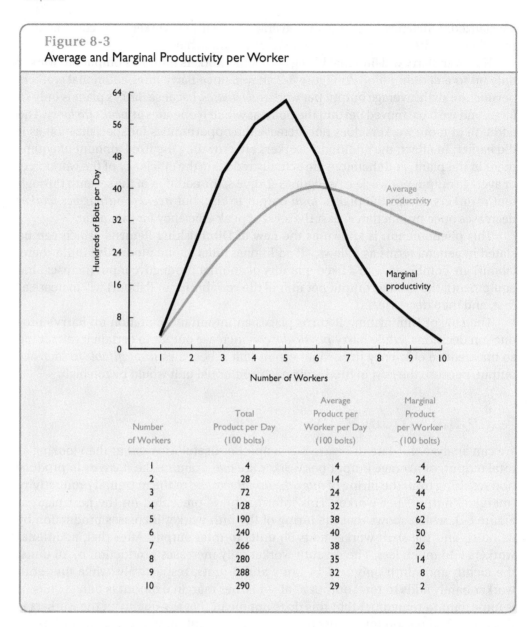

Number of Workers	Total Product per Day (100 bolts)	Average Product per Worker per Day (100 bolts)	Marginal Product per Worker (100 bolts)
1	4	4	4
2	28	14	24
3	72	24	44
4	128	32	56
5	190	38	62
6	240	40	50
7	266	38	26
8	280	35	14
9	288	32	8
10	290	29	2

In general terms, then, we have outlined the situation Barry's firm faces with respect to production costs, and how this will affect its operations. On the basis of these two figures, Barry can make two more calculations that will help to decide exactly what volume of output to produce. These are the average cost per unit and the marginal cost per unit.

Average Cost per Unit

Table 8-1 summarizes the production costs of Barry's bolt plant. The information in the table is based on the production information discussed earlier: *fixed costs* of $120 per day regardless of the level of output, and *variable costs* consisting only of wages of $60 per day for each worker. *Total costs* are fixed costs plus variable costs, and *average cost per unit* is total costs divided by total output. As we saw earlier, at low levels of output, average cost per unit is high, because of high fixed costs per unit. As output increases, the plant operates more efficiently, reaching a minimum average cost per

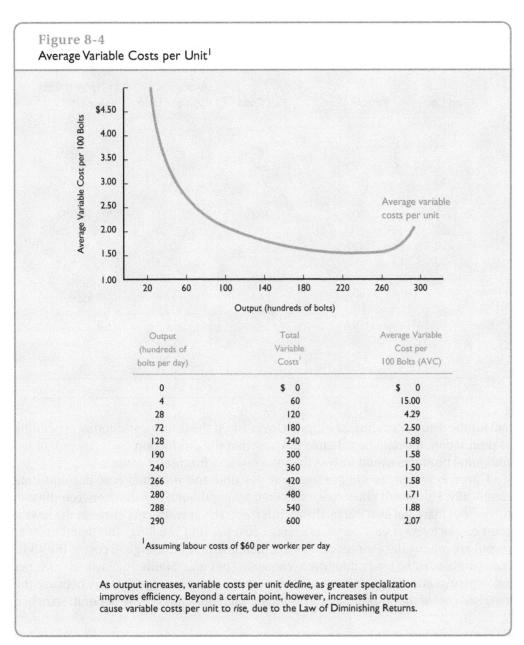

Figure 8-4
Average Variable Costs per Unit[1]

Output (hundreds of bolts per day)	Total Variable Costs[1]	Average Variable Cost per 100 Bolts (AVC)
0	$ 0	$ 0
4	60	15.00
28	120	4.29
72	180	2.50
128	240	1.88
190	300	1.58
240	360	1.50
266	420	1.58
280	480	1.71
288	540	1.88
290	600	2.07

[1] Assuming labour costs of $60 per worker per day

As output increases, variable costs per unit *decline*, as greater specialization improves efficiency. Beyond a certain point, however, increases in output cause variable costs per unit to *rise*, due to the Law of Diminishing Returns.

unit of $2 at a daily output level of 240 units. Further increases in output cause the plant to operate beyond its most efficient level, so that the Law of Diminishing Returns pushes variable costs per unit up again. As a result, average cost per unit increases still further, rising to $2.48 at an output level of 290 units per day.

Marginal Cost per Unit

The last column in Table 8-1 on the next page—marginal cost per unit—requires some explanation. **Marginal cost per unit** is the addition to total costs resulting from the production of one additional unit of output. For instance, when output is increased from 4 units to 28 units, total costs rise from $180 to $240. In other words, it costs $60 more to increase output by 24 units, making the cost of each additional unit (the marginal cost per unit) $2.50 ($60 ÷ 24). These calculations, together with other examples, are shown in Table 8-2 on the next page. Marginal cost per unit can be an important

marginal cost per unit
The addition to total costs resulting from the production of one more additional unit of output.

Table 8-1
The Costs of the Firm

Number of Workers	Total Output per Day[a]	Fixed Costs	Variable Costs	Total Costs	Average Cost per Unit[b]	Marginal Cost per Unit[c]
0	0	$120	$0	$120	—	—
1	4	120	60	180	$45.00	$15.00
2	28	120	120	240	8.57	2.50
3	72	120	180	300	4.17	1.36
4	128	120	240	360	2.81	1.07
5	190	120	300	420	2.21	0.97
6	240	120	360	480	2.00	1.20
7	266	120	420	540	2.03	2.31
8	280	120	480	600	2.14	4.29
9	288	120	540	660	2.29	7.50
10	290	120	600	720	2.48	30.00

[a] Output measured in units of 100 bolts

[b] $\dfrac{\text{Total costs}}{\text{Total output}}$ [c] $\dfrac{\text{Change in total costs}}{\text{Change in total output}}$

tool for the firm in deciding its output. Obviously, if the firm is considering expanding its production, it would be valuable to know that the production costs per unit of the additional products would be less than the revenue from selling them.

Figure 8-5 presents the average cost per unit and marginal cost per unit data graphically. This graph illustrates a fact concerning the relationship between the two curves: the marginal cost curve always intersects the average cost curve at the lowest point on the average cost curve. If average cost per unit is falling, additional units of output are pulling the average cost down, meaning that the marginal cost of the additional units must be lower than the average cost per unit. Similarly, if average cost per unit is rising, additional units of output are pulling the average cost up, because the marginal cost of the additional units is higher than the average cost per unit. So, when

Table 8-2
Calculation of Marginal Cost per Unit

Total Output per Day	Total Costs	Marginal Cost per Unit of 100 Bolts	=	Increase in Total Costs / Increase in Total Output
0	$120			
4	180	$15.00	=	$\dfrac{\$180 - 120}{4 - 0}$
28	240	2.50	=	$\dfrac{\$240 - 180}{28 - 4}$
72	300	1.36	=	$\dfrac{\$300 - 240}{72 - 28}$

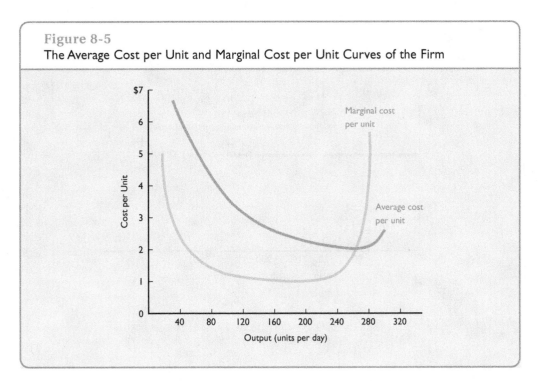

Figure 8-5
The Average Cost per Unit and Marginal Cost per Unit Curves of the Firm

average cost is falling, marginal cost is below the average, and when average cost is rising, marginal cost is above the average—it is only at that point where average cost is at its minimum (neither falling nor rising) that average cost per unit and marginal cost per unit are exactly the same, and the curves intersect. Beyond this output level, as Figure 8-5 shows, marginal cost per unit rises very quickly, as the Law of Diminishing Returns makes it increasingly difficult to increase output by simply adding more workers to the plant.

To summarize information about Barry's production costs, increasing output causes average cost per unit to decrease until it reaches a minimum at an output level around 240 units per day. At output levels beyond these outputs, average cost per unit increases again, and rapidly rising marginal cost per unit makes increasing output beyond a certain point uneconomical. What this "certain point" is—and at what level of output Barry will actually decide to produce—will depend not only on how much additional units *cost* to produce but also on how much additional *revenue* they bring in. To complete our analysis of Barry's bolt firm, we must now consider the revenues, or *sales* of the business.

The Revenue Side

Average Revenue per Unit

We will assume that Barry's is one of many small firms in the highly competitive bolt industry, and that the market price of bolts is $3 per unit (box) of 100 bolts. At this price, the firm can sell as many bolts as it can produce, up to its maximum possible output of 290 units per day. In other words, the demand for Barry's product is perfectly elastic, as shown by the demand schedule and demand curve in Figure 8-6. Figure 8-6 also shows that the *price* of the product can be viewed as the *average revenue per unit*; since the firm can sell as many as it produces for $3 per unit of 100 bolts, the *demand curve* can be viewed as the *average revenue per unit sold*.

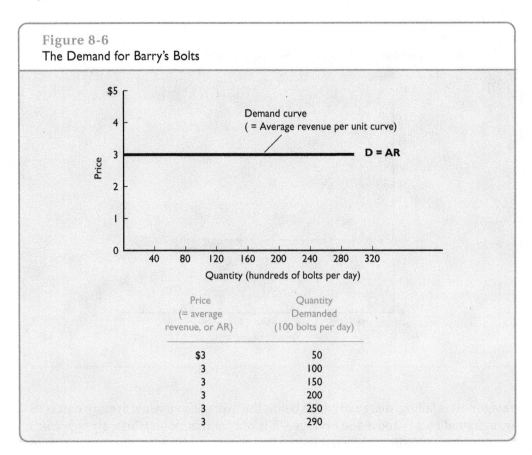

Figure 8-6
The Demand for Barry's Bolts

Price (= average revenue, or AR)	Quantity Demanded (100 bolts per day)
$3	50
3	100
3	150
3	200
3	250
3	290

Marginal Revenue per Unit

From the demand for Barry's bolts, we can develop a table of information concerning the firm's sales revenues, as shown in Table 8-3. Since the firm can only charge $3 per unit, the average revenue per unit is always $3. *Total revenue*, which is simply price (or average revenue) times quantity demanded, rises in proportion to sales. **Marginal revenue per unit** is the addition to total revenue gained from the sale of one more unit. It can be calculated in the same way as we calculate marginal cost per unit, by dividing the increase in total revenue by the increase in units sold; in each case, total revenue

marginal revenue per unit

The addition to total revenue resulting from the sale of one additional unit of output.

Table 8-3
The Revenue Side of Barry's Bolts

Price (= Average Revenue per Unit)	×	Quantity Demanded per day	=	Total Revenue per day	Marginal Revenue per Unit[a]
$3		50		$150	
3		100		300	$3
3		150		450	3
3		200		600	3
3		250		750	3
3		290		870	3

[a] $\frac{\text{Increase in total revenue}}{\text{Increase in quantity sold}}$

rises by $150 and the number of units sold rises by 50, making the marginal revenue per unit $3 at all levels of sales. With the price always $3 per unit, each additional unit sold will always bring in marginal revenue of $3, making the marginal revenue curve identical to the demand curve and the average revenue curve, as Figure 8-7 shows.

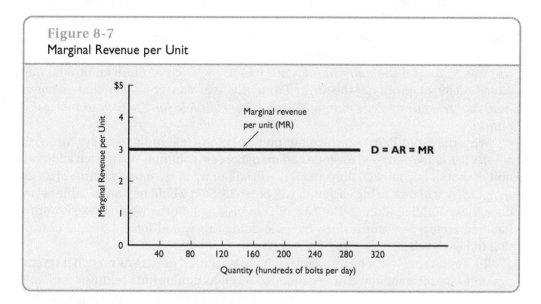

Figure 8-7
Marginal Revenue per Unit

The Most Profitable Output

We now have all of the information about Barry's costs and revenues that the firm needs in order to decide what level of output to produce. Table 8-4 summarizes all of the information we have developed about Barry's costs and revenues and adds a column for total profits, which are total revenue minus total costs. The table shows that low levels of output are unprofitable due to fixed costs, and that profits are maximized at $258 per day by producing 266 units of 100 bolts per day, using 7 workers.

Table 8-4
The Costs and Revenues of Barry's Bolts

Number of Workers	Total Output per day	Fixed Costs	Variable Costs	Total Costs	Total Revenue	Total Profit (+) or Loss (−)Cost	Average Cost per Unit	Marginal Cost per Unit	Marginal Revenue per Unit
0	0	$120	$ 0	$120	$ 0	−$120	—	—	—
1	4	120	60	180	12	− 168	$45.00	$15.00	$3.00
2	28	120	120	240	84	− 156	8.57	2.50	3.00
3	72	120	180	300	216	− 84	4.17	1.36	3.00
4	128	120	240	360	384	+ 24	2.81	1.07	3.00
5	190	120	300	420	570	+ 150	2.21	0.97	3.00
6	240	120	360	480	720	+ 240	2.00	1.20	3.00
7	266	120	420	540	798	+ 258	2.03	2.31	3.00
8	280	120	480	600	840	+ 240	2.14	4.29	3.00
9	288	120	540	660	864	+ 204	2.29	7.50	3.00
10	290	120	600	720	870	+ 150	2.48	30.00	3.00

Tools of Analysis

While it is easy to see why Barry would choose to produce 266 units per day, we can use this simple example to develop other, more sophisticated concepts. Why didn't Barry choose to produce 240 units per day? (This is the output at which the firm operates at peak efficiency and production costs per unit are minimized at $2.) The answer lies in the marginal cost per unit and marginal revenue per unit columns. For each of the extra 26 units (from 240 units to 266 units per day), the *marginal cost* was $2.31 and the *marginal revenue* was $3. So each of these additional units *added* $0.69 of profit to the firm. From this, we can conclude that *whenever marginal revenue exceeds marginal cost, it is profitable for the firm to increase its output.*

Why, then, did Barry not increase output *beyond* 266 units per day? Again, the answer lies in the marginal revenue and marginal cost columns. While each additional unit of output beyond 266 units per day will still bring in *marginal revenue* of $3, the *marginal cost* of producing each unit will be $4.29. So it would be unprofitable to produce these additional units. The Law of Diminishing Returns would make it unprofitable to increase output further, because doing this would force marginal cost per unit to high levels.

To summarize, it will be profitable to increase output as long as marginal revenue per unit exceeds marginal cost per unit. However, as diminishing returns set in, marginal cost per unit will rise, and once marginal cost per unit becomes greater than marginal revenue per unit, it will no longer be profitable to increase production. So profits will be maximized at that level of output at which marginal cost equals marginal revenue—that is, where the marginal cost curve intersects the marginal revenue curve. For example, in Figure 8-8, profits would be maximized by producing 100 units of out-

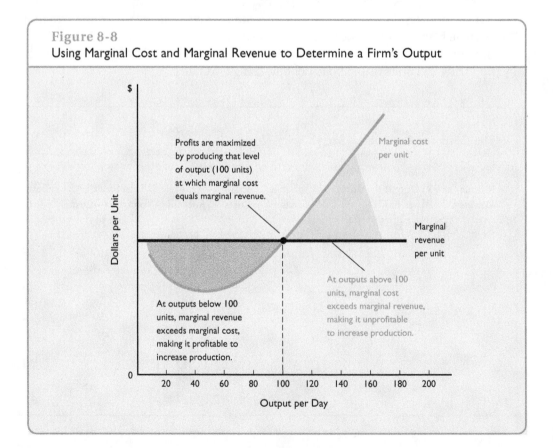

Figure 8-8
Using Marginal Cost and Marginal Revenue to Determine a Firm's Output

Profits are maximized by producing that level of output (100 units) at which marginal cost equals marginal revenue.

Marginal cost per unit

Marginal revenue per unit

At outputs below 100 units, marginal revenue exceeds marginal cost, making it profitable to increase production.

At outputs above 100 units, marginal cost exceeds marginal revenue, making it unprofitable to increase production.

Dollars per Unit

Output per Day

put. In the remainder of this chapter, we will use this approach to analyze the price and output decisions of business firms under different market structures, starting with perfect competition as discussed in Chapter 7.

YOU DECIDE

Making Business Decisions

In the graph in Figure 8-8, the firm will maximize its profits by producing 100 units per day.

QUESTIONS

1. State two different changes in the firm's revenues and costs as shown on the graph that would cause the firm to *increase* its output, and explain *why* output would increase in each case.
2. How would the firm's decision regarding its output change if the price of its product decreased? Explain why this would happen.
3. How would the firm's decision regarding its output change if its production costs (including marginal cost per unit) increased? Explain why this would happen.

Different Market Structures

Perfect Competition

As we saw in Chapter 7, perfect competition is a rare situation in which there are many small firms in an industry, it is easy for new firms to enter the industry, and all firms are selling identical products. The result is the most competitive situation imaginable, in which producers have no control over the price of their products and there is constant downward pressure on profits. Using analysis based on costs and revenues as developed earlier in this chapter, we can now examine the case of perfect competition more closely.

The costs and revenues of the firm in perfect competition will be like those of Barry's Bolts Ltd., which we described as a small firm in a highly competitive industry. The cost curves will have the usual shapes as were described earlier in this chapter, with average cost per unit decreasing as output increases up to a point, then increasing again.[2] The marginal cost per unit curve rises quite sharply beyond a certain output level and intersects the average cost per unit curve at that curve's minimum point, as shown in Figure 8-9. In perfect competition, the existence of many small firms selling identical products ensures that the demand for any one firm's product will be perfectly elastic. So, if the market price of the product is $3 per unit, the demand curve of the individual firm will consist of a horizontal line at a price of $3, as in Figure 8-9. This line will also represent the *average revenue* from each sale (AR) and the *marginal revenue* (MR) for each additional sale, as indicated on the graph.

Figure 8-9 on the next page shows a profitable individual firm in a perfectly competitive industry. *Profits* are maximized by producing the output at which marginal

---

[2] The shapes of the cost curves are determined by physical factors such as the Law of Diminishing Returns; as a result, cost curves have the same general shape regardless of whether the firm is small or large, or in an industry that is highly competitive, oligopolistic, or monopolistic.

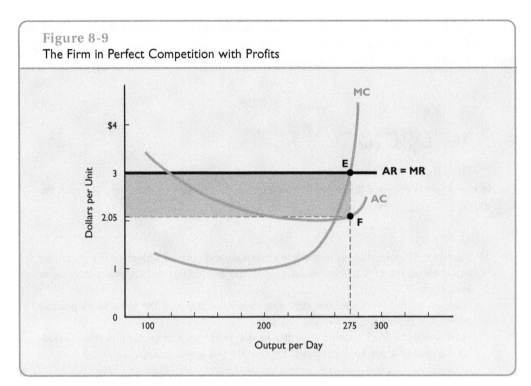

Figure 8-9
The Firm in Perfect Competition with Profits

cost equals marginal revenue (or price), which is 275 units per day, as point E indicates. Total revenue will be $825 per day ($3 × 275 units). Point F indicates that, at an output level of 275 units, average cost per unit is $2.05, and total costs are $564 ($2.05 × 275 units). So total daily profit will be maximized at $261 ($825 – $564), at an output level of 275 units. The shaded area on the graph represents the total profit (275 × $0.95) earned by the firm in this situation.

Dynamics of Perfect Competition

If the firm we have been discussing is a typical firm in the industry, the situation cannot remain as it is shown in Figure 8-9. The profitability of firms in this industry will attract new competitors into the industry, increasing the supply of the product and *reducing its price*. When this happens, the demand curve (labelled AR = MR in Figure 8-9) will move downward as the price declines, reducing the profits of a typical firm. How far can the price fall? Figure 8-10 shows what would happen if the price fell to $1.50: at *every* level of output, average cost per unit exceeds average revenue per unit. As a result, it would be impossible to make a profit at a price of $1.50. By producing 250 units, where marginal cost equals marginal revenue, the firm could minimize its losses, but it would still be losing money.

If the typical firm in the industry were losing money, it is obvious that some firms would have to leave the industry—a polite way of saying that they would go bankrupt. As they left, the supply of the product would decrease, and the price would increase again. How high will the price rise, and at what level will it settle? Figure 8-11 provides the answer: the price will rise to (and settle at) just under $2 per unit, at which point output will be 260 units. At this price, two conditions exist:

(a) marginal cost equals marginal revenue, so that the firm's profits are maximized, and the firm has no incentive to increase or decrease its output, and

(b) average cost equals average revenue, so that profits are zero, providing no incentive for anyone to enter or leave the industry.

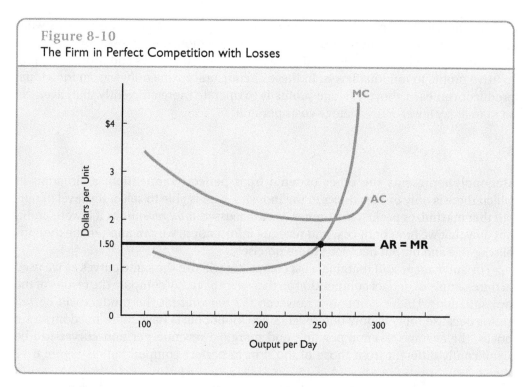

Figure 8-10
The Firm in Perfect Competition with Losses

Since one might wonder why anyone would even stay in a business with no profits, we should define profits more precisely. By *profits* we mean business income *over and above the owner-manager's salary,* which represents the opportunity cost of the owner's time and capital. Viewed differently, we assume that the owner–manager will only continue in business if a certain minimum income level is earned, and include that person's salary in the production costs of the business, as a fixed cost.

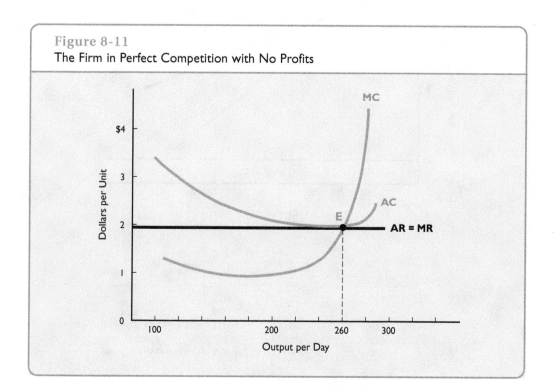

Figure 8-11
The Firm in Perfect Competition with No Profits

In conclusion, then, our marginal revenue/marginal cost analysis confirms what we said in Chapter 7 about the firm in perfect competition: the intense competition in such industries will exert constant downward pressure on prices and profits, tending to drive profits to minimal levels. In these circumstances, the only way an individual producer can earn above-average profits is to operate more efficiently than average, so as to enjoy lower-than-average costs per unit.

Monopoly

Monopoly represents the other extreme from perfect competition: a situation in which there is only *one* producer in the industry, who is able to select the level of output that maximizes profits. In Chapter 7, we discussed *total revenue* as if it were profit, but now that we have both cost and revenue information, we can analyze the monopolist's price and output decisions more precisely.

For our average and marginal cost curves, we will use the same curves as we used in the example of perfect competition so that we can readily compare the results of the two situations. Under monopoly, however, the *demand* for the product will be *less elastic* because there is only one seller. Since monopolists have more freedom to set prices, the average revenue per unit and marginal revenue per unit curves will be significantly different from those of the firm in perfect competition, as Figure 8-12 shows.

As output is increased, marginal revenue per unit falls more rapidly than average revenue per unit, or the demand curve. The reason why marginal revenue per unit

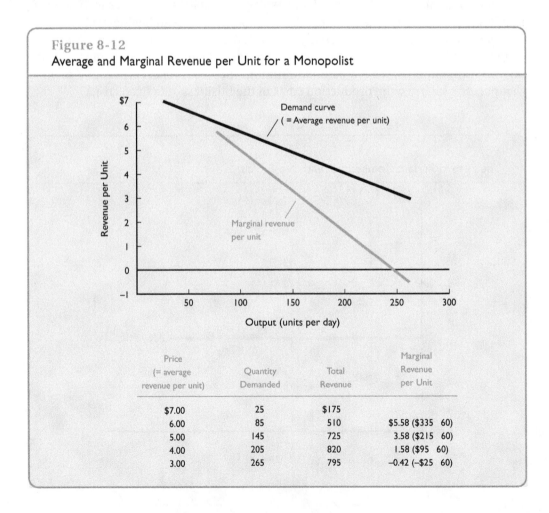

Figure 8-12
Average and Marginal Revenue per Unit for a Monopolist

Price (= average revenue per unit)	Quantity Demanded	Total Revenue	Marginal Revenue per Unit
$7.00	25	$175	
6.00	85	510	$5.58 ($335 ÷ 60)
5.00	145	725	3.58 ($215 ÷ 60)
4.00	205	820	1.58 ($95 ÷ 60)
3.00	265	795	–0.42 (–$25 ÷ 60)

falls so rapidly is that, in order to *sell more units*, the monopolist must *reduce the price*, not only on the additional units sold but also *on all units sold*. For instance, when sales are increased from 85 units to 145 units by reducing prices from $6 to $5, the additional 60 units sold bring in $300 ($5 × 60), but there is $85 less total revenue on the first 85 units, because they are selling for $1 less per unit. So the net marginal revenue on the 60 additional units is $215 ($300 – $85), or $3.85 per unit, as shown in Figure 8-12. As sales increase, the monopolist's marginal revenue curve will fall, and will fall more steeply than the demand curve does—a fact that will have an important bearing on the monopolist's price and output decisions.

Price and Output Decisions

To maximize profits, the monopolist will follow our rule of producing that output at which marginal revenue equals marginal costs. Figure 8-13 shows that doing this will result in a decision to produce 220 units of output per day. Point P on the demand curve shows that, to sell 220 units per day, a price of $3.75 per unit must be charged. Thus, the monopolist will maximize profits by charging a price of $3.75 and producing 220 units per day. At this level of output, the monopolist's average revenue per unit will be $3.75 (the price), and average cost per unit will be $2.10 (from point C on the average cost curve). The average profit per unit will then be $1.65 ($3.75 – $2.10), and the monopolist's total profits will be $363 per day ($1.65 × 220). The shaded area on the graph in Figure 8-13 represents these profits.

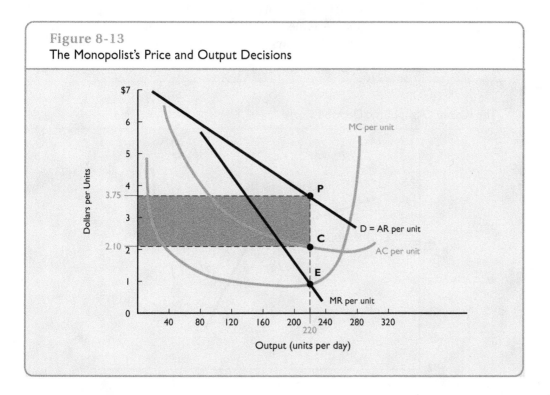

Figure 8-13
The Monopolist's Price and Output Decisions

Monopoly and Competition Compared

In a perfectly competitive industry, we saw that the price of each firm's product would be $1.95, the output of a typical firm would be 260 units per day (Figure 8-11), and that competition would push profits downward toward the minimum level required to keep firms in business. Under monopoly, and using the same cost curves, the price would be $3.75, output would be 220 units (Figure 8-13), and there would be substantial profits.[3] Furthermore, because new firms cannot enter the industry, these profits are secure from competition.

Oligopoly

In Chapter 7, we saw that, while the price and output decisions of oligopolistic industries were of great importance, we could not develop a theoretical basis for analyzing and predicting those decisions. In this chapter, we have developed considerably more sophisticated techniques for analyzing the costs, revenues, and price and output decisions of the firm. However, we are still unable to analyze and predict the decisions of oligopolists precisely, even using these techniques. The problem lies in the nature of the oligopolist's demand curve.

Figure 8-14 shows the demand curve for one firm in an oligopolistic industry in which the firms have agreed upon a price of $6. If this one firm increases its price and the other firms leave their prices at the agreed level of $6, the firm that increases its price will suffer a considerable loss of sales and profits. And if one firm reduces its price, it is reasonable to assume that the other firms will match its price reduction. In that case, the firm that reduces its price will not gain in terms of its market share, and will very likely lose financially. So the demand curve for an oligopolistic firm tends to be "kinked," as Figure 8-14 shows. For price increases, demand is elastic, while for price reductions, it is inelastic. Therefore, a single firm cannot gain by either increasing or decreasing its price. So once the price has been established, there is an incentive for each firm to leave its price at that level, until all the firms agree to a new price.

Marginal cost and marginal revenue analysis does not help us to analyze oligopolists' decisions further. As Figure 8-15 shows, even the most modest kink in the demand

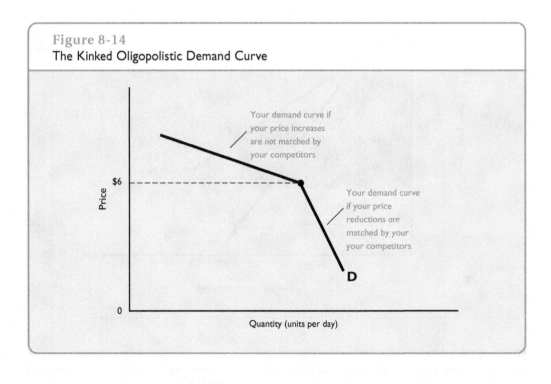

Figure 8-14
The Kinked Oligopolistic Demand Curve

---

[3] For comparative purposes, we have used the same cost curves for the small firm in perfect competition and for the monopolist. This ignores the possibility that the monopolist's costs per unit may in fact be *lower* than the small firm's, due to improved technology and mass-production techniques. We will consider this possibility further in Chapter 9.

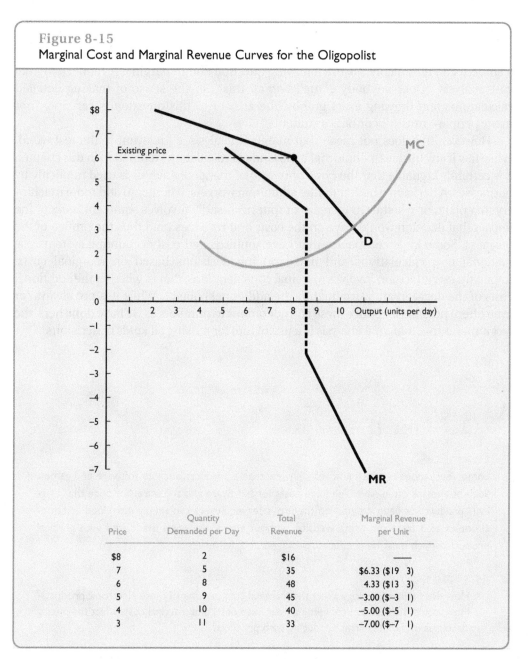

Figure 8-15
Marginal Cost and Marginal Revenue Curves for the Oligopolist

Price	Quantity Demanded per Day	Total Revenue	Marginal Revenue per Unit
$8	2	$16	——
7	5	35	$6.33 ($19 3)
6	8	48	4.33 ($13 3)
5	9	45	−3.00 ($−3 1)
4	10	40	−5.00 ($−5 1)
3	11	33	−7.00 ($−7 1)

curve causes strange changes in the marginal revenue curve. At the level of output where the demand curve is kinked, the marginal revenue curve becomes *discontinuous* (see the dotted line in Figure 8-15), leaving us with no clear intersection point for the marginal cost and marginal revenue curves. As a result of this, marginal cost and marginal revenue analysis cannot help to pinpoint oligopolists' price and output decisions. All we can say is that the existence of a kinked demand curve provides a strong incentive for individual oligopolists to leave their price and output unchanged. As Figure 8-15 shows, it would take a major increase in production costs (upward shift of the marginal cost curve) to cause our oligopolist to reduce output and increase prices, while there is no reduction in cost large enough to induce a price reduction. So all that we can conclude concerning oligopolistic prices through marginal cost and marginal revenue analysis is what we concluded in Chapter 7—that, once set by the industry, oligopolistic prices tend to remain stable until the firm's decide to change them together.

How Realistic Is All This?

A student can reasonably ask the following question about marginal revenue/marginal cost analysis: "Does anybody actually *do* all this?" In the sense of making detailed calculations and drawing exact graphs, the answer to this question is certainly "not many people—mostly economics students."

However, this does not mean that marginal analysis is irrelevant in the real world. While few if any businesspeople make the kinds of calculations referred to in this chapter, it is certainly arguable that the *basic approach* of marginal analysis is used implicitly by businesses. A decision whether to hire additional workers, whether to add more machinery to a plant, or whether to increase output necessarily involves some *estimates* of the impact that decision would have on the costs and revenues (and thus the profits) of the business. Some large companies that have sophisticated cost accounting systems use marginal cost calculations and make pricing decisions based on marginal costs. Implicitly, *every* decision involves marginal considerations; that is, whether the additional costs of the decision are warranted by the additional benefits. While it is not always (or even often) possible to reduce these considerations to numbers as we have done here, the fact remains that marginal analysis is a useful tool for making all kinds of decisions.

YOU DECIDE

Ebusiness Costs

Some ebusinesses produce and sell only electronic products, such as software and games. Such businesses often have high fixed costs for hardware and software, but once the "original" product has been created on the firm's server, buyers can simply download additional copies of it from the firm's website, without any of the costs associated with physical products, which must be produced, packaged, and delivered. ▪

QUESTIONS
1. How does this technology affect the marginal cost per unit of these electronic products?
2. How would the situation concerning their fixed costs and marginal costs affect the pricing strategies of business firms producing such products?

Other Business Decisions

We have seen in this chapter how cost and revenue data (in particular, marginal cost and marginal revenue) can be used to determine the most profitable level of output for a firm. There are two other basic business decisions for which cost and revenue data are vitally important: whether to start a new business and whether to shut down an existing business. For example, the owner of Barry's Bolts can use the cost and revenue data in Table 8-1 to decide:
(a) what volume of sales the firm must achieve in order to justify *starting up* the business, and
(b) how low the firm's sales could fall before the business should be *closed*.

The Start-Up Decision

In deciding whether to start up his business, the owner of Barry's Bolts faces the key question of whether he can sell enough bolts to cover the firm's costs. Because high fixed costs per unit cause the average cost per unit to be high at low levels of output, the firm must achieve a certain volume of sales in order to cover its costs, or break even. To make this decision, the owner will use average cost and average revenue data rather than the marginal cost and revenue data that we used for determining the most profitable level of output.

Figure 8-16 shows the relationship between average cost and average revenue in this way: if the price per 100 bolts (average revenue per unit) is $3, Barry must sell more than 118 units of 100 bolts per day in order to make a profit. At point A, with an

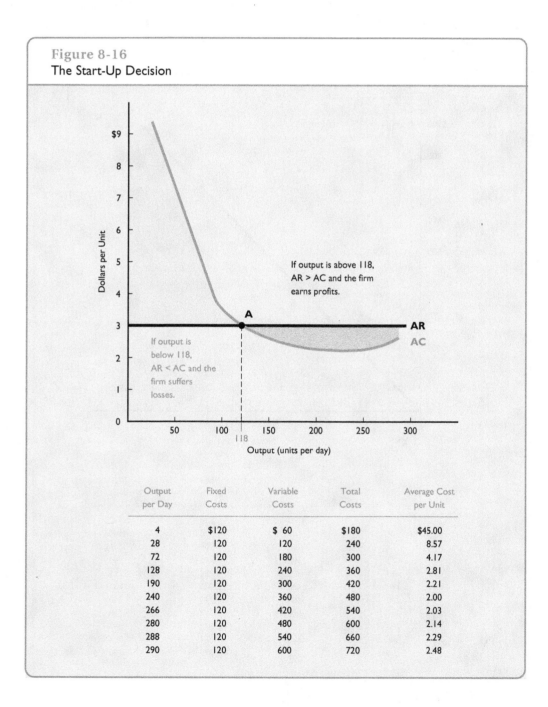

Figure 8-16
The Start-Up Decision

Output per Day	Fixed Costs	Variable Costs	Total Costs	Average Cost per Unit
4	$120	$ 60	$180	$45.00
28	120	120	240	8.57
72	120	180	300	4.17
128	120	240	360	2.81
190	120	300	420	2.21
240	120	360	480	2.00
266	120	420	540	2.03
280	120	480	600	2.14
288	120	540	660	2.29
290	120	600	720	2.48

output of 118 units, average cost and average revenue per unit are equal, making Barry's profit zero—the firm is breaking even.

At output levels below 118 units, average cost exceeds average revenue per unit, and Barry loses money, while at output levels above 118 units, average revenue exceeds average cost per unit, and Barry earns a profit. Unless the firm's owner can realistically plan on sales in excess of 118 units per day, he should not start up in business.

In business terminology, 118 units per day is said to be Barry's *break-even point*, because at this level of output the firm just barely covers its costs, or breaks even. Break-even analysis similar to that shown in Figure 8-16 is useful when considering whether to start a business; however, it is usually done with *total cost* and *total revenue* data, as shown in Figure 8-17 on the next page, rather than with average cost and revenue data.

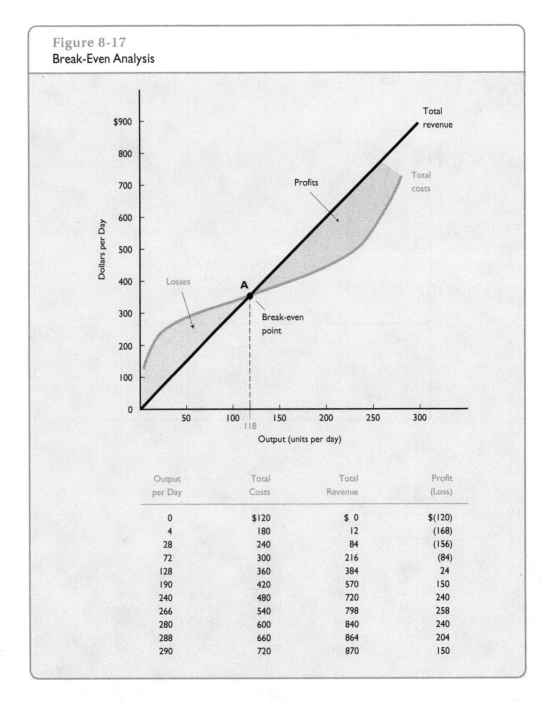

Figure 8-17
Break-Even Analysis

Output per Day	Total Costs	Total Revenue	Profit (Loss)
0	$120	$ 0	$(120)
4	180	12	(168)
28	240	84	(156)
72	300	216	(84)
128	360	384	24
190	420	570	150
240	480	720	240
266	540	798	258
280	600	840	240
288	660	864	204
290	720	870	150

The total cost and total revenue data in Figure 8-17 lead Barry to the same conclusion reached earlier: the firm must sell more than 118 units per day in order to make a profit. At sales of 118 per day (point A), it breaks even, with total revenue equal to total costs. At lower levels of output, total costs exceed total revenue, causing the firm to lose money. Only by selling more than 118 units per day can Barry earn a profit.

Figure 8-17 illustrates another point seen earlier in this chapter: the firm will not maximize profits by producing as much output as is physically possible. If output is increased beyond a certain point, the Law of Diminishing Returns causes costs to increase rapidly, making it unprofitable to increase output further. Rather, profits are maximized at an output level of 266 units per day, as we saw earlier.

The Shut-Down Decision

Suppose that, some time after Barry's Bolts was established, the firm's sales begin to decrease. How low can sales fall before the owner should decide to go out of business?

The key factor in this situation is that, even if Barry stops production, he must still pay his fixed costs, such as rent, interest on debt, and so on.[4] To stop production means incurring fixed costs (losses) of $120 per day. Consequently, it would be better for Barry's Bolts to remain in business (at least in the short run), as long as its losses are *less* than $120 per day. For instance, the table in Figure 8-18 shows that if sales fall to 72 units per day, the firm will lose $84 per day—$36 *less* than the $120 it would lose by stopping production altogether. Why is this so? Because while the firm *is* incurring losses, its total revenue of $216 exceeds its variable costs of $180 by $36. As a result, by continuing production, it can use this $36 to offset some of the fixed costs, so that it loses $84 rather than the $120 it would lose by stopping production completely. The firm is therefore $36 better off (or less badly off) to remain in business producing 72 units per day, than to stop altogether.

As a general rule, we can conclude that as long as total revenue exceeds variable costs, the firm should remain in business rather than close down, because its losses will be smaller. Put differently, only when variable costs exceed total revenue should the firm close. For Barry's Bolts, this occurs when sales fall below 55 units per day, as the graph in Figure 8-18 shows. If the firm cannot sell 55 units per day, it should close down.

These examples show that cost and revenue data can be used not only to determine the most profitable level of output for a firm but also to determine the minimum level of sales required to start up a business, and the level of sales at which a decision is made to shut down the business.

---

[4] These fixed costs must still be paid in the short run; for instance, rent must be paid until his lease expires. Over a longer period of time, *all* costs can be viewed as variable (particularly if the firm goes out of business!).

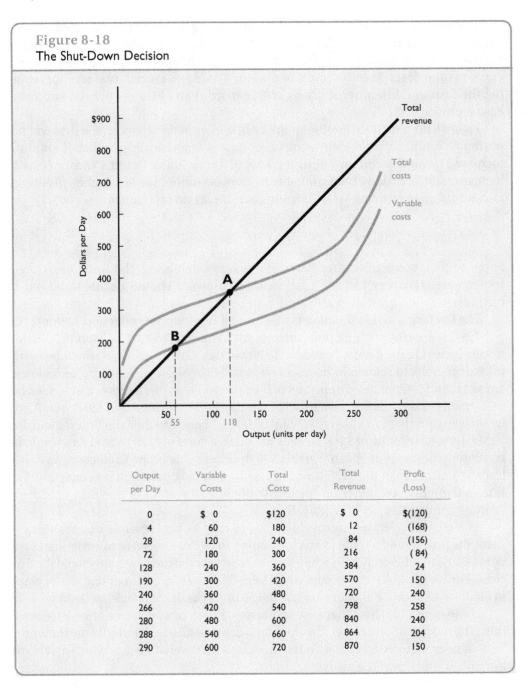

Figure 8-18
The Shut-Down Decision

Output per Day	Variable Costs	Total Costs	Total Revenue	Profit (Loss)
0	$ 0	$120	$ 0	$(120)
4	60	180	12	(168)
28	120	240	84	(156)
72	180	300	216	(84)
128	240	360	384	24
190	300	420	570	150
240	360	480	720	240
266	420	540	798	258
280	480	600	840	240
288	540	660	864	204
290	600	720	870	150

Chapter Summary

1. As output is increased, fixed costs remain constant, while variable costs increase. (L.O. 1)
2. A firm's average costs per unit are high at low levels of output, due to high fixed costs; then, they decline as output increases. Beyond a certain output level, however, average costs per unit rise again, as variable costs per unit increase due to the Law of Diminishing Returns. (L.O. 2)
3. The marginal cost per unit curve will rise quite sharply beyond a certain output level, intersecting the average cost per unit curve at that curve's minimum point. (L.O. 2, 4)

4. A firm's profits will be maximized by producing the output level at which marginal cost equals marginal revenue. (L.O. 3, 4, 5)

5. Under perfect competition, there will be a horizontal demand (or average revenue or marginal revenue) curve, which will be forced downward by competition until the marginal revenue curve intersects the marginal cost curve at the minimum point on the average cost curve. (L.O. 3, 4, 5)

6. The result of this situation will be an equilibrium, in which profits are zero. There is no incentive for each firm to increase or reduce output, and no incentive for firms to enter or leave the industry. (L.O. 5)

7. Under monopoly, as output increases, marginal revenue per unit decreases, falling faster than the demand (average revenue) curve. (L.O. 3)

8. As a result, under monopoly, the marginal cost and marginal revenue curves intersect at a lower level of output than under competition, the result being lower output, higher prices, and higher profits under monopoly than under competition. (L.O. 3, 4, 5)

9. Because an oligopolist's demand curve is "kinked," the marginal revenue curve is not continuous at the existing price and output, providing no clear intersection point for the marginal cost and marginal revenue curves and thus creating an incentive for each oligopolist to leave the price at the existing level once it has been set. (L.O. 3, 4, 5)

10. A firm's revenue and cost data can be used in a similar manner to determine the output/sales level above which profits will be earned and below which the firm should be shut down. (L.O. 6, 7)

Questions

1. You are paying a student $10 per hour to pick strawberries on your farm.
   (a) Explain how the Law of Diminishing Returns will limit the number of hours for which you decide to employ this student.
   (b) Explain your decision using the terms *marginal revenue per box of berries* and *marginal cost per box*.

2. Raj's Raspberry Ranch sells berries at a price of $15 per box. Raj's fixed and variable production costs are indicated in the following table.

Boxes per Day	Fixed Costs	Variable Costs	Total Costs	Average Total Cost per Box	Marginal Cost per Box	Average Revenue per Box	Total Revenue	Marginal Revenue per Box	Profit
0	$20	$ 0	—	—	—	—	—	—	—
10	20	130	—	—	—	—	—	—	—
20	20	250	—	—	—	—	—	—	—
30	20	370	—	—	—	—	—	—	—
40	20	519	—	—	—	—	—	—	—
50	20	680	—	—	—	—	—	—	—
60	20	860	—	—	—	—	—	—	—

   (a) Complete the seven remaining columns in the table.
   (b) The level of output at which profits will be maximized is _____ boxes per day.
   (c) At this level of output, the level of profits will be $_____ per day.
   (d) Draw the average cost per box, marginal cost per box, average revenue per box, and marginal revenue per box curves.

(e) Use the graph that you drew for your answer to part (d) to show the most profitable level of output and sales.

(f) Using the concepts of marginal revenue and marginal cost, explain why your answer to part (e) is the most profitable level of sales and output. Why would it *not* be more profitable to increase output and sales beyond this point?

(g) From the information available, does this appear to be a perfectly competitive industry or not? Why?

3. Petra's Pet Treats sells bags of special pet food to retail stores for a wholesale price of $8 per bag. Following is a table showing Petra's weekly costs and revenues. Complete the remaining columns in the table.

Output (bags per week)	Fixed Costs	Variable Costs	Total Costs	Total Revenue	Profit
0	$800	$ 0	____	____	____
100	800	400	____	____	____
200	800	800	____	____	____
300	800	1200	____	____	____
400	800	1600	____	____	____

(a) In order to break even, Petra must sell _____ bags per week.

(b) Assuming that 400 bags per week is her maximum output, the maximum profit that Petra can earn is $ _____ per week.

4. Petra is considering a different business model, in which, instead of selling to retailers at the wholesale price of $8 per bag, she establishes a website, becomes an ebusiness, and sells directly to consumers (who order over the internet) at a retail price of $15 per bag. However, this ebusiness model will also involve higher costs:

• Due to the cost of the website and other assets she will need, her fixed costs will double from $800 to $1600 per week, and

• Due to higher costs of delivery and customer service, her variable costs will double from $4 to $8 per bag

(a) Complete the following table, showing Petra's costs, revenue and profits.

Output (bags per week)	Fixed Costs	Variable Costs	Total Costs	Total Revenue	Profit
0	____	____	____	____	____
100	____	____	____	____	____
200	____	____	____	____	____
300	____	____	____	____	____
400	____	____	____	____	____

Compare the profits of the conventional business model in question 3 to the ebusiness model in this question, at each level of output and sales shown:

(b) What is less attractive about the ebusiness model? Why does this risk exist?

(c) What is more attractive about the ebusiness model? Why does this opportunity exist?

(d) What will Petra have to achieve in order to avoid the risks and secure the opportunities of the ebusiness model, so that it is more profitable than the conventional model?

(e) What obstacles will she have to overcome in order to achieve the goals outlined in part (d)?

5. Using the terms *marginal revenue* and *marginal cost*, explain why airlines sell tickets at very low prices to people who book a flight at the very last minute (if a seat is available).

Study Guide

Review Questions (Answers to these Review Questions appear in Appendix B.)

1. Identify each of the following as a *fixed cost* or a *variable cost*.
   (a) the monthly rent paid for a firm's office _____
   (b) the paint used to finish a firm's product _____
   (c) the cost of delivering product to buyers _____
   (d) the $100 000 per year paid for leasing of equipment _____
   (e) the salary of the president _____
   (f) the wages paid to production workers _____

2. As a firm's output increases, its total fixed costs
   (a) increase.
   (b) remain constant (do not change).
   (c) decrease.

3. As a firm's output increases, its fixed costs *per unit*
   (a) increase.
   (b) remain constant (do not change).
   (c) decrease.

4. If a firm's sales and output are low, it tends to have losses (or very low profits), in large part because at low levels of sales and output
   (a) its labour costs per unit will be high.
   (b) its variable costs per unit will be lower.
   (c) its prices will be lower.
   (d) its fixed costs per unit will be very high.
   (e) None of the above.

5. As successive units of one production input (e.g., labour) are added to fixed amounts of other inputs (e.g., capital equipment), the average output of the variable input will
   (a) increase at first, then decrease.
   (b) remain unchanged.
   (c) increase at a constant rate.
   (d) decrease gradually.
   (e) None of the above.

6. The phenomenon described in question 5 is known as the _____.

7. As output is increased, average variable cost *per unit*
   (a) falls at first, then rises.
   (b) rises at first, then falls.
   (c) falls continually.
   (d) rises continually.
   (e) None of the above.

8. Marginal cost per unit is
   (a) the net effect of declining fixed costs per unit and rising variable costs per unit as output is increased.
   (b) the total costs divided by the total number of units produced.
   (c) the total variable costs divided by the number of units produced.
   (d) the addition to total costs arising from the production of one more unit.
   (e) None of the above.

9. If output is increased from 25 units to 26 units per day, and total costs increase from $615 to $638 per day, the marginal cost per unit is
   (a) $24.60
   (b) $24.54
   (c) $23.00
   (d) $638.00
   (e) None of the above.

10. Suppose the firm in question 9 can sell the 26th product for $24.
    (a) Its marginal revenue per unit is $_____.
    (b) Should it produce the 26th unit? Why or why not?

11. Complete the last five columns of the following table.

Units of Output per Day	Fixed Costs	Variable Costs	Total Costs	Average Fixed Cost per Unit	Average Variable Cost per Unit	Average Total Cost per Unit	Marginal Cost per Unit
0	$600	$ 0	——	——	——	——	——
5	600	150	——	——	——	——	——
10	600	200	——	——	——	——	——
15	600	225	——	——	——	——	——
20	600	300	——	——	——	——	——
25	600	550	——	——	——	——	——

   (a) As output increases, why do the following cost factors change as they do?
       (i)   average fixed cost per unit
       (ii) average variable cost per unit
       (iii) average total cost per unit
   (b) What does *marginal cost per unit* mean? Why does it change in the way it does as output increases?

Critical Thinking Questions

(Asterisked questions 1 to 4 are answered in Appendix B; the answers to questions 5 to 8 are in the Instructor's Manual that accompanies this text.)

*1. Fluorescent lighting tubes are sold in various lengths. Usually, 48-inch tubes sell for roughly one-third less than smaller tubes that are less than half their length. Obviously, the longer tubes involve more materials and higher materials costs. Then what might explain why the *larger* tube has the *lower* price?

*2. What explains the fact that the classic 939-page *Dr. Spock's Baby and Child Care* sells for the same price as an unremarkable novel of half its length by an unknown author?

*3. Suppose you have the following plans for a new business:
   Fixed costs: $500 per week
   Variable costs: $5 per product
   Price: $10 per product

Output (Units per Week)	Fixed Costs	Variable Costs	Total Costs	Total Revenue	Profit
0	——	——	——	——	——
100	——	——	——	——	——
200	——	——	——	——	——
300	——	——	——	——	——
400	——	——	——	——	——
500	——	——	——	——	——

(a) Complete the table. If you are expecting to sell 400 products per week, what will your weekly profit be?

(b) Suppose that you had been overly optimistic in your planning of your business, and the actual situation turns out to be as follows: fixed costs are $800 per week rather than $500, variable costs are $6 per product instead of $5, and competition limits your price to $8 (instead of $10) and your weekly sales to 300 products (rather than 400).
What will your profit be now?

*4. Sally's Shirts Ltd. sells shirts at a price of $22 each. Sally's fixed and variable production costs are indicated in the following table.

Units of Output per Day	Fixed Costs	Variable Costs	Total Costs	Average Cost per Unit	Average Revenue per Unit	Marginal Cost per Unit	Marginal Revenue per Unit
0	$200	$ 0	——	——	——	——	——
10	200	170	——	——	——	——	——
20	200	320	——	——	——	——	——
30	200	440	——	——	——	——	——
40	200	580	——	——	——	——	——
50	200	800	——	——	——	——	——
60	200	1100	——	——	——	——	——

(a) Complete the five remaining columns in the table.

(b) Draw the curves for the average cost per unit, marginal cost per unit, average revenue per unit, and marginal revenue per unit.

(c) Use the graph that you drew for your answer to part (b) to determine the following:
   (i) The level of output at which profits will be maximized is _____ units per day.
   (ii) At this level of output, the level of profits will be $_____ per day. (Show your calculation of the level of profits.)

(d) Is Sally's Shirts Ltd. operating in a perfectly competitive market?

(e) If this firm is in a perfectly competitive industry and is a typical firm that is making profits, what adjustment will occur in the price of the product, and how will this affect the profits of this typical firm?

5. For the firm whose costs and revenues are shown in the graph below,
   (a) profits will be maximized at a level of output of ___ units per week, and
   (b) at this level of output, profits will be $___ per week. (Show your calculations.)
   (c) Is this firm operating in a perfectly competitive market?
   (d) If this firm is in a perfectly competitive industry and is a typical firm that is making profits, what adjustment will occur in the price of the product, and how will this affect the profits of this typical firm?

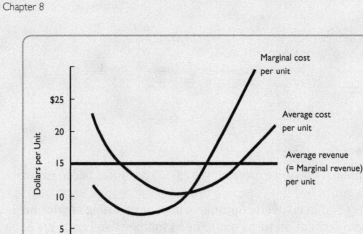

6. Following are the cost and revenue data for tables produced by Peter's Patios Ltd.

If the company charges this price per table:	It will sell this many tables per week:
$38.00	0
33.50	20
29.00	40
24.50	60
20.00	80
15.50	100
11.00	120

The company's fixed costs and variable costs are shown in the following table.

Units of Output per Week	Fixed Costs	Variable Costs	Total Costs	Average Cost per Unit	Average Revenue per Unit	Marginal Cost per Unit	Marginal Revenue per Unit
0	$400	$0	___	___	___	___	___
20	400	180	___	___	___	___	___
40	400	330	___	___	___	___	___
60	400	430	___	___	___	___	___
80	400	560	___	___	___	___	___
100	400	780	___	___	___	___	___
120	400	1080	___	___	___	___	___

(a) Complete the five remaining columns in the table.
(b) Draw the curves for the average cost per unit, marginal cost per unit, average revenue per unit, and marginal revenue per unit.
(c) Use the graph that you drew for your answer to part (b) to determine the following:
   (i)   The level of output at which profits will be maximized is ___ units per week.
   (ii) At this level of output, the level of profits will be $___ per week.
   (Show your calculation of the level of profits.)
(d) Is Peter's Patios Ltd. operating in a perfectly competitive market?

7. For the firm whose costs and revenues are shown in the graph below,

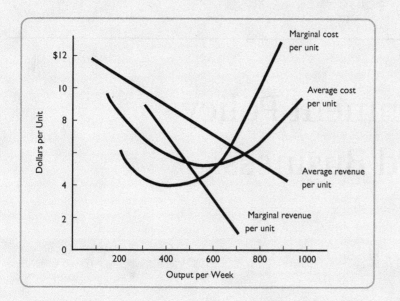

(a) profits will be maximized at a level of output of _____ units per week, and

(b) at this level of output, weekly profits will be $_____. (Show your calculations.)

(c) Is this firm operating in a perfectly competitive market?

8. Kermit's Kandles Ltd. sells candles at a price of $8 each. The following table shows Kermit's fixed and variable production costs.

Units of Output per Day	Fixed Costs	Variable Costs	Total Costs	Total Revenue
0	$400	$0	——	——
100	400	1000	——	——
200	400	1700	——	——
300	400	2200	——	——
400	400	2500	——	——
500	400	3200	——	——
600	400	4400	——	——

(a) Complete the remaining two columns in the table.

(b) Draw the total revenue, total costs, and variable costs curves.

(c) The graph indicates that the minimum level of output (sales) required for this firm to start up in business (its break-even point) is _____ units per day.

(d) The graph indicates that, before this firm should go out of business, its sales should fall below a level of _____ units per day.

(e) Explain the reasons for your answers to (c) and (d).

9. At the end of Chapter 7, we saw that the number of automobile manufacturing companies in North America decreased from about 240 in the 1920s to only 3 major companies in about 40 years. What role do you think the subject matter of Chapter 8 played in this dramatic change in the market structure of the industry?

Use the Web   (Hints for this Use the Web exercise appear in Appendix B.)

1. Visit **http://economics.about.com/od/coststructure/ss/revenue_costs.htm** and do the five-step practice question on marginal revenue and marginal cost.

Government Policy Toward Business

LEARNING OBJECTIVES

After studying this chapter, you should be able to

1. Explain the doctrine of *laissez-faire*, and why government policy toward business in Canada is not based on laissez-faire.

2. State two ways in which government policies support the incomes of farmers.

3. Describe three ways in which government policies assist small businesses, and two types of government actions that have negative effects upon small businesses.

4. Explain why industrial concentration is of concern to governments, and state four reasons for the high degree of industrial concentration in the Canadian economy.

5. State the basic purpose of Canada's Competition Act, and its provision concerning price-fixing.

6. Summarize the arguments in favour of and against governments restricting mergers of large Canadian corporations, and explain how Canada's Competition Act attempts to address both of these arguments.

7. Describe two traditional government methods for protecting consumers against the market power of natural monopolies.

8. Explain why governments have recently opened up some natural monopolies to competition and have privatized some government enterprises.

9. Apply the concepts and facts of this chapter to various situations.

The matter of government policy toward business can be confusing. On the one hand, governments provide a wide range of support to small businesses, such as reduced income tax rates and assistance with financing. On the other hand, there are periodic reports of corporations being fined millions of dollars for conspiring to fix prices, and occasionally executives are even jailed for their behaviour in the marketplace. In this chapter, we will examine these seemingly contradictory government policies toward business. But first, let's start by returning to some of the basics covered earlier.

The Theoretical Ideal of Competition

Chapter 1 stressed the importance of producers being *effective* (by producing things that are useful and wanted) and *efficient* (by producing those items without wasting scarce economic resources). Generally, economists and government policy-makers have tended to prefer competitive industries to concentrated ones, on the grounds that competition serves the consumer best, by promoting both effectiveness and efficiency. In competitive industries, consumer demand pushes businesses to produce whatever consumers will buy, and competition pushes businesses to produce it efficiently. Strong competition among businesses also ensures that consumers will not pay excessively high prices and that producers' profits will be reasonable.

The Theory of Laissez-Faire . . .

If the entire economy consisted of industries that were competitive in this way, it would comprise a self-regulating system for determining the answers to basic economic questions such as what to produce and how to produce it. The marketplace would do such a good job of promoting effectiveness and efficiency that there would be no need for government intervention to improve the operation of the economy.

This theory of a competitive economy that serves the consumer so well that there is little or no need for government regulation or intervention is known as **laissez-faire**. The concept of laissez-faire originated in France at the time of Louis XIV, as a reaction to a web of government regulations of business that had grown so complex and restrictive that it stifled incentives and was actually causing the economy to stagnate. By comparison, a free competitive economy would be much more effective at promoting prosperity.

laissez-faire
The doctrine or philosophy that from the viewpoint of the public interest, it is neither necessary nor beneficial for governments to intervene in the operation of the economy.

. . . Versus Economic Reality

But our modern economy is not as simple as that of the theory of laissez-faire. In much of the economy—the small business sector of Chapter 3—there is a great deal of competition. In these industries, there are many small businesses competing and a considerable number of new ones starting up each year, all to the benefit of consumers.

However, in other parts of the economy, the situation is different. Vigorous competition in an industry is a *dynamic process* rather than a stable situation, and as such, it can lead to quite different results.

At one extreme, in parts of the agricultural sector, there are so many small producers with low incomes that there concerns that *excessive competition* will force too many producers out of business and undermine this important industry.

By contrast, in some industries, a combination of competition and economies of scale can eliminate so many firms that only a few giant ones are left. As we saw in Chapter 7, in industries such as automobile manufacturing, communications, and petroleum refining, the marketplace has become dominated by a few giant corporations, raising concerns that there is *too little competition*, and little chance of new competitors starting up.

In pursuing the goal of vigorous competition, then, governments have found themselves in some cases introducing policies that seek to *restrict and regulate* the market power of large firms with little competition, while in other cases government policies seek to *support and assist* small firms in highly competitive environments.

Government Policies Toward Business

In Chapter 7, we examined the four basic types of market structure:
  • perfect competition, the most competitive possible situation,
  • monopolistic competition, which describes most of the small business sector of the economy,
  • oligopoly, in which industries are dominated by a few large firms, and
  • monopoly, in which there is only one seller.

The market power of firms operating under these market structures ranges from none whatsoever (in the case of perfect competition) to very great (in the case of a monopoly). Accordingly, government policy toward businesses tends to differ from one type of market structure or industry to another. In general, we will find that the more competitive an industry is, the more *supportive* government policy will be, and the less competitive it is, the more *restrictive* government policy is likely to be. In this chapter, we will consider some of the highlights of government policies toward business in Canada, the reasons for the variations in these policies, and some of the problems concerning them. To organize the discussion, we will use the four types of market structure described above.

Government Policies Concerning Competitive Industries

Perfect Competition

The sector of the Canadian economy that most closely resembles perfect competition is *agriculture*. In agriculture, there are large numbers of producers selling products that are more or less identical to those of other farms. Technological advances have increased farm productivity to the point where there is a general tendency to over-supply markets, with the result being low farm prices and incomes. To make matters worse, fluctuations in weather and crop size cause farm prices and incomes to be unstable, as well as generally low.

Because of the extreme competitiveness of agricultural markets and the problems that this creates for farmers, the general thrust of government policy has been to *support farm prices and/or incomes* through a variety of programs.

As we saw in Chapter 6, governments have sometimes employed *price supports* for some farm products. Under this method, the government establishes the price of the farm produce and undertakes to purchase from the farmers at that price any produce that is unsold. As we also saw in Chapter 6, the result of farm price supports will be surpluses of farm produce. To avoid the problem of crop surpluses, governments have sometimes employed *acreage restrictions*. Under such a program, farmers are paid *not* to grow crops on part of their land in order to reduce the supply of farm products and increase their prices.

Canadian governments have several programs under which *direct payments* are made to farmers if crop prices or yields fall below the long-term average. These insurance-like programs are partly funded by farmers themselves, and partly financed by the government. These programs are very important to farmers—in bad years, as much as 75 percent of farmers' net income can come from such government programs.

In addition to this assistance, governments help to increase some farmers' incomes through **marketing boards**. These are government-sponsored organizations of farmers that are intended to restrict how much farmers produce, so as to keep prices higher. As such, a marketing board is a form of price-and-production agreement that is similar to the oligopolistic agreements discussed in Chapter 7, but one that is created by government policy. To protect the high prices charged by marketing boards, the government must provide further assistance by *restricting imports* of cheaper products to prevent these from competing with Canadian products.

marketing boards
Government-sponsored organizations of farmers that support farm incomes by restricting the supply of produce, usually through a system of quotas on individual farmers.

Monopolistic Competition

In monopolistic competition, there are many small firms producing and selling differentiated products or services in a highly competitive environment. This is a reasonable description of the small business sector of the Canadian economy, which, as we saw in Chapter 3, has played a vital role in the creation of jobs.

Because small businesses operate in such a highly competitive environment and face many difficulties as described in Chapter 3, various government programs are available to assist them. Both the federal and provincial governments offer loan guarantees or lower-cost, longer-term financing for small businesses. At the federal level, the Business Development Bank of Canada makes term loans to new or existing businesses that are unable to obtain the required funds from other lenders on reasonable terms and conditions, and offers an extensive management training program. Most provincial governments offer financial help through similar agencies, with loan guarantees arranged through regular financial institutions and screening processes to minimize failure rates.

www.bdc.ca

The federal government's Canada Small Business Financing (CSFB) program makes it easier for small businesses to get loans of up to $500 000 from financial institutions by sharing the risks with lenders. Counselling programs are also available from the federal government and most provinces to assist small business owners with their management problems. Such programs help small businesses that are unable to afford expert counselling, utilizing various people, including Masters of Business Administration students, retired executives, and professional counsellors. Also, marketing programs are offered by all provincial governments. These programs are intended to assist small businesses in the opening up of new markets, both in Canada and abroad, and some are designed to complement programs offered through the federal Export Development Corporation. Some provinces also offer personnel assistance programs to help small businesses find skilled employees, and in some cases, the wages of employees are subsidized by the government in order to aid small businesses in recruiting. Finally, government programs provide research and development assistance in the form of subsidies and by helping small businesses apply new technology in various ways.

www.ic.gc.ca/csbfp

In 2013, the CSBF program supported the investment of almost $2 billion in venture capital into Canadian firms.

www.edc.ca

In total, there is a bewildering array of hundreds of programs for small business offered by the federal, provincial, and municipal governments. According to some

Small businesses benefit
from a lower tax rate of
11 percent on the first
$500 000 of their profits.

www.cfib.ca

Government legislation of
minimum wage rates is a
contentious matter for
many small businesses, as
we will see in Chapter 10.

observers, a major problem facing many small business owners is finding the time to evaluate the wide variety of programs that could be of value, and to work through the extensive paperwork that many of them require. To aid in these matters, some governments have set up information centres to help small businesses determine where to look for aid, and have undertaken to reduce the amount of paperwork involved.

However, not all government policies and programs are helpful to small business. According to the Canadian Federation of Independent Business (CFIB), *taxation* and *government regulation* are the two major impediments to the operations and growth of small and medium-sized businesses in Canada.

Research has shown that labour-intensive small businesses actually pay a higher proportion of their profits to taxes than many larger businesses do. The main reason for this anomaly is that the burden of payroll taxes, such as Employment Insurance, workers' compensation premiums, and taxes for health care, falls most heavily on smaller, more labour-intensive businesses, whose labour costs are a higher proportion of their total costs.

Government red tape and paper burden was the second most frequently identified problem by CFIB members. Small business owners cannot afford the considerable amount of time they are required to divert from managing their operation to filling out government forms relating to statistical information and tax collection—for many, this amounts to 5 to 10 hours per week.

Finally, there is the question of how much assistance should actually be given to small businesses. Sometimes, businesses should be allowed to fail because they are not viable, or the people involved do not have the abilities required to operate a successful business. But neither the government, nor anyone else, knows how to recognize the potential of a new, small business or how much assistance is appropriate. Nonetheless, the importance of small business to the Canadian economy, particularly regarding the growth of employment, has led to a variety of government programs intended to help small businesses, particularly in starting up.

Government Policies Regarding Concentrated Industries

Oligopoly

In Chapter 7, we saw that when an industry is dominated by a few large firms, or oligopolists, it is possible that these firms will agree among themselves to fix prices. It was also mentioned in Chapter 7 that this practice is illegal in Canada, as it is in most countries. However, as we will see, the question of Canadian government policy toward large corporations is considerably more complex than simply outlawing price-fixing.

Industrial Concentration in the Canadian Economy

To the extent that a particular industry or market is dominated by a few firms, it is said to be *concentrated*. Studies have repeatedly shown that **industrial concentration** in the Canadian economy is not only high, but also considerably higher than in the U.S. economy.

This domination of much of Canada's economy by large corporations is viewed with concern by some, especially consumer groups. In the corporate concentration in certain sectors of the economy, they see a dangerous extent of oligopolistic power. On

industrial concentration
The degree to which an industry is dominated by a few firms.

the other hand, defenders of big business argue that large corporations increase the prosperity of Canadians, by making their industry more efficient and better able to compete internationally, a consideration made more important by the trend toward freer trade in recent years.

The debate between critics and supporters of big business becomes more heated whenever there are *mergers* of major corporations, such as those that have occurred in recent years in important industries such as brewing, oil, airlines, steel, retailing, forest products, and bookstores. Critics oppose such mergers on the grounds that they only increase the domination of Canadian markets by fewer and larger corporations. But defenders of the mergers argue that Canadian firms can only succeed in highly competitive international markets if they merge in order to grow larger and more efficient.

In this section, we will consider the reasons for the high degree of industrial concentration in Canada, the debate over whether large corporations are a threat or an advantage to Canadians, and the important question of what government policy toward industrial concentration and mergers should be.

Reasons for Concentration

There are various reasons why some industries come to be dominated by a few large firms. One basic reason is the *elimination of firms by competition*: in a competitive market economy, successful firms will expand, and unsuccessful ones will not survive. A major contributing factor to this tendency is **economies of scale**—as successful firms expand, they use mass-production technology that gives them additional production-cost advantages over their competitors.

economies of scale
Lower production costs per unit made possible by higher volumes of production that permit the achievement of increased efficiencies.

The *small size of the Canadian market* is also a significant factor in Canada's high degree of industrial concentration. With a total market size about one-tenth that of the United States, there is often simply not enough room in Canada for more than a few firms that are large enough to capture the economies of scale that exist in much of modern business.

Finally, *mergers of corporations* also increase corporate concentration. During the 1990s, merger activity in Canada was spurred by the need for Canadian firms to become more efficient and internationally competitive. Following the early 1980s, there was a trend toward increased international competition, or the **globalization** of many markets. This trend, together with the Canada–U.S. Free Trade Agreement (1989) and the North American Free Trade Agreement (1994), not only created more intense foreign competition for many Canadian industries in Canadian markets but also increased export opportunities for Canadian firms. To improve their ability to compete with their larger foreign counterparts in the United States and Europe, some Canadian firms merged with others, so as to gain economies of scale, more complete product lines, stronger marketing networks, better access to financial resources, and so on. For instance, the Molson–Carling O'Keefe merger was intended to increase the efficiency and capacity of the company's Canadian brewing operations while giving it access to the worldwide distribution network of Elders IXL Ltd., Carling's Australian parent company. Similarly, Dofasco's merger with Algoma Steel made it the fourth-largest steel-maker in North America while giving it an expanded and balanced product line that was expected to position the company well for competing in the U.S. market. And the takeover of Canada's MacMillan Bloedel by U.S. giant Weyerhaeuser made the Canadian company a key part of the world's third-largest forest products company.

globalization
The growing internationalization of business, trade, and finance that has characterized the period since the early 1980s.

During the 1990s, merger activity increased sharply in many countries, driven in large part by firms' desire to achieve the scale needed for global competition. This trend was assisted by rising stock prices in the 1990s, since in many mergers one firm uses its own shares as payment to shareholders of the firm being acquired. The lower interest rates of the 1990s also helped firms to finance their purchases of other companies. Another factor was conglomerates' sale of companies as part of the trend toward focusing on their core business. Examples of such sales included Imasco's sale of Canada Trust to the Toronto-Dominion Bank and Molson's sale of Beaver Lumber to Home Hardware.

In Canada, there were as many as 1000 mergers per year, as firms repositioned themselves to deal with international competition both in foreign markets and in Canada. This merger activity has been unprecedented in terms of both the numbers of mergers and the size of many of the enterprises that resulted from these mergers.

The Debate Over Bigness in Business

Critics of big business argue that since the Canadian economy has a high degree of industrial concentration, Canadian consumers are exposed to a high risk of price-fixing by oligopolists. They point to the fact that Labatt and Molson hold a combined market share of about 90 percent of the Canadian beer market as a prime example of unhealthy corporate concentration. In the retail sector, they see evidence of decreasing competition in Hudson's Bay Co.'s purchase of Kmart and its merger of Kmart with its Zellers division, Home Hardware's purchase of Beaver Lumber, the bookstore merger of Indigo and Chapters, and the merger between Superior Propane and ICG Propane. They also point to periodic convictions of corporations for price-fixing and note that the profits of many oligopolists represent a considerably higher rate of return on investment than that earned by an average business.

According to this view, if competition cannot be relied upon to keep prices and profits in check, the government must set down rules for oligopolists to follow and must police their behaviour. In particular, governments must not only prevent price-fixing and other measures that reduce competition but also prevent mergers of companies where these would reduce competition, and possibly even break up excessively dominant corporations into smaller firms if necessary.

Defenders of large corporations argue that these big firms actually contribute to the economic prosperity of Canadians. They emphasize the reinvestment of the profits of big business into capital equipment and improved technology that improve productivity in the Canadian economy.

They argue that this higher productivity benefits Canadians in two ways. First, as we have seen, higher output per worker is the basis for *higher living standards*. By using mass-production technology, large producers can reduce production costs so much that even after their above-average profits are added, the price to the consumer is still lower. If productivity is high enough, it is possible for workers to have high wages, companies to have high profits, *and* consumer prices to be low. And, as supporters of big business point out, if you wanted to show someone a showpiece of Canadian technology, you would probably go to one of the country's vast automobile assembly plants that uses computerized industrial robots and turns out as many as 75 cars per hour.

Second, there is the question of the *international competitiveness* of Canadian producers. Much of Canada's manufacturing industry has historically been small-scale by world standards and, therefore, not very efficient or competitive internationally. So it can be argued that mergers of Canadian firms into fewer but larger and more efficient operations contribute to Canada's international competitiveness. This point is particularly important because so much of the output of the Canadian economy is exported, and so many jobs rely upon the success of Canadian firms in export markets.

"People of the same trade seldom meet together, even for merriment and diversion, but the conversation ends in a conspiracy against the public, or in some contrivance to raise prices."
— ADAM SMITH, *THE WEALTH OF NATIONS* (1776).

"[Mergers] reduce Canadian competition, raise prices for consumers and cause job losses. [We] can't see how any of those things in any way benefit Canadians or the economy."
CONSUMERS ASSOCIATION OF CANADA.

The Policy Dilemma

The arguments for and against bigness in business present government authorities with a very real dilemma in deciding government policy toward industrial concentration. To leave the power of big business unchecked would risk exposing consumers to price-fixing. On the other hand, strong restrictions on big business could limit the growth and efficiency of Canadian firms and their ability to compete internationally.

This dilemma is especially troublesome in Canada, where the situation can be summarized as follows:

(a) industrial concentration in Canada is *substantially higher* than in comparable industries in the United States;

(b) however, the average size of Canada's 100 largest industrial corporations and Canada's 25 largest financial corporations is *much smaller* than the average size of their counterparts in the United States and other developed countries.

This awkwardly contradictory state of affairs is illustrated in Figure 9-1. It shows that many corporations that are sufficiently large to dominate markets and raise concerns about threats to consumers *within Canada* may be relatively small and not competitive by *international standards*. And, in order to become internationally competitive, these firms would have to grow larger, and thus *more* dominant within the Canadian market. These facts make the policy dilemma referred to earlier particularly severe for Canadian policy-makers—while industrial concentration in Canada is presently high enough to support the argument for strong laws restricting further growth and concentration, policies that do so could prevent Canadian corporations from growing to the size needed to be internationally competitive.

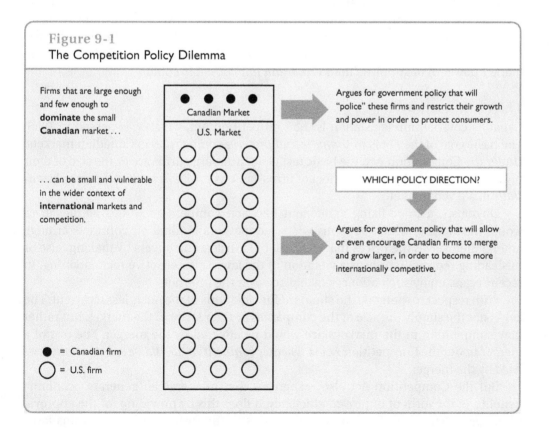

Figure 9-1
The Competition Policy Dilemma

Firms that are large enough and few enough to **dominate** the small **Canadian** market . . .

Canadian Market

U.S. Market

. . . can be small and vulnerable in the wider context of **international** markets and competition.

● = Canadian firm

○ = U.S. firm

Argues for government policy that will "police" these firms and restrict their growth and power in order to protect consumers.

WHICH POLICY DIRECTION?

Argues for government policy that will allow or even encourage Canadian firms to merge and grow larger, in order to become more internationally competitive.

The Changing Economic Environment: Globalization

Historically, Canadian government *trade policy* and *competition policy* were geared to *national markets.* Through its *trade policy,* the government imposed tariffs on imported goods in order to foster the development of Canadian manufacturing industries by protecting them against foreign competition. On the other hand, the government's *competition policy* sought to protect Canadian consumers from price-fixing and other anticompetitive practices by oligopolistic industries (many of which were, themselves, protected by the same government's tariffs against foreign competition). So the government was in the position of trying to *promote competition* among Canadian producers within the Canadian market, while at the same time *restricting competition* from foreign firms in that same market.

The more recent trend toward freer trade has made the concept of gearing policies to national markets less relevant. As nations cut tariffs, international competition became more intense and markets became more international—the process known as *globalization.* As new trade agreements were signed (the Canada–U.S. Free Trade Agreement of 1989, NAFTA in 1994, and the 1995 World Trade Organization agreement), Canadian industry was faced with the prospect of stronger foreign competition. Also, the economic integration of Europe into a single market of 340 million made it likely that North American producers would face stronger competition from larger and more efficient European firms. These trends toward the globalization of markets pushed policy-makers toward thinking more about *international* concerns, especially the ability of their nation to compete in global markets. In this context, big business came to be seen in a less unfavourable light than in the past.

The trend toward freer trade had some major implications for the debate on industrial concentration in Canada. First, freer trade made it more important than ever that in framing its policy regarding big business, the Canadian government take into account the ability of Canadian corporations to compete internationally. Also, the increased competition from imports that would come with freer trade reduced concerns about the market power of large Canadian corporations. In the view of many observers, *freer trade* would do more to protect Canadian consumers against the market power of oligopolists than *Canadian laws* possibly could.

The Competition Act

> "The core of the policy is the likely effect of a proposed merger on competition, whether domestic or foreign."
>
> — WILLIAM STANBURY, UBC FACULTY OF COMMERCE AND BUSINESS ADMINISTRATION.

Canada's competition legislation is the Competition Act, which was passed in 1986. The basic goal of the Act is to *promote and preserve competition* in Canadian markets. Under the Competition Act, the basic test is not how large firms are or the size of their profits, but rather whether the effect of firms' actions is to *lessen competition substantially* in a given market.

Obviously, a price-fixing agreement between competitors would be illegal, as would bid-rigging, which happens when competitors bidding on contracts arrange among themselves the prices that they will bid. Misleading buyers by making false or misleading representations is a violation of the law, as is deceptive telemarketing. In recent years, many such offences take place over the internet.

With respect to mergers, the standard for violations of the Act is less clear-cut. The key is not the simply the size of the companies or their share of the market, but rather how competition in the marketplace would be affected by the merger. The test of a merger under the Competition Act is *whether competition would be substantially lessened* by the merger.

But the Competition Act also recognizes that mergers can generate economic benefits, in the form of improved efficiency. It does this by providing for the approval of mergers that would lead to positive results in the form of efficiency gains large

www.competition
bureau.gc.ca

enough to offset the negative results of reduced competition. And these positive results include improvements in the ability of Canadian firms to compete internationally, both in export markets and against imports into Canadian markets.

The Competition Act is administered by the Competition Bureau, which is a federal agency. The Bureau must be notified of any plan to merge or acquire businesses above a certain size (in 2014, $82 million of Canadian assets or revenues for the target firm, or $400 million of combined Canadian assets or revenues for the firms). After the Bureau has been notified, there is a waiting period for the Bureau to review the proposed merger before the merger can be completed."

The Bureau then reviews the proposed merger or acquisition, considering whether

(a) it is likely to lessen competition substantially.

(b) there are likely to be real gains in efficiency that will exceed, and offset, the lessening of competition.

(c) such gains in efficiency will improve the ability of the merged firms to compete internationally.

The second and third considerations here (b and c)—known as the "efficiency exception"—are the Competition Act's attempt to deal with the policy dilemma described earlier, by allowing mergers that increase efficiency, particularly if they improve the firm's ability to compete internationally. The Act recognizes that a merger could present trade-offs in which both negative effects on consumers and positive effects on efficiencies existed, and it empowers the Bureau to weigh these trade-offs when deciding whether to allow a merger.

Other factors to be considered include barriers to entry to the particular market (which would affect future competition), the extent of foreign competition, the effectiveness of the competition that would remain after the proposed merger, and the availability of alternatives (such as selling all or part of a firm involved in a merger to other firms).

> The Competition Bureau generally will review a merger if the market share of the merged firms would exceed 35 percent.

If the Bureau has concerns about the effect of the proposal on competition, it will seek to negotiate amendments to the proposal with the companies involved. The result is usually a negotiated agreement. However, if the Bureau has doubts, it can also grant conditional approval for a merger and then monitor the competitive conditions in the market following the merger.

If the Bureau and the companies are unable to agree, the matter is taken to the Competition Tribunal for a decision. The Competition Tribunal is chaired by a judge of the Federal Court of Canada, and consists of 12 members, including business and consumer authorities as well as judges. The Tribunal operates under the same procedural rules as a civil court, and its decisions may be appealed to the Federal Court of Canada.

> The purchase of A&P Canada by Metro Inc. gave Metro a market share of 25 percent in Ontario and 30 percent in the Greater Toronto Area.

YOU DECIDE

Canada's Banks: To Merge or Not to Merge?

At first look, Canada's banking industry would appear to be a clear example of market power. The industry has for many years been dominated by the "big five" banks (Royal Bank of Canada, Toronto Dominion Canada Trust, Scotiabank, Bank of Montreal, and Canadian Imperial Bank of Commerce). As measured by assets, the degree of concentration is high— the top three Canadian banks control 60 percent of all banking assets, compared to 45 percent in the United States.

But the situation may not be as simple as it seems at first look. Canada's banks face competition for deposits and loans from roughly 1000 small credit unions (small member-owned financial cooperatives) and caisses populaires (the francophone equivalent of credit unions) across Canada. They also face competition from insurance companies in a variety of financial services. In addition, there is competition from a considerable number of foreign banks, mostly in areas such as business financing and "wholesale" activities involving large deposits. It was expected that due to free trade agreements, the degree of foreign competition would increase in the future.

As a result, various research studies conducted on behalf of the federal government (the Bank of Canada) have concluded that, while more detailed statistics would be helpful, Canada's banking industry is on the whole more like a monopolistically competitive industry rather than the oligopoly that it would appear to be.

Canada's major banks have long argued that they are much less dominant in their industry than is generally supposed, and that Canadian banks need to merge and grow larger so as to be able to compete with their larger foreign counterparts. They point out that the Royal Bank of Canada (Canada's largest bank and a giant by Canadian standards) ranks thirty-fifth in size among world banks, with assets less than one-third of those of the world's largest banks.

In 1998, the Royal Bank and the Bank of Montreal announced their intention to merge, and shortly afterwards Toronto-Dominion Bank and the Bank of Commerce announced similar plans. The announcements stirred up a flurry of controversy, following which the federal government disallowed the mergers. ▪

QUESTIONS

1. How does the banking industry illustrate the complexity of determining what government policy regarding a particular industry should be?
2. In 2002, a technical report of the Bank of Canada[1] found that many of the new computer technologies in banking had high fixed costs and low marginal costs.
   (a) Why would these technologies have high fixed costs and low marginal costs?
   (b) How would these findings affect the debate over mergers of Canada's banks?
3. Have there been any significant developments regarding competition in the Canadian banking industry recently? A Google search for *Canadian banking competition* will provide some information.

---

[1]Charles Freedman and Clyde Goodlet (2002, August). *The Financial Services Sector: An Update on Recent Developments.* Bank of Canada Technical Report No. 91.

Experience with the Competition Act

With respect to mergers, since the Competition Act was passed in 1986, the Competition Bureau has examined on average some 150 merger proposals each year. Most of these have been accepted without challenge; however, in a few cases, the Bureau asked for changes to proposed mergers or challenged them. In several other cases, the merger plans were voluntarily abandoned by the parties following objections by the Bureau. While the names of the companies involved were not revealed, it is reported that several of these plans involved large and well-known firms. Almost all of the Bureau's concerns were resolved through negotiations; only a small number of cases were forwarded to the Tribunal for adjudication.

The most common type of negotiated settlement between the Bureau and the companies involved restructuring proposed mergers through the sale of some assets to competitors. For instance, in order to gain the approval of the Bureau for their merger, Indigo and Chapters agreed to sell 13 superstores and 10 of Chapters' smaller mall-based stores. And when Cineplex Galaxy acquired Famous Players, it had to sell off 35 theatres in 17 cities in 6 provinces. In such cases, the Bureau examines the impact of the proposed merger on competition in various local markets, and if appears that the merger would substantially lessen competition in a market area, it requires that assets be sold to competitors.

With respect to price-fixing, there was general agreement that the new law was more effective than the previous law in that convictions were easier to obtain and penalties were more severe, including a maximum fine of $10 million. Following the passage of the new law, there were several noteworthy cases involving heavy fines.

For example, in 2013, an investigation by the Competition Bureau resulted in the largest fine ever for a bid-rigging offence—a $30 million fine against Yazaki Corporation for its participation in an international cartel with other Japanese suppliers of motor vehicle components. Yazaki secretly conspired with other Japanese manufacturers to submit bids in response to requests for quotations to supply Honda Canada and Toyota Canada with motor vehicle components.

The Competition Bureau's website shows legal cases involving the Competition Act, and the penalties imposed for convictions. To review cases involving convictions, visit www.competitionbureau.gc.ca, search for search for "Penalties Imposed", then click on "Penalties Imposed by the Courts—Competition Bureau. For a summary of each case, click on the name of the company or individual involved.

Most of the offences listed do not involve consumer products that are household names, but rather industrial products sold to other businesses, the higher cost of which increases the prices that consumers pay for the final product. Many cases involve the misleading of buyers, particularly over the internet. And many of the offences are international in nature, raising the question of whether some sort of international legislation is required the era of globalized markets and multinational business transactions.

YOU DECIDE

Beer Competition
Nearly 90 percent of the beer bought in Canada is produced by just two breweries—Labatt and Molson.

QUESTION
1. What could governments do to increase competition in a market that is so strongly dominated by two big firms?

Monopoly

As we saw in Chapter 7, monopoly is the market structure under which there is the strongest market power, because the monopolistic seller has complete control over the supply of the product, and hence its price. In a few cases such as patents on new drugs, governments grant temporary monopoly power to companies as a way of encouraging them to invest in new products, as discussed in Chapter 7. More generally, however, governments see monopolies and their market power of as potentially dangerous.

Natural Monopolies

Nonetheless, there are certain industries in which monopoly is the most logical form of organization. Generally, these industries are *public utilities and services,* such as electricity, water and public transit. The economic rationale for having monopolies in such industries starts with the fact that such utilities often require *very heavy capital investment* in facilities and equipment. This in turn results in *high fixed costs,* such as depreciation and interest on funds borrowed to finance these investments. The best way to keep these fixed costs as low as possible *to each customer* is to spread them over the *maximum possible number of customers.* By giving one producer a monopoly that guarantees it all of the available customers, the natural monopoly should be able to provide the service at a lower cost per customer than would otherwise be possible.

Creating a monopoly in this way will lower the production costs of the firm, but how can the government ensure that the benefits of this efficiency go to the consumer in the form of lower prices, and not to the monopoly itself? A way to protect consumers is for the government to *nationalize* the monopoly, by placing it under government ownership and having the government operate it on a non-profit basis. Canada Post is an example of this approach. Another approach is to leave the monopoly under private ownership but subject its rates (prices) to *government regulation.* The government will regulate the monopoly's rates (prices) in such a way as to permit the company to earn a reasonable rate of return on its shareholders' investment, so as to be fair to shareholders of the utility as well as to consumers.

It may seem that if natural monopolies are owned or regulated by the government, the public will be protected against overcharging. However, the matter of regulating monopolies has not turned out to be quite as simple as that. In order to regulate the prices to be charged by a natural monopoly, the people responsible for determining the regulations must possess considerable knowledge about that industry, its operations, and its costs. The most likely source of people with such knowledge is the industry itself, in the persons of former senior officials of the enterprise being regulated. Even if the regulators come from outside the industry being regulated, they must depend heavily for their information on the management of the monopoly. So the process of regulation is sometimes not the simple, objective, and effective procedure that it is intended to be. It is neither possible nor fair to generalize concerning the effectiveness of regulatory boards, since some seem to be much more effective protectors of the consumer's interests than others.

More recently, some critics have called into question the basic premise that natural monopolies are economically beneficial to consumers. One criticism is that some natural monopolies have charged *excessively high prices,* not because they earn high profits (in fact, many actually lose money), but rather because they employ excessive numbers of people and pay above-market wages and salaries. As a result, critics say, they have developed into inefficient bureaucracies with excessively high labour costs that become the justification for increasing the rates that they charge to their captive customers.

A second reason for questioning the benefits of natural monopolies is that technological progress has created the possibility of *new forms of competition* for established natural monopolies. For instance, new technology now permits competition in long-distance telephone service, and fax machines, email, electronic banking, and telecommunications technology are breaking down Canada Post's monopoly over some kinds of mail service. In a similar way, changes in communications technology are breaking into the field that once was thought to "belong" to cable television companies. These changes suggest that it may prove more beneficial to the public to open up some established natural monopolies to competition than to maintain those monopolies subject to the traditional consumer protections of government ownership or rate regulation.

Whether critics are concerned about the rates charged by natural monopolies or about making alternative technologies and services available to the public, their usual recommendations are to *open up the monopolies to competition* and possibly to *privatize* them (sell them to private investors), with the goal of making them more efficient and effective through some combination of competition and the profit motive.

In some jurisdictions, government-owned electricity generation monopolies are being replaced (or supplemented) by private firms that generate electricity and sell it to the distribution network in competition with each other. This approach brings us back in the direction of laissez-faire, as described earlier in the chapter.

Chapter Summary

1. According to the theory of laissez-faire, government should not intervene in the economy. Canadian government policy is more active, tending to be more supportive of businesses in more competitive industries, and more restrictive toward those in less competitive situations. (L.O. 1)

2. In the case of agriculture, which is the sector of the economy that most closely approximates perfect competition, government policy is quite supportive in a variety of ways intended to both increase and stabilize farmers' incomes. (L.O. 2)

3. With respect to the small business sector, which fits the description of monopolistic competition, many government programs are available, mostly to help small businesses get started. However, small businesses find that two of their main problems—taxation and governmental "red tape"—also arise from the actions of governments. (L.O. 3)

4. Industrial concentration tends to result in market power for producers, which can mean higher prices. The Canadian economy has a high degree of industrial concentration for various reasons, including competition, economies of scale, the small size of the Canadian market, and mergers of firms. (L.O. 4)

5. The purpose of the Competition Act is to promote and preserve competition. Under the Act, price-fixing is illegal and can result in heavy fines. (L.O. 5)

6. Many Canadian industrial corporations are small by international standards. As a result, while it can be argued that government policy should restrict mergers that would increase industrial concentration even further, it can also be argued that it is in Canada's best interests for some firms to merge so as to become more efficient and more competitive internationally. (L.O. 6)

7. The Competition Act is intended to provide the public with protection against anticompetitive behaviour by firms enjoying a dominant position in the Canadian marketplace, while allowing Canadian firms to merge for the purpose of increasing efficiency and thus improving their ability to compete internationally. (L.O. 6)

8. Traditionally, it has been Canadian government policy to allow natural monopolies in many public utilities and services in order to gain cost advantages, and either to place these monopolies under government ownership or to have their rates regulated by government. (L.O. 7)

9. Recently, concerns regarding the efficiency of some government enterprises and the rates they have been charging have led governments in the direction of opening them up to competition and/or privatizing them. (L.O. 8)

Questions

1. (a) Describe three types of government programs that are helpful to small business in Canada.
   (b) What is the opportunity cost of these government programs?
   (c) What are the benefits to Canadians that offset the opportunity costs in part (b)?

2. (a) Why is industrial concentration of concern to government policy-makers?
   (b) Is the overall degree of industrial concentration in Canada lower or higher than in the U.S.?
   (c) State four reasons for the situation described in part (b).

3. Are the following business practices in legal Canada or not? Explain the reasons for each of your answers.
   (a) actions that lessen competition substantially
   (b) price-fixing by producers
   (c) mergers of large corporations

4. Probably the most historic anti-monopoly prosecution involved Microsoft in the United States over the 1998–2002 period. Prosecutors argued that Microsoft's 80 percent share of the market for PC operating systems gave it near-monopoly power. Furthermore, they argued, Microsoft's dominant position in the market was protected by economies of scale: the fixed cost of developing an operating system such as Windows is very high, but the marginal cost of producing additional copies of Windows is very low. This facilitated business practices such as offering its Internet Explorer browser (which was tied to Windows) for free, and made it very difficult for other firms to compete.
   (a) What arguments might Microsoft use in its defence?
   (b) If the prosecution won the case, what remedies might it ask the court to award against Microsoft?
   (c) Make an argument that the facts of the situation justify declaring Microsoft a natural monopoly whose prices and/or profits should be regulated by the government.
   (d) Make an argument that government regulation of Microsoft's prices and/or profits would not only be unnecessary, but also would not be in the interests of consumers.
   (e) Do you know the outcome of the case? It's at **www.usdoj.gov/atr/cases/ f200400/200457.htm**.

5. The Canadian Broadcasting Corporation (CBC) is a federal Crown corporation. Make the strongest possible argument that the CBC
   (a) should be privatized.
   (b) should continue to be a Crown corporation.

6. Which of the following two merger proposals do you think the Competition Bureau would be more likely to accept, and why?

(a) a merger of two furniture manufacturers that would give the new company 65 percent of the Canadian market for a particular type of furniture, or

(b) a merger of two national supermarket chains that would give the new chain nearly 50 percent of the market in many regional areas.

7. Visit the Competition Bureau's website (**www.competitionbureau.gc.ca**) and report on any significant recent developments or cases involving the Competition Act and the Competition Bureau. Search for "Penalties Imposed", then click on "Penalties Imposed by the Courts—Competition Bureau". To see a summary of the facts in each case, click on the name of the company or individual involved. Is there any pattern to the types of cases currently being pursued in the courts by the Bureau?

8. Visit the website of the Business Development Bank of Canada (BDC) at **www.bdc.ca**.
   (a) Who owns the BDC, what is its mission, and how many branches does it operate?
   (b) What services does the BDC provide, and to whom?
   (c) What was the number and total value of loans made by the BDC last year?
   (d) Explain the difference between the activities of the Competition Bureau and the BDC.

Study Guide

Review Questions (Answers to these Review Questions appear in Appendix B.)

1. According to the doctrine of laissez-faire,
   (a) the economy functions best when government regulation and intervention are kept to a minimum.
   (b) the economy cannot function well unless the government takes over the ownership and operation of all businesses.
   (c) the economy functions best if businesses are privately owned and operated, but are subject to extensive government regulations.
   (d) all concentrated industries should be controlled by the government.
   (e) None of the above.

2. The doctrine of laissez-faire assumes that
   (a) all industries are perfectly competitive.
   (b) the economy generally consists of industries that are competitive.
   (c) businesses seek to maximize the welfare of the consumer, and government regulation is therefore unnecessary.
   (d) all business profits are reinvested.
   (e) None of the above.

3. Generally, government policy toward an industry tends to be more *supportive* of industries that are _____, and more *restrictive* toward industries that are _____.

4. *Industrial concentration* refers to
   (a) situations in which one firm controls over half of the sales of an industry.
   (b) the extent to which an industry is dominated by a few firms.
   (c) only those industries in which profits are significantly above the average for the economy as a whole.
   (d) industries in which the major firm(s) concentrate(s) on acquiring the shares of their competition.
   (e) None of the above.

5. Industrial concentration is of interest and concern to economists because
   (a) when a few firms dominate an industry, the potential exists for monopolistic practices such as price-fixing.
   (b) larger firms are sometimes more progressive technologically, and so contribute to higher productivity and living standards.
   (c) it is generally agreed that big business and the domination of industries by a few firms reduce the standard of living of the people.
   (d) Both (a) and (c) are correct.
   (e) Both (a) and (b) are correct.

6. State whether each of the following is a reason why large corporations have come to play such a large role in much of the Canadian economy. Answer *yes* or *no* to each point.
   (a) _____ Larger businesses often enjoy cost advantages due to large-scale production and are thus better able to compete.
   (b) _____ Modern manufacturing often requires such vast amounts of capital investment and large plants that large corporations are required.
   (c) _____ Government prefers large corporations to smaller businesses, and it is government policy to encourage the development of large corporations through tax advantages and other measures.
   (d) _____ Businesses often merge with their competitors.
   (e) _____ The small size of the Canadian market allows for the development of relatively few firms in some industries.

7. The most basic reason for the higher-than-average profit rates of large corporations is that oligopolists
   (a) are more efficient than the average firm.
   (b) advertise more than the average firm.
   (c) pay lower wages than the average firm.
   (d) often compete less intensely regarding prices than firms in competitive industries.
   (e) None of the above.

8. Critics of big business argue that industrial concentration tends to result in
   (a) higher prices and higher output than would be the case in competitive industries.
   (b) lower prices and higher output than would be the case in competitive industries.
   (c) higher prices and lower output than would be the case in competitive industries.
   (d) lower prices and lower output than would be the case in competitive industries.

9. Of the following, which is the *most valid argument* in defence of big business?
   (a) The profits of big businesses (expressed as a rate of return on capital) are not higher than the profits of competitive industries.
   (b) Oligopolists do not agree among themselves to raise prices and restrict output; rather, they compete vigorously on prices.
   (c) While abuses of big business's power (e.g., price-fixing) occurred in the past, these are now prevented by the government.
   (d) Oligopolists constantly strive to improve the quality of their products to the maximum extent possible and to keep their prices low.
   (e) The reinvestment of the large profits of big business in research and development, technological change, and capital investment raises productivity and thus society's standard of living.

10. In determining an appropriate government policy toward large corporations, what factors create a dilemma for Canadian authorities?
    (a) Industrial concentration in Canada is higher than in the United States and other countries.
    (b) Because Canada's largest corporations are much smaller than their foreign counterparts, they are often at a competitive disadvantage in international trade.
    (c) The profits of oligopolistic corporations in Canada are very much higher than in other countries, suggesting that price-fixing is a particularly serious problem in Canada.
    (d) Both (a) and (b) are correct.
    (e) Both (b) and (c) are correct.

11. The basic purpose of Canada's *Competition Act* (1986) is
    (a) to promote and preserve competition in Canadian markets.
    (b) to stop mergers of large corporations.
    (c) to outlaw price-fixing by businesses.
    (d) to break up corporations that are so large that they dominate markets.
    (e) to limit the market share of large corporations.

12. Two business practices that are prohibited by the Competition Act because they reduce competition in markets are
    (a) _____ and
    (b) _____.

13. The Competition Act allows firms to defend proposed mergers on the grounds that the merger would result in _____, and thereby increase the ability of Canadian industry to _____.

14. Suppose that an industry consists of four companies with the following market shares:
    Company A: 30 percent of total industry sales
    Company B: 26 percent of total industry sales
    Company C: 24 percent of total industry sales
    Company D: 20 percent of total industry sales

    Suppose that Company A and Company C want to merge into one larger company that will have more than $400 million in sales or assets.
    (a) Under Canadian law, what must these companies do before they can merge into one company?
    (b) What factors will the federal Competition Bureau consider when reviewing this proposed merger?
    (c) If the Competition Bureau is not satisfied with the proposed merger, what actions might the Competition Bureau take?

15. Under the Competition Act,
    (a) the Bureau of Competition Policy has approved the vast majority of proposed mergers.
    (b) the Bureau of Competition Policy has negotiated significant modifications to some proposed mergers, mostly involving the sale of assets to competitors.
    (c) a large number of proposed mergers have been rejected by the Bureau of Competition Policy.
    (d) a large number of proposed mergers have led to disputes between the Bureau of Competition Policy and the companies involved, which have had to be referred to the Competition Tribunal for a final decision.
    (e) Both (a) and (b) have been true.

16. (a) Some industries are considered to be natural monopolies because
_____.
(b) Two examples of natural monopolies are _____ and
_____.

17. Traditionally, governments have dealt with natural monopolies by
(a) passing laws forbidding them to earn any profits.
(b) taking over the ownership and operation of them.
(c) regulating the prices that they can charge.
(d) Both (b) and (c) are correct.
(e) None of the above.

Critical Thinking Questions

(Asterisked questions 1 to 3 are answered in Appendix B; the answers to questions 4 to 7 are in the Instructor's Manual that accompanies this text.)

*1. In 2001, the Competition Bureau sought an order prohibiting Air Canada from *reducing* its fares below a certain point on certain flights in Eastern Canada that were also serviced by low-cost carriers WestJet and CanJet. Ordinarily, one thinks of the Competition Bureau as opposing the *increasing* of prices by firms. What would explain the Bureau's objection in this case to Air Canada's *lowering* of prices?

*2. Many people dislike the haggling that often characterizes the purchase of a car, and would prefer to buy a car like they buy most other items—the seller tells you the price, and you decide whether or not to buy the product. When Toyota decided to cater to such people by deciding its "best price" for its cars, and instructing its dealers to sell cars at that price, and at that price only, the Competition Bureau objected. Why do you think the Competition Bureau intervened?

*3. Following are the income statements for a manufacturing company with sales of $500 million per year and a service firm such as a restaurant with sales of $500 thousand per year:

	Manufacturing Company	Restaurant
Sales revenue	$500 million	$500 thousand
Non-labour costs	370	320
Labour costs	100	150
Profit	30	30
Payroll taxes (10% of payroll)		
Profit after payroll taxes		

(a) Why are the manufacturing company's labour costs 20 percent of sales revenue, while the restaurant's labour costs are 30 percent of sales revenue?
(b) Finish the table by calculating the payroll taxes and the profits after payroll taxes for each firm.
(c) By what percent do payroll taxes reduce the profit of each firm?

4. The development of a new drug is a very costly venture, involving years of research and testing, and possibly investment in production equipment. On the other hand, once the drug has been developed and mass-production facilities are

in place, the production of additional "copies" of the drug (pills, etc.) is often very inexpensive. Government policy regarding the drug industry is to grant a *patent* to the company that develops a new drug, which gives that company a legal monopoly for a certain number of years. After the patent expires, competing firms can also produce the drug, in generic form.

(a) Compare the drug industry's fixed costs and marginal costs.
(b) How could the situation in part (a) generate economic incentives that slow down the development of new and improved drugs?
(c) Why would the government give a legal monopoly to drug companies?
(d) Why would this legal monopoly be time-limited?
(e) After a patent expires, would you expect the price to fall significantly? Why?

5. Historically, the electricity industry has been treated as a natural monopoly. The facilities that generate electricity (such as hydro-electric plants, coal- or gas-fired plants, and nuclear plants) and transmit it to users over complex systems of wires enjoy such large economies of scale that it was considered both inevitable and beneficial to the public that governments would own them and operate them as monopolies. More recently, however, new technologies such as windmills (visit **www.canwea.ca**) have made it economical to generate electricity on a much smaller scale, with lower fixed costs. This has led to interest in changing the electricity industry, up to and including proposals to privatize entire provincially-owned electrical utilities.

(a) Make an argument that electrical utilities should be privatized.
(b) Make an argument that electrical utilities should be continue to be government-run monopolies.
(c) Is it easier to argue for privatizing the generation of electricity or the transmission of it? Why?
(d) Can you think of some compromise between government-run monopolies and complete privatization that could be beneficial?

6. In the 1970s, Canadian governments introduced marketing boards as a new way of assisting farmers economically. In short, a marketing board is a government agency that has the authority to tell farmers that they cannot produce more than a certain amount of products such as eggs or milk or cheese or chickens. The result of such limitation of supply was, of course, that farmers received much higher prices for these products.

(a) Why would the government establish agencies whose activities would be illegal under the Competition Act?
(b) Who would object to the practices of marketing boards? Why?

Use the Web   (Hints for this Use the Web exercise appear in Appendix B.)

1. In late 2010, the Competition Bureau filed an application with the Competition Tribunal to strike down rules that Visa and MasterCard impose on merchants who accept their credit cards. The Commissioner of Competition alleged that these rules have effectively eliminated competition between Visa and MasterCard for merchants' acceptance of their credit cards, resulting in increased costs to businesses and, ultimately, consumers. Merchants in Canada pay an estimated $5 billion annually in hidden credit card fees. For details of the investigation, visit the Competition Bureau's website at **www.competitionbureau.gc.ca/eic/site/cb-bc.nsf/eng/03325.html**.

10

Labour Markets and Labour Unions

After studying this chapter, you should be able to

1. Explain, with the aid of a graph, how wages are determined in the nonunion sector of the labour force.

2. Give two reasons for the large differences in incomes that exist, and explain why these differences persist.

3. Explain, with the aid of a graph, the effects of a minimum wage law on a low-wage labour market.

4. Explain the collective bargaining process as described in the text.

5. Describe the results of the collective bargaining process in terms of how frequently work stoppages occur and their cost to the economy in working time lost.

6. Explain how disputes over alleged violations of a collective agreement are handled, and explain the difference between and compulsory arbitration and conciliation.

7. Describe the collective bargaining process for unionized employees in essential public services, and give two reasons why the final step in this process is not regarded as ideal.

8. State the trend in union membership as a percentage of the labour force since 1980, and explain the main reasons for this trend.

9. Explain three challenges facing Canada's union movement.

10. Apply the concepts and facts of this chapter to various situations.

In the past few chapters, we have examined *markets for goods and services,* and how prices are determined in these markets by supply and demand, under conditions ranging from highly competitive to monopolistic. In these markets, the sellers are business firms and the buyers are mostly households, or consumers. Markets for goods and services are shown by the flows in the top half of Figure 10-1.

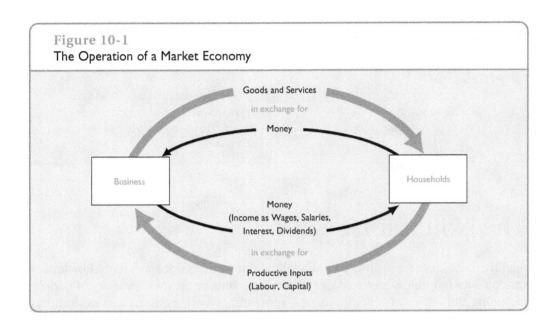

Figure 10-1
The Operation of a Market Economy

The flows in the bottom half of Figure 10-1 show *markets for labour.* In labour markets, the roles of households and businesses are reversed—the sellers are members of households (workers) seeking to sell their labour services, and the buyers are business firms who want to employ people with various skills. The items being "bought" and "sold" are the time and skills of the workers, and the "price" is the wage or salary the workers receive. In labour markets, the supply of various occupational skills interacts with employers' demand for those skills to determine the wages and salaries (or prices) of different types of labour.

In Chapter 7, we saw that markets for products could be described as *competitive* or *concentrated.* In competitive markets, sellers are not organized for the purpose of controlling supply, so prices are determined by the free interplay of supply and demand. In concentrated markets, by contrast, producers can sometimes organize themselves to restrict the supply of the product and keep its price high. These two types of product markets are shown in Table 10-1.

Table 10-1 also shows that labour markets can be characterized in the same way that product markets can. *Nonunion* labour markets are similar to *competitive* industries in that there are large numbers of sellers (workers) who are *not organized* in order to increase their market power and thus gain economically. In contrast, *unionized* groups of workers are more comparable to *concentrated* industries in which business firms are *organized* and band together to gain market power and higher incomes.

In Chapter 1, we saw that one of the three fundamental economic questions is how to divide up the economic pie among Canadians. This allocation is decided by the *incomes* of Canadians, which are mostly determined in the labour markets that we will study in Chapter 10. First, we will consider the nonunion sector of the labour market, then the unionized sector.

Table 10-1
Markets for Products and Markets for Labour

Markets for Goods and Services	Markets for Labour
(a) Competitive Many sellers; *not organized* to restrict competition and control supply and price. Sellers deal as *individuals*.	*(a) Nonunionized* Numerous workers (sellers of labour); *not organized*; deal with buyers (employers) as *individuals*.
(b) Concentrated A few large sellers; sometimes *organized* to restrict competition and influence price by deal *as a group*.	*(b) Unionized* Workers are *organized* by unions to restrict competition among themselves; deal *as a group* with employers in pursuit of higher wages, etc.

The Nonunion Sector

The nonunion sector of the labour force includes both movie stars and fast food workers.

Slightly more than two-thirds of Canada's labour force is not represented by labour unions. The nonunion sector of the labour force embraces a wide variety of people, including the self-employed, managers, most office workers, most service-industry employees (ranging from banking and finance to small-scale service firms such as restaurants and retail shops), and many part-time workers in a variety of occupations.

The incomes of these groups, and of individuals within each group, are determined by a variety of complex factors; however, certain generalizations can be made. Broadly speaking, in the nonunion sector, the forces determining wages and salaries are the *supply of* and *demand for* various types of labour, as shown in Figure 10-2.

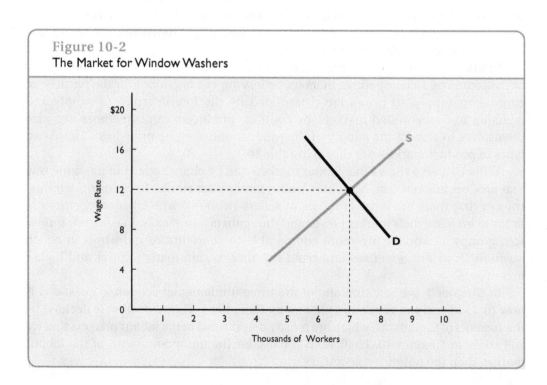

Figure 10-2
The Market for Window Washers

The supply of a particular type of labour (such as the window washers in Figure 10-2) depends on a number of factors, such as the number of people with the required abilities and training and their willingness to work in the field. Also, as the shape of the supply curve shows, higher wages will attract more of these potential workers to actually offer their services to employers. At a wage rate of $8 per hour, 6000 people want to work as window washers, while at a wage rate of $12 per hour, 7000 people will want to work at this job. This is the same relationship that we saw in Chapter 5—higher prices (here, wages) result in a greater quantity supplied (here, labour).

The demand for window washers is called a **derived demand** because it is dependent on, or derived from, the demand for window washing. That is, the higher the demand for window washing is, the higher the demand for window washers will be. However, other factors, such as technological change, can also affect the demand for window washers, by altering the number of workers needed to wash a given number of windows.

derived demand
The demand for a factor of production, which is generated by (derived from) the demand for the good or service that it is used to produce.

Finally, as the shape of the demand curve in Figure 10-2 shows, the number of workers actually demanded (employed) by employers will depend to a significant extent on the wages of those workers—at higher wages, it will not be economical to hire as many window washers as at lower wages. Higher wages might make the price of window washing higher, reducing the "derived demand" for window washers. Also, higher wages would encourage employers of window washers to use labour-saving technology to reduce the number of employees. So a variety of factors underlie the demand and supply curves that determine the wage rate for nonunion workers. In the market for window washers depicted in Figure 10-2, the equilibrium wage rate is $12 per hour, and 7000 people will be employed.

Labour Markets

The Role of Labour Markets

Labour markets perform the important role of allocating labour to various occupations according to the demand of employers and, ultimately, the consumers who buy their products/services. In this role of allocating labour, wages—or, more precisely, *changes in wages*—play an important part. For instance, if the demand for window washing increased, the demand for window washers would increase, causing the demand curve to shift to the right, as shown in Figure 10-3. The result would be an increase in the wage rate of window washers from $12 to $16 per hour, which would attract an additional 1000 people to accept jobs in this field. So, in response to increased consumer demand, employment in this industry has risen from 7000 to 8000. And if the demand for window washing decreased, the market would operate in the opposite direction, as lower wage rates discouraged people from entering this occupation.

In this way, changes in wage rates 'steer' workers toward occupations for which the demand is rising, and away from occupations with falling demand, in the same way that changes in prices 'steer' businesses to produce more of some products and less of others.

short run
The period of time during which the quantities of some inputs cannot be changed.

Labour Markets in the Short Run and the Long Run

Labour markets do not always adjust to changes rapidly and smoothly. In the **short run** (the period when some factors of production are fixed), an increase in wage rates may not call forth an increase in the number of workers, due to the time it takes to recruit and/or train workers. In the **long run** (the period in which the quantities of

long run
The period of time after which the quantities of all inputs can be changed.

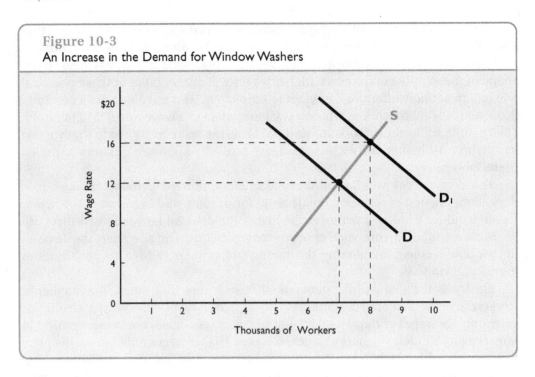

Figure 10-3
An Increase in the Demand for Window Washers

inputs *can* be changed), higher wage rates will attract more people into a field. But in occupations that require a great deal of training, such as medicine, this increase in the number of workers can take considerable time.

The more elastic the supply of labour is, the more smoothly a labour market will operate. Figure 10-4 illustrates this concept by comparing the response of the market for clerical workers and the market for dentists to an identical increase in demand. In the case of clerical workers, homemakers provide a pool of qualified workers who are not working but available for work. This makes the supply quite *elastic*—a relatively small increase in wages and employment opportunities will attract many additional workers into the market. As a result, the increase in demand from D to D_1 causes a large increase in employment (from 100 to 130) and only a small increase in wages (from $10 to $12).

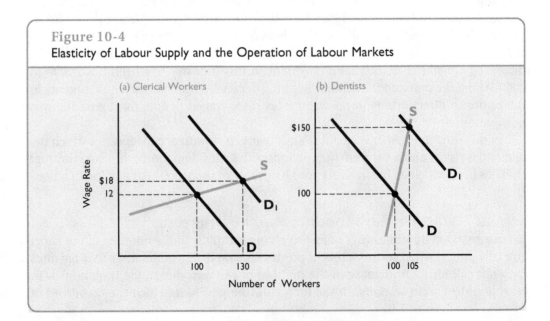

Figure 10-4
Elasticity of Labour Supply and the Operation of Labour Markets

In the market for dentists, the supply of labour is *inelastic*. Almost all the qualified people are already working, and due to the training period required, the number of dentists cannot be increased very much, at least not in the short run. This inelasticity of supply is reflected in the steep slope of the supply curve in graph (b) of Figure 10-4, which shows that even a sharp increase in the wage rate will not bring forth a large increase in the number of dentists on the market. As a result, the same increase in demand as for clerical workers has a quite different effect, causing only a small increase in employment (from 100 to 105) and a very large increase in wages (from $100 to $150), at least in the short run. In the long run, the higher wages would attract additional people into dentistry; that is, the long-run supply curve is likely to become much more elastic.

YOU DECIDE

Canada's Shortage of Skilled Trades Workers

A major economic challenge facing Canada is expected to be a shortage of skilled trades workers. Shortages are expected across the trades in general, and in the construction, mining and petroleum sectors in particular. With many older skilled trades workers soon to retire, Skills Canada (www.skillscanada.com) has estimated that one million more skilled trade workers will be needed between 2014 and 2020. The skilled trades pay good wages, but relatively few young Canadians have been attracted to this type of work.

QUESTIONS

1. With well over a million Canadians unemployed, what explains why shortages of skilled trades workers are already happening, and are projected to grow more severe?
2. What could be done to remedy this situation?

Canadians are constantly going from job to job; from job to unemployment and back; from outside the labour force to a job; and from unemployment to out of the labour force (not seeking work). In a two-year study that tracked a group of Canadians, Statistics Canada found that just 38 percent remained in the same job throughout the two years, and 48 percent averaged more than three transitions. This amounted to 7000 transitions every working hour.

The Dynamic Nature of Labour Markets

The days when a person would settle into one job or one employer indefinitely are long gone. Because of changes in underlying economic factors such as consumer demand, industrial technology, and international competition, as well as changes in general economic conditions such as periodic booms and recessions, labour markets tend to be very dynamic. In some sectors of the economy and some occupational areas, the number of jobs will be expanding, while in others it will be contracting. As a result, in any given year, there is a large flow of people into the labour market, out of the labour market, and between jobs within the labour market. The internet has proven very helpful in this marketplace, through websites such as Workopolis, which make the marketplace much more efficient and effective by providing timely information concerning job opportunities.

Because of these fluctuations, governments provide a variety of programs designed to help workers adjust to changing job markets. Such programs range from the temporary income support provided by Employment Insurance to programs that retrain workers and help them to relocate in order to take new jobs.

www.workpolis.com

Income Differentials

The free interaction of supply and demand in the marketplace generates a tremendous range of incomes (income differentials), from those of star athletes and

The average income of the top 1 percent of Canadian income-earners is about ten times the average income of all Canadians.

entertainers to those of part-time retail workers. In competitive markets, one might wonder why such large income differentials persist over long periods of time. Chartered accountants earn far higher incomes than clerical workers. So why wouldn't more people (including clerical workers dissatisfied with their low incomes) be attracted to become accountants, thus increasing the supply of accountants and reducing the income differential between them and clerical workers?

The answer, of course, lies mainly in the fact that there are often *obstacles* to entering certain occupations. Not everyone has the abilities and skills required to become a chartered accountant, or the opportunity to pursue the education required, so the income differentials between the two groups tend to persist. Similarly, the scarcity of people with the talents to be top athletes or entertainers, or who will undertake unpleasant or dangerous jobs, causes their incomes to be very high compared to incomes for jobs that many people are able and willing to do.

Educational requirements are a major obstacle to entering certain occupations. Sometimes, educational requirements are based on specific knowledge that must be acquired in order to perform a job (such as accounting), while in other cases employers use educational requirements as a handy screening device for applicants (such as the requirement of a university degree for certain jobs).

Because of the cost of higher education, *ability to pay* is sometimes an obstacle to entering certain occupations. For instance, medical and law schools are more accessible to the children of well-off families than poor families. Because of this, many Canadians regard equality of educational opportunities as a key social policy objective, since education is the main way for the children of lower-income families to break out of the "poverty trap."

Obstacles to entering occupations are not the only reason for differences in incomes. Age and experience have a large influence on people's incomes, as most people's incomes are low in their early years of work and peak after age 50. Another factor is *market power*. We saw in Chapter 7 how business firms can obtain market power by acting together; in the second half of this chapter, we will see how some groups of workers do the same thing, by joining together into labour unions.

To summarize, differences in incomes are generated by various factors, including
- abilities and skills,
- educational requirements,
- age and experience, and
- market power.

Minimum Wage Legislation

minimum wage
A legal minimum wage rate set by law.

The fact that, in an open labour market, some groups earn very low wages has led governments to enact minimum wage laws that set legal minimums for the wage rates that employers can pay their employees. In Figure 10-5, the equilibrium or market wage rate is $9 per hour, but the government has set the legal **minimum wage** rate at $12 per hour.

The objective of minimum wage legislation is to increase the incomes of low-wage earners. However, as Figure 10-5 shows, minimum wage legislation also has the side effect of *increasing unemployment*. At the equilibrium wage rate of $9 per hour, 90 000 workers are employed, whereas at a legal minimum wage rate of $12 per hour, only 80 000 jobs exist (point A). There are fewer jobs because the higher wage rate reduces the number of workers that employers can and will employ. Furthermore, the higher wage rate attracts an additional 10 000 workers into the labour force who are looking for work, bringing the total number of people wanting to work to 100 000 (point B), and total unemployment of these workers to 20 000 (the distance AB).

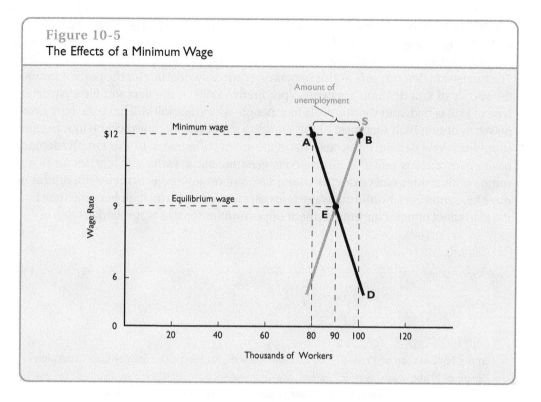

Figure 10-5
The Effects of a Minimum Wage

While there is little doubt that minimum wage laws do reduce the number of jobs, there is also considerable debate as to *how much* they increase unemployment. Generally, employers opposing increases in the minimum wage stress how minimum wage rates kill jobs, while labour unions and other groups that support minimum wages argue that the negative effects on employment are minimal. Supporters of higher minimum wage rates argue that past increases in the minimum wage rate have not been followed by layoffs of employees. However, the effect of higher minimum wages may be more subtle than this, as the *disemployment effect* may arise more from reduced hiring of new workers than from layoffs of existing ones. Then, as workers who left were not all replaced with newly hired workers, the total number of jobs would be reduced. According to labour economists, minimum wage laws create a sort of lottery, in which the winners are the workers who remain in (or get) jobs at the higher wage rates required by the law, while the losers are those who do not get jobs because of the minimum wage. In particular, researchers believe that minimum wages limit employment opportunities for women, many of whom work in service industries such as restaurants, and for younger workers, who are just entering the labour force and often must compete with more experienced workers for jobs.

While the extent of this disemployment effect is uncertain, the basic reality is that in order to lift low-wage earners out of poverty, the legal minimum wage rate would have to be increased substantially from the current levels. And most observers agree that such large increases in the minimum wage rate could have significant negative effects on the job opportunities of the very people the minimum wage was intended to help. So increasing the minimum wage rate would not *in itself* be an effective way to combat poverty. In Chapters 11 and 12, we will consider the problem of poverty and other ways of assisting the poor.

To summarize, in the nonunion sector of the labour force, employees' wages and benefits are largely determined by **individual bargaining** between employees and

Less than 7 percent of the work force work at or below the minimum wage rate. Most are female, young, students or part-timers working in the accommodation, food service, or retail trade industries.

individual bargaining
The process through which workers deal as individuals with employers in negotiating their terms and conditions of employment.

employers. Each worker is free to seek the best deal he or she can get from an employer, and employers are free (subject to legislated rules such as minimum wage laws and employment standards legislation) to seek the best deal they can obtain from workers. The forces that determine how this bargaining process works out for the participants are the supply of and demand for various productive skills. If the demand for a particular type of skill is high and the supply is low, people with that skill will have the bargaining power to obtain high incomes. In the opposite situation, incomes will be low, because supply exceeds demand. Because there are great differences in the supply/demand balance for various skills, labour markets generate some extremely high incomes and some very low ones. Governments attempt to support low-wage earners with minimum wage laws; however, minimum wage rates cannot be made too high because they have the side effect of reducing employment opportunities for low-wage workers.

IN THE NEWS

Hockey Players' Salaries

In the NHL season of 1966–67, the average salary of players for the Stanley Cup Champion Toronto Maple Leafs was 2.7 times the average income of Canadian families. By the 2014–15 season, an average Maple Leaf player's salary was over 40 *times* the average family income of Canadians. ■

QUESTIONS
1. What explains such a large increase in hockey players' incomes?
2. What limits are there on rapid income increases such as these?

The Unionized Sector

collective bargaining
The process through which employers and unions negotiate a new collective agreement.

In the unionized sector of the labour force, the situation is quite different. Individual bargaining is replaced by **collective bargaining**, in which a labour union negotiates with the employer on behalf of *all* the employees represented by the union. The bargaining relationship is thereby considerably altered. The last resort of an individual bargaining on his or her own behalf is to resign (and perhaps be easily replaced, depending on his or her skills), but a union can call a *strike* of *all* the employees it represents. As a result, unionized employees are generally in a stronger position in negotiating with their employers.

Unions in Canada

Labour unions represent about 30 percent of Canada's labour force. As Figure 10-6 shows, the degree of unionization (the percentage of employees who are union members and/or represented by a union) varies widely from industry to industry.

The outstanding feature of Figure 10-6 is the high degree of unionization of government employees—about 75 percent of government employees are unionized, as compared to only 17 percent of private-sector employees.

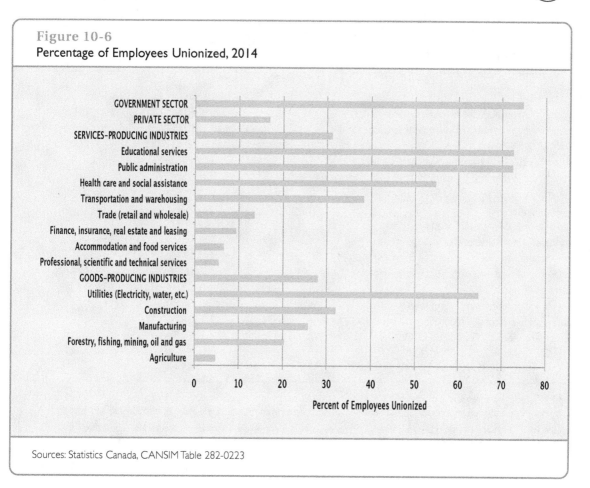

Figure 10-6
Percentage of Employees Unionized, 2014

Sources: Statistics Canada, CANSIM Table 282-0223

The 31 percent unionization rate in service-producing industries is slightly higher than the 28 percent rate in goods-producing industries, but only because the services sector includes most government employees, who are heavily unionized. In private-sector service industries such as retail and wholesale trade, accommodation and food services, and finance, the average unionization rate is below 10 percent.

In goods-producing industries, the average **union coverage rate** of 28 percent is largely due to the 65 percent rate for employees of utilities such as electricity and water, most of whom are government employees. The unionization rate for construction (32 percent) is only slightly higher than the national average, and in manufacturing, the rate has fallen below 26 percent.

The list of Canada's largest unions in Table 10-2 reflects these facts, as half of Canada's largest unions represent government employees, and the 7 largest government-employee unions have nearly one-third of all union members in Canada.

The gender composition of Canada's unionized workforce has changed dramatically in recent years. As recently as 1997, Canada's union membership was 55 per cent male and based mostly in the manufacturing sector, in industries such as automobiles and steel. By 2014, more than half of Canada's union members were women, many of them government sector employees in fields such as health care and education.

Finally, by international standards, the degree of unionization in Canada (30 percent) is neither large nor small, falling between the United States' low level of about 12 percent and the levels of European countries, which often exceed 40 percent.

union coverage rate
The percentage of a group of workers that are union members and/or represented by a union.

Like corporations, unions are quite concentrated—in 2013, the largest ten unions had 50 percent of total union membership in Canada.

Table 10-2
Canada's 14 Largest Unions, 2013

Name	Membership
Canadian Union of Public Employees	630 050
National Union of Public and General Employees	340 000
UNIFOR	308 000
United Food and Commercial Workers Canada	245 327
United Steel, Paper and Forestry, Rubber, Manufacturing, Energy, Allied Industrial and Service Workers International Union	230 700
Public Service Alliance of Canada	187 587
Fédération de la santé et des services sociaux (Federation of Health and Social Services)	129 032
Service Employees International Union	118 991
Teamsters Canada	93 351
Alberta Union of Provincial Employees	80 107
Laborers' International Union of North America	80 000
Elementary Teachers' Federation of Ontario	76 166
FTQ Construction	69 914
Ontario Secondary School Teachers' Federation	65 642

Unifor (Union for Canada) is the result of a merger of the Canadian Auto Workers and the Communications, Energy and Paperworkers unions. It is Canada's largest private-sector union, representing workers in industries ranging from manufacturing and media to forestry and fishing.

Source: Workplace Information and Research Division, Strategic Policy, Analysis, and Workplace Information Directorate, Labour Program, Employment and Social Development Canada.

www.cupe.ca

Some Questions and Answers

How Do Workers Become Unionized?

About 30 percent of Canada's labour force is *represented* by unions. Some workers are *represented* by a union, even though they have not *joined* that union.

A basic principle of Canadian labour law is that most workers have the right to decide democratically whether to form or join a labour union. This process often takes the form of a vote of the employees (known as a *certification vote*) that is conducted by the Labour Relations Board, a government agency that oversees industrial relations. If a majority of workers votes in favour of being represented by a particular union, that union becomes "certified" as the exclusive representative of those employees, meaning that management must deal with the employees *through the union*, rather than deal with them as individuals. (Conversely, if a group of workers no longer wishes to be represented by a particular union, they can vote to decertify it.)

Once it has been certified, a union must by law represent all of the employees in the group for which the union is certified (the "bargaining unit"). And, since all employees in the bargaining unit receive the economic and other benefits of union representation, the general rule is that they all must pay union dues, whether they have formally joined the union or not.

collective agreement

A contract agreed upon by an employer and labour union, specifying the terms and conditions of employment of the employees for a specified period of time.

How Are Collective Agreements Negotiated?

A key service provided to members by their union is the negotiation of their **collective agreement**, or labour contract. The collective agreement sets out all of the terms and conditions of employment for its duration—from wage rates and hours of work to fringe benefits and pensions. The process through which employers and unions negotiate a new collective agreement is called *collective bargaining*. The bargaining process has been compared to buying a used car—both sides open negotiations by demanding more than they are prepared to settle for, as they attempt to get the best possible deal. Then, gradually, as they both become more concerned about the possibility of a strike, the positions of the union and management teams become more reasonable and compatible. Many contract negotiations are settled at this stage. However, it is quite common for the parties to seek assistance before reaching an agreement.

This assistance generally takes the form of *conciliation* (also known as mediation). The conciliator is a neutral person whose role is to *assist the employer and the union to negotiate their own agreement*. Conciliators (unlike arbitrators, which will be discussed later in this chapter) have no authority to decide the outcome of the negotiations by imposing a settlement on the parties. Conciliators are people with broad experience in labour relations disputes, which often proves useful in assisting employers and unions to reach a negotiated agreement without a work stoppage. Sometimes conciliators can use their experience to make helpful suggestions to the negotiators, while at other times conciliators will use various tactics to apply pressure to the negotiators to make concessions and compromises.

Should the employer and the union prove unable to agree upon a negotiated agreement (with or without conciliation), a work stoppage (that is, a strike or lockout) can take place, after the previous collective agreement has expired. Usually, the union will set a strike deadline, and the period before the strike deadline gives both sides an opportunity to reconsider their positions, under growing pressure from the fact that they are facing a strike deadline that is growing closer each day. This pressure can be effective in pushing the negotiators to make compromises in a last-ditch effort to avert a work stoppage. If the parties fail to reach a settlement under pressure of this strike deadline, a work stoppage can occur that will impose losses on *both* sides until an agreement is reached.

Occasionally, the employer will initiate the work stoppage by *locking out* the employees. By setting a deadline for a lockout, the employer can gain control of the timing of a work stoppage, should one take place.

In a work stoppage, the employees will lose wages, and the employer will lose sales and profits. The result is a test of the economic power of the two sides, with the side that has the greatest ability to withstand the economic pressures of the work stoppage more likely to prevail.

Generally, somewhat less than half of contract negotiations are settled before conciliation, about the same number are settled through conciliation, and five percent or less of negotiations end in a work stoppage (usually a strike by the union, but sometimes a lockout by the employer). At whatever stage a settlement is reached, however, it must finally be approved by the membership of the union, through a *ratification vote*.

Why Permit Strikes?

Many people see strikes as a primitive way of settling labour disputes through a form of "trial by combat," and feel that the government should not permit strikes (or lockouts). They would prefer a way of settling labour disputes that is more civilized, reasonable, and fair.

However, it is important to appreciate that a basic premise of labour legislation is that industrial relations disputes are best worked out *by those directly involved*—the employer, through management, and the employees, through their union. As a result, the law does not provide for the government to intervene and impose a decision or a contract on employers and unions. Rather, the law establishes a framework within which unions and employers are expected to *negotiate their own solutions* to their problems, even if that involves a work stoppage.

It is also important to recognize that the threat of a work stoppage plays a very important *positive role* in the collective bargaining process. In a typical year, about 95 percent of all contract negotiations end in agreement without a work stoppage, mainly because *both* the union *and* employer fear the consequences of a stoppage. So the right to strike or lock out (or, more precisely, the *threat* of a work stoppage) serves the important purpose of forcing *both* the employer *and* the union to negotiate seriously, with the usual result being an agreement *without* a work stoppage.

When Are Strikes Not Legal?

This can be a confusing matter, because there are two very different types of disputes that arise between unions and employers. In the one type of dispute, it is quite legal for a strike or lockout to occur, but in the other, it is not (see Table 10-3).

The first type of dispute is the one covered in the previous section—the negotiation of a collective agreement. In such negotiations, it is generally legal to use a strike or lockout (as a last resort), although not until the previous collective agreement has expired. The only exception is essential public services such as police and firefighters, in which work stoppages are generally not allowed by law. These are covered later in this chapter.

There is, however, a second and quite different type of union–management dispute. These are disputes not over the terms of a new contract that is *being negotiated* but rather over *alleged violations of an existing contract.* For instance, suppose that management fires a worker in a way that the worker and the union consider to be a violation of the collective agreement. How should they pursue this matter?

Table 10-3
Two Types of Industrial Relations Disputes

The collective agreement, or labour contract, between an employer and its union sets the terms and conditions of employment for its duration—i.e., constitutes "industrial law" for the parties.

There are two distinctly different types of disputes between employers and unions over the collective agreement:

1. Over Negotiation of the Terms of a New Collective Agreement	2. Over an Alleged Violation of an Existing Collective Agreement
e.g., union wants a 5% wage raise; management offers 1%	e.g., in firing Viv, did management violate the agreement?
⟹ Union and Employer NEGOTIATE	⟹ GRIEVANCE (= Appeal of Management's Decision)
If they cannot agree on terms of the new contract, A STRIKE OR LOCKOUT CAN LEGALLY OCCUR.	If they cannot agree on how to resolve the matter, A DECISION IS MADE BY AN ARBITRATOR (NEUTRAL THIRD PARTY).

The law does not allow strikes (or lockouts) over such disputes. Instead, the worker must file a **grievance**, which is an appeal of management's decision on the grounds that it violates the collective agreement. This will lead to a series of discussions between management and the union to resolve the matter, starting at the lower levels of each organization and moving to higher levels if necessary. If these discussions fail to settle the grievance, the law requires that the dispute be taken to **arbitration**. Arbitration is a court-like process in which a neutral third party (an arbitrator) hears the evidence of both sides and decides whether the collective agreement has been violated. In the example in the previous paragraph of the grievance concerning the firing of the worker, the arbitrator might decide to uphold management's decision, or to reinstate the worker in his or her job with retroactive pay for the time missed from work during the grievance. The arbitrator's decision is binding on both the union and management, who cannot resort to a strike or lockout if they disagree with it.

grievance
An alleged violation of a collective agreement by an employer.

arbitration
The resolution of union–management disputes by the decision of a third party; required by law for grievances that the union and employer cannot resolve by themselves.

Aren't Strikes Costly?

It is true that work stoppages can be costly to those directly involved—the employer loses profits and the employees lose wages. However, the effects of strikes on the nation's economy are greatly exaggerated by the general public. The working time lost due to work stoppages is an extremely small fraction of total time worked in the economy—in recent years, less than one-tenth of one percent.

This is a fraction of the working time that would be lost if all working Canadians were given one additional holiday per year. So, while industrial disputes do impose economic costs on some Canadians, it cannot be argued that strikes *in general* are a threat to the nation's economy.

But What About Public Service Strikes?

While the percentage of total time worked in the economy that is lost due to work stoppages is small, the *impact* of work stoppages on the Canadian public is probably greater than these statistics would suggest, because compared to other countries, a higher proportion of Canada's work stoppages involve *government employees* and thus the interruption of *public services*.

Government employees in Canada enjoy considerably greater rights to unionize and to strike than do their counterparts in most other countries. Since the mid-1960s, it has been a general principle of Canadian labour law that government employees should have similar rights to unionize, bargain collectively, and strike as do employees in the private sector. As a result, governments for the most part have tended to withdraw the right to strike only from employees in *essential* public services, such as police, firefighters, and some hospital workers. As a result, Canada experiences more frequent work stoppages in public services than most other nations do.

In the case of a strike by, for instance, 1500 workers at a soft-drink company, the public can continue to consume the product until inventories run out, and then can switch to other brands of soft drinks until the strike is over. However, a strike by 1500 public transit workers or garbage collectors or teachers will prove much more disruptive, because there is no alternative supplier. Work stoppages in some public services (such as postal service, education, public transit, garbage collection, and health care) have represented a difficult problem in Canadian industrial relations, because they can have a considerable impact on the public and sometimes the economy.

Some say that the solution to this problem is simply to outlaw strikes by government employees. But the matter is not nearly as simple as this. It is not sufficient merely to remove the right of employees to strike—some alternative method must be used to settle their collective bargaining disputes promptly and fairly. Usually, when the right to strike is withheld from a group of employees, the law provides for negotiations and conciliation to take place as described earlier, but requires that if the dispute is not settled through these processes, it must be submitted to *compulsory arbitration*. In arbitration, a neutral third party considers arguments from both management and the union as to what the terms of the collective agreement (wages, benefits, etc.) should be, and then makes a final decision that is binding on both sides. The union cannot strike, nor can the employer lock out the employees.

While the general public tends to see arbitration as a simple solution to the problem, those actually involved in the process are much less satisfied with it. Compulsory arbitration requires that vital decisions be made by an outsider who lacks familiarity with the problems of the employees and management, many of which are often very complex. Another problem is the long delays in the negotiation/arbitration process—it is not uncommon for settlements (and employees' wage increases) to be held up for a year or more after the previous collective agreement has expired. Without the threat of a work stoppage, neither side (particularly the employer) may feel much pressure to negotiate quickly. Also, the arbitration process itself usually lasts several months, during which both sides make extensive submissions, both in writing and at hearings, backed up by large volumes of statistical data and arguments.

Management is not always pleased with arbitration either, because it takes very important matters away from management's control. Major decisions are placed in the hands of an outsider whose decisions cannot be appealed but which may impair management's ability to deliver effectively and efficiently the public service for which the organization is responsible. So arbitration is far from the ideal and simple solution to labour disputes that it may appear to be. For another perspective on the arbitration process, see the "You Decide" box below.

YOU DECIDE

Let's Play Arbitrator

If you think compulsory arbitration of labour contract disputes is a simple matter, take the following opportunity to see the kinds of challenges involved.

A married couple whom you know only slightly are having severe marital problems and disputes, largely because their marriage is not living up to the expectations that each held for it. They agree that it would have been better if, before they were married, they had written up a marriage contract specifying the rights and responsibilities of each partner. However, given the present state of deterioration of their relationship, they are unable to agree on the terms of such a contract. They have asked you, as an impartial third party, to resolve the matter for them in the following way: you will listen to the views and arguments of each of the parties, their proposals for the terms to be included in the contract, and the exact wording of each clause; then you will, on your own, *write for them a complete, detailed marriage contract* that will provide a workable basis for a renewed marriage.

Good luck! ▪

QUESTIONS

1. What is your major strength as the arbitrator of these people's differences?
2. What is your major weakness as the arbitrator?
3. After listening to the positions of each of the parties, will you have a clear picture of the facts of the situation?
4. If one of the parties disagrees with your decision or part of it, how committed will that person be to trying to make your decision work?

The Future of Unionism

Canadian unionism has enjoyed many successes over its long history, not only in terms of the growth of its membership and economic gains for its members, but also through its support of social programs that benefit all Canadians in areas such as health care, safety laws, unemployment insurance, and pensions.

More recently, though, the labour movement faces a number of significant challenges in areas that are vital to its future: the recruitment of union members, unions' relationships with their employers, and their public image.

Recruitment of new members has been a concern of unions since the late 1970s. From the 1940s through the 1970s, total union membership grew quite rapidly, first among manufacturing workers and then among government employees. After the 1970s, however, this trend changed.

While total union membership continued to grow, it grew more slowly than the labour force. As a result, after 1980, the percentage of employees represented by unions decreased, from 38 percent of employees around 30 percent, with most of the decline occurring in the 1980s and 1990s. After 2000, the overall unionization rate remained around 30 percent; however, the rate in some goods-producing industries such as manufacturing continued to decline.

The percentage of men in unionized jobs fell from 42% in 1981 to 29% in 2012; women's unionization rate hovered around 30% during the same period.

This decline was concentrated in private-sector union membership, mostly of males in goods-producing industries. It was caused by two basic and powerful forces for economic change: *technological change* and *international competition* arising from freer trade. Both of these changes cut into employment in many unionized manufacturing industries, as workers were replaced by technology or jobs moved to lower-wage countries. Then in the 1990s the financial problems of Canadian governments restrained the growth of unionized employment in the public sector. So, in two of the most unionized sectors of the economy—manufacturing and government—employment growth was slow, and likely to remain so.

Where, then, could unions recruit new members? The most rapid growth of employment by far was in the *service sector* of the economy—in industries such as retail trade, restaurants, fast food, hotels, entertainment, finance, travel and tourism, recreation, home repairs, day care, landscaping, and so on. Recruiting workers in such industries into unions poses an enormous challenge to unions, for various reasons. Most service-industry employees work in small and scattered businesses with only a few employees, in which owner–managers and employees often work closely together, without the impersonality and "us-versus-them" relationship that makes it easier to unionize workers. In addition, many service-industry workers do not have a long-term attachment to their jobs—many are part-time workers, so such jobs often have a high turnover rate of workers. As a result of factors such as these, the service sector of the economy has tended to be only lightly unionized, and quite resistant to attempts to unionize it.

Unions' relationships with employers have also been challenged by the same economic forces. In the past, Canadian unions in both the private and government sectors had won considerable gains for their members through the adversarial approach of hard bargaining and a willingness to use the strike weapon—confrontation was their style, and it was often effective.

However, freer trade has changed the economic environment. Bargaining with a very profitable oligopolistic manufacturing corporation that has the market power to raise its prices in order to avoid a strike is very different from bargaining with an employer that has low profit margins and whose pricing is limited by foreign competition. Also, unions' bargaining power has been further limited by technological change, which gives employers more options to reduce labour costs by using labour-saving technology.

In short, it had become less easy than it had once been for many private employers to raise prices in order to make peace with their unions, but easier for them to replace workers with technology. And in the government sector, employers' resistance to union demands was also growing, due to financial pressures on governments from their budget deficits.

Because of these changes, it was becoming apparent that the old approach to union-management relationships of confrontation and hostility was no longer sufficient. Both private and public employers faced strong new pressures to keep costs down and increase efficiency, and workers needed financially sound employers in order to have job security. These challenges raised fundamental questions, not only for unions, but also for the management of many enterprises, who were forced to reconsider whether they could expect to manage effectively in this new environment with a traditional authoritarian management style that fostered conflict with their employees rather than the cooperation that they now needed.

The public image of unions has become another growing concern for the labour movement. For many years, many Canadians have perceived unions as beneficial to all Canadians, through their support for social programs in areas such as health care, safety laws, unemployment insurance, pensions, and so on.

More recently, however, this public support for labour unions has been eroding. To some Canadians, it seems that the big battles fought by unions in the past have been won. With employment standards, safety regulations, health care, human rights protections, pensions, and so on all embedded in laws that apply to all workplaces, whether unionized or not, the socially positive effects of union activities seem less evident.

Instead, there has been a growing resentment of unions, and a perception that union members are no longer the underdogs fighting for workers' rights against powerful big corporations, but rather have become "fat cats" who enjoy benefits that other Canadians do not.

This resentment applies to union members in general, but is particularly strong against unionized government employees. To growing numbers of Canadians, the wages, job security, and especially the pensions of government employees are unfairly generous, and impose a burden on the public through higher taxes, and the government employees' unions are to blame for this.

For unions, this means that in addition to facing the more threatening *economic* environment described earlier, they will also probably be facing a more difficult *political* environment, in which public support for government actions to restrict unions could grow.

Chapter Summary

1. About two-thirds of Canada's labour force is not represented by labour unions. In this non-union sector of the labour force, the basic factors that determine wages are the supply of and demand for various skills. (L.O. 1)
2. Supply and demand in labour markets generate a very wide range of incomes; this is in large part due to obstacles to entering certain occupations. (L.O. 2)
3. Minimum wage laws can increase the wages of low-income groups; however, they also have the effect of increasing unemployment among those groups. (L.O. 3).
4. About 30 percent of Canada's labour force is represented by labour unions. The terms and conditions of employment for unionized employees are negotiated by their union and employer through a collective bargaining process, in which a work stoppage can take place as the final step in the process. (L.O. 4)
5. Typically, in about 95 percent of cases, collective bargaining results in an agreement without a work stoppage, and the working time lost due to work stoppages in most years is a very small percentage of total time worked in the economy. (L.O. 5)
6. For disputes over alleged violations of an existing collective agreement, the grievance procedure is used; the final step in this process is a binding decision by an arbitrator. (L.O. 6)
7. For employees in essential public services, strikes are generally not legal; instead, the final step in the collective bargaining process is compulsory arbitration. (L.O. 7)
8. Since 1980, the union coverage rate has fallen from 38 percent to around 30 percent, largely because the most rapid growth of employment has been in the lightly-unionized service sector rather than in the more heavily-unionized manufacturing and government sectors. (L.O.8)
9. Canada's union movement faces challenges regarding maintaining and increasing its membership, its relationships with employers, and its public image. (L.O.9)

Questions

1. In the *nonunion sector* of the labour force, wages and salaries are basically determined by
   (a) the employer, who is free to decide the wages that will be paid.
   (b) the government, which decides what is a fair wage in each case.
   (c) the supply of, and demand for, each particular job skill.
   (d) the minimum-wage laws, as all nonunion employees would be paid less if these laws did not exist.
   (e) the economic and social contribution made by these individuals and groups.
       Explain why each answer that you did *not* select is wrong.

2. The following table shows the market for part-time student labour in Canville.

Wage Rate per Hour	Number of Workers Demanded (Jobs)	Number of Workers Supplied (Job-seekers)
11	800	1200
10	900	1100
9	1000	1000
8	1200	900

(a) In a free market, what will the wage rate be?

(b) If the government imposed a minimum-wage rate of $10 per hour, what would happen in this market?

(c) Explain the reasons for the developments in part (b), with reference to changes on both the supply side and the demand side of this market.

3. Minimum-wage laws that require employers to pay wages above the market equilibrium wage rate tend to

(a) benefit *all workers*, both skilled and unskilled.

(b) benefit *all* unskilled/low-wage workers.

(c) benefit *some* unskilled/low-wage workers.

(d) increase unemployment among unskilled/low-wage workers.

(e) have both of the effects described in (c) and (d).

Explain your answer, using the table in question 2 to illustrate.

4. Suppose that the demand for dentists and house painters simultaneously increased by 25 percent over a short period of time. Which occupation would enjoy the greater increase in incomes over the next few years? Explain why this would be the case, referring in your explanation to the term *elasticity*.

5. In 1980, unions represented 38 percent of Canada's labour force. In recent years, this figure has been about _____ percent. Explain three reasons for this trend.

6. "Strikes are an outdated 'trial by combat' approach to union–management disputes and cost the Canadian economy heavily in terms of lost work. Strikes serve no useful purpose in Canada's industrial relations system, and it would be better for all Canadians if the government simply outlawed strikes and required that all unresolved collective bargaining disputes be decided by arbitration."

Explain why you agree or disagree with this statement.

7. Both conciliators (also known as mediators) and arbitrators sometimes play a role in securing a settlement in collective bargaining between unions and employers.

(a) What is the greatest strength that helps a conciliator in playing his or her role?

(b) What is the greatest weakness that limits a conciliator in playing his or her role?

(c) What is the greatest strength that helps an arbitrator in playing his or her role?

(d) What is the greatest weakness that limits an arbitrator in playing his or her role?

8. Sometimes an approach called *med-arb* (short for *mediation-arbitration*) is used in collective bargaining in situations where a work stoppage cannot take place. In this approach, the bargaining process is the same as described in the text, except that the conciliator (mediator) and the arbitrator *are the same person*. How could this arrangement make that person more effective in both the role of the mediator/conciliator and the role of arbitrator?

9. Visit Statistics Canada's website and find StatsCan's most recent study on minimum-wage workers. To do this, search the site for "minimum wage." Also, do a Google search for "minimum wage" + "Canada."

(a) How many minimum-wage workers are there in Canada?

(b) Who are they?

(c) In which industries and in what sorts of jobs do they work?

(d) Which provinces have the highest and lowest minimum wage rates? (Visit http://canadaonline.about.com/od/labourstandards/a/minimum-wage-in-canada.htm).

Study Guide

Review Questions (Answers to these Review Questions appear in Appendix B.)

Answer questions 1–4 on the basis of the following graph portraying the market for window washers.

1. If the demand for window washers is represented by the curve **D**, the hourly wage rate for window washers will be $ _____ and employment will be _____ workers.

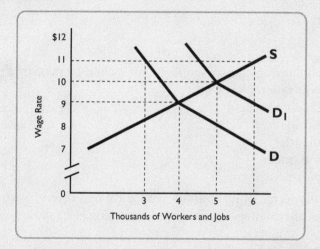

2. If the demand for window washers were to increase as shown by the curve **D₁**, the hourly wage rate would become $ _____. These changes would attract an additional _____ workers into the industry, bringing total employment to _____ workers.

3. If the government were to set a minimum wage of $11 per hour for workers such as window washers, and the demand for window washers was represented by curve **D**, the result would be that
   (a) employment would increase to 6000.
   (b) unemployment would increase to 1000.
   (c) unemployment would increase to 2000.
   (d) unemployment would increase to 3000.
   (e) None of the above.

4. The situation described in the previous question will develop for the following two reasons:
   (a) _____, and
   (b) _____.

5. Most people would agree that medical care is far more important than baseball, but baseball players are paid far more than nurses. Why is this so?
   (a) Baseball players are really entertainers rather than producers of a service.
   (b) Compared to the demand for them, good baseball players are more scarce than nurses.
   (c) Baseball players are more skilled than persons who get less pay.
   (d) The demand for baseball players is greater than for nurses.
   (e) There are fewer professional baseball players than nurses.

6. Large differences in incomes such as those in the previous question tend to persist over long periods of time, largely because
    (a) some occupations make a greater contribution to society than others.
    (b) in some occupations, the demand for labour is persistently large relative to the supply.
    (c) in some occupations, the supply of labour is persistently large relative to the demand.
    (d) there are obstacles to entering some occupations.
    (e) Answers (b), (c) and (d) are all correct.

7. Recently, what percent of Canada's labour force has been represented by unions?
    (a) 10 percent
    (b) 16 percent
    (c) 30 percent
    (d) 38 percent
    (e) 43 percent

8. State whether each of the following types of employment is characterized by a relatively high degree of unionization (*yes* or *no*).
    (a) _____ government employment
    (b) _____ manufacturing
    (c) _____ service industries
    (d) _____ construction trades
    (e) _____ office employment

9. If an employer violates the terms of its contract (collective agreement) with its union (for instance, in the disciplining of employees), the union is legally empowered to
    (a) *sue* the employer in court for breach of contract.
    (b) file a *grievance* against the employer.
    (c) call a *strike* against the employer.
    (d) All of the above.
    (e) None of the above.

10. The final step in the process in question 9 is that
    (a) a neutral third party (an arbitrator) will make a judgment that is binding on both the employer and the union.
    (b) a court may award damages (financial compensation) to the employees.
    (c) fear of the strike or the economic losses arising from the strike will force both the union and the employer to a compromise and settle the matter.
    (d) Both (b) and (c), depending on the course of action chosen by the union.
    (e) Any of the above, depending on the course of action chosen by the union.

11. A strike or lockout is generally legal
    (a) any time there is a dispute between a union and an employer.
    (b) only after the government authorizes a work stoppage.
    (c) as soon as the existing contract (collective agreement) between the union and the employer has expired.
    (d) None of the above.

12. State whether each of the following statements regarding strikes is *true* or *false*.
    (a) _____ They are totally negative in character; they serve no useful purpose in our industrial relations system.
    (b) _____ They play an important role in our industrial relations system because the fear of a strike forces both the employer and the union to compromise in contract negotiations.

(c) _____ Most employers would prefer a system in which strikes are outlawed and unresolved contract disputes are submitted to an arbitrator for a final decision.

(d) _____ They are very costly to society in terms of lost working time and lost output.

13. The proportion of union–management contract negotiations that is settled by negotiation and without a work stoppage (strike or lockout) is generally
    (a) over 90 percent.
    (b) about 75 percent.
    (c) about 60 percent.
    (d) about 50 percent.
    (e) about 35 percent.

14. Which statement best describes the general attitude of unions and management to a legal ban on all strikes?
    (a) Both favour outlawing strikes because this would eliminate costly strikes.
    (b) Unions generally favour such a move, but employers are reluctant to accept it.
    (c) Neither favours such a move because it would require both of them to turn over to an arbitrator the right to decide issues of vital importance to them.
    (d) Employers generally favour such a move, but unions are opposed to it.
    (e) None of the above.

15. Which of the following best describes the usual way of resolving contract disputes in public services that are considered to be essential?
    (a) Contract negotiations take place as usual, and if no agreement is reached, a strike takes place.
    (b) Contract negotiations take place as usual, but if no agreement is reached the dispute is referred to an arbitrator for a final decision—a strike is not legal.
    (c) Essential-service employees are not allowed to form or join labour unions or to strike; decisions regarding wages and conditions of employment are made solely by management.
    (d) Strikes are not legal and no contract negotiations take place—wages and terms of employment are decided by Parliament.
    (e) Contract negotiations take place as usual, except that if no agreement is reached, the dispute is referred to the government for a decision—strikes are not legal.

Critical Thinking Questions

(Asterisked questions 1 to 5 are answered in Appendix B; the answers to questions 6 to 10 are in the Instructor's Manual that accompanies this text.)

*1. Suppose that hairdressers employed by salons organized into a union in an attempt to increase their incomes. What obstacles would their effort encounter with respect to
    (a) the demand side of the market for their labour?
    (b) the supply side of the market for their labour?

*2. Visualize the sorts of developments that would probably occur within both the union and the management negotiating teams as the strike deadline drew nearer. Would these make a settlement more or less likely?

*3. There has been a decline in union membership as a percentage of the labour force since the late 1970s. What would Canada's labour unions have to do in order to reverse this trend? What obstacles would unions have to overcome, and what factors might help them to recruit members?

*4. What explains the fact that from 1981 to 2012, the percentage of men in unionized jobs fell from 42% to 29%, while the unionization rate for women remained around 30%?

*5. Since around 1990, the number of worker-days lost due to strikes and lockouts in Canada has decreased significantly. What might explain this trend?

6. "Only a society with no sense of values would pay an uneducated goon of a hockey player fifty times the income of a police officer or a firefighter." Discuss this statement from the perspectives of *why* such income differentials exist, and whether you agree with the statement.

7. A *lockout* is a work stoppage that is initiated by the employer rather than by its union. Why would an employer lock out its employees rather than let them continue working until they decided to strike?

8. "If employers had profit-sharing with their employees and employee stock ownership plans whereby employees could become shareholders, there would no longer be any need for unions." Do you agree or disagree? Why?

9. To resolve collective bargaining disputes in essential public services, a procedure called *Final Offer Selection* is occasionally used. Negotiations proceed as usual, but if the parties cannot agree on a new contract, each party must make a *final offer* to the other party at a final bargaining meeting, following which further negotiations can occur. If there is no agreement, these two final offers must be presented, *unchanged*, to an arbitrator, who must select as the terms of the collective agreement the offer that is deemed the more reasonable. So *either one or the other* of the offers will become the collective agreement.
   (a) How do you think Final Offer Selection is *intended* to operate in resolving collective bargaining disputes?
   (b) What possible *problem*s might Final Offer Selection encounter in resolving collective bargaining disputes?

10. During recessions such as the early 1980s, the early 1990s, and 2008–09, the worker-days lost due to labour disputes (strikes and lockouts) falls. What could explain this pattern?

Use the Web (Hints for this Use the Web exercise appear in Appendix B.)

1. Visit Statistics Canada's website at **www.statcan.gc.ca** and search for "average earnings of the population 15 years and over by highest level of schooling." What do the statistics in the table tell you about the demand–supply balance at different education and skill levels of the Canadian labour market?

2. The Canadian Labour Congress (CLC) is a national federation of labour unions that represents the concerns of unions across Canada. Visit the CLC's website at **www.clc-ctc.ca**, read its home page then click on *Click, Our Newsletter*, then "*Issues.*" What issues are of concern to the CLC at this time? How are these issues related to economic developments and/or government policies?

Employment and Incomes in the Canadian Economy

LEARNING OBJECTIVES

After studying this chapter, you should be able to

1. Describe the trends in employment in the main sectors of the Canadian economy since 1950, explain the basic causes of these trends, and recognize the consequences of these changes.

2. Give four reasons for the increase in female participation rates and in the percentage of women in the Canadian workforce since 1950.

3. Describe the changing trends in average real family income since 1951, and explain the two basic causes of these changes.

4. Discuss the size of the male–female pay gap and the reasons for that gap.

5. Discuss the reasons for the widening pay gap between skilled workers and unskilled workers.

6. Compare the definitions of *poverty* used by Statistics Canada's Low-Income Cut-Offs (LICOs) and the market basket measure (MBM) approach, and the poverty lines and poverty rates under the two definitions of poverty.

7. Identify four groups that have a strong tendency to be poor, and explain why each group tends to be poor.

8. Apply the facts and concepts of this chapter to various situations.

In Chapter 10, we examined the operation of the labour markets in which Canadians obtain jobs and earn incomes. In this chapter, we will consider more closely two important aspects of those labour markets: (a) the current and future *trends in employment* in labour markets, and (b) two important *trends in Canadians' incomes*—the level of incomes, and how those incomes are divided among various groups, or how the economic pie is divided up.

Employment Trends in Canada

Over the past half-century, major changes have taken place in the nature of the work performed by Canadians. In the broadest terms, as Figure 11-1 shows, the number of people working in the *goods-producing sector* of the economy (industries such as agriculture, forestry, mining, fishing, manufacturing, and construction) has increased quite slowly, while there has been a dramatic increase in employment in the *services-producing sector*, in a wide range of industries ranging from numerous personal services such as restaurants and fast food, retail trade, financial services, tax services, travel services, haircutting, lawn care, dog-walking, and so on, through government and

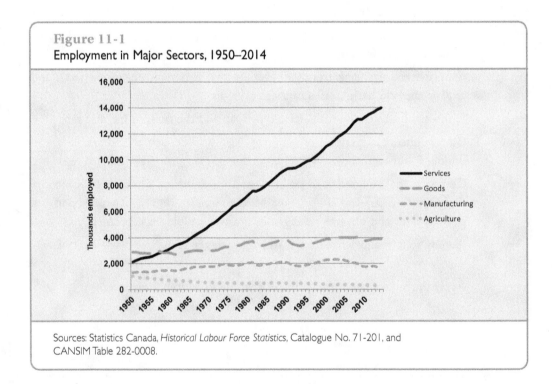

Figure 11-1
Employment in Major Sectors, 1950–2014

Sources: Statistics Canada, *Historical Labour Force Statistics*, Catalogue No. 71-201, and CANSIM Table 282-0008.

community services such as health care and education, as well as business services such as security, information technology, consulting, and research.

The result of these trends, as Figure 11-2 shows, has been that the proportion of Canadians working in the goods-producing sector of the economy has declined from over 56 percent in 1951 to 22 percent by 2014, while there has been a corresponding increase from 44 percent to 78 percent of the work force employed in the service sector of the economy. Table 11-1 breaks this trend down into its component parts: a dramatic decline not only in the proportion but also the actual number of Canadians employed in agriculture; a steady decline in the proportion of employment accounted for by the

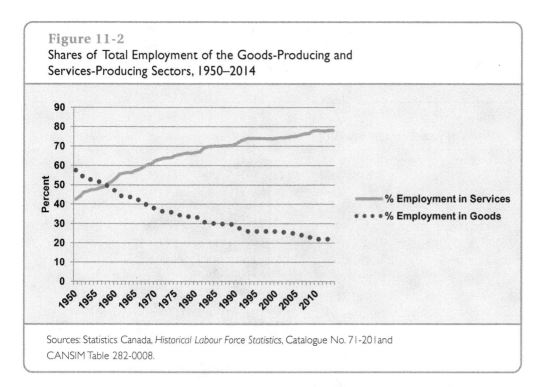

Figure 11-2

Shares of Total Employment of the Goods-Producing and
Services-Producing Sectors, 1950–2014

Sources: Statistics Canada, *Historical Labour Force Statistics*, Catalogue No. 71-201 and
CANSIM Table 282-0008.

manufacturing sector; a slight increase in the proportion of employment provided by
trade, finance, insurance, and real estate; and a dramatic increase in employment in a
variety of community, business, and personal service industries and public administration (or the government sector). From 1976 to 2014, over 91 percent of the increase in
employment in Canada occurred in the service sector of the economy. These trends have

Table 11-1

The Changing Nature of Employment in Canada

	Percent of Total Employment in Each Sector in:						
	1951	1961	1971	1981	1991	2001	2014
Agriculture	18.4	11.2	6.3	3.9	3.5	2.2	1.7
Non-agricultural primary industries	4.4	3.0	2.7	3.1	2.3	1.9	2.1
Manufacturing	26.5	24.0	21.8	18.4	14.7	14.9	9.7
Construction	6.8	6.2	6.0	6.3	5.7	5.5	7.4
Total goods-producing sector	56.1	44.5	36.9	32.7	27.4	25.2	21.7
Transportation, storage, communication and utilities	8.8	9.3	8.7	6.7	6.0	6.0	5.9
Trade (Retail and wholesale)	15.1	16.9	16.5	15.6	16.0	15.8	15.2
Finance, insurance and real estate	3.0	3.9	4.9	6.0	6.6	5.9	6.3
Community, business and personal services and public administration	18.0	25.3	33.0	40.2	45.1	47.8	51.8
Total service-producing sector	43.9	55.5	63.1	67.3	72.6	74.8	78.3
Total all industries	100.0	100.0	100.0	100.0	100.0	100.0	100.0

Sources: Adapted from Statistics Canada, *Historical Labour Force Statistics*, Catalogue No. 71-201 and CANSIM Table 282-0008.

already caused major changes in the ways in which Canadians learn, live, and earn their living, and will continue to do so. In the following sections, we will examine the causes, the effects, and the future implications of these trends

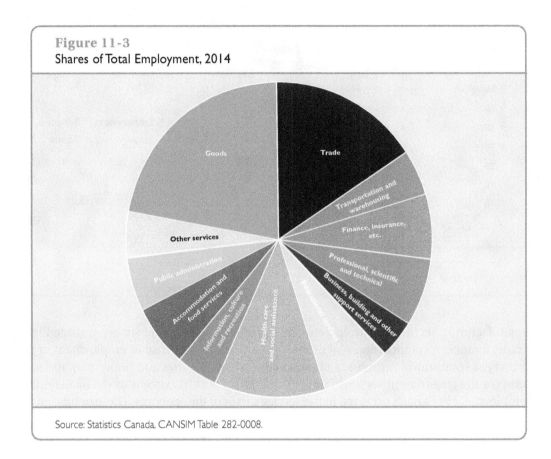

Figure 11-3
Shares of Total Employment, 2014

Source: Statistics Canada, CANSIM Table 282-0008.

In Table 11-1, the category "Community, business and personal services and public administration" includes a wide range of service industries. Figure 11-3 breaks these down into a number of more specific types of industries such as "Accommodation and food services", "Educational services", and so on. A more detailed breakdown would reveal a large number of *specific* service industries within each *type* of industry—for example, the category of "Accommodation and food services" would include hotels, motels, restaurants, fast food service, and a variety of other related services.

Causes of Trends in Employment

To understand why the nature of employment has changed so greatly, we must consider some fundamental changes that have occurred on both the *demand side* and the *supply side* of labour markets in Canada.

The Demand Side

Technological Change

Technological change is the most basic force underlying the changing nature of employment because it has generated major shifts in employers' demand for labour. While technology affects all industrial production methods, it has generally proven easier to apply labour-saving technology to the production of goods, which lend themselves to mass-production techniques, than to the production of services. Many services (such as haircuts, medical services, education, and legal services) are "labour-intensive"; that is, they require a person-to-person delivery. By contrast, the production of many goods can be very "capital-intensive," as the worker-hours per unit of output can be reduced considerably through using capital equipment, including computer-controlled industrial robots.

At the start of the twentieth century, 40 percent of Canada's labour force worked in the *agricultural sector* of the economy. In Canada, as in other nations, the first impact of technological change was in the agricultural sector of the economy, which is well-suited to extensive use of capital equipment. The result was a dramatic increase in agricultural productivity over that century, and a corresponding decrease in the number of workers required in the agricultural sector. Over the twentieth century, the number of agricultural workers decreased by about 400,000, and by 2000, only about 2 percent of Canada's labour force was working in agriculture. Viewed differently, technological change "freed up" large numbers of workers from agriculture, making them available for work in the manufacturing and service sectors of the economy.

Many of the workers no longer needed in agriculture were able to find employment in the *manufacturing sector* of the economy, where employment increased until the late 1970s. However, much of the manufacturing sector is also quite well-suited to mass-production technology. From 1981 to 2013, the output of the manufacturing sector of the Canadian economy increased by about 64 percent, while employment in manufacturing *decreased* by 17 percent. Over the same period, employment in the service sector *grew* by 82 percent. So the decrease in the percentage of the labour force employed in the manufacturing sector that is shown in Table 11-1 has been mainly the result of the introduction of labour-saving technology.

Changes in Consumer Demand

Obviously, the rapid growth in service-industry employment shown in Figure 11-1 could not occur without major increases in the *demand for services*. A key factor in the growth of the demand for services was the process of technological change described in the previous section. By increasing output per worker (productivity), technological change has *increased the standard of living* of Canadians. And, as their living standards rose, people spent an ever-increasing proportion of their incomes on services such as restaurants, entertainment, and travel. Since most service industries are labour-intensive, the rising demand for services generated a vast number of service-industry jobs, sufficient to allow the economy to provide work for the people freed up from the agricultural and manufacturing sectors by technological change. And so, for the most part, the shift of employment from the goods-producing sector of the economy to the service sector was achieved fairly smoothly, without excessive increases in unemployment. As a result, employment has risen very rapidly in the service sector, in fields such as retail trade, food service, sales, accounting, finance, human resources, health care, education, law, computer services, and so on.

International Economic Forces

A third factor that has undercut employment in some manufacturing industries has been the growth of international trade and competition since the 1970s—the process known as *globalization*. Competition from low-wage countries has been especially difficult for Canadian manufacturers in industries such as clothing, footwear, furniture, and assembly operations. Caught between low-productivity labour-intensive production methods, high Canadian wages, and low-wage import competition, many

From 1987 to 2014, the number of jobs for chefs and cooks grew by 73 percent. Employment of labourers *decreased* by 21 percent. (CANSIM Table 282-0009)

Figure 11-4
Shifts in Employment, 1950–2014

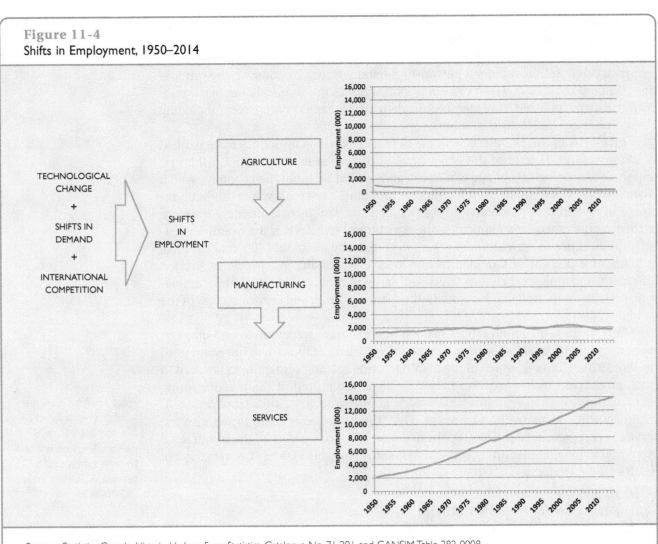

Sources: Statistics Canada, *Historical Labour Force Statistics*, Catalogue No. 71-201 and CANSIM Table 282-0008.

could not continue operating in Canada. Many of those that were able to survive did so through extensive "labour shedding" in order to reduce costs; the result in both cases was a reduction in manufacturing employment in some industries in Canada.

During the twentieth century, then, the nature of the work done by Canadians underwent major changes. Early in the century, most young people stayed and worked on the farm; later, most would go to work in manufacturing plants; now, in the early twenty-first century, the vast majority find jobs in offices or service industries. Similar trends have occurred in all industrialized economies, suggesting that economic progress and change is driven by the same basic technological and economic forces that generate similar results. These forces and their results are summarized in Figure 11-4.

The Supply Side: Working Women

On the supply side of the labour market, there is no doubt that the most dramatic and important development has been the great increase in the number of working women. In 1950, the percentage of women of working age participating in the labour force—

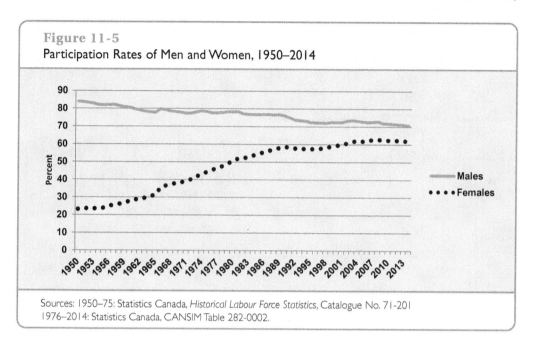

Figure 11-5

Participation Rates of Men and Women, 1950–2014

Sources: 1950–75: Statistics Canada, *Historical Labour Force Statistics*, Catalogue No. 71-201
1976–2014: Statistics Canada, CANSIM Table 282-0002.

the **participation rate**—was 23 percent. By 2014, it was 62 percent. Overall, women comprised 47 percent of the labour force in 2014, compared to less than 22 percent in 1950. These trends are reflected in Figure 11-5, which highlights the rising participation rate of women since the 1950s.

There are several reasons for this remarkable growth of the female work force. Probably the most frequently mentioned factor is the *squeeze on family incomes.* After the mid-1970s, incomes grew more slowly, making it more important for families to have a second income. However, as Figure 11-5 shows, the increase in female participation rates was underway long before this became a factor. This trend suggests that other factors were also at work.

One such factor was the *rising education levels and aspirations of women.* Many more women are completing high school and going on to college and university for higher education than in the past. And, as women's education levels have risen, so have their expectations concerning their jobs, incomes, and careers.

However, these factors only increased the numbers of women *wanting* to work. For this goal to be achieved, there would have to be more *job opportunities* for women.

These opportunities were provided by the rapid growth of the *service sector* of the economy, as described earlier in this chapter. Many women are employed in the service sector, for various reasons. Unlike many goods-industry jobs, most service jobs do not require physical strength so much as the ability to think and to deal with people. Also, many service industries, such as retail trade, provide part-time work, which appeals in particular to working mothers. The importance of the growth of the service sector to the increase in the number of working women can be measured by the fact that, in recent years, over 90 percent of employed women have been working in the service sector of the economy. And this trend appeared likely to continue, as the fastest-growing areas of employment were accounting, human resource management, sales, and advertising—fields in which the number of women was increasing more than three times as rapidly as the number of men.

Finally, many more women are self-supporting than in the past. It is estimated that six in ten women at some time in their life will be self-supporting. More

participation rate
The percentage of people of working age who are participating in the labour force, by either working or looking for work.

On university campuses in recent years, female students have outnumbered males by roughly 4 to 3.

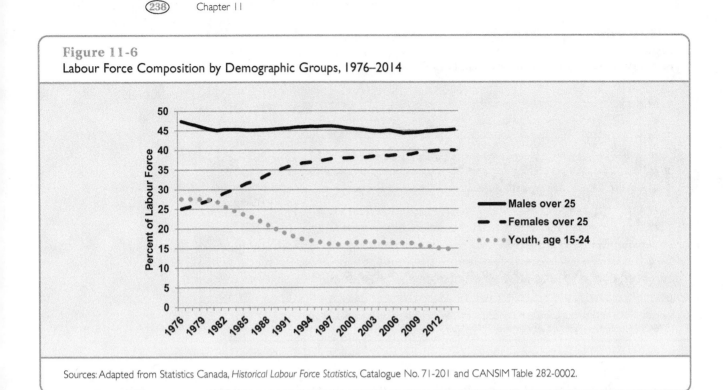

Figure 11-6
Labour Force Composition by Demographic Groups, 1976–2014

- ——— Males over 25
- – – – Females over 25
- · · · · · Youth, age 15-24

Sources: Adapted from Statistics Canada, *Historical Labour Force Statistics*, Catalogue No. 71-201 and CANSIM Table 282-0002.

women are opting for careers, and more marriages break down now than in the past.

Figure 11-6 shows the changes in the composition of the labour force from 1967 to 2014. Due to the rising female participation rates already discussed, the proportion of women in the labour force rose steadily over this period. The 1970s saw a similarly rapid increase in the proportion of *young Canadians* (age 15–24) in the labour force, as the postwar "baby boom" came of working age. However, in the early 1980s, this surge of young entrants to the work force subsided, while the proportion of women in the labour force continued to rise.

Adjusting to Change

The technological and economic forces discussed in this chapter—revolutionary changes in production technology, massive shifts in consumer spending toward services, and the addition of over 5 million women into the work force in less than 40 years—have generated and will continue to generate fundamental changes in the way that Canadians work and live. In the following sections, we will examine some of these changes in the past, the present, and the future.

The urbanization of society was one of the most dramatic effects of technological change in the first half of the twentieth century. As technology reduced the number of workers needed on the farm and drew workers into city-based manufacturing plants, Canada's population became increasingly concentrated into a few large urban areas, with all of the advantages—and disadvantages—of city dwelling. *Rising living standards* were another major result of technological progress, as the increases in output per worker generated by improved technology became the economic basis for a generally rising prosperity among Canadians.

Rising educational requirements were an inevitable aspect of this process because much work became more technical and because many of the new service-industry jobs required specialized knowledge. This trend led to the expansion of the nation's universities and to the establishment of new systems of colleges to provide the "middle-level" skills for which demand grew rapidly as the economy evolved. *Later marriages, working women,* and *higher-income but smaller families* were three other features of the modern society that emerged in the second half of the twentieth century. As noted, the rapid growth of the service industries provided women not only with greatly increased opportunities for employment but also with the prospect of fulfilling and rewarding careers. Longer periods of education and increased interest in women's careers pushed marriage back several years for many, and resulted in much higher family incomes and considerably smaller families than in the past. The *slower population growth* that resulted from these developments eventually led to a government policy of *increased immigration.* To keep the labour force growing at a pace that would provide enough working people to support the baby boomers in their retirement years after 2010, the government increased the inflow of immigration.

Part-time work grew rapidly to over 19 percent of all jobs, in large part due to the rapid growth of service industries such as food service and retail trade, which employ part-time workers. Students and many homemakers welcomed the growth of these part-time job opportunities, but about 30 percent of part-time workers really wanted full-time jobs and were unable to find them. See the "In the News" box below for some facts about how the Canadian labour force has changed since 1976.

IN THE NEWS

Labour Force Facts

From 1976 to 2014 in the Canadian economy:
- the number of jobs increased by 8,124,700, or 83 percent,
- employment in the service sector grew by 7,609,000, or 119 percent,
- employment in the goods-producing sector grew by 515,600, or 15 percent, and
- of the 8,124,700 growth in jobs, 27 percent of the increase were part-time; this brought part-time jobs up to 19.1 percent of total employment (as compared to 12.5 percent in 1976).

QUESTIONS

1. Why do you think part-time employment grew so much faster than full-time employment?
2. Has part-time employment's share of total jobs increased from its 2014 level of 19.1 percent? You can find updated statistics on Statistics Canada's website (www.statcan.gc.ca) by searching for "full-time and part-time employment".

Technology and Employment

After the mid-1980s, the pace of technological change in Canadian industry increased considerably. Such rapid technological change naturally raises fears that new production technology would displace people from their jobs and push ever-higher numbers of people into unemployment, creating economic and social hardship.

Economists tend to be skeptical about such doomsday scenarios. They point out that similar alarms were raised in the past when new agricultural, manufacturing, and computer technologies were introduced. In fact, no long-term increase in unemployment occurred because the effects of technological change on the economy are more complex than they seem. It is generally agreed that technological change can generate *short-term* increases in unemployment by displacing some workers from their jobs. So far, however, this displacement has not created a growing problem of *long-term* unemployment, because there are other, less-noticed aspects of technological change that have positive effects upon employment.

The most important of these has been the rapid growth of employment in the *service sector* of the economy. From 1976 to 2014, employment in service-producing industries grew by 119 percent, while employment in goods-producing industries was growing by only 15 percent, largely due to labour-saving technology. But by increasing output per worker, that same technology raises living standards, which in turn means *higher consumption of services*, and more service-industry jobs. As employers are able to pay higher wages to more productive workers, and as the prices of more efficiently produced goods come down, consumers have more buying power, creating jobs in other sectors of the economy, most notably the *service sector*, which has received a large share of rising consumer spending, as consumers have spent more on services ranging from restaurants to entertainment to financial services to travel and tourism to lawn care and pet care. And since most such services are labour-intensive, this rising consumer spending has generated strongly rising employment in the service sector.

Also, by improving productivity, technological progress enhances the *ability of Canadian industry to compete internationally*. Many Canadian jobs depend on the ability of Canadian producers to export to foreign markets or compete with imports in Canadian markets. Because of this fact, it can be argued that, by improving the efficiency and competitiveness of Canadian producers, technological change could actually support employment.

Figure 11-7 summarizes these factors—the loss of some jobs and displacement of some workers, and the creation of other jobs through increased demand for services and improved international competitiveness. The right side of Figure 11-7 also shows the *process of change* in the labour force, as labour "shifts" from the manufacturing sector to the expanding service sector. Some of the figures shown making this shift are workers who were displaced from jobs by technology, and others are new

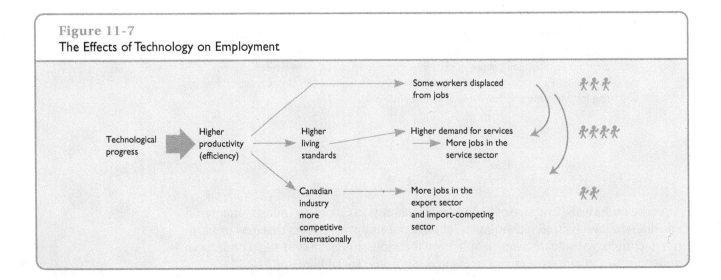

Figure 11-7
The Effects of Technology on Employment

Technological progress → Higher productivity (efficiency) → Higher living standards → Some workers displaced from jobs; Higher demand for services / More jobs in the service sector

Higher productivity (efficiency) → Canadian industry more competitive internationally → More jobs in the export sector and import-competing sector

entrants to the work force who will find work in the service sector rather than in goods-producing industries.

Canada's unemployment rate has been lower in recent years than previously, except during the 2008–09 recession. This indicates that, so far, technological change has tended to *change the nature of work* rather than *reduce the number of jobs*. And, as we have seen, the basic change in the nature of work has been from jobs producing goods to jobs in the service sector. However, making this type of transition to new types of work has required that the labour force adapt to change more than in the past.

Adapting to Change

The key to adapting to change is education and training. It is projected that nearly half of the new jobs created in the future will require more than 16 years of training (a combination of schooling and on-the-job experience) as compared with only 23 percent in 1986.

From the viewpoint of *the individual,* the benefits of education and training are obvious, in the form of a higher probability of finding rewarding employment. Education and training also bring benefits to *business,* in the form of higher productivity. And for *society in general,* investment in education and training is beneficial not only because it improves productivity and prosperity but also because a high-quality labour force tends to attract job-creating business investment.

It is generally agreed that education and training are areas in which Canada needs to improve. Spending on education and training by the Canadian private sector has been low compared to other industrialized countries, and Canada lacks excellent apprenticeship programs such as those of Japan and Germany. While government spending on education in Canada is among the highest in the world, and the average level of educational attainment is high, employers complain that many graduates of Canadian high schools lack the basic literacy and numeracy skills needed to make them productive workers in a modern economy.

Even when there are over a million Canadians unemployed, employers are often unable to recruit qualified workers, and it has been necessary to import certain types of skilled workers. According to a report by the Organization for Economic Cooperation and Development, educational spending should be redirected so as to place greater emphasis on the basic literacy, numeracy, and technical skills needed by a modern workforce.

> "If you think education is expensive, try ignorance."
> — DEREK BOK, FORMER PRESIDENT OF HARVARD UNIVERSITY

www.oecd.org

IN THE NEWS

Technology and Jobs

There have always been fears that new technologies would reduce employment—not just employment in the industries using the new technologies, but also total *employment* in the economy. As the text notes, for many years these fears appeared unfounded, because the rapid growth of jobs in the service sector offset the loss of jobs in industries such as agriculture and manufacturing.

Computer technology did replace labour in some service industries, such as banking and travel agencies, in which computers performed "data processing", or the routine manipulation of masses of structured information. However, it was believed that only humans could perform higher-level tasks requiring the use of judgment to respond to complex and changing situations.

But more recently, machines and computers have moved to new levels of sophistication:

- A machine determines when to administer sedatives to hospital patients.
- A computer diagnoses patients' medical conditions.
- A robot bartender takes customers' orders, then mixes and delivers drinks.
- A computer creates new recipes and a robot performs taste tests on food.
- A computer corrects people's movements while doing physical therapy.

Christopher Steiner's book *Automate This* provides interesting reading about new technologies.

Artificial intelligence now enables machines to *learn* rather than merely follow programmed instructions, and to respond to human language and movement. Algorithms now empower computers to mimic the human mind, and so to do knowledge jobs and service jobs.

Economists are increasingly uncertain about the effects that such technology will have on employment in the future, because those knowledge jobs and service jobs have provided about 90 percent of the increase in total employment in Canada since 1980.

The Optimistic View

Many economists remain confident that the impact of the new technologies will be similar to that of previous technologies. They foresee the effect of the new technologies as assisting workers more than replacing them—for example, a computer might create a "short list" of a patient's possible medical conditions for a doctor to consider, or a "short list" of possible legal precedents for a lawyer, following which a human paraprofessional would sort through, evaluate, and summarize the computer's findings.

They also foresee technology generating rising living standards that will create new service jobs that will offset any loss of jobs due to technology, as has been the case in the past.

The Skeptical View

Others are less confident. One concern relates to the *pace of change*—will workers be able to acquire quickly enough the skills needed to secure jobs in a world of new and rapidly-changing technology? The more fundamental concern, though, is that there might be *fewer jobs*—that technology could reduce the total amount of work needed in the economy in the future.

According to Erik Brynjolfsson, an economist at the Massachussetts Institute of Technology (M.I.T.), "This is the biggest challenge of our society for the next decade. We're going to enter a world in which there's more wealth and less need to work. That should be good news. But if we just put it on autopilot, there's no guarantee this will work out."

And a former U.S. cabinet secretary has said that he no longer believes that automation will always create new jobs. "The answer is surely not to try to stop technical change," he says, "but the answer is not to just suppose that everything's going to be O.K. because the magic of the market will assure that's true." ■

http://web.mit.edu

QUESTIONS

1. Write an optimistic view of how these developments could change people's lives in the future.
2. Write a pessimistic view of how these developments could change people's lives in the future.
3. How could we try to determine if concerns about the negative effect of technology on total employment were correct?

Income Trends in Canada

As Figure 11-8 shows, the average real family income of Canadians has increased considerably since 1951.[1] In fact, average family income in 2011 was more than three times as high as it was 60 years ago, after adjusting for inflation.

More detailed examination of the statistics in Figure 11-8 reveals some significant facts and trends. Average family income rose most rapidly during the 1960s, when it gained almost 40 percent. The 1950s saw the second-greatest gains, of about 27 percent, with the 1970s following with 24 percent. However, most of the growth in living standards occurred between 1951 and 1975, when real income increased at an average rate of 3.4 percent per year. Following 1975, real income per family grew by less than 1 percent per year.

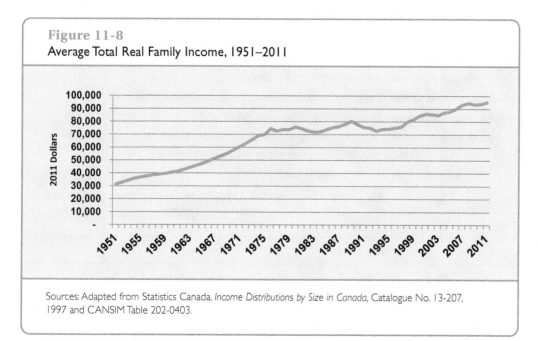

Figure 11-8

Average Total Real Family Income, 1951–2011

Sources: Adapted from Statistics Canada, *Income Distributions by Size in Canada*, Catalogue No. 13-207, 1997 and CANSIM Table 202-0403.

The rapid growth of average real family income until the late 1970s was generated mainly by two factors. The first of these was a significant increase in the number of income-earners per family, mainly the result of *more women working*. The second factor was *rapidly rising productivity*, which, as we have seen, is the most basic source of growing economic prosperity. After the late 1970s, however, the situation changed with respect to both of these factors—productivity growth slowed sharply, and the number of income-earners per family grew less rapidly (and even declined in some years) after peaking at around 1.75. And, when the growth of these two key factors slowed after the late 1970s, so did the growth of average real income per family.

---

[1] *Real income* refers to income after adjusting for inflation. Because of inflation, increases in incomes *seem* larger than they *really are*. For instance, if your income rose by 4 percent but inflation caused the prices of the things you buy to rise by 3 percent, you would be only 1 percent better off, not 4 percent. The figures used in the text and Figure 11-8 show average family income *after allowing for inflation*. For example, in 1951, average family income was about $3,600 in 1951 dollars. But in those days, $3,600 bought about as much as $31,200 would buy in 2011, so Figure 11-8 shows 1951 average family income as $31,200 "in constant 2011 dollars." Adjusting for inflation in this way makes it possible to compare today's incomes with incomes from long ago.

Income by Family Type

Figure 11-8 shows the *average* total income for *all* Canadian families of two or more people, before income taxes. Figure 11-9 provides more detail, by showing incomes for different types of families. The income figures in Figure 11-9 are not directly comparable to those in Figure 11-8, because Figure 11-9 shows incomes after income taxes have been paid. However, they do provide a picture of how the incomes of different types of family compare to each other.

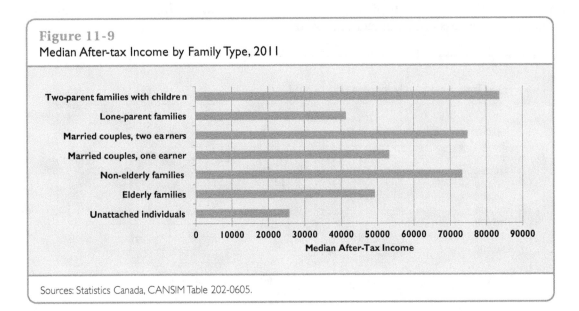

Figure 11-9
Median After-tax Income by Family Type, 2011

Sources: Statistics Canada, CANSIM Table 202-0605.

How Do Americans' and Canadians' Incomes Compare?

For many years, the conventional wisdom has been that Americans enjoy higher incomes than Canadians[2], mainly due to their higher productivity.

However, the situation seems to have become more complex recently, largely due to differences in how income is *distributed* in the two countries. In the U.S. economy, the top few Americans now receive a much higher percentage of total income than in the past, and a much higher percentage than in Canada.

The higher degree of income inequality in the USA is believed to be the result of factors such as a substandard primary education system resulting in many members of

---

[2]There are real difficulties comparing incomes between countries due to factors such as the exchange rates of currencies and differences in taxes. For instance, Canadians pay higher income taxes than Americans, and all Canadians pay a 5 percent federal sales tax (the Goods and Services Tax), which Americans do not, but different provinces and states have different sales tax rates. On the other hand, many Americans pay higher social security payroll taxes than Canadians, and health care in Canada is paid for by taxes, while many Americans pay almost $5000 per person for private health insurance.

the workforce lacking skills, employers not sharing profits with their workers, and less aggressive redistribution of income by U.S. governments (more on this in Chapter 12).

As a result, various studies have recently noted that it seems that while the *average income of all Americans* is still higher than the *average income of all Canadians*, the incomes of *typical* Canadians (or "middle-class" Canadians) might have become higher than those of their American counterparts[3], the moreso when the cost of health care is taken into account. This can happen because of the difference between the *average* (also known as "mean") income and what statisticians call the "*median*" income, which is explained in the box.

A	B	
190	120	
90	95	
50	55	**Median**
40	50	
30	40	
80	72	**Average (Mean)**

In statistics, the "average" (or "mean") is simply the arithmetical average of all of the numbers in a series. In the table, the average in column **A** is 80, and the average in column **B** is 72.

The "median" is the midpoint of a series, in the sense that there as many numbers in the series above it as there are below it. In the table, the median in column **A** is 50, whereas the median in column **B** is 55. In both columns, there are two numbers above these, and two below them.

So the average for column **A** (80) is higher than the average for column **B** (72), but the median for column **B** (55) is higher than the median for column **A** (50). That is because of the different distribution of the numbers in the two columns: in column **A**, the numbers are more concentrated at the top, while in column **B**, the numbers are more widely distributed throughout the table.

The numbers in the table do not represent actual incomes—they are only for illustrating the difference between "average" and "median", and showing how the median can be more representative of a situation than the average. And regarding incomes, the situation in the USA is more like column **A** (higher average income), while in Canada it is more like column **B** (higher median income).

---

[3]This refers to incomes *after* income taxes and benefits received from government. There are studies that indicate that the distribution of income in the United States *before* taxes and government benefits is not very different from Canada and other high-income nations.

Dividing Up the Economic Pie: How Incomes Are Distributed

The previous section indicates that while *average* income is important, another important consideration is how incomes are *distributed* among various occupational groups and between lower-income groups and higher-income groups. This concept of distribution concerns the third of the three basic economic questions from Chapter 1—how the economic pie is divided up among Canadians.

In Chapter 10, we saw how incomes are determined in labour markets, under conditions ranging from the almost free interplay of supply and demand in markets for part-time student labour to markets in which trade unions and professional bodies regulate the supply of labour by limiting how many people can enter some occupations.

On a broader scale, there is the question of how income is distributed among different *income groups*—that is, what share of the economic pie goes to the lowest-income 20 percent of families, to the highest-income 20 percent, and to the various groups in between?

Before we start, we need to make clear exactly what is meant by "income." Statistics Canada uses three measures of income:

- **Market income**, which is income earned in the marketplace; mostly wages and salaries, but also interest, dividends, etc.,
- **Total income**, which is market income plus transfer payments received from governments, such as welfare, Employment Insurance benefits, etc., and
- **After-tax income**, which is total income less income taxes paid.

Table 11-2 is based on the *total income* of families of two or more people. In Chapter 12, we will look at market income and after-tax income, and the differences between them.

As Table 11-2 shows, the distribution of before-tax total income (earned income plus transfer payments from governments) between various income groups has remained remarkably steady over the years, with roughly 40–43 percent of total family income going to the top 20 percent of families, 23–24 percent of income to the second-highest 20 percent, 18 percent to the middle 20 percent, and only 11–12 percent

---

market income
Income earned in the marketplace.

total income
Market income plus transfer payments received from governments.

after-tax income
Total income less income taxes paid.

Table 11-2
Distribution of Total Family Income (before taxes)

	Percentage of Total Income Received by Each Fifth							Average Family Income, 2011
	1951	1961	1971	1981	1991	2001	2011	
Lowest fifth of families	6.1	6.6	5.6	6.5	6.4	6.4	6.3	$29,900
Second fifth	12.9	13.4	12.7	12.9	12.2	11.9	11.3	53,900
Third fifth	17.4	18.2	18.0	18.3	17.6	17.2	16.4	78,000
Fourth fifth	22.5	23.4	23.7	24.1	23.9	23.5	23.3	110,500
Highest-income fifth	41.1	38.4	40.0	38.3	40.0	41.1	42.7	202,800
All families	100.0	100.0	100.0	100.0	100.0	100.0	100.0	95,000

Source: Adapted from Statistics Canada, *Income Distributions by Size in Canada*, Catalogue No. 13-207, 1997 and CANSIM Table 202-0701.

and 6 percent to the second-lowest and lowest 20 percent of families, respectively. These statistics show a degree of inequality in the distribution of income that is not only *considerable*, but also *remarkably consistent* from year to year. For nearly 50 years, the top fifth of Canadian families have had a share of before-tax income roughly seven times as large as the share going to the bottom fifth.

The division of the economic pie is among the most controversial issues in the field of economics, because it raises serious issues of equity. Is the distribution of income reflected in Table 11-2 *fair*? To some, higher incomes represent a *reward* for effort and education; to them, such high incomes not only reflect those people's greater *contribution* to society but also provide *incentives* for Canadians to improve themselves and work harder. To others, these differences in income are much greater than can be explained by differing contributions or by the need to provide incentives. These people view the income-distribution process as one in which a small number of Canadians use their *economic power* to extract an excessive share of the economic pie from the system for themselves, leaving only the crumbs for the poor, who lack the market power to command high incomes.

Which view is correct? How much of this inequality is necessary in order to provide incentives? Is this distribution of income fair or not? The tools of the economist can help to explain *why* such a distribution of income exists, but are of little help in making what are, in essence, subjective value judgments as to whether it is a *fair* or an *appropriate* distribution of income.

However, the controversial nature of this matter does make it important that statistics such as those in Table 11-2 be interpreted carefully and accurately. In particular, the persistent inequality shown by the statistics—over 40 percent of income going to the top 20 percent of families and only 6 percent of income going to the bottom 20 percent of families, decade after decade—creates the impression that these high- and low-income groups comprise the same families, year after year. In particular, the image is generated of the same families stuck with low incomes decade after decade, without hope. While this is certainly the case with some such families, the situation is more complex than this image would suggest. The lowest-income group also includes families whose income is *temporarily* low: for instance, students at school who work only seasonally or part-time, or recent graduates whose low income reflects the fact that they have worked for only part of the year. And, as we will see, the low-income group also includes some families of retired persons whose income is low but who possess considerable assets, such as a paid-for home. So the low-income group is not simply the same group of families year after year, but rather comprises to a significant extent a changing group of households, who flow into and out of the low-income group as their circumstances change.

Finally, the inequalities in the Canadian distribution of income shown in Table 11-2 are not significantly different from those in other industrialized nations. International statistical comparisons are imprecise; however, it seems that income in Canada is distributed a little more unequally than in most European countries and a little less unequally than in the United States.

The Male–Female Pay Gap

For many years, the income differential between men and women has attracted a great deal of attention, commentary, and analysis. Different studies have estimated this pay gap differently, with most concluding that, on average, women earn roughly 70 percent of what men earn for full-time work, as shown in Figure 11-10. The existence of such a large income differential raises questions of gender discrimination in Canadian labour markets.

The average income of the top 1 percent of Canadians is about ten times the average income of all Canadians.

Statistics on incomes are collected each year by Statistics Canada through a survey of about 30 000 households that is known as the *Survey of Labour and Income Dynamics (SLID)*.

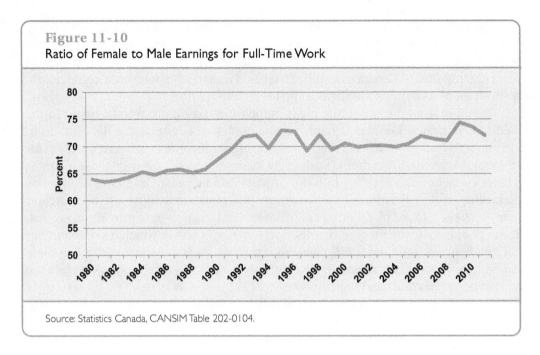

Figure 11-10
Ratio of Female to Male Earnings for Full-Time Work

Source: Statistics Canada, CANSIM Table 202-0104.

However, various studies have shown that most—but not all—of this difference between the incomes of men and women can be explained by economic factors. One such factor is the number of *paid hours worked*—on average, male jobs involve more hours per week *and* more paid overtime hours than female jobs. Most studies estimate that if differences in paid hours worked are considered, the male–female wage gap shrinks by nearly half. Somewhat less than another one-fifth of the gap can be attributed to "productivity factors," such as *training, education,* and *experience.* The fact that many women interrupt their career for child-raising holds back their advancement and incomes. In addition, women have shown a tendency to leave the work force earlier than men—the participation rate for women drops rapidly after age 55, depressing the average income of women by reducing the number of them working during these higher-income years.

Both *marital status* and *age* are also significant factors making women's incomes lower than men's: single women's incomes are about 91 percent of those of single men, while married women earn only 65 percent of what married men earn. And incomes of women in the 15–24 age group are 86 percent of men's, while women over 55 earn only 64 percent of what men earn.

After allowance has been made for the hours worked and productivity factors, there remains a male–female wage gap of about 10 percent that can best be explained by "gender factors." The main such gender factor seems to have been *occupational segregation*: approximately three-quarters of female employees work in five occupational groups—clerical, service, sales, medicine/health care, and education. Since so many women are concentrated into these occupational groups that contain many relatively low-paying jobs, the average income of women in general tends to be below average.

There seem to be at least two basic origins of this occupational segregation. One is *society's stereotypes* concerning the role of women, which probably condition many young women to think in terms of working as secretaries, waitresses, and the like. The other is *selection procedures,* for both hiring and promotion. The people in a given occupational field or workplace tend to hire and promote people with whom they are comfortable and

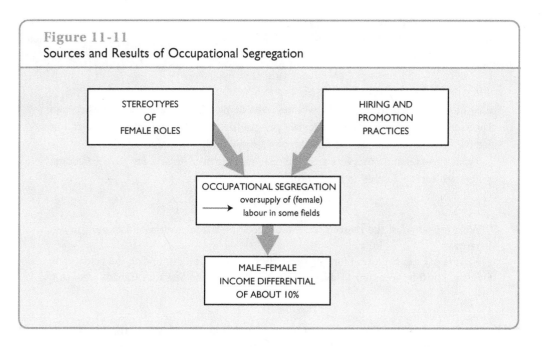

Figure 11-11
Sources and Results of Occupational Segregation

who they believe will "fit in." So if a field is dominated by males, this makes it much more difficult for females to enter it. These two factors are illustrated in Figure 11-11.

Figure 11-11 also shows the economic effects of these forces. If large numbers of women are steered by stereotyping and deflected by selection procedures into a few occupational areas, the result will be an oversupply of (female) labour in those occupations, with low wages the result.

Such male–female wage gaps raise important issues of government policy. If the government wants to reduce the pay gap, one of the most basic steps would be to break down the traditional female stereotypes. The educational system attempts to do this by showing both women and men in non-traditional occupational roles in schoolbooks from the earliest grades. Another basic step would be to change hiring and promotion procedures through *employment equity*, either through persuasion or by legislation. And to deal with the income inequities, there is pay equity legislation. The first step toward dealing with this matter was legislation ruling that people who do the same work must receive the same pay—*equal pay for equal work* legislation. Such legislation has existed for many years in many provinces and is widely accepted. However, its effect is limited to situations where men and women are performing the same jobs. It does not address the main source of male–female wage differences—the fact that women tend to be concentrated in certain types of jobs with below-average pay.

A more controversial approach is the concept of **equal pay for work of equal value**. Under this approach, the "value" of a job is measured by a point system that takes into account factors such as skill, effort, responsibility, and working conditions. Such a system allows the pay of quite different jobs to be compared, by adding up their points: the more points a job has, the more it is "worth."

Equal pay for work of equal value legislation applies to government employees in several jurisdictions. However, the application of the same legislation to private employers is much more controversial, due to concerns regarding employers' ability to compete with other firms that are not subject to such requirements, including foreign competitors.

equal pay for work of equal value
The concept that the values of different jobs may be measured against each other using a point system that incorporates a variety of criteria, including skill levels, effort, degree of responsibility, and working conditions.

IN THE NEWS

Will the Male–Female Pay Gap Narrow in the Future?

Figure 11-10 shows that, as of 2011, women were earning about 72 percent of what men earned for full-time work. The male–female pay gap has narrowed over the long term, but since the early 1990s, the gap has not narrowed significantly.

Nonetheless, some observers are predicting that the male–female pay gap for full-time workers will narrow further in the future. ■

QUESTIONS

1. What are some of the reasons for the expectation that the male–female pay gap will narrow?
2. Has the pay gap narrowed further since 2011 or not? (You can update the statistics in Figure 11-10 by accessing CANSIM Table 202-0104 on the Statistics Canada website.)

For various reasons, the male–female pay gap has been narrowing over time, and many expect that gap to gradually narrow further. Meanwhile, another gap—the gap between the incomes of the skilled and the unskilled—has been *widening*.

The Skills Pay Gap

Over the past few years, there have been growing indications of a widening pay gap between skilled and unskilled workers. The incomes of skilled workers have been rising quite rapidly, while those of the unskilled have been stagnant, or even falling after inflation is taken into account. For example, Figure 11-12 shows that from 1997 to 2014, the weekly wages of professionals in finance and health care increased by

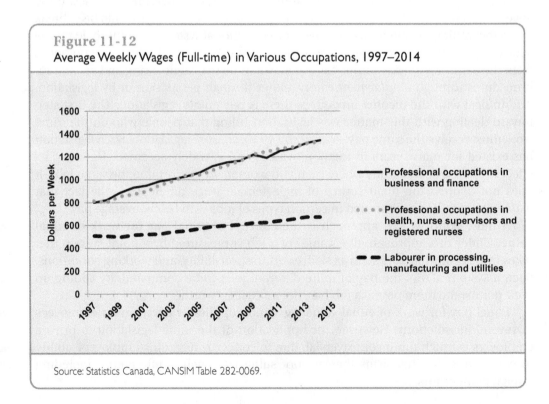

Figure 11-12
Average Weekly Wages (Full-time) in Various Occupations, 1997–2014

Source: Statistics Canada, CANSIM Table 282-0069.

63–68 percent, as compared to a 32 percent increase for labourers. Over the same period, the consumer price index increased by 36 percent, so the real (after-inflation) wages of labourers actually *decreased*.

Many observers link this trend to the decline in lesser-skilled manufacturing jobs caused by changing technology and freer trade. According to the C.D. Howe Institute, ". . . there is evidence that technological change is biased in favour of skilled workers, and wage differentials between skilled and unskilled workers are widening in many industries." Also, free trade and globalization have opened Canadian markets to imports of low-cost, labour-intensive manufactured goods.

In the job market for low-skilled workers, there is an oversupply of labour relative to demand, causing incomes to increase slowly or even decrease, whereas in markets for skilled workers, the opposite is often the case. The result of these effects has been a growing gap between the incomes of skilled workers and those of less-skilled workers.

In 2012, a McKinsey Global Institute report estimated that by 2020, the global economy could see 90 to 95 million more low-skill workers than employers will need.

wwww.mckinsey.com
/insights/mgi

Poverty in Canada

On average, Canadians enjoy one of the highest standards of living in the world, but we have seen that this prosperity is *distributed* far from evenly among Canadians.

How many Canadians have such low incomes that they are living in poverty? According to some estimates, over 5 000 000 Canadians (over 16 percent of the population) are "poor." But other estimates place the number as low as 2 000 000, or even 1 000 000 (3 to 6 percent of Canadians). These widely varying estimates of the extent of poverty arise from the fact that there are very different ways to just *define* what *poverty* actually means.

This is an important debate. By some definitions, poverty is a national crisis that demands massive government action, while according to others, it seems to be a much less widespread problem. First, we will consider the challenges in defining what "poverty" is and measuring how many people are living in poverty.

What Is Poverty?

Defining "poverty" and determining "**poverty lines**" (that is, how low peoples' income must be in order to be considered "poor") is far from a simple task. The most basic problem is that there is no official definition of "poverty" in Canada, and there are different ways of even *defining* what is meant by "poverty".

poverty lines
Income levels below which families or individuals are considered to be poor.

Low-Income Cut-Offs

One definition is that people are poor if their income is too far below the average (or median) income. An example of this sort of definition is Statistics Canada's **Low-Income Cut-Offs (LICOs)**, which have often been used as poverty lines. The lower a person's or family's income is, the higher will be the percentage of its income that must be spent on the basic necessities of food, shelter, and clothing. If income is so low that more than 63 percent of income is spent on these basic necessities (the national average of 43 percent spent on the essentials in 1992 plus 20 percentage points), the LICOs designate it to be a "low income".

Statistics Canada designed the LICOs in order to identify groups of "low-income" Canadians, so as be able to study their characteristics. Their purpose was not to define

Low-Income Cut-Offs
Income levels below which more than 63 percent of income is spent on food, shelter and clothing (20 percentage points higher than the national average of 43 percent spent on the essentials in 1992).

and measure "poverty", and Statistics Canada has stated that it has ". . . clearly and consistently emphasized … that the LICOs are quite different from measures of poverty."

Critics argue that the LICOs are arbitrary, in that they are based on the addition of 20 percentage points to the national average percentage of income spent on essentials. They also argue that using the LICOs as poverty lines means that poverty can never be eliminated, because as incomes in general rise and the percentage of the average income spent on essentials falls, there will always be families and individuals with incomes low enough to be spending more than 20 percentage points more than the average on essentials. This is why the LICOs are considered to designate people as "poor" because their incomes are *too far below the average.*

Market Basket Measure

Market Basket Measure
Poverty lines based on the cost of a "basket" of goods and services required to live above the poverty line, defined in terms of both subsistence and "social inclusion".

The other basic type of definition is the **Market Basket Measure (MBM)**, which attempts to measure a standard of living that is a compromise between subsistence and social inclusion. The MBM represents the cost of a "basket" of consumer goods and services that includes: a nutritious diet, clothing and footwear, shelter, transportation, and other necessary goods and services (such as personal care items or household supplies). Families and individuals with incomes below this level are considered to be poor. The MBM poverty lines also reflect differences in living costs across regions.

Both definitions of poverty can be challenged on the grounds that they are in part arbitrary: the LICOs because they are based on arbitrarily adding 20 percentage points to the percent of income spent on essentials, and the MBMs because it was arbitrarily decided what items to include and not include in the "basket".

To illustrate the levels of income that we are discussing, Table 11-3 shows the after-tax LICOs for 2011.

Table 11-3
Statistics Canada's 2011 after-tax Low-Income Cut-offs

Size of family unit	Rural areas	Community Size			
		Urban areas			
		Less than 30,000[1]	30,000 to 99,999	100,000 to 499,999	500,000 and over
1 person	16,038	18,246	19,941	20,065	23,298
2 persons	19,966	22,714	24,824	24,978	29,004
3 persons	24,545	27,924	30,517	30,707	35,657
4 persons	29,802	33,905	37,053	37,283	43,292
5 persons	33,800	38,454	42,025	42,285	49,102
6 persons	38,122	43,370	47,398	47,692	55,378
7 or more persons	42,443	42,285	52,770	53,097	61,656

[1]Includes cities with a population between 15,000 and 30,000 and small urban areas (under 15,000).
Source: Statistics Canada, CANSIM Table 202-0801

How Many Canadians Are Poor?

Estimates of how many Canadians are poor will of course depend on which definition of poverty is used. According to the after-tax LICO measure, about 3 million Canadians fall below the poverty line, while the MBM measure places the number slightly over 4 million.

From numbers like these, we can calculate the **poverty rate**, which is the percentage of a group (in this case, all Canadians) whose incomes are below the poverty line. For Canada as a whole, the overall poverty rate recently has been estimated to be in the range of 9 percent (using the LICOs) to 12 percent (using MBMs).

But there is an active debate over the accuracy of these estimates. Some argue that the statistics exaggerate the extent of poverty. They note that the income statistics on which poverty rates are based come from Statistics Canada surveys, on which some people underreport their income. Many workers in the food service industry do not report all of their tips, and people tend to underreport their employment insurance and welfare benefits to the survey-takers. Also, the statistics consider cash income only, and an elderly widow with an income of $10,000 per year would indeed be very poor if living on her own, but quite comfortable if living in the home of a family member, with no expenses for food and shelter. According to these critics, the real poverty rate for Canadians as a whole is less than 5 percent.

On the other hand, other people argue that many poor people are not even counted in the statistics, because their lifestyles make it unlikely that they will be picked up in a Statistics Canada survey of households. This debate brings us back to the initial point that is not easy to define and measure "poverty".

poverty rate
The percentage of a group of people whose incomes are below the poverty line.

Who are the Poor?

That said, the statistics on poverty can help us to identify the *characteristics* of the poor, and of groups that tend to be poor. This will help us to understand the nature and causes of poverty, and to develop more effective policies for dealing with it.

Arguably, the most important overall factor influencing the risk of poverty is *family type*. This refers to the subcategories of families and individuals shown in Figure 11-13, which shows the poverty rate for each group as estimated by both the MBM approach and the LICO (after-tax income) approach.

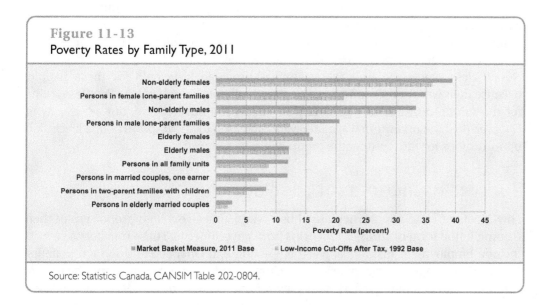

Figure 11-13
Poverty Rates by Family Type, 2011

Source: Statistics Canada, CANSIM Table 202-0804.

Figure 11-13 shows that the highest poverty rates are among *young people* (36-39 percent for young women and 30-33 percent for young men) and *lone-parent families* (as high as 35 percent for women and 21 percent for men). The next-highest poverty rates are at the other end of the age spectrum, where the poverty rates for elderly single women and men are 16 and 12 percent, respectively. The poverty rates for married couples are the lowest.

Statistics on poverty can also be analyzed according to *age* and *sex*. Poverty rates are highest among young people in general, and among older unattached individuals. The high poverty rates among young people reflect factors such as the lower pay earned by newer entrants to the work force due to lack of experience and seniority, as well as the intermittent work and high unemployment rates experienced by many younger people. Causes of low incomes among older unattached individuals include the fact that this group includes a large number of widows, as well as the low pensions received by some older people and problems finding work. However, it should also be noted that whereas the poverty rate for seniors was very high (over 30 percent) in the late 1970s, the highest poverty rates today are among young people.

Across all age groupings, *women* have a higher poverty rate than men, with poverty rates for young women being particularly high. Most of the high poverty rate for non-elderly women can be attributed to the high poverty rates of two subgroups within this group: unattached young women and single-parent mothers.

Poverty rates can also be analyzed according to the *education* of those with low incomes. As would be expected, poverty rates are generally higher for those with less education—for people with less than a high-school diploma, the poverty rate is roughly two or three times as high as for people with a post-secondary diploma or degree.

The Working Poor

While many poor people do not work, a large low-income group that deserves attention is the *working poor*. For this group, low wages and/or intermittent employment mean low incomes despite the fact that they do work considerably.

Generally, more than half of poor Canadians work enough to earn more than half of their total income. These figures show that many of the poor have considerable attachment to the labour force.

Many of these "working poor" earn the minimum wage. Most minimum-wage earners are young people, students and part-time workers; however, some heads of family also work for the minimum wage or less. Many of the "working poor" live on incomes that are actually lower than they would receive if they were on welfare. Nonetheless, the social welfare system has provided little help for these people, because their work activity often makes them ineligible for assistance. People working for the minimum wage rate generally fall below the poverty line, but as we saw in Chapter 10, if the minimum wage rate were increased to above-poverty-line levels, job opportunities for the low-income group could be reduced.

Sources of Income for the Poor

Low-income Canadians, particularly those over 65, receive a high proportion of their income in the form of *transfer payments* from governments. These transfer payments include Employment Insurance, welfare, Canada and Quebec Pension Plan benefits, the federal Old Age Security pension and Guaranteed Income Supplement, the federal Child Tax Benefit and the federal GST credit. For poor seniors, over 90 percent of their income comes from transfer payments, while younger poor people rely upon transfer payments for 40–50 percent of their incomes.

Government transfer payments account for, on average, slightly more than 50 percent of total income for economic families in the bottom 20 percent income group and almost 25 percent for those in the second-lowest 20 percent income group.

In Conclusion

While there are different views as to how *poverty* should be defined and how many poor people there really are, there are some matters upon which there is fairly broad agreement. The risk of having a low income is greatest among single-parent mothers and unattached young people, and lower levels of education increases the risk of poverty considerably.

Women have a higher risk of poverty than men, especially single mothers, younger unattached women with low levels of education, and elderly women living on their own. In the past, seniors have had a high incidence of poverty due to the inadequacy of many pension plans. However, as pensions and government assistance to seniors have improved, and many retirees have benefited from selling their homes at high prices, poverty has become much less of a "seniors' problem" and more of a "youth problem" and "women's problem." Also, child poverty has become more of an issue in Canada in recent years, in large part due to the persistently high poverty rates of younger parents, especially single mothers.

Chapter Summary

1. Due to changes in technology, demand, and international competition, the composition of Canada's labour force has changed greatly since 1950. Employment in the goods-producing sector has increased only slightly, whereas employment in the services sector has increased greatly. (L.O.1)
2. The increased participation of women in the labour market has been the outstanding trend in the labour force since 1950. This trend is due to various factors, including higher education levels and aspirations among women, the need to add to family incomes, the need of more women to be self-supporting, and the growth of job opportunities in the service sector. (L.O. 2)
3. The average real family income of Canadians in 2011 was more than three times as high as in 1951, with most of the increase occurring by 1976. Since then, family income has grown more slowly, due to slower growth of both productivity and the number of income-earners per family. (L.O. 3)
4. There exists a pay differential between men and women of about 10 percent that is attributed to gender factors. In particular, women have tended to be concentrated in certain occupational groupings within which many jobs have below-average incomes. (L.O. 4)
5. There is evidence that the gap between the incomes of skilled and less-skilled workers has been growing wider, probably largely as a result of the effects of technological change and international competition on the demand for labour. (L.O. 5)
6. Canada has no official definition of "poverty". Statistics Canada's after-tax Low-Income Cut-Offs estimate that about 9 percent of Canadians are poor, while the Market Basket Measure standard estimates that about 12 percent are poor. (L.O. 6)

7. The risk of poverty is highest among single young people, lone-parent families, single elderly, and people lacking education and/or skills. (L.O.7)

Questions

1. Describe the changes that have occurred in the distribution of employment between agriculture, manufacturing, and service industries over the past 50 years. Explain three basic reasons for these trends, and explain why you expect them to continue into the future or not.

2. Most observers expect that the rapid increase of the labour force participation rate of women will level off, or at least increase much more slowly in the future. What explains the rapid increase of the female participation rate of the past few decades, and why would it be expected to increase more slowly or level off in the future?

3. After the late 1970s, the growth of real average family income in Canada slowed considerably. What is "real" income, and why did it grow more rapidly before the late 1970s, then much more slowly since then? In the future, what would be the most likely cause of any increases in the real average family income of Canadians?

4. The text describes the pay gap between males and females for full-time work.
   (a) How large is this gap, and what are the reasons for it?
   (b) Would you expect the male–female pay gap to widen or become smaller in the future? Why?

5. The text refers to indications of an increasing gap between the incomes of people with higher levels of education and skill and those with less education and skill. Why has this pay gap been widening? If this gap were to continue to grow, what would be the implications for social trends and problems in Canada? How might government policies help to reduce or ease any such problems?

6. Visit the Statistics Canada website (**www.statcan.gc.ca**) and search the site for *Employment by industry.*

    What are the recent trends regarding employment by industry in Canada, and what might explain these trends?

Study Guide

Review Questions (Answers to these Review Questions appear in Appendix B.)

1. State whether each of the following accurately describes trends in the distribution of employment in Canada over the past half-century. (Answer *yes* or *no* for each.)
   (a) _____ Employment in the service industries has increased much faster than employment in the goods industries.
   (b) _____ Manufacturing workers comprise a smaller proportion of the work force than 50 years ago.
   (c) _____ Agricultural employment has remained almost stable.
   (d) _____ Employment in the service-industry sector of the economy has grown at about the same pace as total employment in the economy.

2. The changes in the labour force described in question 1 have been caused by
   (a) changes in production technology.
   (b) changes in government policies.
   (c) changes in consumer demand patterns.
   (d) increasing international trade and competition.
   (e) Answers (a) and (c) and (d) together.

3. As living standards have increased, the average Canadian family has tended to
   (a) spend more on services, thereby creating more jobs in service industries.
   (b) increase the percentage of its income spent on food products, thereby creating more jobs in the agricultural sector.
   (c) reduce its spending on manufactured goods, which explains the slow growth of employment in the manufacturing sector.
   (d) spend about the same percentage of its income on food, manufactured goods, and services as it always did.
   (e) None of the above.

4. Which of the following are results of the changes in technology and living standards that occurred over the past century? (Answer *yes* or *no* for each.)
   (a) _____ the growth of large cities
   (b) _____ strong annual increases in employment in the manufacturing sector
   (c) _____ rising educational requirements for workers
   (d) _____ larger families
   (e) _____ fewer jobs in the agricultural sector
   (f) _____ increased employment of women
   (g) _____ growth of part-time work
   (h) _____ government policies to restrict immigration

5. If a country's population is 13 million and there are 10 million people of working age and 6.5 million of them participate in the labour force (by either working or seeking work), the labour force participation rate for that country is
   (a) 89 percent.
   (b) 77 percent.
   (c) 65 percent.
   (d) 50 percent.
   (e) None of the above.

6. What has been the trend in male and female labour force participation rates over the past 50 years?
   (a) a slight decrease in the male rate and a large increase in the female rate
   (b) a large decrease in the male rate and a slight increase in the female rate
   (c) an increase in both the male rate and the female rate
   (d) a slight decrease in both the male rate and the female rate
   (e) a slight decrease in the female rate and a slight increase in the male rate

7. In the 1950s, 1960s, and 1970s, average real family incomes in Canada increased quite rapidly, due to
   (a) regular annual decreases in unemployment.
   (b) increases in the number of hours worked per week.
   (c) rising worker productivity.

(d) increases in the number of income earners per family.

(e) Answers (c) and (d) together.

8. After the late 1970s, the growth of average real income per family slowed, due to _____ and _____.

9. Most studies show that women earn about
   (a) 50 percent of what men earn for full-time work.
   (b) 63 percent of what men earn for full-time work.
   (c) 70 percent of what men earn for full-time work.
   (d) 80 percent of what men earn for full-time work.
   (e) 90 percent of what men earn for full-time work.

10. If pay differences due to hours worked, and productivity factors such as training, education, and experience are eliminated, the remaining male–female wage gap that is best explained by "gender factors" is estimated to be roughly _____ percent.

11. The pay gap in question 10 is mainly the result of
   (a) pay discrimination.
   (b) many women having part-time jobs.
   (c) the average age of working women being lower than that of men.
   (d) women interrupting their careers to have babies.
   (e) many women being concentrated in a few job areas that are relatively low-paying.

12. The *poverty line* is
   (a) the percentage of people who are considered to be poor.
   (b) people waiting at the welfare office for their welfare cheques.
   (c) an income that is 50 percent below the national average.
   (d) the income level below which people are considered to be poor.
   (e) None of the above.

13. The *poverty rate* is
   (a) the percentage of any group that has an income below the poverty line.
   (b) the hourly wage rate below which a person is considered to be poor.
   (c) the percentage of families whose income is below the Canadian average income.
   (d) an income less than $20 000 per year.
   (e) None of the above.

14. The use of Statistics Canada's Low-Income Cut-Offs (LICOs) as poverty lines is an illustration of defining the poverty line as an income that is
   (a) not large enough to purchase the necessities of life.
   (b) too far below the average income.
   (c) less than one-half of the national average income.
   (d) less than one-third of the national average income.
   (e) None of the above.

15. If Statistics Canada's after-tax Low-Income Cut-Offs (LICOs) are used as poverty lines, the proportion of Canadians with incomes below the poverty line would be approximately
   (a) 5 percent.
   (b) 6 percent.
   (c) 9 percent.
   (d) 12 percent.
   (e) 16 percent.

16. Under the Market Basket Measure (MBM) standard, a family would be considered "poor" if its income was
    (a) not large enough to purchase a "basket" of goods and services needed to live above the poverty line, defined in terms of both subsistence and "social inclusion".
    (b) not large enough to purchase a subsistence level of bare essentials in terms of food, clothing, and shelter.
    (c) less than one-half of the average income for families of the same size.
    (d) less than one-third of the average income for families of the same size.
    (e) less than one-quarter of the average income for families of the same size.

17. Under the Market Basket Measure (MBM) definition of poverty is used, the proportion of Canadians with incomes below the poverty line would be approximately
    (a) 5 percent.
    (b) 6 percent.
    (c) 9 percent.
    (d) 12 percent.
    (e) 16 percent

18. Three groups with a high risk of poverty are
    (a) _____
    (b) _____
    (c) _____

Critical Thinking Questions

(Asterisked questions 1 to 5 are answered in Appendix B; the answers to questions 6 to 10 are in the Instructor's Manual that accompanies this text.)

*1. "One of the fundamental underlying causes of the great increase in the role played by women in the labour force was technological change." Explain the reasoning behind this statement. Do you agree? Why or why not?

*2. Poor women over 65 outnumber poor men over 65 by about 4 to 1. What might explain why so many more of Canada's older poor people are women than are men?

*3. Some of the *working poor* earn less than they would receive if they went onto welfare and did not work at all. Why, then, do you think they decide to work?

*4. Under many social assistance (welfare) programs, the benefits that people receive are *below* the poverty line. What might explain this seeming inconsistency?

*5. Write an explanation of why some people think that poverty is a very serious problem in Canada, while others believe that it is a relatively small problem. Why is the debate over the extent of poverty an important matter?

6. The labour force participation rate of women decreases quite sharply after age 55.
    (a) Why do you think so many women leave the labour force after 55?
    (b) What effect would this tendency have on the average incomes of women as compared to men?
    (c) Would you expect the participation rate of women over 55 to increase or decrease in the future? Why?
    (d) How would the change in part (c) affect the male–female pay gap?

7. Why do you think women outnumber men by about four to three in university undergraduate programs, and what are the implications of this for the labour force and the male–female pay gap of tomorrow?

Use the Web (Hints for these Use the Web exercises appear in Appendix B.)

1. Visit the Statistics Canada website (**www.statcan.gc.ca**) and search *The Daily* for "family income."

    What are the most recent trends regarding family income in Canada, and what might be the reasons for these trends?

2. Visit the Statistics Canada website and search *The Daily* for "postsecondary enrollment."

    What are the most recent trends regarding male and female university enrollment in Canada, and what might explain these trends?

The Government Sector

After studying this chapter, you should be able to

1. Describe the three key types of programs that comprise Canada's social welfare system.

2. List the four main sources of government tax revenue, and explain the advantages and disadvantages of each of these.

3. Explain the difference between progressive and regressive taxes, and identify taxes as either progressive or regressive.

4. Given data concerning a person's income and income taxes payable, calculate the marginal tax rate paid by that person, and explain how marginal tax rates affect incentives.

5. Summarize how Canadian governments' transfer payments and income taxes redistribute income among Canadians.

6. Describe the purposes of federal government transfer payments to the provincial governments.

7. Distinguish between reasonable and unwise uses of debt, and explain the relationship between a government's budget deficits and its debt and the dangers of excessive deficits.

8. Summarize the problems of growing federal government budget deficits and debt after 1975, how this problem reached a crisis point in 1993, and how measures to resolve it affected health care, education, and income support programs.

9. Explain how government income support programs can create disincentives to work.

We have seen how, in a market economy, the incentives of profits and competition will lead privately owned businesses (the *private sector*) to do a very good job of providing high living standards, by producing goods and services both effectively and efficiently, without government guidance.

However, a market economy will not automatically provide accessible public services such as health care and education, and it generates extreme inequalities in the distribution of income. In addition, a market system provides incentives for various socially undesirable actions by businesses, such as misleading consumers and investors, exploiting workers, using unfair competitive tactics, monopolizing markets, polluting the environment and so on. These problems mean that while the marketplace is the source of many economic benefits, it also has weaknesses, so there is a role for government in a market economy. In this chapter, we will consider various aspects of that role.

As discussed in Chapter 2, the Canadian economy is characterized as a *mixed free-enterprise* economic system. With about 80 percent of economic activity being carried out by private businesses in response to the demand of buyers, the economy is basically "market" in nature. However, there is also a substantial amount of *government involvement* in the economy. As we saw in Chapter 2, governments provide extensive *public services*, such as health care and education, and they own and operate various enterprises, such as the Canadian Broadcasting Corporation and Canada Post. In addition, government taxation and transfer payment programs *redistribute income* from those with higher incomes to those with less, and *government regulations* establish in countless ways the economic "rules of play," to protect consumers, workers, investors, and the environment.

Furthermore, the role of government in the Canadian economy has grown considerably over the years. While the federal government attracts the most public attention, spending by *provincial* and *local (municipal)* governments has exceeded federal government spending since the mid-1960s. The reason is that the provinces have the primary responsibility for education and health care, both of which have expanded greatly since the 1960s.

This growth is reflected in statistics on government spending. Because of population growth and inflation, government spending measured *in dollars* can be expected to almost always increase over time. So it's more meaningful to express government spending as a percent of the size of the whole economy, or the Gross Domestic Product (GDP), which measures the total of all of the economy's output and incomes.

Figure 12-1 shows grand total government spending as a percent of GDP by all three levels of government (federal, provincial, and local) on *all* government programs such as health care, education, police, firefighting, employment insurance, welfare, pensions and so on, plus interest on government debt.

Figure 12-1 shows that government spending grew from about 20 percent of GDP in 1950 to over 50 percent by 1992, which means that government spending was rising considerably faster than the economy was growing. But after 1992, government spending *decreased* as a percent of GDP, as the growth of government spending slowed considerably[1]. Later in this chapter, we will see the reasons behind this major change in the trend.

Impressive though they may be, these spending statistics understate the role of government in the economy by a considerable amount. They do not include the

---

[1] Until the recession of 2008–09, when this trend was temporarily reversed. It is normal for government spending to rise temporarily during recessions, due to increased assistance to the unemployed and spending on job creation projects. In Figure 12-1, this can be seen in the recessions of the early 1980s and early 1990s, as well as in 2008–09.

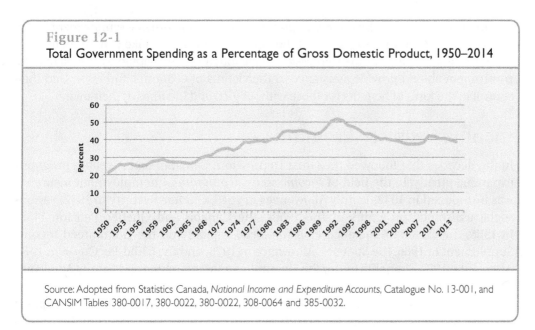

Figure 12-1

Total Government Spending as a Percentage of Gross Domestic Product, 1950–2014

Source: Adopted from Statistics Canada, *National Income and Expenditure Accounts*, Catalogue No. 13-001, and CANSIM Tables 380-0017, 380-0022, 380-0022, 308-0064 and 385-0032.

activities of government-owned *Crown corporations* such as Canada Post and the Canadian Broadcasting Corporation, nor do they include the myriad of *government regulations* of economic activity that have been enacted over the years.

So, the role of government in the Canadian economy has expanded greatly over the past half-century. In this chapter, we will examine the reasons for this growth, and look at recent developments and possible future trends with respect to the role of government in the Canadian economy.

The Growth of Canada's Social Welfare Programs

As we have seen, Canadian governments spend substantial amounts of money on social welfare programs, with most of it going to the three key areas of *income security* (such as Employment Insurance, welfare, and pensions), *health care,* and *education.* Government spending on these programs has risen dramatically during the twentieth century. Why has this happened?

In the most basic sense, the growth of the social welfare system was brought about by the transition from a rural farming society of small communities to a modern, urban society with a large industrial work force, as we saw in chapter 11. In the earlier society of small, closely knit, and stable communities, traditional institutions such as the family, the church, the local community, and private charity were able to provide for the needs of those who required assistance. However, as Canada evolved into an urban society with a large, mobile work force of industrial employees, the situation changed significantly. People and families were exposed to increased risks of loss of income due to unemployment (or layoff), illness, disability, and old age. And as the traditional social institutions became less able to provide support for Canadians who needed it, it became increasingly necessary for governments to provide assistance to those who needed it.

The growth of the government's role acquired considerable momentum from the Great Depression of the 1930s. The Depression destroyed faith in the laissez-faire philosophy

"Income security, health, and education represent central supports of the welfare state."

— ROYAL COMMISSION ON THE ECONOMIC UNION AND DEVELOPMENT PROSPECTS FOR CANADA (OTTAWA, MINISTER OF SUPPLY AND SERVICES).

that the economy could be counted upon to automatically provide employment for all who wanted it and that people could therefore be expected to take care of themselves economically. By doing so, the Depression made much more acceptable the idea that the government should provide assistance to the victims of economic forces beyond their control in the form of benefits for those without jobs and incomes of their own.

Income Security Programs

In the decades that followed the Great Depression, Canada's social welfare programs expanded greatly. In the field of *income security programs*, unemployment insurance was introduced in 1942, Family Allowances in 1945, Old Age Security in 1952, various social assistance programs in the 1950s, the Canada and Quebec Pension Plans in 1965, the Canada Assistance Plan for social welfare and the Guaranteed Income Supplement in 1966, the Spouses' Allowance in 1975, and the Child Tax Credit in 1978. Also, in the 1970s, benefits under the Unemployment Insurance and Family Allowance programs were increased significantly.

Another important, although less visible, way in which governments support people's incomes is through **tax credits** in the income tax system. These tax credits reduce the income taxes payable by Canadians in order to offset a variety of factors that adversely affect their living standards, from children and other dependants to sales taxes and property taxes. Some of these tax credits are structured so that they benefit only lower-income individuals and families, partly by reducing the taxes that they pay, and in some cases entitling them to tax refunds.

tax credits

Credits that reduce the income taxes payable by Canadians in order to off-set a variety of factors that adversely affect their living standards, including dependants, property taxes, and sales taxes.

Health Care

Health care represents the second key element of Canada's social welfare system. Health care can be extremely expensive, exposing individuals and families to the risk of heavy costs and even financial ruin. As a result, it was decided as a matter of social policy that all Canadians should have access to health care without having to pay the costs themselves, giving Canadians one of the more liberal health-care systems in the world. Following the introduction of hospital insurance and medicare programs, government expenditures on health care grew to one of the largest government-spending programs. The Canadian Institute for Health Information (CIHI) estimates total spending on health care in 2014 to be about $6,045 per person.

www.cihi.ca

Education

Education, which represents the third pillar of Canada's social welfare system, is completely financed by tax revenues in the case of primary and secondary education. Post-secondary education is subsidized by governments through grants to colleges and universities that help to keep students' tuition fees down. These government expenditures are justified in part on economic grounds, as an investment in the "human capital" need-ed by a modern economy. Also, government support of education is seen as a key aspect of social policy, as a means of providing equality of opportunity for all Canadians to obtain the education needed for their lives and careers. Canadian governments spend about 5-6 percent of GDP on education, which is neither high nor low by international standards.

Taken together, these programs involve a great deal of government spending. In 2013, program spending (spending on all items other than interest on government debt) by all levels of government in Canada amounted to $697 billion, or nearly $20,000 for every Canadian man, woman, and child. This brings us to the question of how governments raise all the revenues to pay for these expenditures.

Paying For It: Sources of Government Revenues

In 2013, Canadians paid about $579 billion in taxes of various sorts.

There are four basic types of taxes that pay for government spending:

- taxes on *incomes* (personal and business income taxes),
- taxes on *spending* (sales taxes, or **consumption taxes**),
- taxes on *assets* (mainly, property taxes), and
- taxes on *employers' payrolls* (such as Canada Pension Plan and employment insurance premiums).

These taxes raise the funds that provide us with government services and benefits. But each type of tax also brings its own type of costs to the economy, as we will see in the following sections.

Taxes on Incomes

Taxes on incomes such as personal income taxes and business profits taxes are the largest tax source in Canada, mainly because they can be applied to millions of people and businesses. Taxes on incomes raise about 38 percent of all government revenue in Canada.

A key feature of the personal income tax is that the rate of taxation (the percentage of income taken by taxes) can be tailored to people's ability to pay. People with low incomes can pay a low percentage of their income to taxes or none at all, while people with high incomes can be taxed at much higher rates. Taxes that take a higher percentage of the incomes of the "rich" than of the "poor" are known as **progressive taxes**. The most prominent of these is the personal income tax, and in the view of many, this makes the personal income tax a particularly fair tax. And the personal income tax is more progressive than many Canadians believe: the 10 percent of tax filers with the highest incomes pay somewhat more than half of all the personal income taxes paid.

The major limitation regarding income taxes is that if the rate of taxation becomes *too* high, it can have a negative effect on incentives to work, save, and invest. The key here is what economists call the **marginal tax rate**, which is the tax rate payable on any *additional* income that is earned over and above one's present income.

The Marginal Tax Rate

Let's illustrate with an example. If Fred earns $60,000 per year working in a library and pays income taxes of $12,000, he is paying a 20-percent tax rate on his income—on average, he pays 20 cents in taxes on every dollar he earns. This, however, is not Fred's marginal tax rate—his *marginal* tax rate is the percentage of any *additional* income that he earns that goes to taxes. For instance, suppose that Fred works nights as a professional wrestler and earns *an additional* $10,000. If he has to pay $3,500 in income taxes *on this $10,000 of extra income*, his marginal tax rate is 35 percent.

It is the marginal tax rate that affects Fred's incentive to work, because it applies to extra income that Fred can decide to earn or not earn. Even if the tax rate on Fred's main income as a librarian is increased sharply, he has little choice but to continue working—he needs this main source of his income. But a sharp increase in the marginal tax rate on his *extra* income as a wrestler might cause him to decide to retire from the ring, or wrestle less often.

consumption taxes
Taxes levied when consumers buy goods and services; for example, sales taxes.

progressive taxes
Taxes that take a higher percentage of high incomes than of low incomes.

marginal tax rate
The percentage of any additional income that is earned that goes to taxes.

High marginal tax rates can generate disincentives in various ways. As the example of Fred shows, high marginal tax rates can discourage people from working overtime or at a second job. In a similar way, high marginal tax rates could decrease people's incentive to save and invest money in order to earn investment income. High marginal tax rates on business profits can discourage the capital investment that improves efficiency, or even discourage businesses from investing in the country or province with those high tax rates. So while taxes on incomes are their largest source of revenue, governments must avoid making marginal tax rates so high that they create disincentives to work, save, and invest, which would have negative effects on productivity and prosperity.

Taxes on Consumption

Another basic type of tax is *taxes on spending* by consumers. The main such taxes are the sales taxes levied by the federal government (the GST) and provincial governments (the PST), which are in some provinces combined into a harmonized sales tax (HST); however, the very high taxes on tobacco, alcohol, and gasoline are also consumption taxes. Because they tax a broad base of consumer spending, these consumption taxes are a major source of government revenue, providing about 20 percent of total government revenue in most years.

> **regressive tax**
>
> A tax that takes a higher percentage of low incomes than of high incomes.
>
> Patricia earns $40 000 and owns a house on which she pays property taxes of $2000 per year. Her property taxes amount to 5 percent ($2000 ÷ $40 000) of her income. Pat earns $24 000 and lives in an apartment that he rents for $600 per month, or $7200 per year. Of this, approximately 20 percent, or $1440, goes to cover the property taxes paid by the landlord. Pat's property taxes amount to 6 percent ($1440 ÷ $24 000) of his income. In this case, the property tax is regressive—the person with the lower income pays a higher percentage of that income to property taxes than the higher-income person pays.

The main disadvantage of sales taxes is that they are **regressive**—that is, they take a higher percentage of the incomes of low-income earners than from those with high incomes. Certainly, the rich pay *more dollars* in sales taxes than the poor do, because they buy much more. But studies consistently show that the poor pay *a higher percentage* of their income to sales taxes, because their incomes are so low. This is why sales taxes are more burdensome to lower-income people than to those with higher incomes, and why the personal income tax gives lower-income people a tax credit (which is like a refund) for the sales taxes that they have paid.

Taxes on Assets

Another significant source of tax revenue is *taxes on assets*, mainly *property taxes*. These taxes raise about 8 percent of total government revenue, which is less than income taxes and sales taxes; however, they are a major source of revenue for local governments.

Like sales taxes, property taxes are regressive, in that they take a larger percentage of the incomes of low-income people than high-income people[2]. As with sales taxes, the rich pay more dollars in property taxes, but people with low incomes pay a higher percentage of their income to these taxes, as illustrated by the case of Pat and Patricia in the margin note.

> **payroll taxes**
>
> Taxes paid by employers based on the number of their employees or the amount of their payroll.

Taxes on Payrolls

Payroll taxes are levied on employers, based on the *size of their payroll*. These taxes include employment insurance premiums, Canada Pension Plan premiums, workers' compensation premiums, and, in some provinces, a tax to help pay for the costs of health care and post-secondary education. Payroll taxes must be paid whether the employers make a profit or not.

---

[2] People who rent apartments rather than own homes also pay property taxes, which are estimated to typically amount to about 20 percent of their monthly rent.

The problem with payroll taxes is that they amount to taxes on employing people, in the sense that the more people a firm employs, the higher the taxes it must pay. Payroll taxes vary from province to province, and can add up to 10 percent to Canadian employers' payroll costs—that is, to the cost of employing people. Furthermore, the burden of these taxes falls especially heavily on small businesses, many of which are much more labour-intensive than most larger businesses. As a result, payroll taxes are criticized for discouraging hiring by the small business sector, which has created a high proportion of new jobs in Canada in recent years.

How Much Do Government Programs Redistribute Income?

One major aspect of Canada's social welfare system is *public services* such as health care and education, as described earlier in this chapter. The other major component of the social welfare system is *redistribution of income* from people with higher incomes to those with low incomes. Income is redistributed by both the tax system and government transfer payments. Those with higher incomes pay a larger percentage of their incomes to taxes, mainly due to the progressive nature of the personal income tax. And those with lower incomes receive various types of transfer payments, such as welfare, pensions, and employment insurance benefits. The overall result of these programs is the redistribution of income that is reflected in Table 12-1.

There are three definitions of *income* used in Table 12-1:
- *Market income*, which is income earned in the marketplace (wages, salaries, investment income, etc.),
- *Total income*, which is market income plus government transfer payments, such as welfare or employment insurance benefits, and
- *Income after transfers and taxes*, which is total income less income taxes paid.

Table 12-1 shows that in 2011 an average family in the lowest 20 percent of income-earners earned $11,500 in market income and received $18,400 in transfer

Table 12-1

Redistribution of Income by Transfer Payments and Income Taxes, 2011
(for economic families size 2 or more)

	Lowest 20% of incomes	Second 20% of incomes	Middle 20% of incomes	Fourth 20% of incomes	Highest 20% of incomes
Average market income	$11,500	$40,500	$68,500	$103,600	$198,000
Average transfer payments received	+18,400	+13,400	+9,500	+6,900	+4,800
Average total income	29,900	53,900	78,000	110,500	202,800
Average income tax paid	−700	−4,100	−9,600	−17,600	−44,900
Average income after transfers and taxes	29,200	49,800	64,400	92,900	157,900
Net effect of transfers and taxes	+17,700	+9,300	−100	−10,700	−40,100

Source: Adapted from Statistics Canada, CANSIM Table 202-0701.

payments, for a total income of $29,900. It paid income taxes of $700, leaving it with an income after transfers and taxes of $29,200. So, on balance, transfer payments and income tax *added* $17,700 to its income. At the other extreme, an average family in the highest 20 percent group earned $198,000 in market income, received $4,800 of transfer payments, and paid $44,900 in income taxes and, so it *contributed* $40,100 to these redistribution programs.

Table 12-1 shows that *market income* is very unevenly distributed, with the average income of the top 20 percent of income-earners about 17 times the average income of the lowest 20 percent. *Total income*, which includes transfer payments, is less unevenly distributed, with the average income of the top 20 percent of income-earners less than 7 times the average income of the lowest 20 percent. And the average *after-tax income* of the top 20 percent of income-earners is about 5.4 times the average income of the lowest 20 percent, reflecting the higher income tax rates paid by those with higher incomes.

Table 12-2 summarizes the redistribution of income shown in Table 12-1, in terms of each group's share of total income before and after the government programs that redistribute income. The share of total income going to the lowest-income 20 percent of families was increased from 2.7 percent to 7.3 percent by the government's income taxes and transfer payments. At the other end of the scale, government programs decreased the share of total income going to the highest-income 20 percent of families from 46.9 percent to 39.7 percent. The impact on the middle three groups was relatively small, so the main effect of the governmental programs was to redistribute income from the highest group to the lowest group.

Government transfer payments usually account for about half of the total income of families in the bottom 20% income group.

Table 12-2
Shares of Total Income Before and After Government Programs, 2011

Income Group	Share of Total Income, 2011[1]	
	Market Income	Income After Transfers and Income Taxes
Lowest 20%	2.7%	7.3%
Second 20%	9.6%	12.5%
Middle 20%	16.2%	17.2%
Fourth 20%	24.5%	23.3%
Highest 20%	47.4%	39.7%

[1] Economic families with two or more people.

Source: Adapted from Statistics Canada, CANSIM Table 202-0701.

Transfer Payments between Levels of Government

Under Canada's Constitution, the provincial governments have the responsibility for major government programs such as health care, education, and welfare. Since the Constitution was written, government involvement and spending in these areas has grown dramatically, which has greatly increased the provincial governments' need for revenues.

However, under the Constitution, it is the federal government, not the provinces, that has the greatest power collect tax revenues, mainly because the federal government levies the personal income tax, the largest single source of government revenue in Canada. The result is an imbalance, in which the provinces have the greatest spending responsibilities, but the federal government has the greatest taxation power.

To deal with this imbalance, the federal government transfers to the provincial governments some of its own tax revenues, for the purpose of helping the provinces to finance their spending on health care, education, and welfare. In recent, years, these transfers have amount to over 20 percent of the revenues of the provincial governments. And in turn, the provincial governments transfer some of their revenues to local governments, to assist them with their spending responsibilities.

Budgeting Basics

A government uses its budget to plan its revenues (mostly taxes) and expenditures for the next year, much as a family's budget is its financial plan for its income and spending. These budgets have a significant influence on the key "what to produce" decision that we saw in Chapter 1, by directing resources into the production of social services such as education and health care. And as we have just seen, government budgets have considerable influence on the "how to divide it up" question, by transferring income from higher-income Canadians to those with lower incomes.

Uses and Misuses of Debt

Many people think that borrowing and debt are always bad, and should be avoided at all costs; however, borrowing and debt can be part of a good financial plan, and serve quite useful purposes. This is particularly true when the borrowing is for the purpose of acquiring an asset.

For instance, in some years a family might spend more than its income in order to buy an asset such as a house or a car, and borrow money to finance this purchase. Provided that the asset is not too costly for debt repayments to be made out of the family's annual income, such borrowing is considered to be a reasonable decision. After all, the asset will last for years, so it is reasonable to pay for the asset over its lifetime. As shown in Figure 12-2, a decision to borrow to finance the purchase of an asset involves a *one-time* increase in debt, followed by a decrease in indebtedness as the debt is repaid over the life of the asset.

Borrowing to finance a *one-time expenditure* on an asset such as a car is one thing, but borrowing to pay *recurring ongoing expenses* is a very different matter. For instance, if you borrowed to pay the costs of operating the car (say, $300 per month for gas, insurance, etc.), you would be adding to your debt every month. The result would be a steadily rising debt, as shown in Figure 12-3. The situation would be made worse by interest on the debt pushing your debt higher, in a sort of spiral that is the opposite of the well-managed debt portrayed in Figure 12-2.

Government Budget Deficits and Debt

Government budgets and finance can be discussed using these same concepts concerning borrowing and debt, with some differences in terminology.

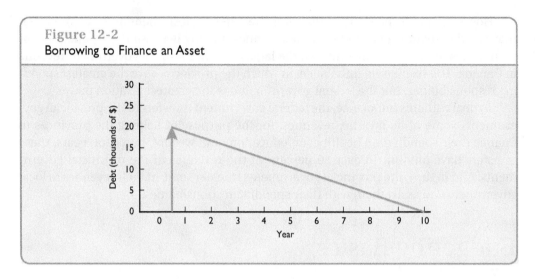

Figure 12-2
Borrowing to Finance an Asset

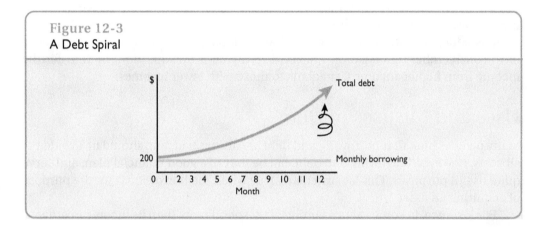

Figure 12-3
A Debt Spiral

Budget deficit

An excess of government spending over government revenues.

When a government's spending exceeds its revenues, it is said to have a **budget deficit**. If the extra spending is for the purpose of building "social assets" such as hospitals or schools, it can be compared to a family's borrowing to buy a house—the government is borrowing to acquire a long-term asset. The government borrows by *selling government bonds*, most of which are long-term in nature—that is, repayable in 10 years or more. Such bonds are mostly bought as long-term investments by large institutional investors, such as pension funds, mutual funds, banks, and so on, although individuals buy them as well. Mostly, they are sold to Canadian investors, although foreign lenders can and do buy them as well.

The relationship between government budget deficits and government debt is shown in Table 12-3. The budget *deficit* is the excess of government spending over revenues for a year. Government *debt*, on the other hand, is the grand total of government borrowing over the years. In Table 12-3, the government starts year 2 with $100 billion of debt from past deficits and borrowing. In year 2, spending ($80 billion) exceeds revenues ($75 billion), so there is a budget deficit of $5 billion. Borrowing to finance the year 2 deficit adds $5 billion to government debt, which increases to $105 billion at the end of year 2. In year 3, another deficit of $8 billion increases the debt to $113 billion. So whenever the government has a budget *deficit*, its *debt* will increase.

If the government's tax revenues and spending are equal, it is said to have a **balanced budget**, and a situation in which tax revenues are larger than government spending is called a **budget surplus**.

balanced budget
A budget in which government spending is equal to government revenues.

budget surplus
A budget in which government revenues are larger than government spending.

Table 12-3
Government Budget Deficits and Debt

Year	Government Spending	Government Revenues	Budget Deficit	Government Debt
1	n.a.	n.a.	n.a.	$100
2	$80	$75	$5	105
3	88	80	8	113

Seeking a Balance: Canada's Experience with Federal Budgets

So, contrary to what many people believe, it is not necessary for the government to balance its budget in every year. Budget deficits are not in themselves bad policy; for example, it could be economically logical to use budget deficits (borrow) to finance the building of social assets such as hospitals or schools[3].

But using budget deficits to pay the government's *annual operating expenses* is a very different matter—these expenses recur each year, so if borrowing to pay them goes on for long, it will lead to steadily rising debt and possibly a "debt spiral", as we saw earlier, in Figure 12-3.

Canada's Deficits Problems

During the 1970s, the federal government made a series of policy decisions that caused deficits and rising debt. First, the government increased spending on various social programs, such as unemployment insurance and pensions, and made commitments to transfer large amounts of federal funds to the provincial governments to help finance their spending on health care, welfare, and post-secondary education.

At the same time, the federal government introduced various tax reductions, which had the effect of depressing its tax revenues. These spending and taxation decisions by the government caused an imbalance to develop between government spending and revenues, so that federal government spending regularly exceeded the government's revenues. Figure 12-4 shows that the federal government's budget deficits after 1974 became not only *large*, but also a *regular annual event* until the late 1990s. This was a borrowing situation like the dangerous one shown in Figure 12-3, not the well-planned one in Figure 12-2.

To finance these large annual budget deficits, the federal government sold large volumes of bonds each year. In the process, the government's debt grew rapidly, as Figure 12-4 also shows. After the mid-1980s, both the size and the rate of growth of the

---

[3] It is also considered reasonable for the government to have budget deficits when the economy is in a recession, order to provide assistance to the unemployed as well as to support total spending the economy. This is covered in *Canadian Macroeconomics: Problems and Policies*, the sister to this text.

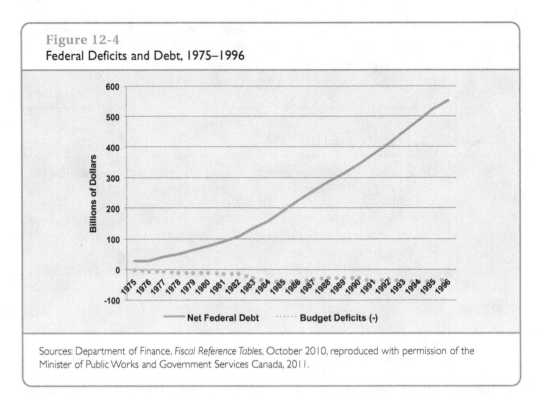

Figure 12-4
Federal Deficits and Debt, 1975–1996

Sources: Department of Finance, *Fiscal Reference Tables*, October 2010, reproduced with permission of the Minister of Public Works and Government Services Canada, 2011.

federal government's debt were becoming serious concerns, and when the federal government reduced its own deficits by limiting its transfer payments to the provinces, this caused the budget deficits of the provincial governments to grow larger.

The Critical Point

Ultimately, a borrower can only borrow for as long as lenders are willing to lend. By 1993, the situation was becoming critical for Canada's governments. The combined budget deficits of the federal and provincial governments amounted to over $50 billion per year. The total net debt of all Canadian governments was over 90 percent of the GDP, and interest payments on the debt were driving it higher, in an upward spiral, as can be seen in figure 12-4.

To finance their massive budget deficits, Canadian governments (mostly the provinces) had for several years been borrowing heavily from foreign lenders. Canada's debt to foreign lenders, about half of which was owed by Canadian governments, was very large, and was rising rapidly.

But by the early 1990s, foreign lenders were becoming concerned about the very heavy debt of Canadian governments. The credit ratings of some provinces deteriorated, forcing the provinces to pay higher interest rates on their bonds in order to attract lenders. These developments forced both the provincial and federal governments to finally confront their budget problems and to make some difficult choices.

"For years, governments have been promising more than they can deliver, and delivering more than they can afford. That has to end. We are ending it."
— FINANCE MINISTER PAUL MARTIN, 1994.

Eliminating the Deficits

As noted at the start of this chapter, Canada's social welfare system is built around the three keystones of *income security programs* (such as employment insurance, welfare, and pensions), *health care,* and *education.* The financial problems of governments were so great that they forced governments to consider the most fundamental changes to these key programs in many years.

The only two ways for governments to reduce their budget deficits are to *increase taxes* or *reduce spending*. Taxes had already been increased so much during the 1980s that further tax increases were considered impossible. The only alternative left was to reduce government spending.

For five years in the mid-1990s, the federal government reduced its program spending (which is all spending except interest on the government's debt) significantly, with the largest cuts falling on federal transfer payments to the provincial governments for health care, post-secondary education, and welfare. This led to various cuts in provincial government spending on these programs, some examples of which follow.

In the field of *health care*, many employees were laid off, particularly nurses, and access to hospital care decreased as many hospital beds were closed. Coverage of some procedures was eliminated, and health-care coverage for Canadians outside the country was restricted. And as the resources of the health-care system were unable to keep up with the demand for services, Canadians faced longer waits for many types of operations.

Post-secondary education also saw large-scale layoffs of employees when provincial grants to colleges and universities were reduced. Students' tuition fees (and student debt) increased considerably, to make up for the reduction in grant revenue. Enrolment in some programs was limited, and class sizes were increased.

Income support programs were also affected. Welfare benefits were reduced by provincial governments, in some cases by more than 20 percent. The federal government reduced the benefits available under the Employment Insurance program, and various benefits that had been available to higher-income Canadians were reduced or eliminated.

After the Pain, the Gain

Over the period from 1993 to 1997, the federal government's financial position improved dramatically, as its budget deficits shrank. This was partly due to the cuts to government spending described earlier, and also to a period of rapid economic

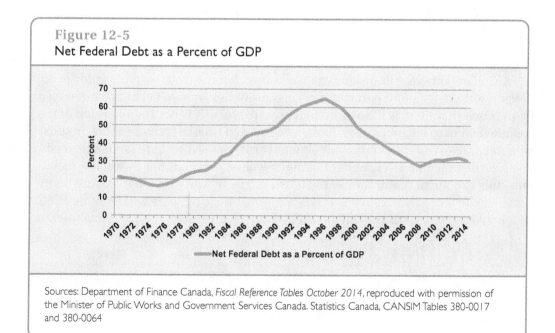

Figure 12-5
Net Federal Debt as a Percent of GDP

Net Federal Debt as a Percent of GDP

Sources: Department of Finance Canada, *Fiscal Reference Tables October 2014*, reproduced with permission of the Minister of Public Works and Government Services Canada. Statistics Canada, CANSIM Tables 380-0017 and 380-0064

growth, which generated more tax revenues for governments from the increases in jobs, incomes, sales, and profits. After 1997, the federal government found itself in the unfamiliar position of having budget surpluses—the first since 1970!

And as the deficits were reduced and turned into surpluses, the problem of federal government debt eased greatly, as Figure 12-5 shows. The combination of less federal borrowing and a rapidly-growing economy (Gross Domestic Product, or GDP) improved the federal government's financial position dramatically, as federal debt as a percent of GDP to decreased from 66 percent in 1996 to less than 29 percent in 2008[4].

YOU DECIDE

How to Use Budget Surpluses?

From 1998 to 2008, the federal government's average budget surplus was $9.5 billion per year. ■

QUESTIONS

1. What are three different types of ways that these surpluses could be used?
2. How much did these surpluses amount to in terms of dollars per Canadian per year? Per month? (Canada's population averaged 31.6 million over this period.)

Transfer Payments and Incentives to Work

Some people welcomed the reductions in welfare benefits described earlier in this chapter, because they believe that welfare benefits are so generous that people receiving them can sit comfortably at home without working. Other people dispute this claim as inaccurate.

To check the actual welfare benefits for your province, Google *welfare rates + the name of your province*.

People who are familiar with the welfare system agree that welfare often does create disincentives to work, but not because welfare benefits are so generous as to make welfare preferable to work. Rather, the problem of disincentives arises because of what happens when someone who is on welfare tries to add to his/her income by doing some work.

A welfare system will discourage welfare recipients from working if for every dollar a welfare recipient earns by working, his or her welfare benefits are reduced by so much that there is little or no incentive to work. It is not the *intention* of the welfare system to kill incentives. Rather, the system tries to focus benefits on those who need them—and the more a recipient earns, the less welfare he or she needs. So as earned income rises, welfare benefits will be reduced. But to welfare recipients, this can mean that if they earn some income by working, their welfare benefits will be reduced by so much that it is not worth working. This has the same effect as a *very high marginal tax rate* on their income: it reduces the incentive to earn

---

[4] The temporary increase in debt as a percent of GDP in 2009–10 was the result of the serious recession of 2008–09. During a recession, the government's budget goes into deficit as the government's tax revenues fall and it has to increase spending on assistance to the unemployed and other measures to ease the impact of the recession.

YOU DECIDE

The Marginal Tax Rate and the Economic Incentive to Work

The *marginal tax rate* is the percentage of any extra income that is earned which goes to taxes. Because it determines how much of any additional income a person gets to keep, the marginal tax rate is very important to the incentive to work; specifically, the higher the marginal tax rate, the lower the economic incentive to do additional work.

We will consider the marginal tax rates of two people. Joan, a teacher, is wondering whether to teach a night course. The course would pay her $1000, but after taxes, Joan would receive only $600, because her marginal tax rate is 40 percent. Joan complains that there is little incentive for her to teach the night course because of these high taxes, which go to support people whom she describes as "lazy welfare bums."

Sandy is on welfare, receiving $800 per month. If she earns $100 per month working part-time, her welfare will be reduced to $720 per month, leaving her $20 better off for having earned $100. In other words, Sandy's marginal tax rate is 80 percent. Sandy declines the job on the grounds that it's not worth the trouble.

QUESTIONS

1. Is Sandy just being "lazy"?
2. If we want to get Sandy off welfare and working, what kinds of changes do we need to make to the welfare system?

income and to get off the welfare system (see the cases of Joan and Sandy in the "You Decide" box).

Studies of this problem have estimated that many recipients of social welfare gain so little by working that if they do work, they are in a similar position to someone who is paying a marginal tax rate of *from 80 to 100 percent*. In some cases, this can work as a "trap" in which welfare recipients become caught indefinitely. To escape from this trap, a person usually has to find a reasonably steady full-time job, so as to break completely clear of the welfare system. But unless one has skills and experience, it is unlikely that this can be achieved, so the welfare cycle tends to go on and on, from year to year, and even from generation to generation.

In an attempt to improve work incentives, some social assistance plans have been modified to allow recipients to earn at least some income without suffering a reduction in their welfare benefits. Such changes do help to improve the incentive for welfare recipients to earn some income by working at part-time jobs. But beyond a certain level of earned income, their welfare benefits are reduced, and if this reduction occurs too rapidly, the same disincentive effect will occur, although at a higher level of earned income.

Advocates of reform to the social welfare system argue that there are real benefits in improving the work incentives in the system. This would help to keep welfare recipients in the work force (even if only combining part-time work with their welfare) and earning both income and self-esteem, rather than passively relying on welfare. Also, by encouraging welfare recipients to earn more, it could actually reduce their reliance on welfare and thus reduce the total amount of welfare benefits that governments pay out, thus helping to reduce the cost to society.

On the other hand, improving incentives is not a simple matter. The more people earn, the less welfare they need, so it is reasonable to reduce benefits as earned income increases. The key is to not reduce benefits so rapidly that there is little or no incentive for welfare recipients to earn income.

Government Benefits and Services in Perspective

Underlying the debate over government benefits and services is the basic economic reality of *scarcity,* as discussed all the way back in Chapter 1, when the people in the island mini-society had to deal with the reality that they did not have the economic resources to produce all of the food, fuel, and security that they needed and wanted. If they decided to produce more of any one item, the *opportunity cost* would be that they would have less of the others.

Concerning government programs, the situation is essentially the same—more resources being employed in the government sector of the economy means that less is available for private consumption by Canadians. So, the opportunity cost of having improved health care or educational services might be that people have to make do with fewer restaurant dinners and video rentals. Viewed from the opposite perspective, if Canadians want lower taxes so that they can have more restaurant dinners and video rentals, the opportunity cost will be reduced government services and benefits.

For nearly two decades after the early 1970s, Canadians seemed to have avoided these realities, as they enjoyed higher levels of *both* private consumption *and* government benefits and services. However, much of this was made possible by borrowing that could not go on forever. By the mid-1990s, economic reality had asserted itself, and Canadians were forced to decide what balance between their private consumption and the level of government benefits and services they wanted for their society. The choice was not an easy one, and ensured difficult decisions and controversy for years to come.

Chapter Summary

1. The three main aspects of Canada's social welfare system are income security programs, health care, and education. (L.O. 1)
2. The four main sources of tax revenues for governments are taxes on incomes (personal and business), consumption taxes, property taxes, and payroll taxes. (L.O. 2)
3. Progressive taxes take a higher percentage of the incomes of the rich than of the poor, while regressive taxes have the opposite effect. (L.O. 3)
4. The marginal tax rate, which is the percentage of additional income that goes to taxes, has important effects on economic incentives to work, save, and invest. (L.O. 4)
5. The effect of Canadian governments' transfer payments and income taxes is mostly to redistribute income from the highest-income 20 percent of families to the lowest-income 20 percent of families. (L.O. 5)
6. The federal government transfers large amounts of revenues to the provincial governments to help pay for the health-care, post-secondary education, and welfare programs for which the provinces are constitutionally responsible. (L.O. 6)
7. If the government has a budget deficit, it must borrow money, and its debt will increase. Borrowing is considered to be a reasonable way to finance the

purchase and construction of assets, but not a sound way to finance operating costs. (L.O. 7)

8. After 1975, the federal government had large annual budget deficits, and accumulated a large and growing debt. By 1993, the situation was so severe that it forced cuts to spending on key government programs such as health care, education, and income support. (L.O. 8)

9. Government income support programs can create disincentives to work if recipients lose too much of their benefits when they earn additional income. (L.O. 9)

Questions

1. (a) What are the three basic types of social welfare programs in Canada, and what are the benefits that they provide for Canadians?
   (b) What is the opportunity cost of these programs?
   (c) How could you assess whether Canadians believe that the benefits of these programs are worth their costs?

2. Suppose the government needs more tax revenue. List the economic and political advantages and disadvantages of increasing each of the following taxes:
   (a) personal income taxes
   (b) corporate income taxes
   (c) gasoline taxes
   (d) consumption taxes (such as the GST)
   (e) payroll taxes

3. Ernie, an accountant, earns $60 000 per year, on which he pays income taxes of $10 000. If Ernie takes on extra work as a night school teacher, his income will increase to $68 000, and his income taxes will increase to $12 800. Ernie's *marginal tax rate* is _____ percent. Show your calculations.

4. Create your own example of how a social welfare system can redistribute income from families with high incomes to families with low incomes. In your example, use the terms *market income, total income,* and *income after transfers and taxes,* and compare the effects of transfer payments and income taxes on a family with a market income of $10 000 and a family with a market income of $100 000. Your example must reduce the annual income gap between these families from $90 000 to $50 000.

5. Sally is on welfare of $700 per month. She has been offered a part-time job that would pay her $300 per month. If she takes this job, her welfare would be reduced to $500 per month. If Sally took the job, her income from working would in effect be subject to a marginal tax rate of _____ percent. Show your calculations.

6. (a) At the start of this year, the government's debt is $300 billion. If the government's spending this year is $220 billion and its tax revenues are $200 billion, the government's budget deficit for the year will be $ _____ billion, and the government's debt at the end of the year will be $ _____ billion.
   (b) Would the building of a hospital be considered a reasonable purpose for the government to borrow money? Why or why not?
   (c) Would paying the salaries of hospital workers be considered a reasonable purpose for the government to borrow money? Why or why not?

7. Make the strongest possible argument for each of the following possible uses of the budget surpluses of Canada's federal government:
   (a) reduction of government debt
   (b) increased spending on government programs (health care, education, etc.)
   (c) reductions in taxes

8. Statistics Canada has statistics on *"consolidated government spending,"* which show the combined spending of all levels of government. Visit **www.statcan.gc.ca** and search for *Consolidated government revenue and expenditures,* then click on "Consolidated government revenue and expenditure." Calculate the percentage increase for each category of government spending over the years shown in the table.
   (a) Which programs seem to have enjoyed the highest priority in recent years? What might explain the emphasis being placed on these programs?
   (b) On which programs has government spending lagged, and what might explain the lower emphasis on these programs?

Study Guide

Review Questions (Answers to these Review Questions appear in Appendix B.)

1. Which of the following are considered to represent the three "keystones" of Canada's social welfare system?
   (a) employment insurance, welfare, and pensions
   (b) education, income security programs, and pensions
   (c) income security programs, education, and health care
   (d) education, welfare, and pensions
   (e) employment insurance, welfare, and government jobs

2. What are the four basic types of taxes listed in the text?
   • Taxes on _____
   • Taxes on _____
   • Taxes on _____
   • Taxes on _____

3. A *progressive tax* is defined as
   (a) a tax that takes a lower percentage of the incomes of the rich than of the poor.
   (b) a tax that takes a higher percentage of the incomes of the rich than the poor.
   (c) a tax that takes an equal percentage of everyone's income.
   (d) a tax that is increased year after year.
   (e) None of the above.

4. Which of the following is an example of a *progressive tax*?
   (a) the personal income tax
   (b) property taxes
   (c) provincial sales taxes
   (d) payroll taxes
   (e) None of the above.

5. A *regressive tax* is defined as
   (a) a sales tax based on the value of goods and services.
   (b) a tax that takes a higher percentage of the incomes of the poor than of the rich.
   (c) a tax that takes a lower percentage of the incomes of the poor than of the rich.
   (d) a tax that takes an equal percentage of everyone's income.
   (e) None of the above.

6. Last year, Nadia's income was $40 000 and her income taxes were $8000. This year, her income is $50 000 and her income taxes are $11 500. Nadia's marginal tax rate is ____ percent.

7. There is a saying among skilled workers that "If you work 5 hours of overtime, the first 2 hours are for the government." This indicates that they believe their marginal tax rate to be about _____ percent.

8. In their song "Taxman," the tax collector tells the Beatles "one for you, nineteen for me." The marginal tax rate implied by this reference is _____ percent.

9. Generally speaking, high marginal tax rates tend to
   (a) reduce the incentive to work.
   (b) not affect the incentive to work.
   (c) reduce the incentive to save and invest.
   (d) increase the incentive to work.
   (e) Both (a) and (c) together.

10. Government tax collection and spending on social welfare redistributes income from Canadians with higher incomes to those with lower incomes. In broad general terms, which of the following best describes the overall effect of these programs on how income is distributed in Canada?
    (a) Income is transferred from the highest-income 40 percent of families to the lowest-income 40 percent of families.
    (b) Income is transferred from the highest-income 20 percent of families to the lowest-income 20 percent of families.
    (c) Income is transferred from the middle-income 20 percent of families to the lowest-income 20 percent of families.
    (d) Income is transferred from the middle-income 20 percent of families to the lowest-income 40 percent of families.
    (e) Income is transferred from the highest-income 40 percent of families to the rest of Canadian families.

11. The federal government transfers some of its revenues to the provincial governments in order to support their spending on three major types of social programs, which are
    (a) health care, education, and public security.
    (b) health care, education, and the environment.
    (c) health care, post-secondary education, and welfare.
    (d) health care, welfare, and public security.
    (e) post-secondary education, welfare, and public security.

12. State whether each of the following would be an economically reasonable purpose for financing expenditures by borrowing money. (Answer *yes* or *no* for each.)
    (a) ____ the purchase of a house by a family
    (b) ____ the weekly purchases of food by a family
    (c) ____ the purchase of machinery by a corporation

(d) ____ the building of a college by the government

(e) ____ the payment of the monthly expenses of operating a college (wages, supplies, etc.)

(f) ____ the purchase of a car by a family

(g) ____ weekly payments for the costs of operating the car (gas, insurance, etc.)

13. A government *budget deficit* exists if
    (a) the government's spending is less than its tax revenues.
    (b) the government's spending and tax revenues are equal.
    (c) the government's spending exceeds its tax revenues.

14. The government raises the money to finance its budget deficits by _____.

15. Suppose the government's debt at the end of last year was $400 billion. If its spending for this year were $170 billion, and its tax revenues for this year were $130 billion,
    (a) its budget deficit for this year would be $_____ billion, and
    (b) its debt at the end of this year would be $_____ billion.

16. The main reason that Canada's welfare system reduces the incentive to work is that
    (a) welfare benefits are so high that many people are encouraged to quit full-time jobs and go on welfare.
    (b) people on welfare are not permitted to seek work.
    (c) when a welfare recipient earns money by working, his or her welfare benefits are reduced, often by so much that there is little or no economic incentive to work.
    (d) there are no government agencies to help those on welfare to find work.
    (e) welfare agencies and social workers encourage people to remain on welfare rather than to seek employment.

Critical Thinking Questions

(Asterisked questions 1 to 5 are answered in Appendix B; the answers to questions 6 to 10 are in the Instructor's Manual that accompanies this text.)

*1. Would tariffs (import duties) on imported goods be a regressive or progressive tax? Explain the reason for your answer.

*2. Which do you think would have more negative effects upon the productivity of the economy and the prosperity of Canadians—a 50-percent marginal tax rate on personal incomes, or a 50-percent marginal tax rate on business profits?

*3. "The government should never borrow money. Borrowing only leads to debt, and debt leads to trouble." Do you agree with this statement? Why or why not? Why might the speaker believe this?

*4. (a) Fill in the columns in the following table for budget deficit/surplus and government debt for each year through 20X4.

			Billions of Dollars	
Year	Government Spending	Government Tax Revenues	Budget Deficit (–) or Surplus (+)	Government Debt
20X1	$110	$100	– $10	$310
20X2	117	105	____	____
20X3	125	110	____	____
20X4	132	114	____	____
20X5	____	____	____	____

(b) Develop a combination of spending reductions and/or tax increases for 20X5 that eliminates the deficits (balances the budget) in 20X5.

(c) What obstacles would the government probably encounter in its efforts to balance its budget in part (b)?

(d) If the budget were to remain balanced in each year *after* 20X5, what would happen to the level of government debt?

*5. If you are receiving employment insurance (EI) benefits, you are allowed to earn up to $50 per week or 25 percent of your regular benefits (whichever is higher) without facing any loss of EI benefits. But all earnings above that limit will be deducted *dollar for dollar* from your weekly EI benefits.

(a) What is the purpose of allowing people receiving EI to earn this income?

(b) What is the marginal tax rate on earnings above the limit?

6. "The government should significantly decrease taxes on *incomes* (both personal incomes and business profits), and make up the lost revenue by significantly increasing taxes on *consumption*, such as the goods and services tax." Explain why the speaker believes that this proposal would improve the operation of the economy in terms of productivity and the standard of living.

7. An alternative to the progressive personal income tax is the *flat tax*, under which everyone pays the same marginal tax rate. Few deductions are permitted, and the tax system is greatly simplified by the elimination of the large number of deductions, exemptions, and tax credits that now exist. Advocates of the flat tax argue that the elimination of deductions, exemptions, and credits enables the tax system to have relatively low *tax rates* but still collect adequate amounts of *tax dollars*. The table below shows a flat tax system with a marginal tax rate of 25 percent and with the first $20 000 of personal income exempt from income tax.

(a) Complete the table.

Income	Taxable Income	Income Taxes	Taxes as a Percent of Income
$ 0	$ 0	$ 0	0
20 000	0	0	0
25 000	5 000	1 250	5%
30 000	———	———	———
50 000	———	———	———
100 000	———	———	———
200 000	———	———	———
300 000	———	———	———

(b) Is the flat tax progressive, regressive, or neither? Why?

(c) If a flat tax were introduced, what do you think would be the keys to making it a tax that would be acceptable to the general public as a reasonably "fair" tax?

(d) What political obstacles would there be to introducing a flat tax in Canada?

8. "The 'disincentive problem' with welfare in Canada is that welfare benefits are so generous that people would rather sit on their chairs at home and take welfare than get up and go to work." Is this an accurate description of the problem of disincentives in Canada's income support programs as described in this chapter? Explain the reasons for your answer.

9. What do you think would have happened after 1993 if Canadian governments had *not* reduced their spending and deficits?

10. One proposed reform for health care is to charge a *user fee* of perhaps $5 to $10 for every visit a person makes to a doctor or a hospital emergency room. What would be the main arguments in favour of such user fees, and why do many people oppose them?

Use the Web   (Hints for this Use the Web exercise appear in Appendix B.)

1. The recession of 2008-09 caused the federal government's debt as a percentage of GDP (see Figure 12-5) to increase in for the first time in 14 years. Has the federal government's debt resumed its downward trend as a percentage of GDP? For the debt figures, visit **www.statcan.gc.ca** and search for "federal government debt" ("net federal debt" is the figure to use), and for the GDP figures, search for "gross domestic product."

2. Do you know the marginal tax rate that you are paying? Visit **www.ey.com** and search for "personal tax calculator."

Environmental Economics

After studying this chapter, you should be able to

1. Explain in terms of *private costs, social costs,* and *externalities* why there are economic incentives to pollute the environment.

2. Use a production-possibilities curve and the concept of opportunity cost to show why a cleaner environment can be regarded as similar to any other good or economic benefit.

3. Summarize the implications of the Law of Diminishing Returns for decision making regarding environmental protection.

4. Explain how economic analysis of the costs and benefits of a pollution control program can help in designing the program and deciding who should pay its costs.

5. Describe the operation, advantages, and disadvantages of each of the following pollution control strategies: direct regulation, taxes on pollution, tradable pollution credits, lawsuits for damages, and government subsidies.

6. Explain the operation, advantages, and disadvantages of each of the following waste management strategies: landfills, incineration, recycling, and "pay to throw" plans for garbage collection.

7. Explain the *greenhouse effect* and concerns about global warming.

8. Apply the facts and concepts of this chapter to various situations.

In 1969, the Cuyahoga River in Cleveland, Ohio was declared a fire hazard after it caught fire for at least the twelfth time. Today, the river is much cleaner.

Since the 1960s, the environment has been a public issue in Canada and other countries. During the late 1960s and early 1970s, concerns over air and water pollution led to the first legislation governing air and water pollution. From the mid-1970s to the mid-1980s, however, environmental issues took second place to "bread and butter" economic concerns caused by unusually severe inflation and unemployment. Following the mid-1980s, a combination of better economic times and serious pollution problems such as acid rain brought environmental issues back to the forefront.

More recently, however, environmental problems have moved to a larger and more threatening scale, with growing concerns about climate change and global warming that make earlier concerns about air and water pollution seem minor by comparison. According to some projections, the environmental consequences of our economic growth could threaten our future, or even our existence.

But much public discussion of environmental issues is not productive. Rather than focusing on the *causes* of environmental problems and setting realistic *objectives* and effective *strategies* for dealing with it, discussion of environmental issues too often focuses on predictions of catastrophe and on *fixing blame*, usually on someone else. Often, the problem is simply blamed on "industry," with the implication that if industry (that is, someone else) behaved more responsibly, there would be no environmental problems.

A more productive approach is to analyze the *causes* of environmental problems. By doing so, we can not only gain a better understanding of these problems, but also formulate government policies that are most likely to be effective in dealing with them.

Economic analysis of this sort shows that environmental problems are much more than the result of industrialists' negligence. Environmental problems are deeply rooted in the very nature of our society and our economy, in at least two fundamental ways. The first of these is our desire for material benefits. To a significant extent, pollution is a by-product of the high levels of consumption and production that we have come to enjoy. One of the most telling illustrations of this reality is the fact that the largest single source of air pollution in North America is not industry, but rather our own automobiles. The second reality is that there are strong *economic incentives to pollute* the environment. Whether you are a corporation dumping waste into the water and air, or a driver disconnecting the emission controls on your car to save on gas, it is to your short-run economic advantage to pollute the environment. From the viewpoint of the *individual* person or business, pollution pays. However, the *collective* effect of millions of individuals behaving in this way can be serious—even catastrophic—environmental damage in the longer run.

The Economic Incentive to Pollute

As noted in Chapter 2, in a market system, the profit motive provides important economic incentives for businesses to produce what consumers want and to produce it as efficiently as possible. These incentives contribute greatly to the economic prosperity of consumers.

But the profit motive also generates socially undesirable incentives. One of these is for producers to join together in price-fixing agreements, as discussed in Chapter 7. Another is the economic incentive to pollute the environment.

In discussing this problem of incentives, economists distinguish between two types of costs of producing a product:
 (a) private (internal) costs, and
 (b) social (external) costs.

Private costs are ordinary production costs such as labour and materials. These costs are paid by producers, and are ultimately included in the price paid by the consumer. Because these costs are contained *within* the production/consumption system, they are called *internal costs.*

Social costs are the costs to the environment, and thus to society at large, of actions such as the dumping of industrial wastes into the air and water. These costs may or may not be measurable in dollar terms, but they are real and often high, including health problems and costs for those affected. Because they are not paid for by the business that *produces* the product and not included in the price of the product paid by the consumer who *uses* the product, but rather are *passed on* to the environment and to society at large, they are called *external costs.*

The economic incentive is for producers to *minimize* their internal costs by being as efficient as possible. This encourages them to use economic resources such as labour and materials as efficiently as possible. It also encourages them to *maximize* their external costs by dumping as much of their waste as possible into the environment rather than paying to prevent or clean up the resultant pollution. It is important to note that such behaviour is economically beneficial (in the short run)not only to the *producer* (who gets higher profits) but also to the *consumer* (who gets the product at a lower price). But the result can be serious effects upon the environment.

Externalities

When the production or the consumption of a product inflicts incidental costs such as pollution on others, and these costs are not paid by those who inflict them, economists say that an **externality** exists. This is also known as a *spillover effect,* because the effects of some people's actions spill over onto others. Pollution is among the most serious of these effects. In our pursuit of material prosperity, we—consumers as well as producers—are choosing to avoid paying some important costs of our prosperity, and choosing to pass these on instead to our environment, with potentially serious results.

As we have seen, the marketplace can solve many important economic problems. However, pollution is not a problem that the marketplace will solve on its own—the incentives within the market system tend to *generate* pollution, not reduce it. As a result, government action will be required to deal with this problem.

The Cost of a Cleaner Environment

Another fundamental reality of environmental economics is that pollution is mostly the by-product of the consumption and production of goods that most people are fond of having and reluctant to do without. You may be upset about the quality of air in your community, but are you willing to reduce your driving by one-third and do without your air conditioning in order to reduce air pollution from cars and electrical generating plants? Alternatively, would you be willing to pay significantly more for these and other consumer products in order to pay for the costs of making the producers' plants and the products themselves less damaging to the environment?

Many people have been reluctant both to accept these realities and to pay the cost, preferring instead to view the situation with alarm while blaming others. Such attitudes could explain the reluctance of many politicians to mount an effective attack on environmental problems. If government leaders believe that voters are unwilling to

private (internal) costs
Production costs, such as labour and materials, that are paid by producers and ultimately included in the price paid by the consumer.

social (external) costs
Costs that are not paid by producers, but rather passed on to society at large.

externality
An incidental cost, or side effect, inflicted on others by the production or consumption of a product. Also known as a *spillover effect.*

pay the cost of a cleaner environment, their efforts will tend to consist of strong words but weak action. For instance, they will tend to pass impressive-sounding legislation, but enforce it ineffectively.

At the most basic economic level, a cleaner environment is like any other good or economic benefit: we can have more of it if we are prepared to accept less of other things. As we saw in Chapter 1, the fact that society has limited economic resources means that using more of these resources to produce one thing necessarily means having less available to produce other things. The people of the island mini-society of Chapter 1 could have used one of their workers to clean up the island, but that would have meant they would have to do without the food, fuel, or security that this person could have provided. A cleaner environment does have opportunity costs.

Similarly, if in our modern economy we choose to devote more of our economic resources, such as capital and labour, to producing pollution control equipment and thus a cleaner environment, we will have less of other products, or a lower standard of living. Viewed from a different perspective, if producers have to install costly pollution-control equipment, their production costs and the price consumers pay for their products will be higher. For instance, the cost of capping greenhouse gas emissions at 1990 levels has been estimated to be an additional 8 cents per litre on the price of gasoline—$300 to $400 per year for an average driver. This is a trade-off, like other economic choices, that we somehow have to make.

The trade-off between consumer goods and a cleaner environment can be shown with a production-possibilities curve of the sort discussed in Chapter 1 and illustrated in Figure 13-1. We could choose point A, at which we would have the maximum possible amount of consumer goods but devote no resources to pollution control and therefore have the dirtiest possible environment—perhaps one in which we would have to wear gas masks to work. At the other extreme, we could choose point B, at which we would have the cleanest possible environment, but a very low standard of living due to extremely strict environmental controls that highly restricted the production of consumer goods and made them more costly.

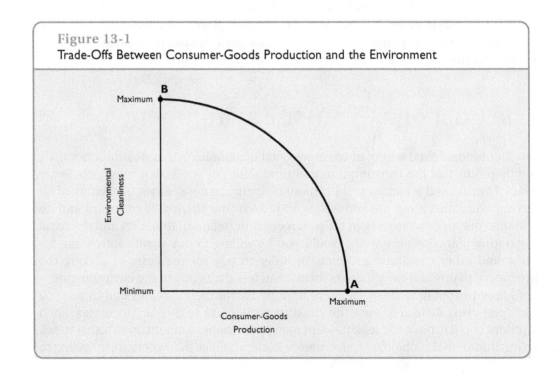

Figure 13-1
Trade-Offs Between Consumer-Goods Production and the Environment

Points A and B represent the two extremes of environmental decision making. In reality, it would be reasonable to expect a choice somewhere between A and B that represents an *acceptable balance* between our material wants and the quality of our environment.

The trade-off between a cleaner environment and fewer consumer goods is the way that *the economist* sees the issue. *The consumer* sees it in terms of having to *pay higher prices* for products in order to cover the costs of pollution control measures and equipment used in their production, leaving the consumer with less money to spend on other things. The result is the same—a trade-off in which the outcome is a cleaner environment and a lower standard of living (consumption per person). The money that consumers must pay for emission controls on their automobiles cannot be spent on other consumer goods and services.

Diminishing Returns and the Environment

As with other economic benefits, the cleanup of the environment is subject to the Law of Diminishing Returns described in Chapter 8. That is, it may prove quite easy to reduce the level of pollution by, say, 20 percent, through relatively simple and inexpensive measures. However, to achieve a further 20-percent reduction of pollution may well involve higher costs, while improvements beyond this are likely to prove even more costly. To reduce pollution to very low levels could prove so costly that it might well be considered not worth doing.

This reality makes it all the more important that we have reasonable estimates of the costs of pollution (and thus of the benefits to be gained by reducing pollution) and of the costs of pollution-control measures, so that we can make rational decisions concerning pollution control. This would enable us to use our antipollution resources so as to achieve the maximum possible beneficial results.

Environmental Decision Making and Cost–Benefit Analysis

Economists cannot tell society *which one* of the various possible combinations of environmental cleanliness and consumption is best, or *whether we should* improve our environment by *x* percent at the cost of a *y*-percent reduction in the volume of our consumption. These are decisions for the people of a society to make, mainly through their governments.

However, economic analysis can assist in the decision-making process by providing estimates of the *costs* and *benefits* of any given level of pollution; that is, who loses due to the pollution, and how much, and who gains economically due to the pollution, and how much?

For instance, suppose a pulp-and-paper company is polluting a river. Those who benefit from this situation would include the company itself, its shareholders, and employees. Less obvious beneficiaries would include consumers of paper, who get cheaper paper, and the local community, which benefits from the employment created by the paper mill, the taxes paid by the mill, and the spending of money by mill employees. Some of the social costs of the pollution could be estimated, such as damage to commercial fishing and tourism, water purification costs, and health costs.

Other costs, such as damage to wildlife and the quality of the environment, would be more difficult to determine. However, it would be possible at least to estimate the costs and benefits of the situation as it is now, and estimate the benefits and costs of reducing the volume of pollution.

Such estimates can help in making decisions concerning the following matters:

(a) *The objective of the pollution control program:* Is the target the total elimination of the pollution, or would the Law of Diminishing Returns make this target too costly? What would be the benefits and the costs of reducing the pollution by 90 percent? 80 percent? 70 percent? Having estimates of the costs and benefits of these decisions can be quite helpful in setting targets for pollution control programs.

(b) *How to attack the problem:* As we will see shortly, there is a variety of possible approaches to protecting the environment. If we know who benefits and who loses from the situation, and the economic incentives involved, we should be better able to devise the most effective approach.

(c) *Who should pay the costs of attacking the problem:* Depending on the costs and benefits involved, it may be appropriate for the cost to be paid by the producer and/or the consumer and/or the government. Economic analysis can help to determine who should pay these costs.

The Current Environmental Situation

www.ec.gc.ca

Until the late 1960s, the environment *seemed* capable of handling most industrial by-products—those that were not recycled by natural processes seemed to be spread sufficiently thinly so as not to constitute a serious concern. During this era, the prevailing attitude was summed up in the catchphrase "the solution to pollution is dilution." By the early 1970s, however, growing problems of air and water pollution made it clear that dilution was *not* the solution. Growing public concern led to legislation targeted at *specific* problems such as gases polluting the air, chemicals polluting the water, acid rain, and so on. More recently, however, environmental concerns have moved to a much larger, even global, scale, due to *more general* problems such as climate change and global warming.

While the marketplace will solve many economic problems, environmental pollution is not one of these. So, environmental problems call for action by governments, not only on a national level but also internationally.

What Can Governments Do?

We have seen that the basic reason for pollution is that there is an incentive for producers and consumers to pass on the external costs of their activities to the environment and to society at large. From the economic viewpoint, then, the objective of antipollution policy should be to *internalize* the external costs of pollution, so that those who benefit from pollution are forced to *pay all of the costs* arising from their activities. Then polluters will have an incentive to take steps to reduce or eliminate their pollution. The following sections describe four ways of doing this: *direct regulation and fines, taxes, tradable pollution credits,* and *legal liability.* In addition, we will consider the possibility that, in some cases, governments should pay for, or *subsidize,* pollution control. Finally, we will examine the question of *waste management.*

Direct Regulation

By far the most common form of government antipollution action is *direct controls*. Under this approach, the polluter is required by law, or by a government agency empowered by law to set pollution standards, to reduce the pollution to a certain level. The emission controls set by governments for automobiles are probably the best-known form of pollution control by direct regulation. The most common penalty for violating the law is fines.

While regulations appear to be simple ("pollution is bad, so make it illegal"), in practice, matters are more complex. The main problem is the setting of the limit, or standard, for the pollution. From the environmental viewpoint, it would seem desirable to set a standard of zero pollution, or ban pollution outright. However, as we have seen, it would prove extremely costly (and in some cases technically impossible) to achieve zero pollution. So outright bans are used only for substances that have such extremely severe environmental effects that they must be banned at virtually any cost. Generally, direct controls allow some pollution, but specify the acceptable limits. Setting such standards is a difficult and controversial matter, especially when the environmental costs and the costs of pollution control are not completely known. Almost always, polluters complain that the costs of meeting the standards are excessive and will result in lost jobs, while environmentalists complain that the standards are so lax that serious pollution will continue.

Once the standards have been set, there remains the problem of enforcing them. Enforcement of complex regulations requires considerable resources, mainly in the form of qualified inspectors. Environmentalists argue (often with justification) that governments tend to pass environmental legislation but fail to provide the resources to enforce it effectively.

On the other hand, very strict enforcement of some environmental laws can generate problems of a different sort. An example is provided by California, where the city of Los Angeles and farmers in the state's central valley depend upon water pumped from the San Joaquin River in Northern California. Because of this pumping of water, the delta smelt, a small fish that inhabits the San Joaquin River, became a candidate for the endangered species list. To save the delta smelt would require very costly changes to the complex systems that deliver water from Northern California to the south. When a proposal was made to build a reservoir that would hold winter rain runoff and reduce the amount of water that had to be pumped from the delta smelt's habitat, environmentalists discovered on the site of the proposed reservoir the home of a single family of rare kit foxes—another endangered species. This was not a unique case—residential and commercial/industrial developers found that governments frequently stopped their projects when antigrowth activists discovered some rare animal or plant on the site. While California had led the way in the environmental movement of the 1980s, there was by the 1990s a political backlash against excessive regulation, which was perceived as preventing socially and economically desirable projects. In economic terms, the regulations were considering only the *benefits* of measures to protect the environment, and not taking into account their *costs*.

Finally, it is essential that the penalties for violating environmental protection laws be sufficiently high to discourage polluters. Often, both the risk of prosecution for violating pollution control legislation and the fines levied on violators have been so low that the economic incentive is to take one's chances by ignoring the law, and pay the fines if caught.

Notwithstanding these difficulties, direct controls are the most common form of pollution control. When properly set and enforced, and with adequate penalties, direct controls can force polluters to pay the costs of pollution prevention or cleanup. By forcing producers—and consumers of the products, if their prices rise—to pay these costs, direct controls have the effect of internalizing at least some of the previously external costs that had been passed on to the environment and society at large, thus providing incentives to stop or at least reduce the pollution.

Taxes on Pollution

Another approach to pollution control is to levy a *tax on polluters* (a *pollution tax*) equal to the external costs caused by their pollution. Such a tax would force polluters to pay the full external costs of their activities. More importantly, it would provide an incentive for polluters to invest in pollution control equipment. For instance, suppose that a firm is paying pollution taxes of $150 000 per year. If by investing $1 million in pollution control equipment, it can cut its pollution so as to pay no pollution tax, it would save itself $150 000 per year—a rate of return of 15 percent (after tax) on the investment of $1 million. Such a rate of return would warrant investing the $1 million in pollution control equipment.

While attractive in theory, this approach also has certain disadvantages. In many cases, it may be difficult if not impossible to measure the external costs imposed by a polluter, making it very difficult to establish the amount of pollution tax to be paid. In addition, the pollution control authorities would have to monitor each polluter's performance so as to levy the appropriate taxes. Finally, there are political obstacles to this approach. While economists see pollution taxes as an incentive to invest in pollution control equipment, the public tends to see them as a licence to pollute that wealthy firms will cheerfully pay while continuing to destroy the environment. As a result of these problems, governments have seldom employed this approach, and have relied mostly on direct controls.

Tradable Pollution Credits

The objective of a system of *tradable pollution credits* is for an industry to achieve an acceptable level of pollution at the lowest possible cost. Under this system, the government establishes an overall acceptable level of pollution for an industry—say, 100 000 tonnes of sulphur dioxide (SO_2) emissions per year into the air. Each producer in the industry is then allocated a share of the total credits, which gives each producer the legal right to emit a certain amount of SO_2. Older plants, which are the most difficult and costly to upgrade environmentally, will tend to pollute in excess of the amount permitted by their credits, while newer plants with better equipment will pollute less than allowed by their credits, giving them surplus credits. Rather than invest in very costly pollution-control equipment, owners of the older plants can buy pollution credits from newer, cleaner plants. Over a period of time, the government will reduce the total allowable pollution limit for the industry, which will increase the value (price) of the tradable pollution credits. This will give producers increased incentives to develop pollution-cutting innovations, so as to provide themselves with more surplus pollution credits that they can sell at higher prices to firms with higher pollution levels. In effect, *overall* emissions targets for the industry are met, while *within* the industry emissions are shifted from plants where the unit cost of pollution control is low to plants where it is high.

Advocates of tradable pollution credits argue that not only is this system a more efficient way of controlling pollution, but it also provides the best *incentives for firms to develop continual improvements in pollution-reducing technology*, by literally

On the Chicago Climate Exchange, companies buy and sell pollution credits.

www.chicagoclimatex.com

creating a profitable market for pollution-control technology. By contrast, they say, direct regulation tends to freeze pollution control technology, by dictating that firms use certain equipment to control pollution, without providing incentives to do better. This system is used in the United States to reduce emissions from over 100 coal-burning electrical utilities in the Midwest, and the U.S. Environmental Protection Agency has auctioned 150 000 one-tonne pollution permits to electrical utilities for about US$21 million.

Environmentalists and much of the public tend to dislike tradable pollution credits, on the grounds that this policy seems to make pollution socially acceptable, through the government selling licences to do it and promoting a market for those licences. The main limitation on this approach in Canada is that much of Canadian pollution comes from relatively few sources, making it more difficult to establish an effective market such as could exist among over 100 U.S. electrical-generating utilities. On a smaller scale, Ontario Hydro practised something like this by shifting sulphur dioxide emissions between its power stations in order to minimize the cost of meeting increasingly lower emission limits set by the government.

Lawsuits for Damages

Another way to force polluters to pay for the external or social costs of their activities is to allow the victims of their pollution to *sue them* for damages. If damages could be proven and the amount established, such lawsuits—whether by groups of citizens, other businesses, or governments—could provide an incentive for polluters to invest in pollution-control equipment, in the same way as pollution taxes can. This approach is seen as a useful part of antipollution policy, but the complexities, cost, and time involved in taking a lawsuit to court have tended to restrict it to a minor role.

Subsidies

Much of Canadian industry operates in highly competitive world markets, which require that the industries manage costs very effectively. Canadian businesses often argue that if Canada forces them to invest in costly pollution control equipment, they will be placed at a competitive disadvantage vis-à-vis foreign competitors who are not subject to such requirements. In the extreme, these costs might become so high that Canadian producers are unable to compete and must close. A variation of this argument is that corporations—both Canadian and foreign—will tend to establish new plants outside of Canada, where pollution controls are less strict and costly. This argument can be quite telling, because it places protection of the environment in direct conflict with another very high policy priority—jobs for Canadians. Such concerns are particularly high in communities that rely on one industry for employment, such as pulp-and-paper towns.

If pollution control regulations would really seriously impair a firm's competitive position, government policy-makers are faced with a difficult choice—should they allow the firm to continue to pollute at an unacceptable rate, or impose regulations that might cost the firm's employees their jobs? In either case, an undesirable social effect will result. In such circumstances, it may be justifiable for society at large, through the government, to use public funds to subsidize the cost of pollution control equipment, so as to permit businesses to reduce their pollution without causing severe economic hardship.

Waste Management

Each year, Canadians dispose of nearly 800 kilograms per person of garbage. Where should all this waste *go*?

There are three basic alternatives for dealing with the vast amounts of waste generated by a modern industrial society: *landfills, composting, incineration,* and *recycling*. Each of these has its own advantages and disadvantages, from the perspective of economics and the environment.

Landfills

Landfills (less elegantly known as garbage dumps) occupy a somewhat paradoxical position because while they are the *least costly* way of dealing with waste, they are very *unpopular politically*. Few issues will generate hostility in a community more quickly and strongly than the prospect of becoming host to a garbage dump. Consequently, there are few tasks for a government as politically awkward as finding a location for a new landfill site.

Notwithstanding its unpopularity, landfilling is clearly by far the lowest-cost means of disposing of waste. In most countries, even with rising government standards required for landfill sites, the cost of dealing with waste through landfilling is between 40 and 75 percent of the cost of incineration, the next-cheapest method. At least, then, the cost savings associated with landfilling raises the possibility of governments offering remuneration to communities that agree to provide landfill sites.

> The problem of landfill space is more a matter of politics than geology. It is estimated that if Canada continued to produce municipal waste at the present rates of use for 1000 years, the total waste could all fit into a space less than 50 kilometres square and 10 metres deep.

Composting

According to Environment Canada, biodegradable materials such as food waste make up about 40 percent of all residential waste in Canada, which make it essential to divert organic materials from landfills. Many communities encourage this through composting programs (often using "green bins" provided by the community).

The benefits of composting include not only much more efficient use of the available landfill sites, but also the compost that is produced by these programs, which can be used in home gardening, agriculture, and horticultural industries. According to Statistics Canada, by 2014 more than 61 percent of Canadian households were participating in some form of composting, nearly double the rate that composted in 1994.

Incineration

As noted, incineration is the second-cheapest method of disposing of waste. Even if incineration produces energy that can be sold, it is still one-third to one-half more costly than landfilling. This is partly because government standards for incineration have also been rising, to protect against air pollution from incinerators. Rules governing air emissions from incinerators can require that as much as half the capital cost of a new incineration plant consist of air-pollution control equipment.

> "Many people love recycling. It seems to meet some deep need to atone for modern materialism, by saving some of the materials from the rubbish bin."
> — THE ECONOMIST

Recycling

In a sense, recycling is the opposite of landfilling, in that it is the most politically popular but least economical means of dealing with waste. Despite the popular appeal of recycling, the economics of recycling have often not worked out very well. Many recycling schemes have (at least so far) been costly money-losers, largely due to a lack of planning on the part of governments.

Seizing upon recycling as a popular way to reduce the volume of garbage to be sent for landfilling or incineration, governments have often established very ambitious recycling targets. The result has been mountains of recyclable materials—more than can be sold to recyclers. This oversupply of recyclables—collected at considerable cost to the government—drives the market price of recyclable materials to very low levels. As a result, the governments lose money when they sell the materials to recyclers. In the case of household waste, which requires extensive collection and sorting, the price that can be gotten for the recyclables rarely covers even a fraction of the cost of collecting and sorting them. In the case of some waste plastic, the price has been negative; that is, the governments have had to pay companies to take the waste for recycling.

In part, the costs of the recycling process itself are a problem. The collection and sorting of recyclable materials is a labour-intensive and therefore quite costly process. Then there are the costs of recycling the waste into usable materials. Even when the waste "raw materials" are very cheap, the cost of processing them into finished products is often higher than producing products from new materials. For recyclers, the "bottom line" is that they must compete with companies that produce materials from virgin raw materials. This is a particularly serious problem if new raw materials are available at a low price, as many have been in recent years.

As a result of factors such as these, while recycling has certainly grown, it has not yet been able to play the role in waste management that was hoped for or expected. There is nothing inherently faulty with recycling; indeed, it is conceptually the most attractive way of dealing with waste. However, recycling can become economical enough to play its potential role in waste management only if the right combination of technology, labour costs, and materials costs occurs.

Recycling: The Government at Work

One area in which recycling can be helpful is with respect to household garbage. The recycling of some types of garbage, including paper, tin cans, and bottles, not only provides reusable materials but also reduces the volume of garbage and the strain on disposal facilities.

A major obstacle to recycling household garbage is sorting it into different categories, such as paper, glass, cans, and other materials. This task is most easily and economically done at the household level, but there is no direct economic incentive to do so. In fact, such sorting involves a cost to householders: the opportunity cost of the time spent to sort the garbage.

Many municipalities encourage households to recycle by providing free containers for recyclable garbage (a form of government subsidy) and by providing considerable publicity stressing the advantages to their community of using these containers. So, by spending a relatively small amount of public money, governments have been able to promote environmentally beneficial recycling.

Recycling: The Market at Work

A major environmental concern is the exhaustion of certain types of nonrenewable natural resources, such as minerals. Some futurists have painted economically disastrous scenarios in which the world runs out of many such resources.

However, market forces appear to be capable of dealing, at least in part, with this concern. As the most attractive low-cost sources of some minerals have depleted, their prices have risen. These rising prices have provided incentives for both consumers and producers of these minerals to do some useful things. Faced with higher prices, users of these minerals have found ways to economize on their use

A Japanese scientist has projected that more than half of the world's consumption of paper could be produced from the waste of banana plantations, rather than by cutting down trees.

and/or find substitutes. Meanwhile, rising prices have not only encouraged the development of new sources of such materials, but also have made it more economical to *recycle* them. In effect, higher metal prices can change scrap metal into an economically viable alternative to mining.

In such circumstances, the market provides the necessary economic incentives for recycling, as recycled metals become cheaper than newly mined minerals. Even 20 years ago, the Western world was obtaining 48 percent of its lead, 38 percent of its copper, 25 percent of its aluminum, 24 percent of its zinc, and 21 percent of its tin from recycling.

The Environment Industry

While many people see private industry and the environment as being in direct conflict with each other, the fact is that Canada is developing a significant *environment industry*. One rapidly growing part of this industry is waste collection. In part, this is due to the lower costs of private waste management firms as compared to government operations.

Other aspects of the environment industry involve consulting and equipment installation and maintenance. Statistics on the waste management industry are not easy to come by, but by some estimates there are more than 3500 environmental equipment and service firms operating across Canada. Nonetheless, compared to European nations, Canada's environment industry has been described as "less developed."

Making Polluters Pay

In the previous sections, much has been made of the costs of waste disposal. This has led to proposals that would require polluters themselves to pay for the amount of garbage that they generate. In theory, such schemes would not only force polluters to pay, but would also provide incentives for them to reduce the amount of their pollution.

At the household level, this approach takes the form of pay-to-throw schemes for garbage collection of the type run in many U.S. cities. Most such plans charge a fixed fee for a basic garbage collection service (say, two cans or bags per week) and extra fees for additional garbage (say, $1.00 per can or bag).

On the face of it, such schemes appear rather successful. One study for the World Resources Institute estimated that a fee of $1.50 on each 32-gallon (145-L) garbage container would cut the volume of waste by 18 percent.

But where does this 18 percent of volume of garbage *go*? A good deal of it still went out in people's garbage containers, but in a more compressed form. This compression was achieved by a manoeuvre known as the "Seattle stomp," after that city introduced a pay-to-throw scheme. In one city, the average weight of a container filled with garbage rose by 42 percent. Worse, however, was an increase in illegal dumping, as people threw their garbage onto public (and private) property and into ditches and rivers in order to avoid extra charges. And when Seattle's pay-to-throw plan was introduced, local charities found their drop-offs and doorsteps swamped with bags of unwanted "donations" that often seemed to resemble garbage.

Ultimately, then, a policy that seeks to force polluters to pay high costs through what amounts to a "garbage tax" will encounter the problem that it gives them a strong incentive to dump their garbage illegally. A more logical policy would be to tax not garbage, but rather consumption. The tax revenues could then be used to subsidize recycling and proper garbage disposal, giving people an incentive to use these socially beneficial methods rather than an incentive to dump illegally.

Global Warming and the Greenhouse Effect

In recent years, global warming has emerged as the major environmental issue. Environmentalists claim that greenhouse gases generated by humans are driving temperatures upwards, with potentially catastrophic effect. The Canadian Council of Ministers of the Environment (CCME) reports that the area of the Canadian Arctic permanently covered by sea ice has decreased by one-quarter since the late 1960s, and that a shorter ice season has made survival more difficult for polar bears in Hudson Bay. Skeptics assert that global warming concerns are the result of "junk science" and are completely unwarranted.

www.ccme.ca

Out of all this confusion, a few facts can be gleaned. The most basic fact is that greenhouse gas emissions are mainly (about 80 percent) generated *by consumers*, not by producers (industry). While the amount of energy used by industry to *produce* goods and services has been *decreasing*, per person energy use by Canadian *consumers* has been *increasing*.

What is Canada's contribution to greenhouse gas emissions? *In total*, not much— only 2 percent of world emissions. But that is not because Canadians are virtuously thrifty with energy; it is simply because Canadians represent only one-half of 1 percent of the world's population. On a *per person* basis, Canadians are just about the biggest energy consumers in the world, and we have a poor track record of improvement.

Our lifestyle is tied to high energy consumption. We use energy to transport ourselves, to heat us in winter and cool us in summer, to fuel our industrial activity, and to operate the myriad of electrical appliances that we use daily. Even much of our leisure time is spent consuming energy through travel, the use of recreational vehicles, equipment that uses electricity, and so on.

The simple fact is that current large-scale energy sources generate significant amounts of pollution. The main problem is the burning of fossil fuels, mainly gasoline. The automobile is the largest single source of air pollution, accounting for about 40 percent of greenhouse gas emissions. It is followed by the coal and oil burned to generate much of the electricity that our lifestyle requires.

Some of the pollutants from the burning of fossil fuels can be controlled, but not all. The most intractable pollutant is *carbon dioxide*, which, unlike other pollutants from automobiles, cannot be controlled with pollution-control equipment. The resultant ongoing large-scale emission of carbon dioxide into the air has contributed to the **greenhouse effect**—the global warming trend that environmentalists fear will cause disastrous climatic changes around the world, including the raising of ocean levels, widespread flooding of coastal areas, and weather changes such as hurricanes.

The Outlook for the Environment

What is the outlook for improving our environment? Certainly, public concern has increased the pressure on both governments and business to pay more attention to protecting the environment. However, there remains the reality of the trade-off discussed earlier in this chapter—that there are real costs to be paid in order to achieve a cleaner environment. The key to an effective attack on pollution, then, is not whether the public is *concerned* about the environment, but whether people are *willing to pay* to protect and improve the environment.

greenhouse effect
The global warming trend that environmentalists fear will cause disastrous climatic changes around the world, including the raising of ocean levels, widespread flooding of coastal areas, and weather changes such as hurricanes.

The glaciers of the Himalaya Mountains are melting at such a rapid pace that the long-term water supply of much of India and China is threatened.

According to the Canadian Wind Energy Association, Canada could meet 20 percent of its electricity needs from wind energy.

Canadians cannot be proud of their own track record regarding the environment. In a Conference Board of Canada study that measured air pollution, garbage production, energy consumption, water usage, and many other factors, Canada ranked 15th of the 17 countries studied, with only the United States and Australia ranking lower.

Regarding environmental threats, the performance of Canadians, like that of other people, has been mixed. Some significant progress has been made in dealing with *specific and immediate* problems such as certain air and water pollutants, or waste management and composting. However, human beings appear to be much less capable of dealing with *longer-term* threats, regardless of how large and serious these may be. The most potentially serious of these is of course climate change, but the decisions required to address this problem force an unattractive trade-off upon people: are they willing to *pay now* (in the form of some sacrifices in their material standard of living) in order to avert a threat of uncertain size and form at some uncertain time *in the future*?

So far, people have been reluctant to deal with this problem. And as living standards and fossil-fuel energy consumption rise in developing countries, the global problems of carbon dioxide and climate change seem likely to continue to grow.

"Encouraging more sustainable consumption is crucial." Conference Board of Canada

At present, the only way to control carbon dioxide emissions is through conservation; that is, by controlling and reducing our energy consumption (see the *In the News* box on gasoline taxes). This approach would require changing from a value system based on economic growth and high and rising living standards to one that embraces values such as conservation and quality of life, and accepts limits on our standard of living and energy consumption. But this would mean such a drastic change in people's values, attitudes, and lifestyle that political leaders are reluctant to confront the problem with policies.

So we continue to hope that somehow, technology will manage to solve the problem by separating energy consumption from the problem of accumulating carbon dioxide. Unless that can be done, a fundamental conflict will persist between our high-energy-consumption lifestyle and the only environment in which we have to live.

www.canwea.ca

IN THE NEWS

Higher Taxes on Gasoline?

Gasoline prices in North America are much lower than in Europe and Japan, mainly because Canadian and U.S. governments do not tax gasoline as heavily as other countries.

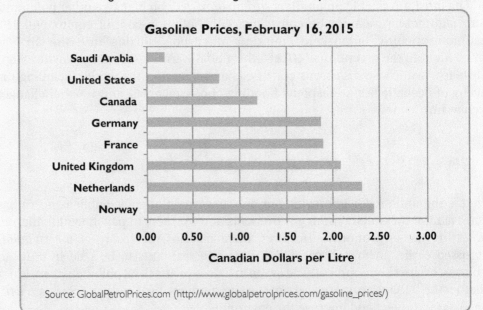

Gasoline Prices, February 16, 2015

Source: GlobalPetrolPrices.com (http://www.globalpetrolprices.com/gasoline_prices/)

Considering the serious concerns regarding emissions from automobiles, air quality, global warming, and dependence on oil from the Middle East, some observers argue that the single most logical policy for the Canadian and U.S. governments would be to increase the taxes on gasoline considerably.

QUESTIONS

1. What is the logic of proposing higher gasoline taxes and prices?
2. Why do the Canadian and U.S. governments seem unwilling to even consider this proposal?
3. Would you vote for a political party that made this proposal a keystone of its election platform?
4. How have gasoline prices changed since February 2015? You can find gasoline prices at http://www.globalpetrolprices.com/gasoline_prices/.

Chapter Summary

1. There are economic incentives for both producers and consumers to pollute, by passing the external costs of their production or consumption on to the environment. (L.O. 1)
2. There is an economic trade-off in which society can have a cleaner environment if it is willing to accept a lower level of production and consumption of goods and services. (L.O. 2)
3. As with other economic benefits, the cleanup of the environment is subject to the Law of Diminishing Returns: as the level of pollution is lowered, it becomes increasingly costly to reduce it further. (L.O. 3)
4. Economic analysis of the costs and benefits of pollution control can help in making decisions concerning the objectives of a pollution control program, how to attack the problem, and who should pay the costs of the program. (L.O. 4)
5. Some types of action that can be taken to protect the environment are direct regulation, taxes on pollution, tradable pollution credits, lawsuits for damages due to pollution, and government subsidies to help pay the cost of pollution controls. (L.O. 5)
6. With respect to waste management, landfilling is the lowest-cost disposal method, incineration is second-lowest, and recycling the highest-cost way of dealing with waste. Taxes on consumption and subsidies for proper garbage disposal and recycling are considered more environmentally effective than taxes on garbage itself, which tends to generate environmentally damaging illegal dumping. (L.O. 6)
7. The burning of fossil fuels generates *greenhouse gases*, which environmentalists believe are contributing to the potentially serious problem of global warming. (L.O.7)

Questions

1. "The pollution problem is most fundamentally a problem of economic incentives leading people to behave self-destructively, and the solution to pollution is for governments to change those incentives so that people behave environmentally responsibly."

Explain the speaker's viewpoint, using the terms *private costs*, *social costs*, and *externalities*.

2. (a) Draw a production-possibilities curve to illustrate that a cleaner environment can be viewed as involving similar "trade-offs" to those involved with increasing the production and consumption of any other good.
   (b) How does the curve show the opportunity cost of a cleaner environment?
   (c) How does the Law of Diminishing Returns complicate the task of seeking a cleaner environment?

3. (a) Which method of handling household and industrial waste is the most politically popular—landfills, incineration, or recycling?
   (b) Why, then, is this method not used more frequently?

4. A city is suffering from severe air quality problems, mostly due to emissions from cars.
   (a) Who benefits from this emissions/pollution situation?
   (b) Who bears the costs of the pollution?
   (c) The city's residents are pressuring the city government to "pass a law" limiting the pollution, but why is direct regulation not a simple solution to this problem?
   (d) Using the concepts of costs, benefits, and incentives, explain how a road toll system could be used in a situation such as this.
   (e) Is this a situation in which government subsidies for public transit should be considered? What would you like to know before using taxpayers' money to reduce the cost of public transit to riders?

5. "Setting pollution-control standards is simple—the standards should require that pollution be reduced to the maximum extent possible using modern technology. In fact, the objective of any pollution-control program should be to reduce pollution to zero."

   Do you agree with the above statement or not? If not, how should pollution-control standards be determined?

6. One approach to waste management is to charge householders a fee for every bag of garbage that is collected.
   (a) How is this policy intended to work?
   (b) Explain some unintended negative environmental effects that this policy is likely to have, and why these effects would probably occur.
   (c) The effects in (b) would not occur if governments collected garbage for free and paid for this service by taxing products when they were purchased rather than when they were thrown away, by increasing the sales tax. Why do you think that governments have not implemented such an alternative policy?

Study Guide

Review Questions (Answers to these Review Questions appear in Appendix B.)

1. State whether each of the following is an example of a *private cost* or a *social cost*.
   (a) Wages paid to employees
   (b) The effects of sulphur dioxide emissions from a plant
   (c) Interest payments to bondholders

(d) The cost of the company's annual social event

(e) Traffic congestion caused by a company's warehouse

2. In attempting to maximize its profits by reducing costs, a producer is likely to conclude that

(a) minimizing social costs is less important than minimizing private costs.

(b) private costs should be replaced by social costs whenever possible.

(c) social costs should be minimized.

(d) Both (a) and (b).

(e) None of the above.

3. The basic reality is that a cleaner environment is like any other good: if we want more of it, we will have to accept _____.

4. Because of the Law of Diminishing Returns,

(a) pollution will diminish to nearly zero if you keep coming back at the problem.

(b) technology has made it easier to push pollution to very low levels.

(c) the cost of reducing pollution by a given amount increases, the further pollution is reduced.

(d) it is often not economically feasible to reduce pollution to zero.

(e) Both (c) and (d) are correct.

5. Direct regulation of polluters

(a) is not a policy that is popular with the general public.

(b) is the most common form of government antipollution policy.

(c) will only be effective if there is adequate enforcement and penalties for violators are sufficiently heavy.

(d) is a relatively rare form of government antipollution policy.

(e) Both (b) and (c) are correct.

6. Taxes on pollution

(a) can create an incentive for polluters to invest in pollution control equipment.

(b) are not a policy that is popular with the general public.

(c) are the most common form of government antipollution policy.

(d) Both (a) and (b) are correct

(e) None of the above.

7. Tradable pollution credits

(a) are a commonly-used approach to reducing pollution.

(b) can provide incentives for firms to improve their pollution-reducing technology.

(c) are not a policy that is popular with the general public.

(d) Both (b) and (c) are correct.

(e) None of the above.

8. Lawsuits for damages from pollution

(a) are costly and difficult to organize and win.

(b) are very seldom pursued.

(c) are a major concern of companies with bad pollution records.

(d) Both (a) and (b) are correct.

(e) None of the above.

9. Which method of handling household and industrial waste is least costly?

(a) landfills

(b) incineration

(c) recycling

(d) Both (b) and (c).

(e) None—all methods cost roughly the same.

10. State whether each of the following statements concerning recycling is *true* or *false*.
    (a) T or F
       It is by far the most economical method of dealing with waste.
    (b) T or F
       Most recycling projects have proven to be very profitable.
    (c) T or F
       The large quantities of recyclable materials collected have often driven the prices at which they can be sold to recyclers to very low levels.
    (d) T or F
       Recycling is a very popular concept with the public and with governments.
    (e) T or F
       Producers often find it less costly to use virgin raw materials than recycled materials.

11. The *greenhouse effect* refers to
    (a) the use of carbon dioxide to grow plants.
    (b) a global warming trend.
    (c) the political impact of the Green Party on election results.
    (d) the environmental impact of the clearing of the Amazon rain forest.
    (e) None of the above.

12. Of all greenhouse gas emissions,
    (a) about 20 percent come from consumers and 80 percent from producers (industry).
    (b) about 40 percent come from consumers and 60 percent from producers (industry).
    (c) about 50 percent come from consumers and 50 percent from producers (industry).
    (d) about 60 percent come from consumers and 40 percent from producers (industry).
    (e) about 80 percent come from consumers and 20 percent from producers (industry).

13. Canada is the source of about
    (a) 2 percent of the world's greenhouse gas emissions.
    (b) 5 percent of the world's greenhouse gas emissions.
    (c) 10 percent of the world's greenhouse gas emissions.
    (d) 20 percent of the world's greenhouse gas emissions.
    (e) 25 percent of the world's greenhouse gas emissions.

14. On a per person basis,
    (a) Canadians consume much less energy than people in other countries.
    (b) Canadians consume slightly less energy than people in other countries.
    (c) Canadians consume about the same amount of energy as people in other countries.
    (d) Canadians consume slightly more energy than people in other countries.
    (e) Canadians are among the biggest consumers of energy in the world.

15. In making progress regarding the protection of the environment, Canada has
    (a) made the least progress of any developed nation.
    (b) lagged behind most developed nations.
    (c) been among the leaders among developed nations.
    (d) been the leader among developed nations.

Critical Thinking Questions

(Asterisked questions 1 to 4 are answered in Appendix B; the answers to questions 5 to 8 are in the Instructor's Manual that accompanies this text.)

*1. "The real problem with pollution is that people do not understand the side-effects of their actions. What is needed to combat pollution, therefore, is a comprehensive educational program pointing out how pollution is caused and the threat it is to all of us." Do you agree or disagree with this statement? Why?

*2. "The real problem with pollution is that it pays to pollute. And as long as it pays to pollute, consumers and producers will continue to foul our environment."
   (a) Do you agree or disagree with this statement? Explain fully.
   (b) What are the implications of this reality for government environmental policy?

*3. "The thing that people just have to learn to accept is that if we want more of a cleaner environment, we will have to put up with less of something else."
   (a) Explain what the speaker means, using the term *opportunity cost.*
   (b) Why do you think many people are reluctant to accept these realities?

*4. One source of pollution is throwaway drink containers.
   (a) Identify some of the costs and the benefits of using such containers.
   (b) Identify the advantages and disadvantages of each of the following approaches to the problem of throwaway drink containers:
      (i) prohibition of throwaway containers
      (ii) taxes on throwaway containers

5. In many cities, the problems of both traffic and pollution from automobile emissions are made worse by high numbers of cars with only one occupant. An interesting approach to managing this problem is *HOT lanes*, which stands for a combination of high-occupancy (HO) and toll (T) lanes. Certain traffic lanes are reserved for the use of cars with multiple occupants (HO), which pay no toll. Single-occupant vehicles can also use these lanes, but only if they pay a toll. *HOT* lanes are primarily a traffic management strategy, but also deliver environmental benefits.
   (a) In what ways would *HOT* lanes reduce air pollution?
   (b) What factors would have to be taken into consideration when deciding the toll rate for single-occupancy vehicles?
   (c) Modern computer technology allows the toll rate for single-occupancy vehicles to be different at different times of the day. How would you expect the toll rate to change during heavy-traffic periods, and why would this be done?

6. The text notes that the Law of Diminishing Returns leads to the logical conclusion that beyond a certain point, rising costs of additional pollution reduction tend to make it not worthwhile. Under what circumstances would this generalization *not* be an appropriate guideline for government policy concerning the environment?

7. Norway has perhaps the highest gasoline prices in the world, due to its very high taxes on gasoline.
   (a) Explain how such high gasoline prices would have positive effects on the environment.
   (b) How does Norway provide an excellent example of the trade-off between a cleaner environment and a higher standard of living?
   (c) Higher taxes on gasoline would not only benefit the environment, but also would provide governments with much-needed funds for key social pro-

grams such as health care and education. Why, then, have governments in Canada and the United States not imposed higher taxes on gasoline?

8. Do you believe that the values of your generation concerning the environment and material goods and services are different from those of your parents' generation? Would you be more prepared than your parents were to reduce your standard of living in order to create a cleaner environment? If your answer is *yes*, what might explain why your views are different? What might explain an answer of *no*?

Use the Web (Hints for these Use the Web exercises appear in Appendix B.)

1. Google "climate change in Canada". What are the current issues and developments in Canada regarding climate change?

Into the Future

LEARNING OBJECTIVES

After studying this chapter, you should be able to

1. Define the term *resource wealth mentality* and explain how this term could be applied to Canadian attitudes and government policies in the past.

2. Provide three reasons for the phenomenon known as *globalization*, and explain how it has presented Canada with major economic challenges and opportunities.

3. State three characteristics that help to make a nation's economy attractive to investment in high-technology industries in the globalized world economy.

4. Describe changes that Canada made to its policies regarding trade, government finances, and other matters in response to globalization, and explain how these changes were intended to help Canada to prosper in the globalized world economy.

5. Describe the demographic challenges that Canada faces in the future, and explain the changes that will help Canada to deal with these challenges.

For many years, Canada was an economically comfortable country, with high living standards and extensive government social programs for its people. In fact, Canada was consistently rated as one of the best countries in the world in which to live.

However, in the period from the late 1980s through the much of the 1990s, Canadians experienced considerable economic change and discomfort as the country grappled with some major economic challenges. The most fundamental of these challenges was the changing international economic environment known as *globalization*. In addition, there were the problems of *government deficits* and *debt*, and the related problem of *high taxes*. Another basic problem was the *slow growth of productivity* in the Canadian economy, which threatened both the standard of living of Canadians and the ability of Canadian industries to compete in the globalized world economy. How Canada addressed these issues would largely determine the economic prosperity of Canadians in the future.

Dealing with these challenges would involve fundamental changes in both government policies and in the Canadian economy itself. Before we consider these changes, however, we will review the background to this situation—the basic nature of the Canadian economy and government policy orientation that existed in the past.

Canada Before the 1990s

Economically, Canada is a relatively small country, with an economy about one-tenth the size of the United States' economy and a population similar to California's. From Canada's very beginning as a nation, its economic prosperity was largely due to exports of natural resources and resource products, mainly to the United States.

Canada used its prosperity to develop quite an extensive social welfare system, as was described in Chapter 12. Canadian governments established a broad range of social welfare programs for individuals and families (such as education and health care), an extensive support system for weaker and less efficient producers (including tariff protection for manufacturers, subsidies for farmers, and assistance of various sorts for many corporations in difficulty), and various forms of aid to economically weaker regions (including equalization payments, regional development grants, and subsidies to people and businesses in those regions). In the words of Professor Michael Porter,

> Traditionally, Canadians have lived in a relatively insulated environment brought about by paternalistic government policies, a history of market protection, and the accumulated attitudes and experiences of both individuals and businesses.
>
> This old economic order, as we call it, was a system where many prospered. However, because the old order generally provided insulation from external pressures and fostered limited internal pressures, many of the critical requirements for upgrading to more sophisticated and sustainable competitive advantages in Canadian industry have been missing or are only weakly present.[1]

Porter describes a Canada that had traditionally relied upon exports of natural resources and resource products as its basic source of economic prosperity. These exports, together with substantial inflows of foreign (mainly U.S.) business capital investment, provided Canadians with the foreign currency with which they purchased the imported goods and services that supported their high living standards.

---

[1] Michael E. Porter, *Canada at the Crossroads: The Reality of a New Competitive Environment* (October 1991; a study prepared for the Business Council on National Issues and the Government of Canada).

According to some critical observers, Canada had developed a **resource wealth mentality**—the view that wealth is not so much something that you *create* as something that *happens to you* through processing and selling resources that you are fortunate enough to own. With economic wealth so readily provided by resource exports and foreign investment, government policy in Canada tended to be less concerned with *creating wealth* than with promoting a *fair distribution of wealth*, by providing assistance to individuals, businesses, and regions that needed it.

In short, with high living standards supported by their exports of natural resources and by foreign investment, with tariffs to protect much of their manufacturing sector from import competition, and with government social welfare programs that sheltered them from competition and economic hardship, Canadians were able to enjoy a comfortable and secure economic prosperity.

> **resource wealth mentality**
> The view that society's economic wealth is derived mainly from the sale of natural resources, as opposed to efficiency in the production of goods and services.

Pressures for Change: Globalization and Competition

During the 1980s, a variety of factors combined to generate such a large increase in international trade, investment, and competition that this phenomenon would come to be known as *globalization*. The main source of globalization was *freer trade*, as nations lowered tariff barriers and markets were opened to international competition. Other important factors were *improved computer, communications, and transportation technology* that lowered the costs of doing business internationally and facilitated trade and investment on a global scale. With new technology, came worldwide markets for many more goods and services. Designers, manufacturers, and retailers became able to communicate with each other more quickly and more effectively all around the world than was possible in the past within one country. And, with increased international competition came higher productivity and lower costs and prices.

Challenges and Opportunities

The increased competitiveness of the new global economy presented Canada with some major challenges. The most basic of these was the problem of Canada's lagging productivity growth, which was noted earlier. Much of Canada's manufacturing sector was not very efficient, having produced only for the small Canadian market and with tariff protection against foreign competition. Such industries were ill-prepared for the stronger international competition associated with globalization. And, despite the importance of trade to the domestic economy, Canadian producers and governments were slow to adapt to this new, more competitive international environment. Rather than look outward to the opportunities presented by the global economy, Canada sought to maintain the old order described above, by protecting its less efficient producers against competition, with tariffs and government subsidies. Partly as a result of this protectionism, the efficiency, or productivity, of much of the Canadian economy failed to keep pace with improvements in other nations. As the 1980s progressed, Canada became less and less internationally competitive, especially in manufacturing.

But globalization brought tremendous opportunities as well as threats. For Canadian producers that *could* compete, there was the opportunity to break out of the small Canadian market and into much larger foreign markets. The Canada–U.S. Free Trade Agreement of 1989 alone secured Canadian firms' access to a market *ten times* the size of the small Canadian market.

Coping with Change

In the new, globalized world economy, it is more important than ever for a nation to be efficient and competitive and to be an attractive location for business investment. Multinational corporations, including Canadian firms, search the world for the most economical locations for their activities. If a country can attract business investment and the jobs and production that this investment brings, that country will prosper economically. If it fails to attract investment, it will fall behind economically.

What makes a country an attractive location for business investment? Many people think that the answer is cheap labour, but this is not usually the case. Low-wage labour is only important for labour-intensive manufacturing industries such as clothing and footwear. But in many industries, such low-wage, semi-skilled labour has already been replaced to a great extent by technology.

To modern, high-technology industries, the key attraction is not cheap labour, but rather *skilled people* with *specialized knowledge*. In addition, a nation needs to have excellent *transportation and communication links* to the rest of the world, in order to function effectively as part of the new world economy.

From this perspective, a nation's key strategic assets economically are no longer its cheap labour or its natural resources, but rather the *quality of its labour force* and its transportation/communications *infrastructure*—the knowledge and skills of its people, and the support systems for linking the productive use of those skills into the global economy so that they can access markets and partners around the world. In addition, a nation's taxation system must be attractive to employers, investors, and skilled workers.

If a country has these qualities, it will tend to attract business investment and prosper economically. Its productivity will be high, the standard of living of its people will be high, and its industries will be internationally competitive. Its skilled workforce will earn high incomes and its government will have a strong tax base, which can be used to invest further in better schools, research, and transportation and communications systems. These features will attract more investment, and the cycle of prosperity can be continued. For an economically small nation such as Canada, globalization offers the additional opportunity of increasing its exports into larger foreign markets, if its producers are able to compete.

For nations that lack a skilled workforce and communications and transportation infrastructure, the opposite kind of cycle can take place. Unable to attract capital with their labour forces' skills and their infrastructure, such nations would be forced to resort to low wages and low taxes as inducements for businesses to invest there, and would be able to compete only in labour-intensive, low-wage industries.

Into the Future

The mid-1980s witnessed the beginning of a significant shift in the emphasis of government policy in Canada, a key purpose of which was to adapt to the globalized world economy. Less emphasis was placed on government support for individuals and industries, and increased emphasis was being placed on market forces, private enterprise, entrepreneurship and incentives for work, investment, productivity, and the creation of wealth. In short, the policy emphasis shifted from the *redistribution* of wealth toward the *creation* of wealth.

In this context, the 1989 Free Trade Agreement with the United States represented a landmark decision for Canada, by signalling Canada's intention to participate more fully in the increasingly globalized markets of the world. As such, it was the most visible part of a basic shift in Canadian policy toward an emphasis on productivity, competitiveness, and an outward-looking internationalism rather than on more inward-looking nationalistic policies that sheltered Canadian industries from international competition. The Free Trade Agreement was regarded not as an end in itself, but rather as the first step toward Canada's becoming productive and competitive on a global scale.

In support of this general change in policy direction, there were many shifts in a wide variety of government economic policies in the years that followed. After the mid-1990s there was a significant *decrease in the size of government spending* as a proportion of the economy, as we saw in Chapter 12. This meant *changes to Canada's social welfare programs* that placed more emphasis on training and work, rather than passively receiving benefits as in the past. Employment Insurance benefits were reduced, new restrictions were placed on frequent claimants, and there was more emphasis on retraining the unemployed rather than simply supporting their incomes. The budgets of many government operations became more restricted, forcing them to place more emphasis on improving efficiency.

The business sector was not exempt from these changes, as *government subsidies to business* were reduced; also, the *privatization* of government-owned enterprises such as Air Canada and Canadian National Railways forced them to operate more efficiently and without the subsidies that they had received when owned by the government. Also, there was *deregulation* of some industries, in which government regulations had restricted the entry of new competitors and/or controlled production and/or prices. To improve productivity performance, the government deregulated some of these industries, such as airlines, financial services, and communications, such as long-distance telephone service.

After government finances had been gotten in order, there were a series of *reductions in personal and business income taxes* after 2000, which was a reversal of past trends. And, as discussed in Chapter 9, there was more emphasis on support for the *small business* sector of the economy, as a major provider of employment growth in the future.

Taken together, these new policies represented a significant shift in Canadian economic policy. As noted earlier, government policies had traditionally been directed largely toward *redistributing economic wealth*, through an extensive social welfare system. But to improve productivity and competitiveness, the new Canadian policies emphasized the *creation of wealth*. This required incentives for enterprise, entrepreneurship, and investment, as well as increased emphasis on competition and efficiency.

In a broad strategic sense, the new direction of government policy was to shift the emphasis in the Canadian economy from *security and consumption* toward *efficiency and investment*—or from benefits that exist mainly in the present to longer-term gains.

Future Challenges

Foreseeing the future is risky at best, but in the field of demographics, at least you know what's coming at you. Looking ahead, Canada's future economic success will depend to a large extent on how successfully the country can deal with certain demographic challenges that are already manifesting themselves. Most of these challenges relate to the most important resource of any economy: its labour force.

The aging of the baby boomers—that large group born from 1946–66 who for decades have comprised the "heartland" of Canada's labour force—is one of these challenges. The boomers have begun to retire, and by 2030 the vast majority of them will have left the labour force.

As the number of retirees rises, Canada will have to deal with an unprecedented number of dependent seniors (age 65 or older). The extent of this problem is measured with a statistic known as the **senior pendency ratio**, which is the ratio of seniors (age 65 or older) to the working-age population. In 1971, there were only 15 seniors per 100 Canadians of working age, by 2015 this had risen to about 25, and by 2056 Statistics Canada projects that there will be 50 seniors for every 100 Canadians of working age.

Canadians will have to find solutions to the costs associated with such a large seniors population, in terms of their the cost of pensions, the higher health care costs for an aging population, and the costs of caring for a growing number of dependent seniors unable to live on their own.

Another way of looking at this problem is that retirement of the boomers could leave the economy with a *labour shortage*, in the sense of too few workers relative to the number of seniors. With a larger percentage of the population no longer working, it will become more important than ever that the *productivity* of those who *are* working be as high as possible.

Technology may make this possible, particularly the new technologies discussed in Chapter 11; however, this would require a *labour force* that possesses the education and skills to work with new and rapidly-changing technologies.

This brings us to the second great challenge: the labour force of the future will have to be more educated and skilled than the generation that preceded it. As we saw in Chapter 11, the combination of technological change and free trade have been

senior dependency ratio. the ratio of seniors to the working-age population

When the retirement age of 65 was established, most people didn't live long after 65.

IN THE NEWS

The Greying of Canada

As the graph shows, the proportion of Canada's population over the age of 65 will grow rapidly. ■

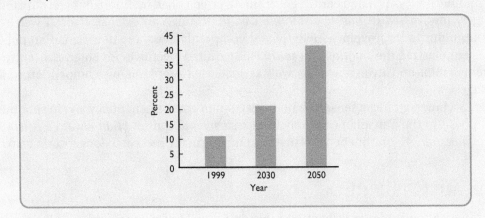

QUESTIONS

1. Why are such large increases in the seniors population forecasted?
2. What are the implications of this trend for the living standards of Canadians?
3. What could the government do to reduce the negative economic effects of an aging population?

creating an imbalance in the labour forces of the economically developed countries, in which there has been a growing "skills pay gap" that reflects shortages of many skills, but also surpluses of less educated and skilled labour.

To deal with all of the challenges described above, Canada will need a twenty-first century labour force with the education and skills for the future. This will require large-scale investment in human capital—not only more money spent on education and training, but also more effective ways of promoting the learning of the skills and attitudes that will be required for success in a workplace that will be both more demanding and more rewarding.

Canadians want a great deal from their economic system. They want prosperity for themselves in the form of high levels of private personal consumption, high levels of government services (including a strong social welfare system, health care, and education), economic security, and protection of the environment. To provide of all these, the Canadian economy must be prosperous and productive. Only by becoming more productive, more efficient, and more competitive will Canadians find it possible to achieve all their economic and social goals.

Chapter Summary

1. Traditionally, Canada relied heavily upon natural resource exports to create much of its economic wealth, while government policies aimed more at redistributing income and providing social welfare programs than at promoting productivity, the creation of wealth, and competitiveness. (L.O. 1)

2. The increasing globalization of the world economy presented Canada with major economic challenges, the main one being the need to become more efficient and internationally competitive than in the past. Globalization also offered opportunities, as large markets outside of Canada opened up. (L.O. 2)

3. In the globalized world economy, a knowledgeable and skilled labour force and excellent transportation and communication links to the rest of the world are important in attracting business investment and the jobs and economic wealth such investment brings. (L.O. 3)

4. After the mid-1980s, in an attempt to improve the nation's productivity and competitiveness, Canadian government policy shifted away from redistribution of wealth and protection of industries from foreign competition, and more toward wealth creation and economic internationalism. (L.O. 4)

5. In the future, the aging of Canada's population will require a work force with the education and training that will make its productivity higher than in the past. (L.O. 5)

Questions

1. Briefly describe Canada prior to the 1990s in terms of
   (a) the basic source of its economic wealth, and
   (b) the general thrust of its government economic policies.

2. (a) What is the phenomenon known as *globalization*?
   (b) How did globalization present Canada with both threats and opportunities economically?

3. (a) In what ways would Canada have to change its government economic policies in order to take advantage of the opportunities of globalization and deal with the threats that it presented?
   (b) Describe at least four changes that Canada made to its government economic policies in response to globalization, and explain the intended results of each of these policy changes.

4. Google "concerns of Canadian seniors".
   (a) Overall, does the life of Canadian seniors appear to be satisfactory?
   (b) What issues are currently of concern to Canadian seniors?

Study Guide

Review Questions (Answers to these Review Questions appear in Appendix B.)

1. Canada's traditional source of economic prosperity was in the
   (a) exporting of manufactured goods.
   (b) exporting of resource-based raw materials.
   (c) establishment of social welfare programs.
   (d) earning of income from investments in other countries.
   (e) Both (a) and (c).

2. A *resource wealth mentality*
   (a) refers to the view that in order to prosper economically, a society must use *all* of its economic resources (labour, capital and land) efficiently and effectively.
   (b) refers to the view that economic prosperity comes mainly from processing and selling natural resources, rather than efficient and effective production of goods and services.
   (c) can lead to the belief that the government's role is to ensure that the country's economic wealth is distributed fairly among its citizens.
   (d) Both (b) and (c) are correct.
   (e) None of the above.

3. In the *globalization* process of the 1980s and 1990s, international trade increased greatly due to various forces, including
   (a) _____
   (b) _____
   (c) _____

4. Globalization presented Canada with both
   (a) opportunities, in the form of _____ and
   (b) threats, in the form of _____.

5. In the globalized world economy, Canada's major *disadvantage* was
   _____.

6. Which of the following factors is most important to multinational high-technology corporations in deciding in which countries to locate their production facilities?
   (a) sources of cheap raw materials
   (b) low wage rates

(c) a highly educated and skilled work force

(d) Both (a) and (b).

(e) None of the above.

7. To improve Canada's ability to compete in the globalized world economy, it was necessary for governments to place more emphasis on policies that would
   (a) improve the productivity of Canadian industry.
   (b) control the growth and market power of large corporations.
   (c) redistribute income from the rich to the poor.
   (d) provide more protection for Canadian jobs against foreign competition.
   (e) None of the above.

Critical Thinking Questions

(Asterisked questions 1 to 3 are answered in Appendix B; the answers to questions 4 to 7 are in the Instructor's Manual that accompanies this text.)

*1. How did the 1989 Canada–U.S. Free Trade Agreement symbolize a fundamental shift in the direction and goals of Canadian economic policy, and how did the new policy objectives differ from those of the past?

*2. What role can improvements in productivity play in helping Canada to meet its economic challenges and achieve its potential?

*3. If the federal government had budget surpluses, how could these be used to promote more rapid increases in the productivity of Canada's labour force in the future?

4. In the view of economists, the game (industry) of professional hockey provides a good example of how globalization, or the internationalization of markets, presents Canadians with both challenges and opportunities. Explain why this is the case, taking into account the perspectives of both players and teams.

5. What role can the internet play in helping Canada to meet its economic challenges and achieve its potential?

6. What changes to Canada's educational system would you suggest in order to help Canada to meet its economic challenges and achieve its potential?

7. If you could make *one* change to Canadian government economic policies aimed at increasing productivity in the Canadian economy, what would that change be?

Use the Web   (Hints for this Use the Web exercise appear in Appendix B.)

1. Google "government policy and productivity". What recent developments have occurred regarding government policies to promote increases in the productivity of Canada's labour force?

15W

The Agricultural Sector

Please reference the MyEconLab as MyEconLab with eText for Microeconomics, 11/e via www.pearsonmylabs.com.

The Politics of Economics

Answers to Boxed Questions

Chapter 1: What Is Economics?

YOU DECIDE: **The Scarcity Problem on a Personal Level**

1. As the situation is described, most people would say "no" to this question because the opportunity cost is too high. Because you have borrowed a total of $400 at the high interest rates that are charged on credit cards, the repayments will cut into your future spending on consumer goods and services by considerably more than $400. These high interest rates add so much to the cost of buying things on credit cards that they should make people more careful when "paying with plastic." But for many people, the opposite happens—buying on credit is so easy that they do so without considering how costly it is. Buying on credit is simply paying for things out of your future income, and paying the lender for the use of the money in the meantime. This does not mean that one should never buy on a credit card—just that, before doing so, one should consider whether getting the item sooner is worth paying so much extra for it. Finally, if you conclude that getting the item right away is important to you, are there other ways to borrow the money and at a lower rate of interest?

2. Most personal finance advisers suggest paying the outstanding balance on credit cards on time each month, to avoid interest charges. Then the credit card becomes a convenience rather than a burden. But this requires that you restrain your credit card spending each month to the amount that you can afford to repay. If this sort of self-discipline is not your style, the safest type of card to carry is a debit card that allows a vendor to take the money directly from your account.

YOU DECIDE: **Measuring Your School's Performance**

1. To measure the *effectiveness* of a school, you need to first consider the real *goal(s)* of the school. For a community college whose programs are geared to the job market, the success of graduates in finding jobs and rewarding careers would be a good indicator of effectiveness. A transfer institution would consider the success of graduates in securing admission to university as a key indicator of effectiveness. High schools might place more importance on graduation rates, as well as graduates' success in securing admission to postsecondary education.

2. Measuring the *efficiency* of a school could involve *physical* or *financial* measures. Physical measures would include statistics such as number of students per teacher, class size, and number of classes per teacher. The efficiency with which the facilities are used could be measured by statistics on number of teaching hours per day/week/year, and by data on square metres per student. Financial measures of efficiency would include things such as cost per student, cost per student/hour taught, etc.

3. Some ways to increase the efficiency of a school would be to increase the number of students per teacher, by increasing class sizes and/or the number of classes that each teacher must teach in a week or year. Also, longer school hours and longer school years would increase efficiency in the use of facilities.

4. This question is intended to raise the question of whether pursuing one goal (in this case, efficiency) might have negative effects upon the achievement of the other goal (here, effectiveness). The potential for conflicts between the goals of efficiency and effectiveness arises from the possibility that larger classes and

heavier class loads for teachers would make it more difficult for students to get the feedback and assistance that is important to their learning.

Chapter 2: Canada's Economic System

YOU DECIDE: **To Subsidize or Not to Subsidize?**

1. The opportunity cost of subsidizing public services depends on what one assumes would have been done with the funds if they had not been used to subsidize those services. If one assumes that the funds would have been spent on other government programs, the opportunity cost would be less of other government services, such as health care or education. If, on the other hand, one assumes that the funds would have been returned to the public via tax reductions, the opportunity cost would be the goods and services that the public could have bought with those funds.

2. A good case can be made that public transit and college programs in business and technology should be selected for subsidization. As noted in the text, a market system will tend to under-produce such public services, because people will only pay as much for them as warranted by the benefits that they receive from them *as individuals,* whereas the purchase and provision of these services bring *broader social benefits.* Specifically, the more people use public transit, the less traffic and pollution there will be, to the benefit of *all* of the people of the city. Also, such basic infrastructure makes the city more attractive for businesses to locate and invest. And a more educated work force contributes to higher productivity and economic prosperity, not only for the graduates but also for society at large.

It is more difficult to claim widespread social benefits for the other two items listed. Government support for a symphony orchestra does bring cultural benefits, but these are enjoyed by a smaller segment of society than the beneficiaries of public transit and education. The same can be said of subsidizing campsites, which primarily benefits citizens who like to camp, at the expense of those who choose not to camp.

The "bottom line" regarding subsidization may be this: how convincingly can you explain to some who does *not* use the subsidized service (public transit, education, orchestra or campsites) that using their tax money to subsidize it actually does *benefit them*?

Chapter 3: Business Organization in Canada

YOU DECIDE: **Update to the Saga of Dan's Doughnut Dens**

1. *Sole proprietorship:* This is easy to start, and provides the owner-manager with strong incentives as well as independence. On the other hand, sole proprietorships tend to suffer from a lack of management expertise since few individuals are strong in all aspects of management; partly for this reason, the workload of the owner-manager is often very heavy. If the business earns a high income, taxes on this income will be high since it will be taxed as the personal income of the owner. If, on the other hand, the business is unsuccessful, the personal liability of the owner can place his or her personal assets at risk.

Partnership: The partnership has advantages and disadvantages similar to the sole proprietorship's, except that a partnership can add management talent and capital. However, there is the disadvantage of potential conflict between the partners. In the event that the business fails, general partners have unlimited liability.

Corporation: Limited liability is a major advantage in two ways. First, the owners' (shareholders') personal assets are not at risk, but more importantly, this makes it much easier for a corporation to raise capital by selling shares to the public. Beyond a certain level of profits, tax rates on corporations are lower than on the personal income(s) of the owner(s). However, the process of incorporating a business is costly, and a possible risk (that Dan experienced) of selling shares is that control of the corporation may be lost.

2. 45.0% + 5.1% = 50.1% = control of the corporation by Dan and Ermyntrude.

3. First, Dan should determine his *objective(s)*—what does he want to accomplish through this business? For instance, does he want to become the biggest doughnut shop operator in the city or the country (or in the world), or would he be happy to be a small independent player in this market? From this starting point, logical *strategies* can be developed for achieving his objective(s). Throughout the story, Dan seemed

to let himself be carried along by events or be reacting to situations, rather than proactively pursuing strategies in order to reach objectives.

4. Mainly because larger businesses generally need to raise considerable amounts of capital, and the corporate form of organization is best suited to this task due to its ability to issue shares to the public.

IN THE NEWS: Self-Employment in Canada

1. A key factor in the growth of self-employment (and small business generally) has been the growth in the *service sector* of the economy. A modern economy is capable of producing large volumes of *goods* with relatively few workers by using high-technology production methods. The high output per worker generated by this technology also increases people's standard of living, and consumers with higher living standards tend to buy more services, such as travel, entertainment, restaurants, and so on. And while the production of *goods* is often best suited to large mass-production facilities (big business), *services* are generally most effectively delivered by smaller enterprises that are convenient to the consumer. For instance, your car may have been built in a mass-production plant in Kansas City, but you get it repaired and washed by small business operators near your home.

Much of the growth of self-employment has been associated with the growth of the service sector, described above. In addition, the downsizing of many Canadian corporations and government agencies during the mid-1990s forced many people into self-employment. Also, some employers laid off employees and then re-engaged them as self-employed "contractors," which saved the employers from having to pay payroll taxes and allowed the employees-turned-contractors to deduct work-related expenses from their incomes for tax purposes.

2. The rapid growth of employment opportunities in the service sector coincided with greater social and economic self-sufficiency among women, a result of their increased levels of education and career expectations. Growing numbers of women entrepreneurs have successfully established themselves in the expanding service sector, because it is so well suited to small businesses and self-employment.

3. There is a general expectation that these trends will continue. The driving forces behind these trends—technological advances and rising demand for services—seem likely to continue.

YOU DECIDE: Sales and Jobs

1. Honda is a *manufacturing* company that is "capital-intensive"—it uses a great deal of capital equipment such as industrial robots, and relatively little labour in its production of automobiles. Canadian Tire, on the other hand, is a retailer, which is a *service* company. This means that it is by nature "labour-intensive", because it takes a lot of worker-hours to stock shelves, service customers, and check out buyers. Put differently, it takes a lot more worker-hours to handle a million dollars of retail sales than to produce a million dollars worth of cars.

YOU DECIDE: A Competitive Market for Education?

1. The pressure of competition could push schools to improve the quality of the education they offer in order to attract students and "sales income," much as many private schools do.

2. There might be a "quality control" problem. Some schools might offer education that *looks* attractive, but is in fact inferior in order to attract business.

3. The main thing would be *consumer knowledge*; the better-informed parents are about the educational "product" being offered, the more likely they are to make good choices, thus placing more pressure on schools to provide high-quality education.

It should be noted that in school systems in which students are free to attend the school of their choice and in which schools' operating grants from government(s) vary directly with enrolment each year, there is already a de facto "market system" in operation.

Chapter 4: The Demand Side of Markets

YOU DECIDE: The Economics of Smoking

1. Demand is more inelastic for adults than for youths, because the same price increase causes a smaller reduction in smoking by adults.

2. There are two logical explanations for the more inelastic demand of adults. First, having smoked for longer, they are more addicted to tobacco. And second, adults generally have more disposable income than youths.

3. IF—and this is a *big* if—the same coefficient of elasticity applies to a very large price increase as applies to a 10 percent price increase, a price

increase of more than 60 percent would be required. (Since a 10 percent price increase cuts youth consumption by 8 percent, the price increase would have to be a little more than six times as large.)

Chapter 5: The Supply Side of Markets

IN THE NEWS: **Price and Supply**

1. Rising demand for oil was causing the price of crude oil to increase, which sent a signal through the market to producers that they should seek ways to increase production. And the rising price made it profitable for producers to exploit higher-cost production alternatives, which had not been economical in the past, when oil prices were lower.

2. Producers of "fracked" oil need the price of oil to be over $70 per barrel in order to be profitable. There are two types of risk for them, one on the supply side of the market and another on the demand side.

   On the supply side, such a rapid expansion of fracking could lead to an oversupply of crude oil, which could drive the price down below the $70 level needed for most producers to be profitable, especially if Saudi Arabia did not reduce its own output in order to stabilize prices.

   On the demand side, if prices for gasoline and heating oil remained high, this might cause consumers and businesses to economize on their use of these products, such as by buying more fuel-efficient cars, switching to alternative sources of fuel and heating, and so on.

Chapter 6: The Dynamics of Competitive Markets

IN THE NEWS: **Commercials During the Super Bowl**

1. Advertisers buy *exposure to an audience* who will see their commercials. The Super Bowl draws a massive audience of over 130 million people, which makes sponsors willing to pay extremely high rates to advertise on the show; that is, it increases the demand for advertising time greatly.

2. On the supply side, the supply of commercial time is obviously both *low* (there are only so many minutes of commercial time during a football game) and extremely *inelastic* (the amount of commercial time cannot be increased even if the price rises to very high levels).

IN THE NEWS: **The World Market for Oil**

1. In 2007 and the first half of 2008, the demand for crude oil increased very strongly, due to a world economic boom, with an added surge of demand from the rapidly-growing Chinese economy. The inelastic world supply of oil was unable to keep up with the rising demand, so the price rose very sharply.

2. In 2008–09, the situation regarding the demand for crude oil reversed: the demand for oil fell sharply due to a sudden and serious recession in the United States and other countries. The result was a very sharp decrease in the price of oil—the reverse of the situation in 2007–08.

   The point to note here is that the price fluctuations of 2007–09 were caused by changes on the *demand side* of the market for crude oil. The sharp price decline of 2014–15 was mainly caused by developments on the *supply side* of the market—specifically, the increase in supply due to "fracking" in the United States.

3. The supply curve would still be inelastic up to the price at which a significant amount of "fracked" oil came onto the market—beyond that price, the supply curve would become considerably more elastic—that is, it would bend to the right. As of spring 2015, it was still uncertain what that price would actually be. A commonly-cited figure for the average cost per barrel of fracked oil was $70; however, it was believed that many producers had lower average costs, and that technological advances would lead to even lower costs before long.

   Whatever the critical price needed for "fracking" to be profitable turns out to be, this would mean that once the price reached that point, it would be less likely to increase much further, which explains why a Saudi Arabian prince said in January 2015 that the world would "never see $100 per barrel oil again".

YOU DECIDE: **Markets for Assets**

1. If the price of an asset were expected to *fall*, the situation would be the opposite of the one portrayed in the box: the supply (selling) of it would increase as some owners of it would sell it before the price fell further, while the demand for it would fall, as prospective buyers waited for the price to fall further. The combination of increased supply and reduced demand would cause the price of the asset to fall further and faster.

2. The prices of such assets would be considerably more unstable than the prices of ordinary goods and services—they would tend to rise and fall more often, and by larger amounts.

3. Eventually, the price would reach such a high level that a growing number of people would not expect it to rise further. This change in expectations would cause less buying of it (a decrease in demand) and more selling of it (an increase in supply). The price would stop rising, and would probably fall. If this caused an expectation that the price would fall further, this could generate a rapid decrease in its price, as selling activity increased but there was a lack of buyers.

YOU DECIDE: The Internet and Markets

1. Buyers should pay lower prices, because the internet in effect brings more competing sellers into the market, as anyone who has used bizrate.com knows very well.

2. The experience has been the opposite of question 1: people who have posted their garage sales on the internet have received *higher* prices. The generally accepted reason is that the internet postings attract more competing buyers to these "mini-markets."

3. The purpose of this question is to focus back onto the *market basics* involved in this item: in question 1, the effect of the internet is to bring *more sellers* into the marketplace, which depresses prices. In question 2, the internet brings *more buyers* into the marketplace, which supports higher prices. That is, the key is not the internet per se, but rather how the internet affects the marketplace.

Chapter 7: Market Structures

YOU DECIDE: Coffee Crop Control

1. The seemingly strange behaviour of farmers (plantation owners, actually), burning part of their crop distracts from the simple reality that this is merely a measure to restrict the supply of coffee on world markets so as to secure a higher price for it. Economically, it is the same tactic as OPEC's pumping less crude oil, or car companies shuttering plants and laying off workers a few months before the end of a model year. The difference is that in agriculture, weather and other uncertainties mean that producers cannot effectively control production as required

over the course of the year. Rather, they have to wait until the end of the crop year, *then* control the supply.

2. For such a plan to achieve its objective, *all* the major players in the world market would have to agree to participate in restricting the supply. There would have to be a reasonable amount of trust among them, such that none would "chisel" on their agreement. And, of course, the demand for coffee would have to be inelastic.

3. As usual, we should consider both the demand side and the supply side of the market. If the demand for coffee were elastic, the plan to raise prices would fail—but have *you* ever seen someone stagger into a Starbucks or Tim Hortons in the morning, review the prices posted on the wall, deliberately count his or her money, and depart? So the only problems that could arise are on the supply side, and the main ones are that some producers might fail to stick to the agreement to destroy part of their crops, and that an "outside" producer might enter the market. This is what actually did happen when Vietnam became the world's second-largest coffee producer in the late 1990s.

IN THE NEWS: OPEC

1. For such a small reduction in supply to cause such a large increase in price, demand must be very *inelastic*. This behaviour is what one would expect of the demand for oil, at least in the short run. Buyers of gasoline and fuel oil are not in a position to quickly change the equipment (vehicles and furnaces) in which they use petroleum products, so demand would be inelastic.

2. The key to achieving higher prices is to restrict the production (supply) of oil. But OPEC only controls 35 to 40 percent of world crude-oil production. If the higher prices that OPEC was seeking were to lead non-OPEC producers to increase their production, OPEC's price objective would not be achieved. In addition, the objective of a higher price would necessarily involve lower production quotas for each member of OPEC. But members of OPEC have often been known to cheat on their production quotas. If some OPEC members were to pump oil in excess of their quotas, the world

supply of oil would be higher than OPEC had planned—and the price would be below OPEC's target.

YOU DECIDE: The International Diamond Monopoly

1. There is a real possibility that more diamonds will be found than can be absorbed by the market at current prices. Furthermore, the high prices of diamonds create an incentive to find more of them. If De Beers were to be unable to buy all such newly found diamonds, they might be sold on the open market, driving prices downward.

2. If the monopoly is charging high prices, its high profits will attract competitors. These could take the form of new firms producing the same product or substitutes. The change in DeBeers' strategies over the years supports this view; on the other hand, BeBeers did manage to exercise monopoly power for a long time.

Chapter 8: The Costs and Revenues of the Firm

YOU DECIDE: Making Business Decisions

1. An increase in the price or a reduction in the firm's production costs would lead to an increase in output. A higher price would shift the point where marginal revenue per unit = marginal cost per unit (MR=MC) to the right, because it would be profitable to produce additional units. Lower costs would also cause higher output, because lower production costs of additional units would make it profitable to produce them.

2. If the price fell, the firm would reduce its output. The marginal revenue per unit line on the graph would shift downward, pushing the intersection point of the MR and MC curves to the left. The lower price would make it unprofitable to produce some units that had been profitable at the previous price.

3. An increase in production costs would also lead the firm to reduce its output, because the higher costs would make it unprofitable to produce some units that had been profitable when costs were lower.

YOU DECIDE: Ebusiness Costs

1. The marginal cost of additional units is *very* low; selling additional units does not require paying for any more labour or materials.

2. Such a combination of high fixed costs and low marginal costs supports a very aggressive pricing strategy, for two reasons. First, such low marginal costs mean that additional units can be priced very low and still sold profitably. And second, such low prices would increase sales volume, which would spread the firm's high fixed costs over a larger number of units. High fixed costs tend to dictate a fairly high break-even point, and low prices help the firm to achieve this level of sales.

Chapter 9: Government Policy Toward Business

YOU DECIDE: Canada's Banks: To Merge or Not to Merge?

1. The fact that the five largest banks control a very large proportion of the total assets in the banking industry suggests that the banking industry is highly concentrated. However, a more detailed look at the industry reveals that banks do face competition in the various markets in which they operate; for instance, taking deposits, making loans, financial services, and so on.

2. (a) The high fixed costs would reflect the heavy investment in the electronic equipment and technical infrastructure required to support it. In addition, experience has shown that such sophisticated systems also involve significant initial investments (fixed costs of a different sort) in employee training. Once these investments are in place, the capital equipment handles most additional business itself, at a very low (marginal) cost. For example, people used to pay bills by cheque, which required paying workers to process each transaction at a significant marginal cost per transaction. With online banking, the bank's computer processes bill payments at a very low marginal cost per transaction.

   (b) Technical Report No. 91 could add weight to the banks' argument that in modern high-technology banking, there are significant economies of scale that give larger banks a competitive advantage over smaller ones, by spreading their high fixed costs over a larger number of customers and transactions. The Canadian banks (which are small by international standards) could argue that they should be allowed to merge in order to achieve these economies of scale.

What is not (yet) clear is just *how large* banks must actually be in order to achieve these economies of scale—is it the case that the larger a bank grows, the lower its marginal costs will be, or do these economies of scale "stall" at a certain point? And if so, at what point, and how much would Canadian banks need to grow to reach that point? Or might they already be large enough to have reached that point?

YOU DECIDE: Beer Competition

1. Even with assertive monitoring by the Competition Bureau, there would still be only two major competitors. With the aging of the population, the beer market has been growing very slowly, so there is no room for more Canadian breweries as competitors. So if the government really wanted to increase competition, the best way would be to open up the Canadian beer market to foreign competitors. This is in fact what did happen, thanks in large part to free trade agreements.

Chapter 10: Labour Markets and Labour Unions

YOU DECIDE: Canada's shortage of skilled trades workers

1. As noted, one basic reason for the projected shortages is that many skilled trades workers are relatively old and will be retiring before long. But why are relatively few young Canadians interested in skilled trades careers? Many people say that this is because there is a social stigma attached to skilled work that involves working with your hands, sometimes outdoors. So young people are encouraged by their parents and high school teachers to go to university and college rather than enter the trades, which are perceived to be of lower status.

Another problem is that many apprenticeship programs create bottlenecks that restrict entry into the trades. In some cases, apprenticeships are quite long and/or wages are relatively unattractive; also, provincial government regulations often limit the number of apprentices that employers can hire.

2. In various European countries, no social stigma exists concerning the trades: a skilled trades certificate is considered to have the same social and economic value as a university degree. In Germany, Switzerland, Austria and Denmark, about two-thirds of young high school students at the age of 16 enrol in paid apprenticeship programs and graduate at 19 ready for work and without student debts.

Also, easing of provincial restrictions and higher wages for apprenticeships would help to attract more young people into the skilled trades.

IN THE NEWS: Hockey Players' Salaries

1. The "short answer" to this question is that the demand for NHL hockey players grew by a factor of 5 (from 6 teams to 30), while the supply of players of NHL calibre did not. However, this explanation seems insufficient to account for such a massive increase in players' salaries.

According to people who follow the National Hockey League, the reasons for the rapid increase in salaries were more complex, and were rooted in a combination of free agency, salary arbitration, and a very wide gap in the financial conditions of the rich (big-market) teams and the poor (small market) teams. Under their collective bargaining agreement (CBA or labour contract), at a certain stage in their respective careers, players who had been tied to one team could become *free agents* and sign with the team that bid the most for their services. In this free agent market, some rich teams (most notably the New York Rangers) were willing to pay extremely high salaries for a few key players who might help them to win the Stanley Cup.

The NHL's labour contract also provided that at an earlier point in their careers, players who were not yet free agents and who had salary disputes with their team could apply for *salary arbitration*, in which an arbitrator would decide the player's salary. In these arbitrations, players were able to use the salaries paid by rich teams to key free agents as benchmarks for their own salary claims. For example, if the New York Rangers signed free agent Pierre Slapshotte for $10 million a year, Yuri Skormor could argue to an arbitrator that the Calgary Flames should have to pay him $8 million because he scored 80 percent as many points as Slapshotte. So the huge salaries paid to a few key players by a few rich teams spread to players on the poor teams.

2. The high cost of players' salaries became a problem for the league. Several of the smaller-market teams with lower revenues were losing large amounts of money.

In a free-market "survival of the fittest" situation, as many as one-third of the teams might have gone bankrupt. But the NHL would not let this happen, perhaps because it believed that its image as a growing and popular sport could not withstand such a blow. So, in the negotiations for a new labour contract with its players, the NHL decided that there must be a dramatic decrease in players' salaries—a decrease large enough to keep the small-market teams with lower revenues in business.

When the players refused to accept this, the 2004–05 season was lost to a work stoppage when the league locked the players out. The final settlement included many concessions by the players, including salary rollbacks of 24 percent.

YOU DECIDE: Let's Play Arbitrator

1. You are neutral, and because of this neutrality, both sides accept you as arbitrator.
2. You are still an "outsider"—you have not actually *lived with* the problems that you are trying to resolve.
3. No. You will only know *what you have been told* by two people who are probably not interested in the facts so much as in getting a decision from you that suits them.
4. There is a real risk that this person will feel no commitment to making your decision work. It is too easy for this person to rationalize that the decision was made by someone else.

Chapter 11: Employment and Incomes in the Canadian Economy

IN THE NEWS: Labour Force Facts

1. In large part, the growth of part-time employment is the result of the growth of the *service sector* of the economy. While the production of goods lends itself to full-time work such as in manufacturing plants, services such as retail trade, restaurants, and entertainment often tend to be delivered at peak periods, making part-time employment particularly well suited to these industries.

However, financial pressures on employers also seem to be a factor in decisions between hiring full-time and part-time employees. During the economic boom of the second half of the 1980s, part-time employment *decreased* from 17.0 percent of all jobs to 16.6 percent. During the recession of the early 1990s, part-time employment increased to 19.1 percent by 1993, but in the boom of the late 1990s, it *fell again*, to 18.1 percent. So at least in some cases, employers seem to prefer full-time workers, but will hire more part-timers when pressed financially.

2. The Statistics Canada's webpage also contains some interesting breakdowns of part-time employment by age and sex.

IN THE NEWS: Will Technology Cause Unemployment?

1. The optimistic view is that much more output could be produced with fewer hours of work, allowing people to enjoy *both* a much higher material standard of living *and* more leisure time. The typical workweek could be reduced to 4 or even 3 days, so as to spread the available work (and income) among the maximum number of people. Alternatively, some of the labour freed up by technology could be allocated to socially useful public tasks, such as creating and maintaining infrastructure, recreation facilities, parks, etc.

2. The pessimistic view is that the available work would not be widely shared, perhaps because many people would lack the skills to work effectively in the new high-technology environment. This would lead to a surplus of less-skilled workers, the result of which would be a combination of depressed wages and high unemployment for the less-skilled. Society would evolve into two "tribes" of people: a busy and well-paid group, and a large group of very poor people with frustration in their minds and time on their hands—not a healthy situation.

3. If technology were to replace labour on such a new large scale, this could show up as a *shorter workweek*, if things went well as in #1. If the

unhappy situation in #2 happened, this would probably show up at first as a rising *unemployment rate*, but later (and more significantly) as a falling *labour force participation rate*, as growing numbers of people of working age stopped not just working, but even *looking for work*.

IN THE NEWS: **Will the Male–Female Pay Gap Narrow in the Future?**

1. The main reason for expecting that the male–female pay gap will narrow in the future is that more young women than men are pursuing post-secondary education. On university campuses today, women outnumber men by about four to three, and young males are particularly likely to become high school dropouts. Another important factor will be the retirement of older women, for whom the pay gap is largest (33 percent for women aged 45–54) and their replacement by younger women, for whom the pay gap is smaller (19 percent for women aged 15–24).

   Looking farther into the future, because more women will have well-paying careers rather than being second-income earners in the family, more of them will probably work past the age of 55. This would add to the average income of women.

   On the male side of the picture, the loss of higher-paying (mostly male) manufacturing jobs due to technological change could depress the average male pay rate.

Chapter 12: The Government Sector

YOU DECIDE: **How to Use Budget Surpluses?**

1. (a) Pay down government debt.
   (b) Increase spending on programs such as health care, education, etc.
   (c) Reduce taxes
2. $9.5 billion is $9,500,000,000.

   $9,500,000,000 divided by 31 600 000 = $300 per Canadian per year, or $25 per month. (So $9.5 billion isn't really as huge as it sounds at first.)

YOU DECIDE: **The Marginal Tax Rate and the Economic Incentive to Work**

1. No. She is merely responding logically to the incentives presented to her by the system. If Joan faced a marginal tax rate of 80 percent and decided not to teach night school because of it, her middle-class friends would probably say that she was behaving rationally and that the tax system was virtually forcing her to turn down this extra work.
2. Sandy needs to be allowed to keep a higher proportion of any income that she manages to earn. In other words, her welfare benefits should not be reduced so rapidly when she earns money that her incentive to work is destroyed.

Chapter 13: Environmental Economics

IN THE NEWS: **Higher Taxes on Gasoline?**

1. The argument is that higher gasoline taxes and prices would discourage excessive consumption of gasoline, and that the resultant conservation of gasoline would reduce the automobile emissions that are the main source of air pollution. (In the short run, the demand for gasoline would probably be inelastic—people would not suddenly sell their SUVs and buy more fuel-efficient vehicles. In the longer run, more adjustments are possible—in the 1970s and 1980s, people did in fact switch to more fuel-efficient vehicles following the very large increases in gasoline prices.)
2. There are three answers to this question— politics, politics, and politics. Consumers love cheap gasoline, and are very hostile to taxes that increase the price of their gas. Politicians will never forget that, in December of 1979 the fledgling Progressive Conservative government of Joe Clark was defeated after it proposed an 18-cent-per-litre tax on gasoline that would have benefited both federal finances and the environment.

Chapter 14: Into the Future

IN THE NEWS: **The Greying of Canada**

1. The increase in the seniors population reflects the aging of the *baby boomers*—the large number of Canadians who were born from 1946 to 1966. The oldest baby boomer turned 65 in 2011; the youngest turns 65 in 2031. Many of these baby boomers will live to about 80 or more.
2. The implications of this trend for the living standards of Canadians are not positive. With so many more people retired, Canadian society will have a lower proportion of its total popula-

tion working than in the past. Another way of looking at it is that a smaller proportion of working Canadians will have to produce enough to provide for themselves plus a larger proportion of non-working Canadians.

To illustrate, imagine a deserted island economy with 20 people. Two are too young to work, 16 are of working age, and 2 are too old to work. If 10 of the 16 work (62.5 percent), then *10 workers have to support 2 retired people.* If 4 more retire, then 6 will be too old to work. If 2 are still too young to work, that leaves 12 of working age. Even if 8 of them work (66.7 percent), *8 workers have to support 6 retired people.*

3. One major thing that governments could do to reduce the negative economic effects of an aging population would be to increase the age of retirement. This would keep more older people working, so fewer would be in retire-ment. Another key policy would be to increase immigration of young people with the skills required by Canadian employers, so as to replenish Canada's labour force as the baby boomers retire. Also, any government policies that would encourage more Canadians of working age to work would help, as would policies that would increase productivity. The more each working Canadian produces, the less serious would be the problem of supporting the increased number of retired people. One way or another, the key is to keep output as high as possible despite the loss of so many baby boomers from the workforce.

Other approaches are less attractive, as they would require either that retired Canadians accept a lower living standard in the form of reduced pensions, or that working Canadians accept a lower living standard because of higher taxes to support the retirees.

Chapter 1

1. e
2. b
3. b
4. d
5. b
6. e
7. a
8. b
9. a
10. d
11. c
12. a
13. (a) 2 kg of vegetables
    (b) 4 kg of vegetables
    (c) 6 kg of vegetables
    (d) 6 kg of vegetables
    (e) 12 kg of vegetables
    (f) 8 kg of vegetables
    (g) 20 kg of vegetables
14. d
15. b

1. (a) Your car will not be fixed, so the opportunity cost will be whatever the use of your car would have provided for you. Maybe you'll forgo the income you could have earned if you had been able to get to work, or maybe you'll miss out on some social or recreational opportunities.
   (b) Your mother will be very disappointed about not getting to go to the concert. The opportunity cost of getting your car fixed will be whatever the consequences of her disappointment are for you. (You know these better than anyone else. . . .)

2. The obvious opportunity costs are related to the cost of your attending school—the things that you could have bought with the money spent on tuition, books, and so on. The less obvious opportunity cost is the foregone income that you could have earned if you had not gone to school.

3. Not at all—Rajinder has many more dollars, but still has only has a limited number of dollars. Every dollar that Rajinder spends on one thing means that there is one less dollar available to spend on other things.

4. (a) This is intended to improve effectiveness, by telling management what customers like and dislike about the company's products and services.
   (b) This is intended to improve efficiency, by motivating workers to produce products at a faster rate.
   (c) This is intended to improve both effectiveness and efficiency. If the robots produce products with precision, they will be more effective than workers, and if they produce products rapidly enough, the cost per product will be lower than with workers.

5. (a) This is intended to improve effectiveness, by telling the college what students like and dislike about the college's programs, courses, and services.
   (b) This is intended to improve efficiency, by increasing the number of students taught by each teacher. The increase in efficiency could be measured by an increase in teacher productivity (output per worker), or by a decrease in the cost per student.

1. In answering this question, don't look for the words *effectiveness* and *efficiency*; articles are unlikely to use these exact terms. Instead, look at an item and ask yourself whether you can apply the concepts of effectiveness and efficiency to it.

Chapter 2

REVIEW QUESTIONS

1. e
2. e
3. c
4. c
5. d
6. c
7. e
8. c
9. c
10. e
11. (a) T
    (b) T
    (c) F
    (d) T
    (e) F
12. (a) F
    (b) T
    (c) T
    (d) F
    (e) T
13. (a) T
    (b) T
    (c) T
    (d) F
    (e) T
14. c
15. d
16. e
17. e
18. b
19. c

CRITICAL THINKING QUESTIONS

1. (a) Market element: Consumers are directing the use of economic resources by buying more goat meat, which will cause its price to increase, which will encourage more production of goat meat. No government action is involved.
   (b) Command element: Governments are directing the use of economic resources toward education by using tax funds to finance education at no cost to users.
   (c) Market element: The oversupply will drive prices down, which will encourage buyers to buy more computers, and producers to adjust their production. No government action is involved.
   (d) Command element: Due to concerns that the merger of two such large firms would create monopoly-like power in the marketplace, the government is directing that the merger not take place.
   (e) Command element: The government is directing that the market's distribution of income (division of the economic pie) be altered so that lower-income citizens receive a larger share.
   (f) Market element: This situation was essentially the negotiation of a price (the compensation of players) by private buyers (the hockey clubs) and private sellers (the players). The decision was made by these parties, not the government.
   (g) Command element: The tax system established by governments is directing that higher-income citizens pay a larger share of the cost of government programs.
2. Assuming no changes in production costs per product,
   (a) the price of product A would rise by $2, and the profit per product would increase by $2/$7, or 29 percent.
   (b) the price of product B would fall by $1, and the profit per product would decrease by $1/$7, or 14 percent.
   (c) produce more of product A and less of B. Note how relatively small changes in *prices* can have significant effects on *profits* and on producers' *incentives*.
3. Corporations—this is merely one form that business enterprises can assume. But for a market system to function properly, there must be markets and prices. It is through price changes in markets that producers are given incentives to adjust production in response to the demand of buyers. And, of course, it is the profit motive that gives producers the economic incentive to do so.
4. (a) Competition among producers not only pushes producers to use resources effectively and efficiently; it forces them to *keep prices down*. If there were no competition

(that is, a monopoly), the producer could charge much higher prices. The same idea applies to producers getting together and agreeing on their price, which is illegal in Canada. Probably the most attractive aspect of the market system is that it does a good job of benefiting consumers, who are portrayed as "kings of the marketplace."

(b) However, if there were no competition, producers, not consumers, would be the dominant force in markets.

USE THE WEB

1. and 2. These questions are intended to show how a sophisticated information system such as the internet can improve how markets function, by making communications between buyers and sellers easier and faster.

Chapter 3

REVIEW QUESTIONS

1. T
2. F
3. T
4. T
5. T
6. T
7. T
8. F
9. T
10. T
11. F
12. F
13. F
14. T
15. T
16. F
17. F
18. T
19. T
20. e
21. c

CRITICAL THINKING QUESTIONS

1. CFIB provides two important services for its members that they could not afford to do on their own. The first of these functions is political lobbying to persuade governments to consider the concerns of the small business community when deciding their economic, taxation, and other policies that affect small business. Another function is the conducting of research of interest and value to the small business community.

2. The most frequently cited reason for people wanting to be in business for themselves is psychological rather than economic—they are independent in nature and prefer working for themselves, even if this involves less income and security than working for a large corporation. For some people, another reason is the possibility of striking it rich by establishing a very successful business.

3. Payroll taxes are taxes based on the size of an employer's payroll, or the number of its employees. Small businesses are particularly concerned about payroll taxes because small businesses tend to be more *labour-intensive* than larger businesses, often because small businesses provide services and/or use less high-technology production methods.

   This means that for labour-intensive businesses, labour costs are often a higher percentage of their total costs than for large firms such as big manufacturers. In turn, this means that payroll taxes, which in effect add to a firm's labour costs, are often more burdensome for small businesses than for large ones.

4. In support of government ownership and operation of such enterprises, it can be argued that they have contributed greatly to the economic development and unity of Canada, by providing energy (especially electricity) and key transportation and communication infrastructure such as railways, air service, postal service, and radio and television. In addition, it can be argued that these government enterprises made these services available to all Canadians, whether or not the size of their communities was large enough to make it profitable to provide that service.

5. Critics of government-owned-and-operated enterprises argue that they are inefficient and ineffective, largely because they lack a profit motive and have no competition. In addition, critics say, many government enterprises pay above-market wages to their employees, which adds to their inefficiency and costs. In turn, this means that many of these enterprises lose money and have to get subsidies

from governments, which involves opportunity costs because those governments could have spent those taxpayers' funds on other important public services, such as health care or education.

USE THE WEB

1. This is another example of how the internet makes vital information about markets readily available to people.
2. This question relates to the section in Chapter 3 about the problems of small business, and how various agencies offer assistance of different sorts to small businesses. For an idea of how an incubator works, visit the various sections of the website, such as the one on success stories.

Chapter 4

REVIEW QUESTIONS

1. a
2. decrease
3. (a) unwilling
   (b) unable
4. (a) substitute
   (b) do without (buy less)
5.

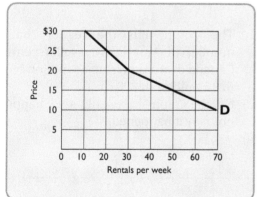

6. b
7. a
8. a
9. c
10. a
11. b
12. a
13. a
14. b
15. b

16. Neilson's chocolate ice cream
   chocolate ice cream
   ice cream
   dairy products

CRITICAL THINKING QUESTIONS

1. Note that in both graphs, the quantity demanded is 100 units per week at a price of $5. So our starting point is that, in both graphs, total revenue is $500 per week at a price of $5. Next, we check what would happen to total revenue if the price increased to $8.

   Graph A shows an elastic demand, because at a price of $8, total revenue *decreases* to $400 per week ($8 x 50 units). And graph B shows an inelastic demand, because at a price of $8, total revenue *increases* to $640 per week ($8 x 80 units).

2. (a) From $2 to $3: inelastic—total revenue increases, from $100 to $120 thousand
      From $3 to $4: unitary elasticity—total revenue is unchanged at $120 thousand
      From $4 to $5: elastic—total revenue decreases, from $120 to $100 thousand
   (b) At a price of $2 per dozen, most consumers seem to be willing to accept a price increase to $3, probably because they do not see attractive substitutes at a price of $3 for cobs of corn. However, when the price reaches $5, buyer resistance increases, as more people are unwilling to pay such a price. When a dozen cobs of corn costs you $5, substitutes seem more attractive than when it costs you $3.

3. (a) inelastic—the tradition of the Christmas turkey dinner would make price less of a consideration at Christmas.
   (b) elastic—with the alternative of DVDs available, people would become more resistant to increases in the price of movie tickets.
   (c) elastic—this adds another substitute for the products of the existing pizzerias, which would make it more difficult for them to increase their prices.

4. (a) air conditioners—these are less of a necessity than furnaces (in Canada's climate); it is easier to do without them or substitute for them.
   (b) automobiles—if the price of both autos and licences rose 20 percent, the fact that in some cases the purchase of a car can be postponed would cause their sales to decrease more than those of licences,

which are *required* in order to drive a car. Another factor would be the high price of a car as compared to a licence.

(c) telephone service—while the demand for both these items would be inelastic, there are more substitutes for telephone service than for electricity—for example, instant messaging on the internet.

(d) new autos—see (b) above; plus, when you need a replacement part in order to get the use of your car back, are you going to refuse to buy it because it is expensive?

5. (a) The demand for SUVs would decrease, so the demand curve for SUVs would shift to the left.

(b) These are complementary goods, because gasoline is bought in combination with an SUV.

6. (a) When the price of gasoline goes up sharply, most consumers complain loudly but keep buying nearly as much gas as before. At this point in time, they are trapped—they already own (or are leasing) their vehicle, and it would be costly to change to a more fuel-efficient one. These facts keep the demand for gas high (inelastic, really), which in turn contributes to high gas prices.

(b) If the price of gas *remains* high (which would lead more drivers to expect that it would continue to be high), the behaviour of consumers changes. When the time comes to replace their vehicle, more drivers buy a fuel-efficient one. This decreases the quantity of gasoline that they buy, which could be regarded as a decrease in demand and/or more elastic demand. In addition, people discover alternatives that economize on gas, such as carpooling, which they can exercise if the price of gas goes up.

USE THE WEB

1. To monitor trends over the five years shown, calculate the *percentage increase* for each year over the previous year. Doing this will allow you to easily compare the trend in the statistics for your province with the trend in the much larger statistics for Canada as a whole. Trends in new housing starts are affected by various factors, including mortgage interest rates, the condition of the economy (boom or recession), and population growth.

2. *The Daily* is used by Statistics Canada to release new statistics on all sorts of matters, which are kept in an archive. Its releases often contain both up-to-date statistics and explanations for recent trends shown by the data.

Appendix 4A

REVIEW QUESTIONS

1. (a)

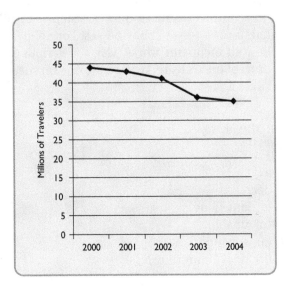

(b) The graph tells the reader that the number of American travellers entering Canada decreased from 44 million in 2000 to 35 million in 2004.

(c) No, the graph shows only *what* happened, not *why* it happened.

2. (a)

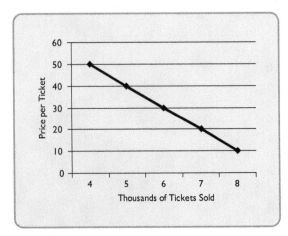

(b) The graph tells the reader that if the price of tickets is higher, people will buy few tickets, and at lower prices they will buy more tickets.

(c) Yes, because the graph shows the relationship between the price of tickets and how many tickets people will buy.

3. (a)

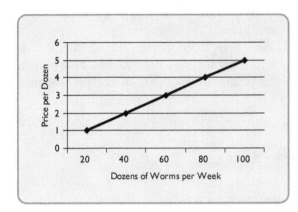

(b) The graph tells the reader that if the price of worms is higher, the children will pick more worms and offer them for sale.

(c) Yes, because the graph shows the relationship between the price of worms and how many worms people will gather and offer for sale.

Chapter 5

REVIEW QUESTIONS

1. b and e
2. c
3. d
4. (a) concentrated
   (b) competitive
   (c) concentrated
   (d) competitive
5. d
6. a
7. e
8. b
9. a
10. a
11. b
12. b
13. d
14. c
15. c
16. d

17.

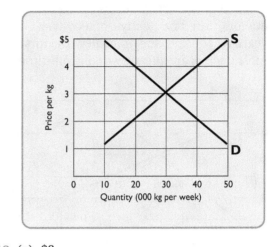

18. (a) $3
    (b) 30 000
19. c
20. b

CRITICAL THINKING QUESTIONS

1. The supply curve would shift from S to S1, as shown in the following graph.

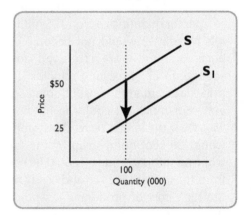

   Assume that retailers have 100 000 pairs of unsold summer shoes. Earlier in the season, they were charging $50 a pair for these shoes, but now that the season is nearly over, they reduce the price to $25. This reflects an increased willingness to sell this product, which takes the form of a price reduction rather than the increase in the amount offered for sale that is usually associated with such a shift in the supply curve.

2. The supply of retail clerks would be more elastic. If the price (that is, the wage rate) of retail clerks increased, the quantity of "clerk labour" supplied could increase considerably. Sources of labour could include young people who have left school, part-time student workers (more of them plus longer hours of work), homemakers,

retired people, and so on. An increase in the incomes of doctors would also bring forth more doctors, but not nearly so readily—it takes years to educate and train new doctors, and most doctors are already working full-time.

3. (a)

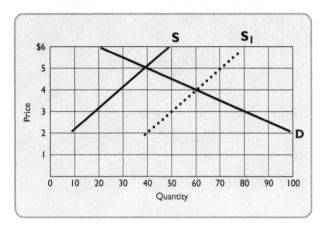

The equilibrium price is $5.

(b) See the dotted supply curve (S1); the new equilibrium price is $4.

4. (a) The supply curve would become much steeper for quantities beyond 85 million barrels per day. It would not become vertical, because *some* more crude oil could be squeezed out of existing oilfields if higher prices warranted the cost of doing so; however, not much oil could be obtained this way. Over the longer term, the supply curve would be kept quite steep by the fact that while additional crude oil could be obtained from those more remote and costly sources, the high cost of producing it would mean that its price would be high.

(b) The implication is that if the demand for oil continues to increase, the price is likely to not only stay high, but probably increase further.

(c) If something were to happen that increased the supply of crude oil, the price of oil would not increase, and could even fall. A similar development could occur if a substitute for oil (or for the gasoline that is made from oil) were developed.

5. This is a situation in which supply becomes inelastic because of limited plant (refinery) capacity. The problem in this case is an *inelastic supply of gasoline*, rather than a limited supply of crude oil (which has usually been the reason for rapidly rising gasoline prices).

Unless refinery capacity were increased, even large increases in the price of gasoline would fail to bring forth a larger quantity of gasoline supplied.

USE THE WEB

1. Clicking on the "New and Used" section beside a book will show you a list of a number of sellers of used copies of that book. The more sellers there are, the more competitive that market should be.

2. Check how many dealers are offering that particular car for sale; more sellers in a particular market area indicates a more competitive market.

Chapter 6

REVIEW QUESTIONS

1. increase, increase
2. decrease, decrease
3. decrease, increase
4. increase, decrease
5. b
6. a
7. $3, 50 units per week
8. c
9. (a) The quantity supplied would increase to 80 per week.
   (b) The quantity demanded would decrease to 20 per week.
10. b
11. (a) The quantity demanded would increase to 70 per week.
    (b) The quantity supplied would decrease to 30 per week.
12. b
13. c
14. d
15. a

CRITICAL THINKING QUESTIONS

1. (i) This would cause the demand for the product to increase. The demand curve would shift to the right, causing both price and quantity to increase.
   (ii) This is an increase in supply. The supply curve would shift to the right, causing the price to decrease and the quantity to increase.
   (iii) The demand curve would shift to the left (and become more elastic), so both price and quantity would decrease.

(iv) This is a decrease in supply, so the supply curve would shift to the left (or upwards, depending on how you look at it), which would cause the price to increase and the quantity to decrease.

(v) A shortage would develop, as in Figure 6-9.

(vi) Demand would decrease, so the demand curve would shift to the left. Both price and quantity would decrease.

(vii) The tax adds to the cost of producing and selling the product, so the supply curve would shift upwards by $2, reflecting the added cost. The result would be an increase in the price and a decrease in the quantity.

(viii) The supply curve would become vertical or nearly vertical at an output of 70 units per week, and the price would increase to where the new supply curve intersects the demand curve.

(ix) A surplus would develop, as in Figure 6-8.

(x) Both the demand curve and the supply curve would shift to the right; the equilibrium quantity would rise but the result could be either an increase or a decrease in the equilibrium price, depending on whether the demand or the supply increased by more.

2. (a) an increase in supply—a large harvest of corn has generated lower prices that are encouraging higher consumption.

(b) an increase in demand—a cold winter has increased the demand for natural gas and caused prices to rise.

(c) a decrease in demand—the demand for boat rentals is down, possibly due to bad weather; and marinas have cut rental rates in an attempt to offset this.

(d) a decrease in supply—a poor harvest of strawberries has caused higher prices for the reduced amount on the market this year.

3. (a) The starting point in the graph is that the market is represented by demand curve D and supply curve S, and the equilibrium price (rent) is $1000 per month and the equilibrium quantity is 500 apartments. The influx of renters increases the demand from D to D1, which causes rents to increase from $1000 per month to $1300.

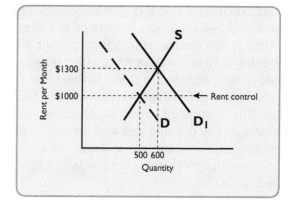

(b) If monthly rents are allowed to rise to $1300, the supply curve tells us that the quantity of apartments supplied will increase from 500 to 600. But if the town limits rents to $1000, the quantity supplied will only be 500, and there will be a shortage of apartments. Builders will build apartments in other towns, where they can charge the market rate for rent.

4. This is an interesting phenomenon that has been observed in various centres. The most common explanation for it is that early in the morning the demand for gas is more inelastic, because most buyers of gas are commuters who are in a hurry and, if they need gas, do not shop around for the best price—they just stop at the first station they see, or go to their usual station. Later in the day, more gas is bought by people who are not in such a hurry, and can take more time to compare prices.

5.

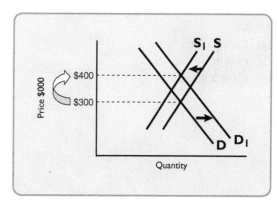

Initially, demand is represented by D and supply by S, and the equilibrium price is $300 000. Let's assume that because there is a general expectation that housing prices are going to rise rapidly, two things happen in this market:

(a) more buyers want to buy now, to beat the price increases, which increases demand to D1, and

(b) some sellers decide to postpone putting their houses onto the market for a while, hoping to get considerably higher prices at that time. This will decrease the supply (temporarily) to S1.

    The combined effect of *expected* rising prices on the demand side and the supply side of the economy can cause prices to actually increase sharply (in this example, from $300 000 to $400 000).

USE THE WEB

1. The statistics that you will see are not the prices of individual items, but rather something that statisticians call "indexes". These are averages of the prices in each category, such as food, shelter, etc. These averages (indexes) are adjusted so that the average for each category = 100.0 in a base year (2002 in this case).

    So what these index numbers measure is not prices of items, but rather *how much these averages of prices of types of items have increased* from any one year to another year. For example, the index for food was 135.5 in 2014 and 132.4 in 2013, so in 2014, the average price of the items in the "food" category increased by 2.3 percent (135.5 minus 132.4 divided by 132.4). And within the "food" category, there would be many items whose prices would have changed in various ways such that the *average* of their prices had increased by 2.3 percent.

Chapter 7

REVIEW QUESTIONS

1. (a) many small firms
   (b) easy to enter
   (c) identical products
2. a
3. c
4. d
5. e
6. d
7. b
8. a
9. increase their prices
10. (a) The producers make an agreement concerning price and output.
    (b) The producers maintain that agreement.
    (c) Newcomers and foreign competitors are kept out of the market.
    (d) The demand for the product is inelastic.

11. a
12. e
13. e
14. there is only one producer of a product.
15. c
16. control the supply of its product.

CRITICAL THINKING QUESTIONS

1. (a) Perfect competition
   (b) He is one of many small producers of identical products.
   (c)

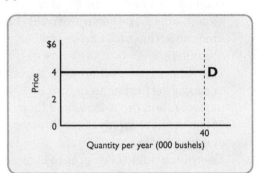

   (d) 40 000 bushels (as much as he can)
   (e) His sales would fall to zero.
   (f) No. He can already sell all that he can produce at the market price, so cutting his price would serve no purpose.
   (g) No. His product is identical to that of all the other farmers, so advertising would serve no purpose.
   (h) He should increase the efficiency of his farm, so as to get his cost of producing a bushel of wheat down. That would increase his profit per bushel sold.
2. (a) monopolistic competition
   (b) His business is one of many small firms in an industry that is easy to enter, and his product is not identical to those of his competitors—it is differentiated.
   (c)

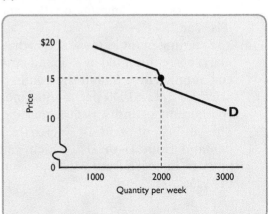

(d) (i) He should differentiate his product from those of his competitors.

(ii) He should make his production methods as efficient (low-cost) as possible.

(iii) Advertising makes sense, so as to bring the features of his products and services to people's attention.

(iv) His product differentiation gives him the opportunity to increase prices a little, but the fact that there are many competitors to whom his customers can switch limits how much he can increase prices. The more differentiated his product and the more loyal his customers, the higher his prices could be. On the other hand, he may decide not to increase his prices much or at all, so as to secure a loyal customer base.

3. The most basic reason why competitive industries generally have low prices and low profits is that producers are unable to control or restrict the supply of their product or service. And the main reason why they cannot restrict supply is that it is *easy for new firms to enter* their industry. This is very much in contrast with the situation in the next question.

4. (a) Barriers to entry are factors that prevent new firms (competitors) from starting up in an industry in competition with established firms. Examples of barriers to entry include the amount of capital needed to start a business, consumer acceptance and problems achieving the level of sales needed to operate profitably, and various other factors described in Chapter 7.

(b) The above-average profit rates of oligopolists will tend to attract new competitors that could undermine the oligopolists' market power and profits. Barriers to entry can prevent new competitors from doing this.

5. (a)

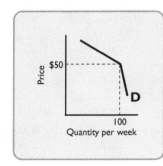

Since there are only a few firms in the industry, what will happen when this one firm increases its price will depend on what the other firms do with *their* prices.

(b) If this firm increases its price and the other firms do not increase their prices, this firm's sales will fall considerably. Its demand will be *elastic*, and a price increase will cause its sales revenue to decrease.

(c) If this firm decreases its price, we have to assume that the other firms will decrease their prices, too. In this case, this firm's price will be lower but its sales will only be slightly higher, so its sales revenue will decrease. For a price decrease, demand will be *inelastic*.

(d) The situations in parts (b) and (c) create an incentive for firms in this industry to agree on the price that they will all charge; then, the incentive for each firm is to neither increase nor decrease its price until all the firms agree upon a new price.

USE THE WEB

1. Be sure to select *Dealer Listing*—the objective is to see how many dealers are offering each car, not how many private sellers there are. Then be sure to count the *number of dealers* offering that car, not the number of vehicles for sale.

Chapter 8

REVIEW QUESTIONS

1. (a) fixed
   (b) variable
   (c) variable
   (d) fixed
   (e) fixed
   (f) variable
2. b
3. c
4. d
5. a
6. Law of Diminishing Returns
7. a
8. d
9. c
10. (a) $24
    (b) Yes. Producing and selling the twenty-sixth product adds more ($24) to the firm's revenues than it adds to its costs ($23).

11.

Units of output per day	Fixed Costs	Variable Costs	Total Costs	Average Fixed Cost per Unit	Average Variable Cost per Unit	Average Total Cost per Unit	Marginal Cost per Unit
0	$600	$ 0	$ 600	n.a.	n.a.	n.a.	n.a.
5	600	150	750	$120	$30	$150	$30
10	600	200	800	60	20	80	10
15	600	225	825	40	15	55	5
20	600	300	900	30	15	45	15
25	600	550	1150	24	22	46	50

(a) (i) Average fixed cost per unit decreases as fixed costs are spread over more units.

(ii) Average variable cost per unit decreases at first, then increases, as the Law of Diminishing Returns causes average output per worker to increase at first, then decrease.

(iii) Average total cost per unit decreases at first as fixed cost per unit and variable cost per unit fall, but, after output reaches a certain level, will increase as a result of rising variable costs per unit due to the Law of Diminishing Returns.

(b) Marginal cost per unit is the cost of producing one additional unit.

As output increases, the Law of Diminishing Returns causes marginal cost per unit to decrease at first, then to increase.

CRITICAL THINKING QUESTIONS

1. One possible explanation is that the longer tubes are used much more commonly than the shorter ones. Consequently, the longer tubes are mass-produced to a greater extent than the smaller ones. As a result, the longer tubes could have the lower production costs (particularly fixed costs) per unit, despite their larger size and the greater amount of materials in them.

2. In publishing, there are *heavy fixed costs* associated in the development and production of a book. Books with high sales volume such as Dr. Spock's spread these fixed costs over a very large number of copies, making the fixed cost *per copy sold* lower than for books with shorter print runs.

3. (a)

Output (units per week)	Fixed costs	Variable costs	Total costs	Total revenue	Profit
0	$500	$ 0	$ 500	$ 0	–$ 500
100	500	500	1000	1000	0
200	500	1000	1500	2000	500
300	500	1500	2000	3000	1000
400	500	2000	2500	4000	1500
500	500	2500	3000	5000	2000

At sales of 400 products per week, the weekly profit will be $1500.

(b)

Output (units per week)	Fixed costs	Variable costs	Total costs	Total revenue	Profit
0	$800	$ 0	$ 800	$ 0	–$ 800
100	800	600	1400	800	–600
200	800	1200	2000	1600	–400
300	800	1800	2600	2400	–200
400	800	2400	3200	3200	0
500	800	3000	3800	4000	200

At sales of 300 products per week, fixed costs of $800 per week, variable costs of $6 per product and a price of $8, the firm will have a weekly loss of $200.

4. (a)

Units of output per day	Fixed Costs	Variable Costs	Total Costs	Average Cost per Unit	Average Revenue per Unit	Marginal Cost per Unit	Marginal Revenue per Unit
0	$ 200	$ 0	$ 200	———	———	———	———
10	200	170	370	$ 37.00	$ 22.00	$ 17.00	$ 22.00
20	200	320	520	26.00	22.00	15.00	22.00
30	200	440	640	21.33	22.00	12.00	22.00
40	200	580	780	19.50	22.00	14.00	22.00
50	200	800	1000	20.00	22.00	22.00	22.00
60	200	1100	1300	21.67	22.00	30.00	22.00

4. (b)

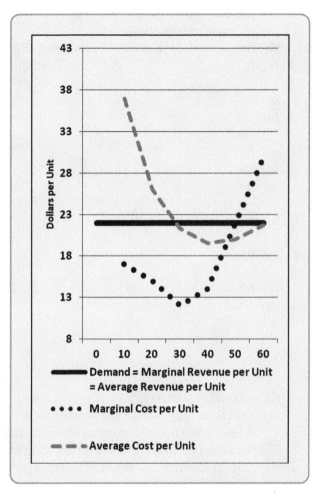

(c) (i) 50 units
   (ii) $100 (average revenue = $22.00; average cost = $20.00, so profit is 50 units x $2.00 each)
(d) Yes, as indicated by the perfectly elastic demand curve.
(e) The price would be forced downward by competition, reaching an equilibrium level of about $19.50, where the AC curve is at its lowest point. Profits would then be zero, having been eliminated by competition.

USE THE WEB

1. This is a good practice exercise in working with the concepts of this chapter.

Chapter 9

REVIEW QUESTIONS

1. a
2. b
3. competitive; concentrated

4. b
5. e
6. (a) yes
   (b) yes
   (c) no
   (d) yes
   (e) yes
7. d
8. c
9. e
10. d
11. a
12. (a) price-fixing and bid-rigging
    (b) false or misleading representations
    (c) deceptive telemarketing
    (d) mergers of firms, if these would lessen competition substantially
13. increase efficiency; compete internationally
14. (a) They must secure approval from the federal Competition Bureau.
    (b) The Competition Bureau will consider whether the proposed merger would lessen competition substantially. In addition, it will consider whether the proposed merger would likely result in gains in efficiency that would increase the ability of the merged companies to compete internationally.
    (c) The Competition Bureau would seek to negotiate changes to the proposed merger that would preserve competition in affected markets, such as the sale of some operations and assets to competing firms. If the Bureau and the companies proposing the merger cannot agree, the matter is taken to the Competition Tribunal for a decision.
15. e
16. (a) The very heavy capital investment in these industries makes their fixed costs so high that in order to keep costs to users down, they should be made monopolies so that they can have the maximum number of users
    (b) public transit, water utilities, postal service
17. d

CRITICAL THINKING QUESTIONS

1. The key to understanding this matter is that the basic goal of the Competition Act is to promote *and preserve* competition in Canadian markets. Smaller regional airlines had made several complaints that Air Canada

was pricing its flights *below its costs*, with the objective of driving the smaller airlines out of business. This sort of practice (described in Chapter 7 as "predatory pricing") does indeed reduce prices in the very short run, but by driving competitors out of business, it reduces competition and makes it easier to increase prices after that.

2. The Competition Bureau objected because, by in effect dictating the price that dealers could charge for its cars, Toyota was interfering with competition in the marketplace. This is different from price-fixing, which is an offence that involves competing producers agreeing on a price. In cases such as the Toyota one (known as *resale price maintenance*), a producer takes action that prevents retailers from competing regarding the price of its producer—an action described in law as "maintaining the resale price" of the product.

3. (a) The restaurant is labour-intensive; that is, it needs a lot of labour in order to cook and serve food and beverages. The manufacturing firm, on the other hand, is capital-intensive: many of its operations are carried out by machinery rather than by labour. As a result, labour costs are a higher proportion of the restaurant's total costs than of the manufacturer's total costs.

(b)

Manufacturing	Company	Restaurant
Sales revenue	$500 million	$500 thousand
Non-labour costs	370	320
Labour costs	100	150
Profit	30	30
Payroll taxes (10% of payroll)	10	15
Profit after payroll taxes	20	15

(c) Payroll taxes reduce the manufacturing firm's profits by 33 percent ($10/$30), and they reduce the restaurant's profits by 50 percent ($15/$30).

USE THE WEB

1. Look on the Competition Bureau's website for updates to this case.

Chapter 10

REVIEW QUESTIONS

1. $9 per hour; 4000 workers
2. $10 per hour; 1000 workers; 5000 workers

3. d
4. (a) the number of people seeking work would increase to 6000, while
   (b) the number of jobs would decrease to 3000
5. b
6. e
7. c
8. (a) yes
   (b) yes
   (c) no
   (d) yes
   (e) no
9. b
10. a
11. c
12. (a) false
    (b) true
    (c) false
    (d) false
13. a
14. c
15. b

CRITICAL THINKING QUESTIONS

1. (a) On the supply side of the market for hairdressers, the union's problem would be that it could not prevent lower-price competition from non-union hairdressers who refused to join the union, and from self-employed hairdressers.
   (b) On the demand side, the key factor would be the elasticity of demand for hairdressing. If the demand were relatively elastic (for instance, if higher prices caused people to go to the hairdresser less often), a union could only achieve large increases in hairdressers' incomes if it were prepared to accept a significant reduction in the number of (unionized) jobs in the industry. And a larger problem could be that the presence of non-union hairdressers as a substitute would make the demand for unionized hairdressers more elastic, which would further reduce the number of jobs for unionized hairdressers.

2. As the strike deadline draws nearer, pressure on the negotiators for *both* sides to reach a negotiated settlement becomes more intense, for various reasons. The first of these is simply the fact that time is short, and rapidly getting shorter.

   Second, with time so short, it is less likely that the negotiating teams can hope that the conciliator (assuming that one is still there) will be able to come up with a magical solution *for them*—if a solution is to be found, they will have to *find it themselves*. The time has come (or will soon come) to stop playing negotiating games, and make your very best offer.

Third, both sides will understand (and fear) that the passage of the strike deadline will make the situation much more unpredictable and dangerous for them. As long as they are negotiating, they have some control over the process, but once a strike starts, they are into economic warfare, the outcome of which is uncertain—in other words, you could *lose*.

By placing growing pressure on both negotiating teams, these factors make a negotiated settlement more likely, especially in the hours just before the strike deadline.

3. Chapter 10 notes that a major reason for the decline in union membership as a percentage of the work force has been *changes in the nature of employment*. In highly unionized fields such as manufacturing and government, job growth has been slow. In contrast, most of the growth of employment has been in the service sector, which is not highly unionized. Unions cannot change these trends in the types of work, so for union membership to grow again as a percentage of the labour force, unions would probably have to recruit more members in the service sector of the economy. Many service industries are not easy to unionize. Often, firms are small in size, much of the work is part-time, and worker turnover is high. Unions would probably target service industries in which employers are larger, such as banking and big retailers; however, most of these firms tend to resist union recruiting efforts very strongly. If employees of these firms felt that they were being underpaid and/or treated unfairly by management, they would be more likely to join a union, as groups of employees at some Wal-Marts have periodically tried to do.

4. The main reason why the percentage of men in unionized jobs fell so much while the unionization rate for women remained steady is that the factors that were driving change (international competition and technological change) had their greatest impact on goods-producing industries such as manufacturing, in which most of the workers tend to be men. By contrast, jobs in service industries, which employ mostly women, tend to be less vulnerable to both international competition and technological change.

5. Unions tend to bargain more aggressively (and strike) when they have reason to believe that employers will give them much of what they want in order to avoid a strike. After 1990, unions realized that three factors were making it less likely that going on strike would be successful.

The first of these was that in the short run, the recession and slow economic growth that followed were making employers much less profitable. The second and third factors were more long-run in nature. One was that many Canadian manufacturers were facing increased foreign competition, which cut into their profits and limited their ability to raise prices, and the other was that a growing number of unionized manufacturing workers faced the risk of being replaced by new technology such as computerized industrial robots.

USE THE WEB

1. Many people think that having a high level of education more or less entitles someone to a higher income, but people's incomes are determined by supply and demand. So, when you compare the income figures for different education and skill levels, think in terms of the supply of and demand for the services of people who possess that education or skill level.

2. The CLC takes positions on a wide range of economic, social, and political issues. In reviewing the CLC's position on any given issue, ask yourself how the CLC's recommendations would affect union members.

Chapter 11

REVIEW QUESTIONS

1. (a) yes
   (b) yes
   (c) no
   (d) no

2. e

3. a
4. (a) yes
   (b) no
   (c) yes
   (d) no
   (e) yes
   (f) yes
   (g) yes
   (h) no
5. c
6. a
7. e
8. slower increases in the number of income earners per family and in worker productivity
9. c
10. 10 percent
11. e
12. d
13. a
14. b
15. c
16. a
17. d
18. Young females, female one-parent families, young males, male one-parent families

CRITICAL THINKING QUESTIONS

1. The reasoning behind this statement is that most women work in service industries and office work rather than in goods-producing industries such as manufacturing, construction, and agriculture, and that because of technology, job growth has been much more rapid in service industries than in service industries. Chapter 11 describes how employment in goods industries has grown only slowly, while employment in service industries has grown very rapidly, creating growing numbers of job opportunities for women. One obvious reason for these trends is changes in production technology, which has cut into employment in goods industries. A less obvious but equally important effect of technological change has generated a much higher standard of living, which in turn has increased consumer demand for the services that provide employment for many women. The argument is that without technological change, most jobs would still be in the goods-producing industries, which tend to be male-dominated.

That said, another perspective is that, for various reasons, the time had come for women to insist on a role in the workforce, and that they were going to go out and compete with men for jobs in any case, whether those jobs were in traditional goods-producing industries or in service industries.

2. The main reason for such a striking statistic is probably the demographic fact that women live significantly longer than men, so that there are many more women than men in the over-65 population. Also, in part, these statistics reflect the fact that women past retirement age have lower incomes than men. Many of those with their own pensions have lower pensions than men because their incomes were on average lower than men's, while widows often live on two-thirds or one-half of their husbands' pensions.

3. For most of the working poor, it is a matter of pride—they do not wish to be dependent upon social assistance. Does this make them noble contributors to society or illogical people who don't exercise their most economically advantageous alternative? And what does it say about the economic alternatives offered to them by society?

4. There are three alternatives here, the last two of which seem the most likely:
   • governments know that the poverty lines are valid and have decided to provide welfare benefits that are too low for people to live on,
   • governments believe that the poverty lines are not valid and that people can live on less, and/or
   • governments believe that if they provide welfare benefits equal to the poverty line, these will be so high that many people will choose to remain on welfare, creating financial problems (and political problems with taxpayers) for the government.

5. First, there is no official definition of "poverty" in Canada, and no agreement regarding what "poverty" even means. Some people consider people to be poor only if their income is so low that they cannot afford the essentials of life. Others argue that people with higher incomes can still be considered "poor", as long as their income is far enough below the average or median income.

Second, whichever concept of poverty is used, translating it into an actual definition requires some quite arbitrary decisions. If the LICOs are used, are people "poor" if their incomes are 50 percent below average? 40 percent? 30 percent? 20 percent? 10 percent? If the Market Basket Measure standard is used, what items should be included in the basket? A telephone? A computer? Internet access? A cell phone? A smartphone? There's lots of room for disagreement on these details, and these details influence the level of the poverty line.

And third, there are real problems gathering data for estimating the extent of poverty. Statistics Canada collects the income statistics through surveys, and some people underreport their incomes. Also, poverty lines consider only cash income, whereas people with a low cash income can live comfortably under certain circumstances, such as the widow living with family members who has a low income but no expenses for food or shelter.

USE THE WEB

1. *The Daily* often includes both statistics and the causes of changes in the statistics.
2. *The Daily* often includes both statistics and the causes of changes in the statistics.

Chapter 12

REVIEW QUESTIONS

1. c
2. (a) taxes on incomes (personal and business)
   (b) taxes on spending (sales taxes, or consumption taxes)
   (c) taxes on assets
   (d) taxes on payrolls
3. b
4. a
5. b
6. 35 percent ($3500/$10 000)
7. 40 percent (2/5)
8. 95 percent (19/20)
9. e
10. b
11. c
12. (a) yes
    (b) no
    (c) yes
    (d) yes
    (e) no
    (f) yes
    (g) no
13. c
14. borrowing money (mostly by selling government bonds)
15. (a) $40
    (b) $440
16. c

CRITICAL THINKING QUESTIONS

1. They would be regressive, because import duties add to the prices of imported products, in the same way as sales taxes do. And sales taxes take a higher percentage of the incomes of the poor than they take of the incomes of wealthier Canadians.

2. The key to this question is not which of these choices one might prefer, but rather what the effect of such tax rates on the economy would be, particularly in terms of their effect on incentives to work and to invest. To answer this question requires looking beyond the fact that higher personal income taxes would leave people with less take-home pay, and asking what effects these scenarios would have on productivity and therefore on living standards.

   A 50-percent marginal tax rate on personal incomes would represent a significant increase (the average marginal tax rate is now around 40 percent). The key question is whether such a marginal tax rate would cause many people to refuse to do additional work, such as overtime or a second job. To the extent that people declined to do additional work, efficiency would be impaired.

   A 50-percent marginal tax rate on business profits would represent an even larger increase than for workers in the previous paragraph. The key question here is how such a marginal tax rate would affect the decisions of businesses—would they reduce their investment in equipment that increases efficiency, or, even worse, would some multinational businesses decide not to invest in Canada?

   We know from experience that marginal tax rates in the 50-percent range do not kill the incentive to do additional work for most Canadians. We do not know how similar tax rates would affect business decisions to make investments that would increase their efficiency, only that the potential for negative effects could be considerable. And if business investment were severely affected, the impact on the Canadian economy could be serious.

3. The statement is a very simplistic one, based on the notion that debt is bad. As the text points out, there are situations in which borrowing by governments is certainly reasonable. The clearest such case is when a government borrows in order to purchase or build a costly asset, such as a hospital or a college; by borrowing, the government can provide the public with the use of the asset much sooner, and the public's taxes can pay off the debt over a period of time. Households can make good use of debt in this way (e.g., to buy a house), so can businesses (e.g., to acquire plant or equipment), and so can governments.

The speaker might be (mistakenly) comparing all government borrowing to the misuse of credit cards by some consumers, who go excessively into debt not to acquire assets, but rather just to increase their consumption spending beyond their income. Or perhaps the speaker is thinking back to Canada's experience of the 1975–93 period, as described in Chapter 12. Or maybe the speaker does not trust elected governments to manage their finances soundly in the face of political pressures to give voters benefits above and beyond the taxes that they pay.

4. (a)
   (b) The figures in year 20X5 (1) balance the budget solely by reducing spending so that spending and tax revenues are both $114 billion. The budget is balanced.

   The figures in year 20X5 (1) balance the budget solely by increasing tax revenues so that tax revenues and spending are both $132 billion. The budget is balanced.

   These are just examples. Any combination of spending cuts and tax increases that added up to a total of $18 billion in 20X5 would also balance the budget.
   (c) The spending reductions and tax increases in part (b) are *big*. The spending cuts amount to nearly 14 percent of all government spending, and the tax increases require boosting the tax burden by nearly 16 percent. Changes in government spending and/or taxes on such a large scale would inevitably generate a great deal of political opposition from groups that would be adversely affected.
   (d) The government's debt would remain stable (in this example, at $355 billion).

5. (a) The purpose is to provide people who are receiving EI benefits with an incentive to work, at least to a certain extent. There had been many complaints from employers that EI was creating an incentive for people to *not* take jobs that were available, especially if these might be short-term jobs that would leave the worker unqualified to go back on EI when the job ended. For example, fish canneries in communities with very high unemployment rates sometimes found themselves unable to recruit workers.
   (b) 100 percent—for every dollar that you earn over the limit, your EI benefits are reduced by one dollar. You get to keep none of your earnings, which is a marginal tax rate of 100 percent.

USE THE WEB

1. Use the "Net federal debt" statistics at the bottom of the table on the Statistics Canada website.

Chapter 13

REVIEW QUESTIONS

1. (a) private cost
   (b) social cost
   (c) private cost
   (d) private cost
   (e) social cost
2. d

		Billions of dollars		
Year	Government Spending	Government Tax Revenues	Budget Deficit (−) or Surplus (+)	Government Debt
20X1	$110	$100	− $10	$310
20X2	117	105	− 12	322
20X3	125	110	− 15	337
20X4	132	114	− 18	355
20X5 (1)	114	114	0	355
20X5 (2)	132	132	0	355

3. less of other things (goods); that is, a lower standard of living
4. e
5. e
6. d
7. d
8. d
9. a
10. (a) F
    (b) F
    (c) T
    (d) T
    (e) T
11. b
12. e
13. a
14. e
15. b

CRITICAL THINKING QUESTIONS

1. The problem with this view is that it assumes that, once educated about the negative social effects of their actions, people and businesses will willingly take actions that cost them economically in order to live up to their social obligations. In other words, it does not really address the problem that there are economic incentives to pollute. So, for this approach to be effective in dealing with pollution, people would have to be persuaded to voluntarily accept the costs of reducing their pollution, without any assurance that others would do the same.

2. (a) This is an unattractive statement, but it is accurate. As Chapter 13 notes, both producers and consumers of a product gain economically from not having to pay the social costs of their actions. If a company saves $1 per product by dumping waste into the air or water, the company will save on the costs of disposing of the waste, and consumers of the product will probably enjoy lower prices as well.

    (b) This reality means that governments must actively intervene in order to protect the environment; the marketplace and the incentives of the marketplace will make pollution problems worse, not better. So government environmental policy needs to start from the realization that it must overcome the economic incentive to pollute, using incentives and/or penalties that change people's behaviour.

3. (a) In effect, we can "produce" a cleaner environment by investing in pollution-control equipment. And since the resources used to produce a cleaner environment cannot be used for other purposes, there is an opportunity cost of improving the environment in terms of lower production of other things. For consumers, this opportunity cost takes the form of higher prices for the products that they buy, leaving them less money to spend on other things.

    (b) In general, people dislike the economic reality of opportunity cost; they would rather be able to have more of all things, and not have to face the reality that more of one thing means less of others. Regarding the opportunity cost of a cleaner environment, there are probably other factors. Most individuals do not see themselves as benefiting from pollution (unlike some industries, for example), so they cannot see why they should pay for cleaning it up. And many people feel that pollution is caused by others (mostly industry), so others should bear the costs of cleaning up and protecting the environment.

4. (a) The main benefit is simply convenience and cost, for both consumers and producers. For consumers, the main cost saved is the time and effort of carting empties around, while for producers the collection and recovery/reuse of reusable containers is a labour-intensive task that can be quite costly. All of these are private costs.

    The main costs are social costs, such as the economic costs of cleaning up all the discarded throwaways and the extra use of scarce landfill sites, and the littering of the environment with throwaways.

    (b) (i) Prohibition would eliminate the costs in a quite simple manner. It would also eliminate the consumer's having any choice in the manner (such as paying a higher price for the convenience), and may seem to some to be a somewhat drastic approach to dealing with a problem that generates litter but is not life-threatening.

(ii) Taxes on throwaways could discourage the use of these containers, depending on how high the taxes were. They would leave consumers the choice of paying more for the convenience of throwaways (i.e., "internalize" the external costs), and the tax revenues could be used to pay for cleanups, to subsidize recycling, etc. However, they would not completely eliminate the problem.

Chapter 14

REVIEW QUESTIONS

1. b
2. d
3. (a) trade agreements that reduce barriers to trade
   (b) improvements in communications technology
   (c) improvements in transportation technology and costs
4. (a) improved access to larger foreign markets
   (b) increased competition from foreign imports
5. Much of its industry was not efficient enough to compete internationally.
6. c
7. a

CRITICAL THINKING QUESTIONS

1. In the past, government policy had stressed the goal of a fairer distribution of economic wealth, and had sheltered Canadian manufacturing industries from international competition— the "resource wealth mentality" described in Chapter 14. The 1989 Free Trade Agreement with the United States signalled a basic shift in Canadian policy toward an emphasis on creating economic wealth and competing internationally. This shift in policy increased the importance of goals such as increasing productivity and improving the ability of Canadian industry to compete internationally.

2. As a small country that relies heavily on exports for its economic prosperity, Canada needs its industries to be able to compete internationally. And a key to competing internationally is to have high productivity, since high output per worker per hour helps to keep production costs low.

3. Budget surpluses could be used to finance tax reductions that were meant to increase incentives for businesses to invest in productivity-increasing equipment, and for people to work, save, and invest. Budget surpluses could also be a source of funds for government spending programs that would increase productivity; these could include programs such as research and development and education and training.

Glossary

administered prices A term used to describe prices that have been fixed by sellers. See price-fixing.

after-tax income Total income less income taxes paid.

arbitration The resolution of union–management disputes by the decision of a third party; required by law for grievances that the union and employer cannot resolve by themselves; used to settle disputes over the terms of new collective agreements in cases where strikes of essential employees are prohibited.

balanced budget A budget in which government spending is equal to government revenues.

board of directors A group of people elected by the shareholders of a corporation to provide direction to the management of the corporation.

budget deficit An excess of government spending over government revenues.

budget surplus A budget in which government revenues are equal to government spending.

capital (equipment) The tools, equipment, machinery and factories used to increase production per worker.

cartel A formal agreement among producers to coordinate their price and output decisions for the purpose of earning monopoly profits.

coefficient of elasticity The percentage change in quantity demanded that results from a 1-percent change in price.

collective agreement A contract agreed upon by an employer and labour union, specifying the terms and conditions of employment of the employees for a specified period of time.

collective bargaining The process through which employers and unions negotiate a new collective agreement.

command system An economic system in which economic decisions are made mainly by the government, in a centralized manner.

competitive industry An industry that consists of many small firms and is easily entered by new competitors.

complementary good A good that is bought in combination with another good.

concentrated industry An industry that is dominated by a few large firms and is not easily entered by new competitors.

consumption taxes Taxes levied when consumers buy goods and services; for example, sales taxes.

corporation A business firm that is a separate legal entity from its owners, or shareholders, each of whose liability is limited to the amount of his or her investment in the firm.

Crown corporations Corporations owned by a government and that are ultimately responsible, through a cabinet minister, to that government.

demand The entire relationship between the various possible prices of a product or service and the quantity demanded at each price, expressed through either a schedule or a graph.

deregulation Policies to reduce government regulation of business, with the intention of promoting efficiency.

derived demand The demand for a factor of production, which is generated by (derived from) the demand for the good or service that it is used to produce.

ebusinesses Businesses using processes and activities based on electronic information and data exchanges via the internet and the World Wide Web.

economics The study of the decisions a society makes concerning the production of goods and services and the division of these among its people.

economies of scale Lower production costs per unit made possible by higher volumes of production that permit the achievement of increased efficiencies.

effectiveness A measure of how well an economy performs in terms of producing goods and services that are needed and wanted.

efficiency A measure of how well an economy performs in terms of producing high volumes of goods and services at a low cost per item.

elastic demand The term used to describe demand if a price increase causes a reduction in total sales revenue.

elastic supply A situation in which the quantity supplied increases readily when the price increases.

equal pay for work of equal value The concept that the values of different jobs may be measured against each other using a point system that incorporates a variety of criteria, including skill levels, effort, degree of responsibility, and working conditions.

equilibrium price A price determined in the marketplace by the interaction of supply and demand.

equilibrium quantity The quantity sold (bought) at the equilibrium price.

externality An incidental cost, or side effect, inflicted on others by the production or consumption of a product. Also known as a spillover effect.

fixed costs Production costs that remain constant, regardless of the level of output (for example, rent).

general partners Partners who take an active part in the management of the business and who have unlimited personal liability for its debts.

globalization The growing internationalization of business, trade, and finance that has characterized the period since the early 1980s.

greenhouse effect The global warming trend that environmentalists fear will cause disastrous climatic changes around the world, including the raising of ocean levels, widespread flooding of coastal areas, and weather changes such as hurricanes.

grievance An alleged violation of a collective agreement by an employer.

Gross Domestic Product (GDP) A measure of the total value of goods and services produced and incomes earned in a country in one year.

individual bargaining The process through which workers deal as individuals with employers in negotiating their terms and conditions of employment.

industrial concentration The degree to which an industry is dominated by a few firms.

inelastic demand The term used to describe demand if a price increase causes an increase in total sales revenue.

inelastic supply A situation in which quantity supplied does not increase readily when the price increases.

inputs Economic resources, such as labour, capital equipment, and natural resources, that are used to produce goods and services.

labour The largest single productive input available to any economy, labour includes all of the productive talents of the people of a society, mental as well as physical.

laissez-faire The doctrine or philosophy that from the viewpoint of the public interest, it is neither necessary nor beneficial for governments to intervene in the operation of the economy.

land Short form for all the natural resources available to a society's economy as economic inputs.

Law of Diminishing Returns A physical law stating that, if additional units of one productive input (such as labour) are combined with a fixed quantity of another productive input (such as capital), the average product per unit of the variable input (labour) will increase at first and then decrease.

limited partner A partner who invests in a business but takes no active part in the management of it, and whose liability is limited to the amount invested.

long run The period of time after which the quantities of all inputs can be changed.

Low-Income Cut-Offs Income levels below which more than 63 percent of income is spent on food, shelter, and clothing (20 percentage points higher than the national average of 43 percent spent on the essentials in 1992).

marginal cost per unit The addition to total costs resulting from the production of one more additional unit of output.

marginal productivity (per worker) The increase in production resulting from the hiring of one additional worker.

marginal revenue per unit The addition to total revenue resulting from the sale of one additional unit of output.

Marginal Tax Rate The percentage of any additional income that is earned that goes to taxes.

Market Basket Measure Poverty lines based on the cost of a "basket" of goods and services required to live above the poverty line, defined in terms of both subsistence and "social inclusion".

market income Income earned in the marketplace.

market power The ability to raise one's prices; usually associated with a dominant or monopolistic position in the market.

market structure Term used to describe the organization and nature of a market or an industry, particularly whether it is competitive or concentrated in nature.

market system An economic system in which economic decisions are made mainly by consumers and privately owned producers, in a decentralized manner.

marketing boards Government-sponsored organizations of farmers that support farm incomes by restricting the supply of produce, usually through a system of quotas on individual farmers.

minimum wage A legal minimum wage rate set by law.

monopolistic competition A term describing industries that consist of many small firms, where entry to the industry by new firms is easy, and where the products or services of individual firms, while basically similar, are differentiated from each other to a degree.

monopoly A situation in which there is only one seller of a particular good or service.

natural monopoly An industry, such as public utilities, that by its nature lends itself to a monopolistic form of organization.

non-price competition Competition between sellers based not on price but rather on factors such as product differentiation and advertising.

oligopoly A situation in which four or fewer firms account for at least half of the sales of an industry.

opportunity cost The concept that the real economic cost of producing something is the forgone opportunity to produce something else that could have been produced with the same inputs.

output The goods and services produced by a society using its productive inputs.

participation rate The percentage of people of working age who are participating in the labour force, by either working or looking for work.

partnership A business firm owned by two or more persons, with each person bearing full legal liability for the firm's debts.

payroll taxes Taxes paid by employers based on the number of their employees or the amount of their payroll.

perfect competition A term describing industries that consist of a large number of small firms, where entry to the industry by new firms is easy, and where all firms in the industry sell identical products.

perfectly elastic demand A situation in which any price increase above the market price will cause a firm's sales to fall to zero; represented by a horizontal demand curve.

poverty lines Income levels below which families or individuals are considered to be poor.

poverty rate The percentage of a group of people whose incomes are below the poverty line.

price-fixing Agreements among oligopolists to raise their prices above levels that would prevail in a competitive situation.

price-maker Term used to describe the position of the dominant firm(s) in a concentrated industry, which can influence the price of the product.

price-taker Term used to describe the position of the individual small firm in a competitive industry, which is unable to influence the price of its product and is forced to accept (take) whatever price is determined in the market.

price control (ceiling) A legal limit on a price or on increases in a price, which holds the price below its equilibrium level.

price leadership A technique of price-fixing in which one firm (the price leader) sets its price and the rest of the firms in the industry follow suit.

price support (floor) An artificially high price, held above the equilibrium level by the government.

private (internal) costs Production costs, such as labour and materials, that are paid by producers and ultimately included in the price paid by the consumer.

private corporation A private corporation has fewer than 50 shareholders.

Privatize The process of selling government enterprises (usually Crown corporations) to private interests.

product differentiation Attempts by individual firms to distinguish their products or services from those of their competitors.

production-possibilities curve A curve that shows the economy's potential output, assuming that economic inputs are fully employed and efficiently utilized.

productivity Output per worker per hour; a measure of efficiency.

profits Those funds left from a business's sales revenues after all expenses have been paid; such funds are therefore available (after taxes have been paid) for dividends to shareholders and reinvestment in the business.

progressive taxes Taxes that take a higher percentage of high incomes than of low incomes.

proxies Legal instruments that allow a shareholder's right to vote at shareholders' meetings to be delegated to another person, either with or without specific instructions as to how that vote will be exercised.

public corporation A public corporation has 50 or more shareholders.

recession A period during which the economy's output is falling and unemployment is high.

regressive tax A tax that takes a higher percentage of low incomes than of high incomes.

resource wealth mentality The view that society's economic wealth is derived mainly from the sale of natural resources, as opposed to efficiency in the production of goods and services.

scarcity The problem that, while economic inputs (and thus potential output) are limited in availability, people's wants and needs are apparently unlimited.

senior dependency ratio The ratio of seniors to the working-age population.

shareholders The owners of shares (stocks) in a corporation; shareholders may or may not have voting rights and their liability is limited to the amount invested.

short run The period of time during which the quantities of some inputs cannot be changed.

social (external) costs Costs that are not paid by producers, but rather passed on to society at large.

sole proprietorship A business firm owned (and usually managed) by a single person who bears full legal liability for the firm's debts.

standard of living A measure of the economic prosperity of the people of a society, usually expressed in terms of the volume of consumer goods and services consumed per household or per person per year.

subsidies Payments by the government of part of the cost of a service in order to reduce the cost to the user of the service.

supply curve A graphical representation of a supply schedule.

supply schedule A table depicting the relationship between the price of a product and the quantity supplied (offered for sale).

tax credits Credits that reduce the income taxes payable by Canadians in order to offset a variety of factors that adversely affect their living standards, including dependants, property taxes, and sales taxes.

total income Market income plus transfer payments received from governments.

unionization rate The percentage of a group of workers that is unionized.

variable costs Production costs that vary with the level of output (for example, direct labour and materials).

World Trade Organization (WTO) An international organization through which 149 member nations negotiate and enforce rules for international trade.

Index

MICROECONOMICS SCOREBOARD

CANADA'S LARGEST 10 CITIES

SOURCE: STATISTICS CANADA, CANSIM TABLE 051–0034

	POPULATION, 2007
Toronto	5,509,874
Montreal	3,695,790
Vancouver	2,285,893
Ottawa – Gatineau	1,168,788
Calgary	1,139,126
Edmonton	1,081,275
Quebec	728,924
Hamilton	720,426
Winnipeg	712,671
London	469,714

EDUCATIONAL ATTAINMENT, (POPULATION AGE 15+, 2009)

SOURCE: STATISTICS CANADA, CANSIM TABLE 282–0004

Total, all education levels	27 309 200
0 to 8 years	7.0%
Some high school	14.1%
High school graduate	19.9%
Some postsecondary	8.3%
Postsecondary certificate or diploma	30.6%
University degree	20.2%
Bachelor's degree	13.9%
Above bachelor's degree	6.3%

PERSONS PER SQUARE KILOMETRE (2009)

SOURCE: STATISTICS CANADA, CANADA AT A GLANCE, 2010.

	PERSONS PER SQUARE KILOMETRE
Japan	338
United Kingdom	249
Germany	230
Italy	195
France	113
Mexico	53
United States	32
Canada	3

HOME	0	0	2
VISITORS	0	0	0
PERIOD	1	2	3

MICROECONOMICS SCOREBOARD

POPULATION BY PROVINCE AND TERRITORY, 2014
SOURCE: STATISTICS CANADA, CANSIM TABLE 051-0005

Canada	**35,675,834**
Newfoundland and Labrador	526,837
Prince Edward Island	146,524
Nova Scotia	943,932
New Brunswick	754,643
Quebec	8,236,310
Ontario	13,730,187
Manitoba	1,286,323
Saskatchewan	1,129,899
Alberta	4,145,992
British Columbia	4,657,947
Yukon	36,758
Northwest Territories	43,795
Nunavut	36,687

EDUCATIONAL ATTAINMENT, POPULATION AGE 15+
SOURCE: STATISTICS CANADA, CANSIM TABLE 282-0004

	Percent of Population	
	2009	2014
0 to 8 years	6.9	5.6
Some high school	14.1	12.1
High school graduate	20.0	20.8
Some postsecondary	8.3	7.0
Postsecondary certificate or diploma	30.6	31.3
University degree	20.1	23.1
Bachelor's degree	13.8	15.8
Above bachelor's degree	6.3	7.3